Global Outlook on Financing for Sustainable Development 2025

TOWARDS A MORE RESILIENT AND INCLUSIVE ARCHITECTURE

OECD
BETTER POLICIES FOR BETTER LIVES

Please cite this publication as:
OECD (2025), *Global Outlook on Financing for Sustainable Development 2025: Towards a More Resilient and Inclusive Architecture*, OECD Publishing, Paris, https://doi.org/10.1787/753d5368-en.

ISBN 978-92-64-54906-7 (print)
ISBN 978-92-64-83042-4 (PDF)
ISBN 978-92-64-90428-6 (HTML)

Global Outlook on Financing for Sustainable Development
ISSN 3079-2126 (online)

Photo credits: Some elements of the cover design adapted from © Freepik.com.

Corrigenda to OECD publications may be found at: https://www.oecd.org/en/publications/support/corrigenda.html.

Foreword

Understanding the global trends affecting the Financing for Development (FfD) Agenda

The biennial flagship Global Outlook on Financing for Sustainable Development provides a comprehensive analysis of major trends impacting the global financial system and financing for the Sustainable Development Goals (SDGs). The report addresses the interconnected crises hindering progress towards the 2030 Agenda, including the impacts of the COVID-19 pandemic, the climate crisis, rising inequalities, fragility and the growing financial gaps in developing countries. By offering multidisciplinary insights, it highlights the interdependence of economic and social systems and the urgency of collective action for fairer, inclusive global growth.

The Outlook serves as a critical resource for development co-operation providers by raising the importance of new systemic challenges, fostering policy coherence for sustainable development and demystifying the complexity of emerging co-operation actors and financial modalities. Through its evidence-based recommendations, it aims to help the OECD and its members shape the international response to development challenges, as custodians of norms and standards for sustainable development finance.

From Addis Ababa to Seville: taking stock of progress and setbacks

Ten years after the adoption of the Addis Ababa Action Agenda (AAAA) in 2015, this edition takes stock of progress and setbacks, analysing emerging challenges in financing sustainable development. Its comprehensive review of the AAAA commitments allows the international community to assess how well the framework has responded to evolving global dynamics, and where adjustments are needed to better align with the 2030 Agenda and Paris Agreement. By examining the seven action areas of the AAAA, it provides critical insights into systemic barriers, highlighting innovative solutions and actionable pathways for strengthening the global financing architecture, and ensuring it remains fit for purpose in the post-2025 era.

Statistical annexes, at the end of each chapter starting from Chapter two, provide a paragraph-by-paragraph assessment of the AAAA, with key data points tracking progress against relevant SDG targets and indicators. The data points are mainly drawn from the UN's Sustainable Development Goals Extended Report 2024 and its statistical annexes. Trend data in are in constant USD 2015 prices unless otherwise indicated.

Formal input to the Fourth International Conference on Financing for Sustainable Development (FfD4)

The OECD inter-directorate task force, led by the Development Co-operation Directorate (DCD), prepared fact sheets and statistical annexes to monitor progress on the seven action areas of the AAAA with critical analysis and key data points. Submitted to the United Nations and Member States to inform preparations for the FfD4 Elements paper, they align with international processes and have been finalised as chapters two to eight within this report. To ensure inclusivity, the drafts were made publicly available for feedback, reflecting the OECD's commitment to broad consultation and collaboration with stakeholders. Through its fact sheets and statistical annexes, the Outlook enhances accountability and transparency, equipping countries with tools to measure progress and improve the effectiveness of their financing strategies.

The OECD response to FfD4 challenges

Faced with significant challenges, including escalating financing gaps and geopolitical tensions, the FfD4 Conference needs to balance ambition with practicality in addressing sustainable development priorities. Inclusive governance and policy coherence are critical to overcoming these hurdles, as disparities in decision-making structures and resource allocation undermine global trust and cooperation. In response, the OECD's Global Outlook on Financing for Sustainable Development offers practical support to FfD4 negotiators, with evidence-based insights and recommendations to align priorities, foster equity and integrate diverse stakeholder perspectives. By emphasising inclusive decision-making processes that amplify the voices of developing countries, and leveraging its expertise in policy coherence, the OECD aims to help craft a financing framework that is resilient, actionable, and capable of meeting the post-2025 sustainable development agenda.

Acknowledgements

This 2025 edition of the Global Outlook on Financing for Sustainable Development was prepared under the overall leadership of Pilar Garrido, OECD Director for Development Co-operation (DCD). Olivier Cattaneo, Head of the Policy Analysis and Strategy Unit in DCD, and Rachel Morris, Policy Analyst, led the drafting of the report. Contributing authors were Clemence Decisy, Jieun Kim, with valuable research support by Apolline Greiveldinger and additional support provided by Gabriele Cristofaro.

The OECD's inter-directorate Task Force on Financing for Development (FfD), under the guidance of Deputy Secretary-General Mary Beth Goodman, advanced technical and high-level meetings to prepare strategic guidance on inputs for the Fourth International Conference on Financing for Development (FfD4), led by Pilar Garrido with Carmine Di Noia, Director for Financial and Enterprise Affairs (DAF), Ragnheiður Elín Árnadóttir, Director of the Development Centre (DEV), Manal Corwin, Director of the Centre for Tax Policy and Administration (CTPA), Alvaro Pereira, Chief Economist to the Economics Department (ECO), Jo Tyndall, Director for the Environment Directorate (ENV), Elsa Pilichowski, Director for Public Governance (GOV), Andreas Schaal, Director for Global Relations and Cooperation (GRC), Jerry Sheehan, Director for Science, Technology and Innovation (STI), Dominic O'Shea, Director for the Resource Management and Partnerships Unit (SWAC), Marion Jansen, Director for Trade and Agriculture (TAD), Romina Boarini, Director for the Centre on Well-Being, Inclusion, Sustainability and Equal Opportunity (WISE) Important comments and analysis were provided by members of the OECD inter-directorate Task Force on Financing for Development (FfD), including Yasmin Ahmad, Fares Al Hussami, Brilé Anderson, Catherine Anderson, Geraldine Ang, Silvia Appelt, Jose Antonio Ardavin, Wiebke Bartz-Zuccala, , Aussama Bejraoui, Eric Bensel, Marisa Berbegal Ibanez, Elena Bernaldo de Quiros, Francesca Bertolino, Thomas Boehler, Alexander Bohmer, Emily Bosch, Joao Paulo Braga, Monica Brezzi, Juan Casado Asensio, Raffaella Centurelli, Mario Cervantes, Cibele Cesca, Tea Cimini, Carlos Conde, Wouter Coussement, Rita Da Costa, Pietrangelo De Biase, Caio De Oliveira, Marc De Tollenaere, Antoine Dechezlepretre, Harsh Desai, Elise Desplanques, Ben Dickinson, John Drummond, Kerri Elgar, Marta Encinas-Martin, Abdoulaye Fabregas, Margherita Fadda, Chiara Falduto, Sam Foxall, Camilo Gamba Gamba, Valérie Gaveau, Carolina Guerra, Anibal Guerrero Aguilar, Alejandro Guerrero-Ruiz, Laura Gutierrez, Michelle Harding, Jenny Hedman, James Hermanson, Paul Horrocks, Tomas Hos, Renwick Irvine, Raphael Jachnik, Julian Kath, Georgina Kelly, Megan Grace Kennedy-Chouane, Anthony Kiernan, Anita King, Fatos Koc, Emilie Kothe, Benjamin Kumpf, Hirofumi Kyunai, Martina Lejtreger, Iris Mantovani, Virginie Marchal, Vasiliki Mavroeidi, Laura Mc Donald, Ida McDonnell, Louise Menard, Sebastian Nieto Parra, Jose René Orozco, Julian Paisey, Cecilia Piemonte, Jan Rielaender, Cécile Sangare, Nejla Saula, Rachel Sberro-Kessler, Kerstin Schopohl, Rolf Schwarz, Jens Sedemund, Vincent Siegerink, Ernesto Soria Morales, Tomasz Kozluk, Joseph Stead, Hector Tajonar de Lara, Ozlem Taskin, Tatyana Teplova, Harry Tonino and Jacqueline Wood. Additionally, Joelle Bassoul, Catherine Bremer, Karena Garnier, Masato Hayashikawa, Ola Kasneci, Henri-Bernard Solignac-Lecomte, Yumiko Sugaya and Lucia Zarama assisted in the production process. Susan Sachs provided editorial review.

Member states provided valuable inputs and comments, including the United States Agency for International Development (USAID), the Permanent Delegation of Italy to the International Organizations in Paris, the New Zealand Delegation to the OECD and the Permanent Mission of Austria to the OECD.

Editorial

The 4th International Conference on Financing for Development in Seville on 30 June - 3 July 2025 offers a rare opportunity to renew the global financing framework for achieving the Sustainable Development Goals (SDGs) and to address the growing SDG financing gap.

Total financing for sustainable development grew from USD 4.31 trillion in 2015 to USD 5.24 trillion in 2022, an increase of 22%. However, annual financing needs to achieve the SDGs by 2030 surged by 36% over the same period, from USD 6.81 trillion in 2015 to 9.24 trillion in 2022, driven by climate challenges, the COVID-19 pandemic, supply chain disruptions and rising food and energy prices. If the SDG financing gap continues to grow at its 2015-2023 rate, it will reach USD 6.4 trillion by 2030.

The current USD 4.0 trillion SDG financing gap has significant implications, particularly for low-income countries (LICs). While the early 2000s saw LICs narrow the gap in their GDP per capita with high-income nations at a rate of 0.5% per year, the trend has reversed since 2015, with LICs falling further behind by 1.1% annually. Compounding this, rising debt burdens now put pressure on critical investments in health, education, and climate resilience. In 2024, 24 countries faced high risk of debt distress, up from 16 in 2015.

The 4th International Conference on Financing for Development is an opportunity to develop practical strategies to bridge the financing gap. Innovation in financial and policy tools is essential. This includes policy and incentive reforms in OECD countries to better align finance with the SDGs, improving the investment climate in developing countries, and a reform of multilateral development banks, which is underway.

Strengthening domestic resource mobilisation is a cornerstone of sustainable development financing. At 11% in 2022, the tax-to-GDP ratio in LICs remains below the 15% threshold that is necessary for providing key public services. Efforts to increase tax revenues, improve transparency, enhance compliance and build taxation capacity must continue, which the OECD will continue to support through our joint initiative with the United Nations Development Programme (UNDP),Tax Inspectors Without Borders.

Official development assistance (ODA) remains an essential source of sustainable development financing. In 2023, ODA reached an all-time high of USD 223 billion in current prices or USD 194 billion in 2015 constant prices, up by 48% from USD 131 billion in 2015 for OECD Development Assistance Committee member countries. Further support is needed to strengthen core capacities and institutions in developing countries through country-programmable aid, budget support, technical assistance and capacity building. Equally important is the quality of financing: resources must align with the principles of development effectiveness to ensure they drive meaningful outcomes, supported by the Global Partnership on Effective Development Co-operation co-hosted by the OECD and UNDP.

Remittances have grown steadily since 2015, reaching USD 476 billion in 2023, but transfer costs remain high at 6.4%, more than double the SDG target of 3%, leading to USD 16 billion in losses for developing country households annually. Increased access to banking services, enhanced market competition and wider access to new payments technology can help reduce remittance costs. Foreign direct investment (FDI) inflows to ODA-eligible countries reached USD 335 billion in 2022, similar to USD 338 billion in 2015.

Initiatives such as the joint OECD-African Union Commission African Virtual Investment Platform or the FDI Qualities Policy Toolkit can help leverage FDI and optimise its quality.

This special edition of the OECD *Global Outlook on Financing for Sustainable Development* provides policymakers and negotiators with key evidence, data and analysis to inform their country positions ahead of the forthcoming 4th International Conference on Financing for Development, and ultimately to help optimise the impact of a new financial framework for development. The OECD will continue to support countries in scaling up sustainable development financing, including by providing sound data and analysis for the Conference, and beyond.

Mathias Cormann,

OECD Secretary-General

Table of contents

FIGURES

TABLES

Abbreviations and acronyms

AAAA	Addis Ababa Action Agenda
AI	Artificial Intelligence
BEPS	Base Erosion and Profit Shifting
COP29	29th Conference of the Parties (UN Climate Change Conference)
CPI	Climate Policy Initiative
COVID-19	Coronavirus Disease 2019
DAC	Development Assistance Committee
DSSI	Debt Service Suspension Initiative
EMDCs	Emerging Markets and Developing Countries
FAO	Food and Agriculture Organization
FDI	Foreign Direct Investment
FfD4	Fourth International Conference on Financing for Development
GDP	Gross Domestic Product
G20	Group of Twenty
GFCF	Gross Fixed Capital Formation
GNI	Gross National Income
GPEDC	Global Partnership for Effective Development Co-operation
HICs	High-Income Countries
IFFs	Illicit Financial Flows
IMF	International Monetary Fund

INFFs	Integrated national financing frameworks
JETPs	Just energy transition partnerships
LDCs	Least Developed Countries
LICs	Low-Income Countries
LMICs	Lower-Middle-Income Countries
MDBs	Multilateral Development Banks
MICs	Middle-Income Countries
NBFIs	Non-Bank Financial Institutions
NDCs	Nationally Determined Contributions
NGFS	Network of Central Banks and Supervisors for Greening the Financial System
ODA	Official development assistance
OECD	Organisation for Economic Co-operation and Development
PPG	Public and Publicly Guaranteed
SDS	Sustainable Development Solutions
SDG	Sustainable Development Goal
SIDS	Small Island Developing States
TOSSD	Total official support for sustainable development
UN	United Nations
UNCTAD	UN Trade and Development
UNDP	United Nations Development Programme
WHO	World Health Organization
WMO	World Meteorological Organization

Executive summary

The Fourth International Conference on Financing for Development (FfD4), set to take place in Seville in 2025, marks a pivotal moment for the global community. In a context of widening financing gaps and debt pressure, escalating climate and other crises, and the urgent need to deliver on the Sustainable Development Goals (SDGs), FfD4 offers a critical chance to renew the global financing framework, aligning ambitions with actionable solutions to the challenges of our time. As the clock ticks toward 2030, this is the moment to revitalise collective efforts, ensuring no country is left behind in the transition to a sustainable and resilient future.

The global economy has shown resilience since the COVID-19 pandemic, with growth rebounding from a 3.4% contraction in 2020 to 3.2% in 2024, but long-term growth prospects remain weak, with forecasts for 2029 at 3.1%, the lowest in decades. Low-income countries (LICs) face stagnant growth, and the gap between them and high-income countries (HICs) has widened. Geopolitical shifts, trade fragmentation and economic sanctions have worsened conditions. Despite a 22% increase in financial flows to developing countries since 2015, the SDG financing gap has grown by 60% to reach USD 4 trillion in 2022, and resources remain insufficient to meet rising needs. Additionally, rising interest rates and increasing debt in developing countries are crowding out critical investments in health, education, and climate goals.

In that context, the report identifies **three priorities for negotiators seeking to renew the financing framework and action plan in Seville**, and accelerate progress toward the SDGs:

1. **Aim for a meaningful and politically feasible FfD4 outcome.** Restoring trust among nations is critical to achieving consensus on renewing the financing framework.
    - **Reform existing international development co-operation platforms** to promote inclusivity and collaboration. Institutions inherited from the mid-twentieth Century need to adapt their governance to the new geoeconomic context and embrace new challenges in a more inclusive and collaborative way. The renewed framework should better articulate the actions of established platforms in charge of designing, measuring, monitoring and accounting for development cooperation results. This includes: articulating Integrated National Financing Frameworks (INFFs) with country platforms; clarifying and ringfencing the definition of official development assistance (ODA) and strengthening collaboration between international forums on financing for development and the OECD Development Assistance Committee (DAC); further promoting participation by all countries in the International Forum on Total Official Support for Sustainable Development (TOSSD); or utilising the updated Global Partnership for Effective Development Cooperation (GPEDC) monitoring framework to empower countries to take the lead in designing and implementing development strategies.
    - **Reaffirm core development co-operation effectiveness principles.** The FfD4 intends to place developing countries in the driver's seat. Long-standing effectiveness principles will therefore require more thorough implementation and monitoring. Country ownership and better coordination among stakeholders are essential to reducing the fragmentation of donor policies that generate high transaction costs for partners. High-impact investments require better aligning financing flows with development priorities and improving coordination mechanisms. An updated GPEDC

monitoring framework could advance inclusivity, transparency, and alignment with country systems.

- **Improve policy coherence for sustainable development (PCSD).** Actors like the OECD could accelerate efforts to improve the measurement of the transboundary impacts of policies that exacerbate global inequalities, and help governments make them more coherent with the objective of global, sustainable development. For example, reforming fiscal policies, tax systems and subsidies in high-income countries can better align financial flows with SDG and Paris Agreement targets.

2. **Update the FfD4 framework to walk the crest line towards a bold yet pragmatic post-2025 agenda**. Since the adoption of the Addis Ababa Action Agenda (AAAA) in 2015, the COVID-19 pandemic, climate change, shrinking fiscal space and other challenges have shifted financing needs and priorities. To accelerate progress towards the SDGs, negotiators need to strike a delicate and sustainable balance between ambition and practicality.

    - **Close "negative feedback loops"**. Unless adequate financing is provided to tackle them, negative trends such as climate change, reduced human capital or excessive debt accumulation will self-perpetuate. The high short-term costs of investments in education, clean energy or infrastructure are necessary to yield long-term economic benefits and break those vicious circles.
    - **Accelerate the "alignment of the trillions"**. Global assets –worth USD 461 trillion in 2022– must be redirected towards mending SDG financing gaps. Eliminating harmful practices like fossil fuel subsidies (USD 1.53 trillion in 2022), fostering financial transparency, and advancing sustainability taxonomies can drive impactful investments. Targeting financial leakages like high remittance fees and illicit flows can unlock billions annually. Reforming multilateral development banks (MDBs) to triple lending by 2030 in just and sustainable transitions is crucial.
    - **Identify new financing resources and levers for transition**. Just transition strategies, carbon pricing and green finance reforms can mobilise resources for SDGs while addressing differentiated responsibilities and needs. Tools like debt-for-nature swaps and ocean and bioeconomy initiatives can unlock additional resources. Stronger nationally owned strategies can chart clear pathways towards the interlinked goals without undermining environmental, social and economic progress.

3. **Reinforce the monitoring of the FfD4 framework for heightened accountability and transparency, with clear and actionable deliverables.** This report identifies at least 70 relevant SDG targets and proxy indicators to track financing progress and adapt strategies.

    - **Agree to clear and actionable deliverables accompanied by well-defined targets and indicators**. Focusing on measurable outcomes aligned with global goals is key to maximising the impact of all sources of financing for development. This report demonstrates the potential of new metrics and safeguards to make resource allocation more equitable, enhance accountability and effectively track contributions towards achieving SDGs.
    - **Encourage tailored FfD4 commitments**. Seville should not be the end, but the beginning of a process. The new framework should call to develop a companion implementation plan with suggested actions by different actors such as the OECD DAC, the Finance in Common Summit, groups of multilateral development banks, the UN-led Global Investors for Sustainable Development Alliance and philanthropies, among others. These actions could be continuously monitored, and progress reported to the UN on a regular basis.
    - **Foster adaptive learning, driving continuous improvements in how financing contributes to the SDGs and beyond.** Drawing from processes like Voluntary National Reviews (VNRs) and Integrated National Financing Frameworks (INFFs), FfD4 should facilitate data-driven decision-making and capacity-building. For example, improved reporting systems and technical assistance for statistical capacity can strengthen global monitoring efforts, ensuring real-world impacts and maximising accountability.

1 Preparing post-2025: Transformation amid geo-economic tensions

The 2025 Fourth International Conference on Financing for Development (FfD4) in Seville, Spain, will have to tackle complex challenges. This chapter presents a snapshot of the geo-economic landscape in which these negotiations will unfold and explores prospects for accelerating the transition towards sustainable development. It highlights the key takeaways from a ten-year stocktake of each of the seven action areas of the Addis Ababa Action Agenda (AAAA), to strengthen preparations for the FfD4 agreement and contribute to establishing a robust financing framework for the 2030 Agenda.

1.1. A world of geo-economic tensions

The global economy shows resilience amid multiple shocks, with inflation receding steadily and various economic indicators pointing towards a soft landing. But high economic uncertainty affects global financial stability and long-term growth prospects, while rising geopolitical tensions threaten to fragment global co-operation and impede development progress. An analysis of convergence against income and Sustainable Development Goal (SDG) indicators shows that developing countries are at risk of further falling behind.

Economic stabilisation masks a slowdown in long-term growth prospects

In the first years following the Addis Ababa Action Agenda (AAAA) until the COVID-19 pandemic (2015-19), the global economy grew at a steady pace. However, low-income countries (LICs) were faring less well than most other countries. Many LICs were affected by a decline in prices for commodities such as oil and metals, which was due to a slowdown in growth in the People's Republic of China (hereafter China) and weakening global demand. This not only reduced export revenues but also led to significant depreciation of LICs' currencies. As a consequence, these countries experienced low, and even negative, economic growth and high levels of inflation. In the years between the AAAA and the COVID-19 pandemic, LIC economies were stabilising as inflation was decreasing and economic growth picking up again (Figure 1.1).

After being hit by multiple crises since 2020, the global economy has shown resilience overall. The COVID-19 pandemic caused an unprecedented disruption to the global economy, affecting cross-border capital flows and global trade. The global economy contracted sharply by 3.4% in 2020, down from a growth forecast of 2.5% at the beginning of the year (International Monetary Fund, 2020[1]). Supply chain disruptions due to the pandemic were followed by an energy and food crisis triggered by Russia's full-scale invasion of Ukraine and a surge in global inflation. However, economic activity recovered relatively quickly. Global output grew at an estimated annualised rate of 3.2% in the first half of 2024 and is expected to stabilise at this level over 2024 and 2025[1] (OECD, 2024[2]). Ongoing adjustments to supply chains and logistics have led to greater efficiency and stability, helping production and distribution. Inflation has continued to fall this year in most countries.[2]

However, the recovery masks changes in the structural make-up and growth potential of the global economy. The medium-term global growth forecast for 2029 is 3.1%, the lowest in decades.[3] Since the global financial crisis, global growth forecasts have consistently been revised downward. Private investment as well as productivity and labour force participation rates remain below pre-pandemic trends (Cho et al., 2024[3]), contributing to a gradual shift towards a low-growth environment that could impede the green transition and global poverty reduction (International Monetary Fund, 2024[4]; OECD, 2024[2]).

Economic conditions in lower-income countries are weaker than in advanced economies. Inflation in these countries remains at elevated levels amid a global easing of price pressures (Figure 1.1, Panel B). In several developing economies, elevated international food, fuel and fertiliser costs have hit particularly hard and resulted in severe cost of living crises. Food price inflation in LICs hit a peak at 32% in April 2023, and while it decreased again to 17% in December 2023, the rates are still higher than pre-pandemic levels (e.g. 12% in December 2019) (Food and Agriculture Organization, 2024[5]). Weak local currencies in developing countries exacerbated the inflationary pressures. These pressures caused emerging economies and developing countries to grow more slowly than expected. Economic growth in LICs was low at 1.0% in 2022 compared with 3.9% in lower middle-income countries (LMICs), 4.1% in upper middle-income countries (UMICs), and 2.4% in high-income countries (HICs) (Figure 1.1, Panel A).

Figure 1.1. Amid a global recovery, low-income countries are still struggling with low growth rates and high inflation

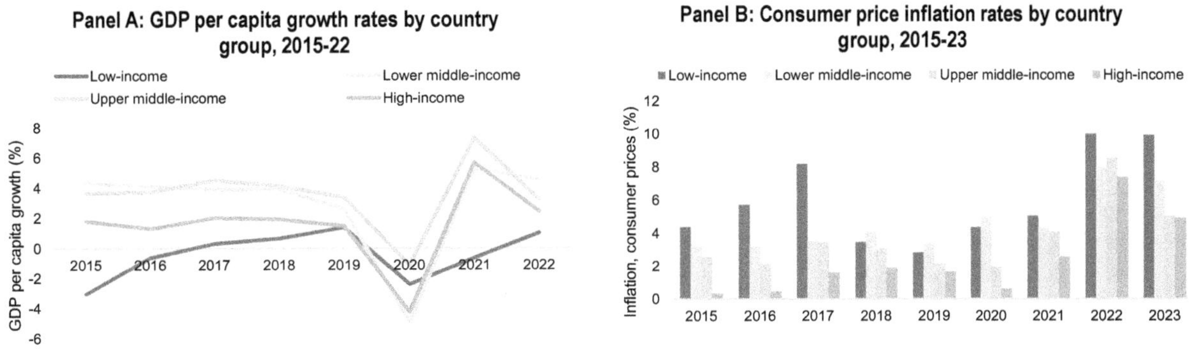

Source: Authors' calculations based on World Bank Group (2024[6]), *Data Bank, World Development Indicators* (database), https://databank.worldbank.org/source/world-development-indicators.

Geopolitical shifts and new patterns of trade and financial flows are increasing fragmentation of the global economy

A phenomenon referred to as geo-economic fragmentation (Aiyar et al., 2023[7]) **has been accelerating in recent years due to an increasing number of geopolitical events and conflicts.** In 2023, there were 56 active conflicts, the highest number since the end of the Second World War (Institute for Economics & Peace, 2024[8]). Events such as Brexit, trade disputes between the United States and China, trade flow restrictions associated with the COVID-19 pandemic as well as international conflicts and geopolitical tensions reflect rising protectionist sentiments and have collectively fractured the economy into distinct geopolitical blocs (D'Orazio, Ferriani and Gazzani, 2024[9]). Growing support for populist and isolationist parties in many Western countries both reflects and is driving these shifts.

Shifts in trade policy reflect geo-economic fragmentation. Concerns about supply chain resilience and national security have prompted an increasing number of cross-border trade restrictions. About 2 000 new restrictions on trade were reported in 2022, up from about 752 in 2019, according to Global Trade Alert data (Figure 1.12, Panel A). Trade flows between geopolitical blocs dropped by 10% in 2022 (Carluccio et al., 2024[10]). This reduced trade between geopolitical blocs can disrupt the spillover of technology and know-how, leading to projected welfare losses as large as 12% in some regions (Góes and Bekkers, 2022[11]).

In turn, fragmentation also affects cross-border financial flows. Financial sanctions have increased since the global financial crisis (Figure 1.12). Financial institutions restrict ties with jurisdictions considered to be high risk due not only to profitability concerns but also to risks of money laundering and terrorism financing high compliance costs, sanctions, increased geopolitical competition, political instability, and conflicts (OECD DAC Network on Governance, forthcoming[12]). Such a practice of restricting or terminating business relationships may negatively affect capital flows and financial inclusion in developing countries. For example, anti-money laundering and counter-terrorist financing standards can have unintended consequences in countries with weak supervisory and regulatory capabilities (Financial Action Task Force, 2021[13]). Analysis by Kida and Paetzold (2021[14]) of data from 89 emerging and developing countries found that inclusion on a Financial Action Task Force black or grey list imposed significant costs on countries in the form of reduced capital, foreign direct investment (FDI) and portfolio inflows that amounted to an equivalent to 7.6% of their gross domestic product (GDP) on average.

Figure 1.2. The number of trade restrictions and sanctions increased substantially since 2010

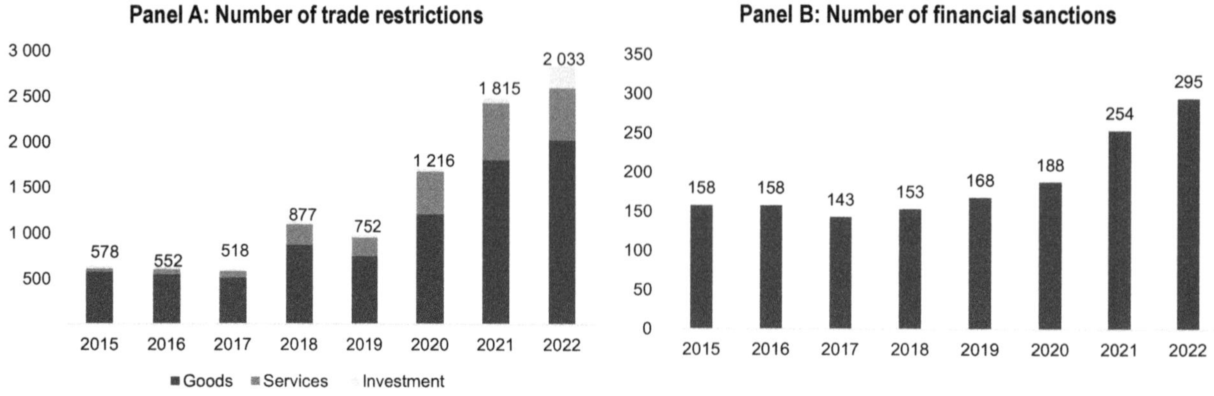

Source: Panel A: Authors' calculations based on Global Trade Alert (2024[15]), *Data Center* (database), https://data.globaltradealert.org. Panel B, Authors' calculations based on Syropoulos et al. (2024[16]), "The global sanctions data base – Release 3: COVID-19, Russia, and multilateral sanctions", https://doi.org/10.1111/roie.12691; Felbermayr et al. (2020[17]), "The global sanctions data base", https://doi.org/10.1016/j.euroecorev.2020.103561; Kirilakha et al. (Kirilakha et al., 2021[18]), "The global sanctions data base: An update that includes the years of the Trump presidency", https://doi.org/10.4337/9781839102721.

Economic and SDG convergence between countries has slowed and even reversed

The low-growth environment and multiple crises affected the pace of conversion between advanced and developing economies. While medium-term growth prospects have been consistently and globally revised downwards since the global financial crisis, the trend is more pronounced for developing countries. As shown Figure 1.3, catch-up rates of LICs, measured as the average annual change in their distance to the GDP per capita level in HICs, were at 0.5% in the early 2000s but subsequently reversed to -0.5% between 2008-14 and to -1.1% between 2015-22, meaning that HICs and LICs further diverged rather than converged. Catch-up rates of middle-income countries (MICs) have also decreased in recent years. For LMICs, convergence with HICs accelerated from 0.7% over 2000-07 to 2.1% over 2006-14 before catch-up rates dropped to 0.1% in 2015-22; for UMICS, convergence with HICs remained stable over 2000-06 and 2007-15 at 1.8% and 1.9%, respectively, before declining to zero percent over 2015-22. Based on OECD long-term economic growth forecasts, divergence between LICs and HICs is expected to continue over 2023-30, while convergence between MICs and HICs will be slower than it was over 2000-07 and 2008-15.

Geo-economic fragmentation, the rise of artificial intelligence (AI) and other trends shaping the global economy are likely to further dampen economic convergence. For instance, if trade barriers are applied across all sectors, forcing countries into exclusive trade relations within different geopolitical blocs, it is estimated that worldwide GDP would decrease by 2.3% (Bolhuis, Chen and Kett, 2023[19]). Advanced economies and emerging markets would lose 2.1% and 2.5%, respectively, and LICs would experience output losses of 4.3% (Figure 1.3, Panel B). LICs would lose more because of their high exposure to commodity trade including with China, whose growth has decelerated in recent years (Box 1.1). LICs also tend to be more commodity intensive and often specialise in the exports of key commodities, especially metals and energy. Likewise, advanced economies stand to benefit from AI sooner than emerging market and developing countries because their economies tend to be more knowledge- and technology-intensive[4] (Cazzaniga et al., 2024[20]).

Figure 1.3. The slowdown in convergence will continue due to geo-economic tensions

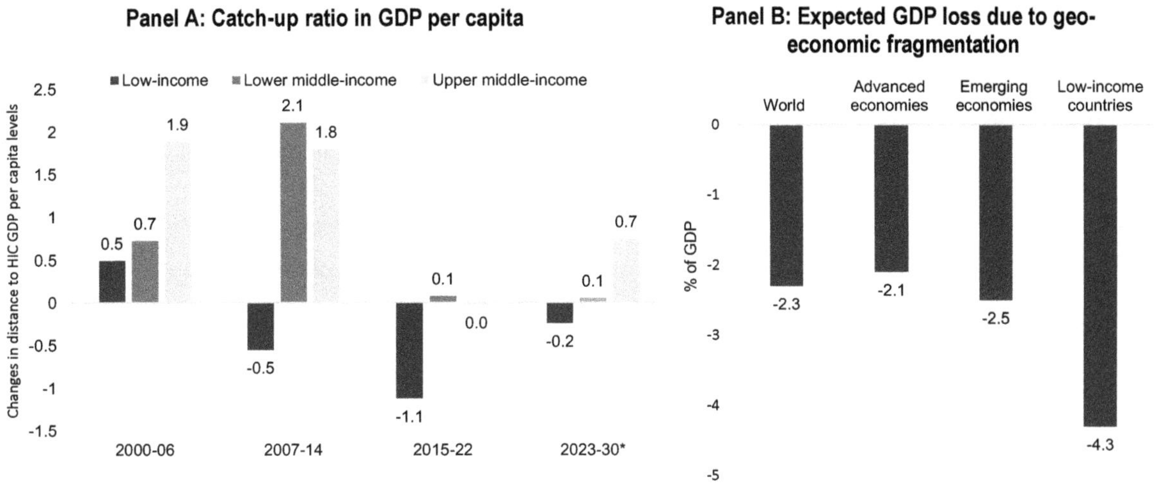

Note: * The 2023-30 ratios are OECD projections.
Source: Panel A: Authors' calculations based on OECD internal model and forecasts. Panel B: Authors' calculations based on Bolhuis, Chen and Kett (2023[19]), "Fragmentation in global trade: Accounting for commodities", https://www.imf.org/en/Publications/WP/Issues/2023/03/24/Fragmentation-in-Global-Trade-Accounting-for-Commodities-531327.

Box 1.1. Developing countries in sub-Saharan Africa are especially vulnerable to the structural slowdown in China's economy

From 1979 to 2018, China experienced an average annual growth rate of 10% and lifted over 800 million people out of poverty. Given their extensive trade and investment linkages with developing countries, China's rise also had far-reaching impacts on developing countries elsewhere, notably in Africa. The value of goods trade between China and Africa has grown at a compound annual growth rate of 16.1% from about USD 9.9 billion in 2000 to USD 260.8 billion in 2022 (Chakrabarty, 2024[21]).

The slowdown in Chinese demand, the resulting impact on commodity prices and ongoing cuts in Chinese financing are expected to affect African countries. In 2022, China's growth rate was a mere 3%, and it is gradually rebalancing its economy away from an export- and investment-led growth strategy to higher domestic consumption and what the Chinese leadership has termed "better quality growth" by focusing on sustainability and high-tech sectors (Chakrabarty, 2024[21]). According to Chen, Fornino and Rawlings (2024[22]), a 1 percentage point decline in China's GDP growth causes a 0.25 percentage point decline in sub-Saharan Africa's GDP growth within one year. At the same time, China's loan disbursements to Africa, which peaked in 2016, have also declined steadily from USD 28.8 billion in 2016 to USD 1.0 billion in 2022 (Global Development Policy Center, 2024[23]).

To adapt to the changes induced by China's economic slowdown and reduce their dependence on China, African countries will need to diversify their economies more, including through increased intra-African trade (Abdel-Latif et al., 2023[24]).

Source: Chakrabarty (2024[21]), "Shrinking Chinese demand, loan volumes weaken Africa's growth prospects", https://www.orfonline.org/expert-speak/shrinking-chinese-demand-loan-volumes-weaken-africa-s-growth-prospects; Chen, Fornino and Rawlings (2024[22]), "Navigating the evolving landscape between China and Africa's economic engagements", https://doi.org/10.5089/9798400267840.001; Global Development Policy Center (2024[23]), *Chinese Loans to Africa Database*, https://www.bu.edu/gdp/chinese-loans-to-africa-database/, Abdel-Latif et al. (2023[24]), "China's slowing economy will hit Sub-Saharan Africa's growth, https://www.imf.org/en/News/Articles/2023/11/09/cf-chinas-slowing-economy-will-hit-sub-saharan-africas-growth.

Convergence between SDG Index scores in HICs and developing countries advanced at a fast pace immediately after the AAAA in 2015 but has slowed significantly in recent years. Prior to the COVID-19 pandemic, LICs progressed faster on the SDG Index from 2015-19 (+1.6 points) than did HICs (+0.7 points). Since 2020, however, the SDG Index score of HICs has slightly improved (+0.3 points) while that of LICs has stagnated (+0.1 points) (Sachs, Lafortune and Fuller, 2024[25]). As seen in catch-up rates, the trend in recent years has been towards divergence rather than convergence. After 2019, the difference with HICs' SDG Index scores increased by 2.6% for LICs, indicating there was divergence in SDG performance (Figure 1.4).

Figure 1.4. Convergence in terms of SDG performance has slowed in recent years

Convergence in SDG Index scores with high-income countries

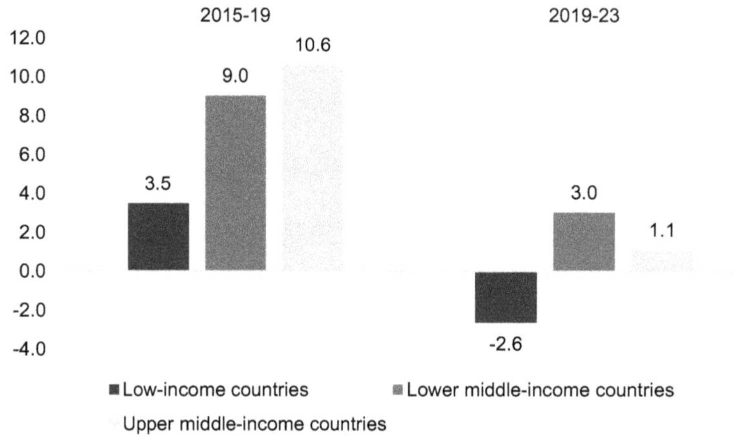

Source: Authors' calculations based on Sachs, Lafortune and Fuller (2024[25]), *Sustainable Development Report 2024: The SDGs and the UN Summit of the Future*, https://sdgtransformationcenter.org/reports/sustainable-development-report-2024.

1.2. Rising sustainable finance needs

Growing macroeconomic vulnerabilities point to escalating financing needs. The widening SDG and climate financing gaps risk derailing progress and leaving vulnerable populations further behind, as discussed above. This section looks beyond these immediate challenges to explore the evolution of total financial flows since the adoption in 2015 of the 2030 Agenda (along with the SDGs and the AAAA) and the Paris Agreement. Over this nearly ten-year period, progress has been mixed, signalling a pressing need for stronger links between macroeconomic policies and financing strategies to tackle both current challenges and the looming risks ahead.

Financing for sustainable development has rebounded

The COVID-19 crisis had an unprecedented impact on financing for sustainable development, leading to sharp declines in financial flows. Available financing for sustainable development in developing countries (excluding China) decreased from USD 4.6 trillion in 2019 to USD 3.9 trillion in 2020, a drop of USD 774 billion or 17% (OECD, 2022[26]). Available government revenue (after debt service payments) experienced the largest absolute decline over the period, falling by USD 689 billion, or 22%, from USD 3.1 trillion to USD 2.4 trillion (OECD, 2022[26]). This decline was greater than during the 2008-09 global financial crisis: specifically, three times bigger in LICs, twice as severe in LMICs and four times greater in UMICs (OECD, 2022[26]). The pandemic also set back external private finance in developing countries by USD 700 billion over 2019-20, a 60% larger decline than seen after the 2008-09 crisis (OECD, 2020[27]).

Since 2020, volumes of all sources of financing called for in the AAAA have increased, a sign of resilience despite the challenges posed by the COVID-19 pandemic. As shown in Figure 1.5, total available financing for sustainable development flows in developing countries (excluding China) reached USD 5.24 trillion in 2022 (in 2015 constant prices), a notable 22% increase from USD 4.31 trillion in 2015 and a 9% increase from pre-pandemic levels (USD 4.79 trillion in 2019). Total financial flows include public and private financing such as available government revenues, debt service, public concessional (official development assistance [ODA]) and non-concessional (loans only) funds, FDI, remittances, and philanthropic flows.

Figure 1.5. Financing for sustainable development in developing countries has shown resilience

Trends in flows by volume, 2015-22

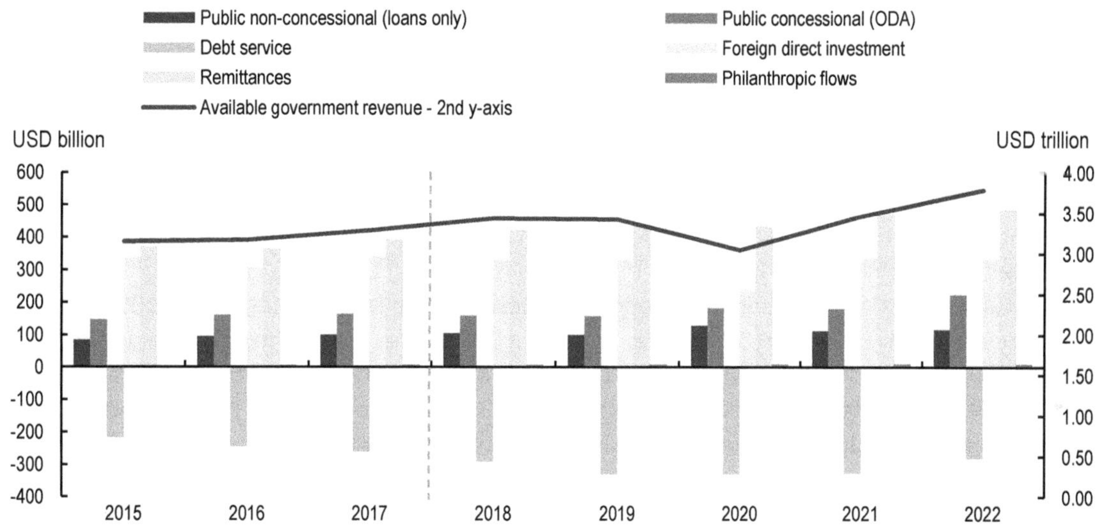

Note: Calculations include ODA-eligible countries (excluding China) and are based on 2015 constant prices. Public non-concessional funds, debt service, FDI, remittances and available government revenues flows are deflated using the GDP deflator of the US Federal Reserve Bank of St. Louis. Public concessional (ODA) and philanthropic flows are deflated using the OECD Development Assistance Committee (DAC) deflator. Available government revenue consists of government revenue minus debt service. This analysis is inspired by the ONE Campaign's Trillions Tracker and covers the period from 2015 (adoption of the AAAA) through 2022. Figures prior to 2018 are calculated using the cash flow method; figures from 2018 onward are based on the grant equivalent method. (Where available, 2023 figures are also included in the main body of text following Figure 1.5.)

Source: Authors' calculations. Public non-concessional flows are calculated from gross disbursements of non-concessional loans provided by official bilateral and multilateral sources and draw on long-term public and publicly guaranteed (PPG) debt data from World Bank Group (2024[28]), *Data Bank: International Debt Statistics* (database), https://databank.worldbank.org/source/international-debt-statistics. Debt service payments, including both principal and interest on long-term PPG debt, are calculated using World Bank (2024[29]), International Debt Report 2024, http://hdl.handle.net/10986/42444. Government revenue figures are derived from general government revenue data in International Monetary Fund (2024[4]), *World Economic Outlook, April 2024: Resilience Amid Divergence*, https://www.imf.org/en/Publications/WEO/Issues/2024/04/16/world-economic-outlook-april-2024. Public concessional flows (ODA) from all official donors, presented as gross disbursements, and philanthropic flows are sourced from the OECD (2024[30]), *OECD Data Explorer, DAC1: Flows by donor (ODA+OOF+Private) (database)*, http://data-explorer.oecd.org/s/9w. FDI inflows are based on UNCTAD (2024[31]), *Foreign direct investment: Inward and outward flows and stock, annual* (database), https://unctadstat.unctad.org/datacentre/dataviewer/US.FdiFlowsStock. Remittances are based on World Bank Group (2024[32]), *Data: Personal remittances, received (current US$)* (database), https://data.worldbank.org/indicator/BX.TRF.PWKR.CD.DT.

The next paragraphs analyse the trends in financial resources depicted in Figure 1.5 over 2015-22, adding the 2023 data point when available.

Available government revenue (after debt service payments) has rebounded since the COVID-19 crisis and in some cases even surpassed pre-pandemic levels. At the start of the pandemic, available government revenue in ODA-eligible countries (excluding China) dropped by 11% from USD 3.42 trillion in 2019 to USD 3.04 trillion in 2020, but quickly recovered to reach USD 3.46 trillion in 2021 and USD 3.79 trillion in 2022, a 9% increase over the previous year (Figure 1.5). Between 2015 and 2022, when the volume was USD 3.15 trillion, available government revenue increased by 20%, or 2% annually, and increased in all income groups: +21% in least developed countries (LDCs) and other LICs, +30% in LMICs, and +15% in UMICs (World Bank Group, 2024[28]) (Figure 1.6). At the same time, however, the share of available government revenue in financing for sustainable development has declined. Its ratio went from 2.7 times that of other financing sources in 2015 to 2.1 times in 2022. From 2015 to 2022, tax revenue as a percentage of GDP increased from 16.8% to 17.5% on average in developing countries (UN, 2024[33]). Nevertheless, the tax-to-GDP ratio remained below the effective tax rate of 15% in LICs (11.44% in 2022) and in LDCs (13.2% in 2022)[5] (UNU-WIDER, 2023[34]). In comparison, the average total tax revenue as a percentage of GDP in OECD countries increased from 32.9% in 2015 to 34% in 2022[6] (OECD, 2023[35]).

The drop in available government revenue was driven in part by debt service, which increased substantially as a response to the crisis, particularly in LDCs and other LICs and LMICs. All developing countries' net interest payments on public debt reached USD 847 billion in 2023, and more than half of developing countries allocate at least 8% of government revenues to interest payments (UNCTAD, 2024[36]). As shown in Figure 1.5, debt service for ODA-eligible countries (except China) increased from USD 217 billion in 2015 to USD 280 billion in 2022, with a peak of USD 329 billion in 2019. This represents a 29% increase over the period or a 4% increase annually. Over 2015-22, the rise in debt service reached alarming levels in LDCs and other LICs (62%) and LMICs (61%), though it increased only by 8% in UMICs. Over 2019-21, during the pandemic, debt service represented 9% to 10% of government revenues compared with 6% in 2015. In 2022, it fell to a 7% share. At the onset of the pandemic, in May 2020, the Group of Twenty (G20) launched the Debt Service Suspension Initiative (DSSI) to help prevent a further rise in debt burdens. The initiative enabled 48 of 73 eligible countries to redirect resources towards addressing the crisis and protecting vulnerable lives. By its conclusion in December 2021, the DSSI had suspended USD 12.9 billion in debt payments for participating developing countries.

Remittances have grown steadily since 2015. They are the second-largest source of financing to developing countries (excluding China) and the largest *external* source. They amounted to USD 476 billion in 2023, slightly down from USD 486 billion in 2022 but up from USD 370 billion in 2015 – a 31% increase over the period 2015-22 or 4% annually (Figure 1.6). While remittances increased in all income groups, the rise is more pronounced in UMICs (+48%) than in LDCs and other LICs (+24%) and in LMICs (+26%). Since 2015, remittances have been the largest source of external finance flows to LMICs, surpassing the volume of both public concessional flows and FDI. However, in the fourth quarter of 2023, the global average cost to send USD 200 remained elevated at 6.4%, which is 0.2 percentage points higher than in 2022 and more than double the 3% target set in SDG 10.c.1 (Migration Data Portal, 2024[37]).

After substantially declining during the crisis, FDI flows have rebounded, albeit unevenly, across developing countries. The latest available figures for global FDI flows indicate a total of USD 802 billion in the first half of 2024 (OECD, 2024[38]). In 2023, FDI inflows to ODA-eligible countries (excluding China) amounted to USD 286 billion, a 15% decrease from 2022. Nevertheless, FDI inflows to developing countries also have demonstrated resilience over time. FDI reached USD 335 billion in 2022, closely aligning with the 2015 level of USD 338 billion and significantly rebounding from the 2020 volume of USD 238 billion. This represents a marginal 1% decline over the entire period of 2015-22. However, not all income groups experienced this rebound in FDI: flows declined by 42% in LDCs and by 84% in other LICs but decreased by only 2% in LMICs and increased by 8% in UMICs (Figure 1.6). For LDCs, the drop can be explained by an exceptional peak in 2015. In the case of UMICs, they were the most affected during the pandemic due to their stronger integration in global capital markets, but they also recovered faster as a result.

Public concessional (ODA) and non-concessional flows played a countercyclical role, mitigating the effects of the COVID-19 crisis. In 2023, total ODA from all official donors to developing countries reached a record high of USD 233 billion (in 2015 constant prices) as donors increased support for Ukraine and provided more humanitarian assistance to developing countries.[7] Of this total, DAC countries' contribution amounted to USD 194 billion; contributions from non-DAC countries and multilateral organisations amounted to USD 15 billion and USD 23 billion, respectively (OECD, 2024[39]; OECD, 2024[30]). Public concessional (ODA) and non-concessional (loans only) flows significantly increased over 2015-22. Public concessional (ODA) flows from official donors to developing countries excluding China reached USD 224 billion in 2022, an increase from USD 147 billion in 2015 (+52% over the period or 6% annually). ODA flows increased by 21% in LDCs, 29% in other LICs, 85% in LMICs and 5% in UMICs over the same period (Figure 1.6). Public non-concessional flows totalled USD 116 billion in 2022, up from USD 84 billion in 2015 (+38% over the period or 5% annually). The 75% increase in multilateral non-concessional flows, from USD 49 billion in 2015 to 86 billion in 2022, compensated for the 13% decrease in bilateral non-concessional flows from USD 35 billion in 2015 to USD 30 billion in 2022 (Figure 1.6). The countercyclical nature of international public finance helped offset the shortfall in other external financing flows, though it could not fully make up for the losses (OECD, 2022[26]).

Philanthropic flows represent a small share of the total financial flow volume of financing for sustainable development. Philanthropic flows amounted to USD 9.9 billion in 2022 compared with 3.5 billion in 2015 (+185% over the period or 23% annually), though this increase was largely due to improved data coverage (OECD, 2024[40]).

Figure 1.6. Increases in financial flows in developing countries varied across types and income groups

Trends in flows, percent change per year, 2015-22

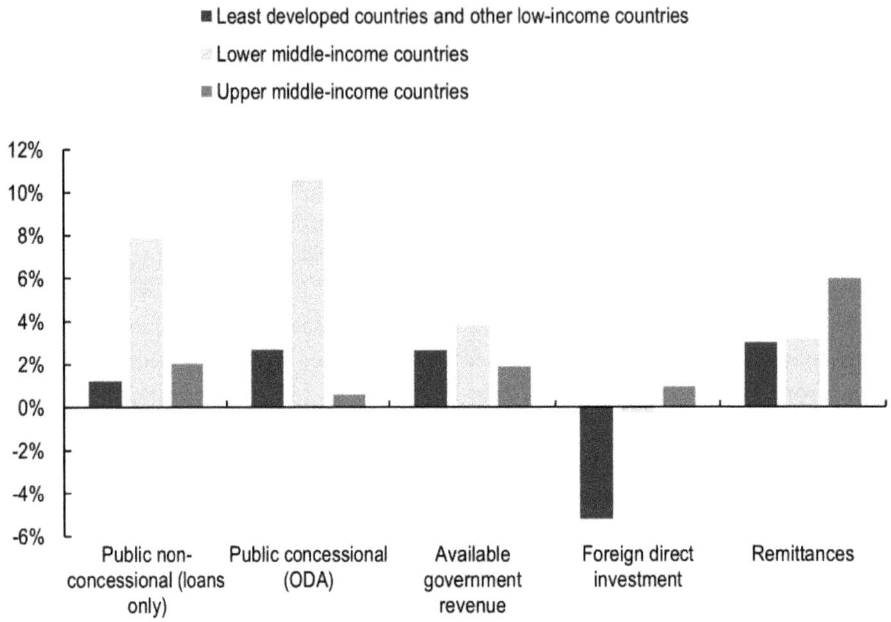

Note: Calculations cover ODA-eligible countries excluding China and are based on 2015 constant prices. Public non-concessional, debt service, FDI, remittances and available government revenues flows are deflated using the GDP deflator from the US Federal Reserve Bank of St. Louis. Public concessional (ODA) flows are deflated using the DAC deflator. Available government revenue consists of government revenue minus debt service. Other LICs data are included where available. Calculations were conducted collaboratively by the ONE Campaign and the authors.
Source: Public non-concessional flows are calculated from gross disbursements of non-concessional loans provided by official bilateral and multilateral sources, drawing on long-term public and publicly guaranteed (PPG) debt data from International Monetary Fund (2024[4]), *World Economic Outlook, April 2024: Resilience Amid Divergence*, https://www.imf.org/en/Publications/WEO/Issues/2024/04/16/world-economic-outlook-april-2024; World Bank Group (2024[28]), *Data Bank: International Debt Statistics* (database), https://databank.worldbank.org/source/international-debt-statistics (released in December 2023), which is also the source of data for debt service payments, including both principal and interest on long-term PPG debt. Government revenue figures are derived from general government revenue data in International Monetary Fund (2024[4]), *World Economic Outlook, April 2024: Resilience Amid Divergence*, https://www.imf.org/en/Publications/WEO/Issues/2024/04/16/world-economic-outlook-april-2024. Public concessional flows (ODA) from all official donors, presented as gross disbursements, are sourced OECD (2024[30]), *OECD Data Explorer, DAC1: Flows by donor (ODA+OOF+Private) (database)*, http://data-explorer.oecd.org/s/9w. FDI inflows are based on UNCTAD (2024[31]), *Foreign direct investment: Inward and outward flows and stock, annual* (database), https://unctadstat.unctad.org/datacentre/dataviewer/US.FdiFlowsStock. Remittances are based on World Bank Group (2024[32]), *Data: Personal remittances, received (current US$)* (database), https://data.worldbank.org/indicator/BX.TRF.PWKR.CD.DT.

Resources remain insufficient to meet accelerating financing needs

The SDG financing gap has widened significantly since the COVID-19 crisis. In 2014, just prior to the formal adoption of the SDGs, the United Nations (UN) estimated that the annual financing gap for achieving sustainable development in developing countries was USD 2.5 trillion, reflecting the need for enhanced investments in economic infrastructure (power, transportation, telecommunications, water and sanitation, etc.); food security; social infrastructure (education, healthcare, etc.); and environmental sustainability (UNCTAD, 2014[41]; UN, 2023[42]). Financing for implementing the SDGs was already off track but in 2020, after COVID-19 struck, the gap ballooned to USD 3.9 trillion – a 56% increase in just six years. The pandemic further intensified the so-called scissor effect in SDG financing, meaning the combination of rising needs and declining resources (OECD, 2020[27]). Two main factors in developing countries were responsible: the USD 689 billion drop in available government revenue over 2019-20, which represented over 80% of the total decline in sustainable development financing, and the USD 907 billion increase in government spending in response to the COVID-19 emergency. This emergency expenditure accounted for nearly 30% of total government revenues in 2019 and exacerbated the challenges these countries faced in mobilising domestic and external financial resources (OECD, 2022[26]). The widening gap also reflects systemic challenges such as insufficient public and private investments, debt vulnerabilities, and limited fiscal space in many countries (OECD, 2020[27]).

The annual financing gap for achieving the SDGs has reached alarming levels, with the latest estimates ranging from USD 3 trillion to USD 4 trillion. The UN Trade and Development (UNCTAD) estimated that the SDG investment gap in developing countries amounts to USD 4 trillion per year from 2023 to 2030 (UNCTAD, 2023[43]). According to the G20 Independent Expert Group (2023[44]) and Bhattacharya et al. (2023[45]), the estimated annual gap in 2023 was USD 3 trillion in emerging markets and developing countries (EMDCs) excluding China, including USD 2.5 trillion in public spending. According to the ONE Campaign (2024[46]), annual public spending (and planned expenditures) on climate and development rose by approximately USD 700 billion between 2019 and 2022 but represent 29% of the amount needed to close the financing gap, leaving an outstanding gap in official finance of nearly USD 1.75 trillion (Table 1.1).

Table 1.1. Various estimates show the annual SDG financing gap is substantial and growing

Estimates of the SDG financing gap (USD trillion)

	Total SDG financing needs **by 2030**	*Of which climate-related financing needs are*	SDG financing gap before COVID-19	SDG financing gap **by 2030**	*Of which the climate-related financing gap is*	Countries
UNCTAD			2.5 *(in 2014)*	3.8-4.3 Midpoint: 4	2.2	Developing countries
Bhattacharya et al. (2023)	5.4	2.4		3	1.8	EMDCs excluding People's Republic of China
Independent Expert Group for the 2023 G20 Summit				3		EMDCs excluding People's Republic of China
OECD				3.9 *(in 2020)*		ODA-eligible countries, excluding People's Republic of China
Climate Policy Initiative		9			5.5	Global

Note: The figures are in USD trillions. The amounts are based on an annual investment basis by 2030.
Source: UNCTAD (2023[47]), *World Investment Report 2023: Investing in Sustainable Energy for All*, https://unctad.org/publication/world-investment-report-2023; Bhattacharya et al. (2023[45]), *A Climate Finance Framework: Decisive Action to Deliver on the Paris Agreement – Summary*, https://www.lse.ac.uk/granthaminstitute/publication/a-climate-finance-framework-decisive-action-to-deliver-on-the-paris-agreement-summary/; G20 Independent Experts Group (2023[44]), *Strengthening Multilateral Development Banks: The Triple Agenda - Volume 1*, https://www.gihub.org/resources/publications/strengthening-multilateral-development-banks-the-triple-agenda-report-of-the-g20-independent-experts-group/; OECD (2022[26]), *Global Outlook on Financing for Sustainable Development 2023: No Sustainability Without Equity*, https://doi.org/10.1787/fcbe6ce9-en; Buchner et al. (2023[48]), *Global Landscape of Climate Finance 2023*, https://www.climatepolicyinitiative.org/publication/global-landscape-of-climate-finance-2023/.

Needs are expanding at a faster pace than available resources, driving the widening SDG financing gap, including for climate-related goals. While total available resources grew by 22% between 2015 and 2022, the SDG financing gap increased by 60%, or nearly three times faster (Figure 1.7). Based on their 2015-22 growth rate, when volumes increased from USD 4.31 to USD 5.24 trillion, total available resources for financing sustainable development are projected to reach USD 6.37 trillion by 2030, a 48% increase from 2015. However, if the SDG financing gap continues to grow at its 2015-22 rate, when it increased from USD 2.5 to 4.0 trillion, it is expected to reach USD 6.4 trillion by 2030, which would be a 156% increase since 2015. It should be noted that these are conservative estimates given the challenges and uncertainties that lie ahead until 2030.

Figure 1.7. Needs are projected to continue growing faster than available resources in developing countries up to 2030

SDG financing gap, 2015-30 (estimated)

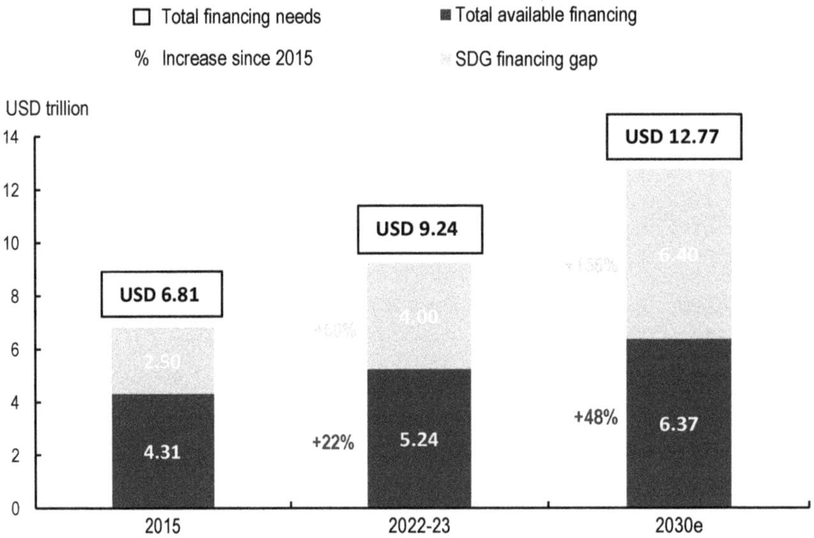

Note: For the second column, total available financing is based on 2022 figures, while the SDG financing gap is assessed for 2023. The 2015 and 2023 SDG financing gaps are based on UNCTAD estimations. Total available financing figures are based on authors' calculations and 2015 constant prices. Authors' calculations for the estimated 2030 financing needs are based on the growth rates for total available financing and the SDG financing gap from 2015 to 2022.
Source: Authors' calculations and UNCTAD (2023[47]), *World Investment Report 2023: Investing in Sustainable Energy for All*, https://unctad.org/publication/world-investment-report-2023.

The response to the climate crisis is a main driver of the growing financing needs. Bhattacharya et al. (2023[45]) estimate that USD 2.4 trillion will be needed annually for climate-related investments in EMDCs other than China by 2030; this represents a more than fourfold increase (+433%) from the 2019 investment baseline (Figure 1.8). At the sector level, USD 1.5 trillion will be required for the energy transition alone, USD 250 billion for adaptation and resilience, USD 300 billion for loss and damage,[8] USD 300 billion in natural capital and sustainable agriculture, and USD 75 billion for a just transition[9] (Bhattacharya et al., 2023[45]).

More than half of the annual SDG financing gap relates to climate, predominantly the energy transition. According to UNCTAD (2023[43]), more than half of the SDG financing gap, or USD 2.2 trillion annually, is associated with the energy transition, while the energy investment gap has grown by 100%, or USD 1.1 trillion, since 2015. This latter gap refers to investments in clean energy including renewables, energy efficiency, and all related transition technologies and sources (UNCTAD, 2023[43]). The biodiversity sector requires another USD 300 billion to support nature conservation, sustainable fishing, ocean pollution control and sustainable forestry (Zhan et al., 2023[49]). Van Tilburg et al (2024[50]) highlight that, based on analyses by the G20 Independent Experts Group (2023[44]) and Bhattacharya et al. (2023[45]), the annual climate-related financing gap could amount to USD 1.8 trillion annually by 2030. At the same time, developing countries (excluding China) are falling behind in the energy transition. LICs and LMICs accounted for only 7% of global clean energy spending in 2022, for example, highlighting a significant disparity in investment distribution (Bhattacharya et al., 2023[45]). Global investments in clean energy reached a record high in 2023, driven primarily by rapid growth in solar photovoltaic technologies and electric vehicles. More than 90% of the investment surge since 2021 occurred in developed countries and China.

The adaptation financing gap is growing. As illustrated in Figure 1.8, USD 250 billion will be required annually for adaptation and resilience by 2030 (Bhattacharya et al., 2023[45]). The UN Environment Programme estimates that USD 215 billion per year will be needed for all developing countries, an amount that represented 0.56% of their combined GDP in 2021. While the absolute costs are highest for UMICs and LMICs, adaptation costs as a percentage of GDP are significantly higher for LICs (3.5%) than for LMICs (0.7%) and UMICs (0.5%). Additionally, while they contribute little to the causes of climate change, people living in LDCs and small island developing states (SIDS) are disproportionately more vulnerable to climate hazards and more likely to die from climate-related disasters. For LDCs and SIDS, estimated needs amount to 0.7% and 2.0% of GDP, respectively, or a total of USD 29 billion annually – approximately 12% of the modelled adaptation costs for all developing countries (United Nations Environment Programme, 2023[51]). Adaptation finance provided and mobilised by developed countries amounted to USD 32.4 billion in 2022, and while this was a significant increase from the USD 10.1 billion in such financing in 2016, the current level of investment is still not sufficient to meet growing adaptation needs (OECD, 2024[52]). The highest adaptation costs are associated with river flood protection, infrastructure and coastal protection and are concentrated in East Asia and the Pacific and Latin America and the Caribbean, among others (United Nations Environment Programme, 2023[51]).

Figure 1.8. Annual climate financing needs could more than quadruple by 2030

Projected annual climate financing needs by 2030, by activities, versus other SDG financing needs

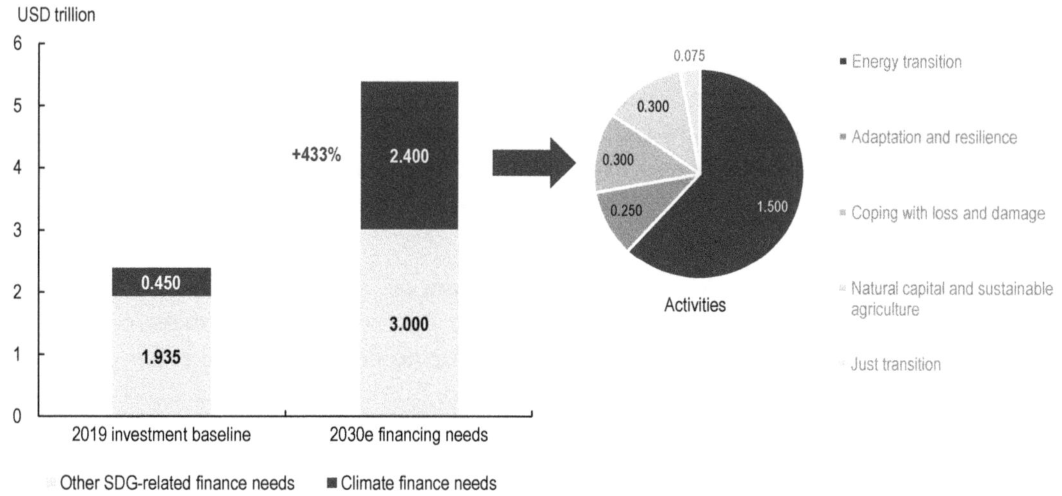

Note: The 2030 estimates reflect the annual needs.
Source: Bhattacharya et al. (2023[45]), *A Climate Finance Framework: Decisive Action to Deliver on the Paris Agreement – Summary*, https://www.lse.ac.uk/granthaminstitute/publication/a-climate-finance-framework-decisive-action-to-deliver-on-the-paris-agreement-summary/.

The second-largest SDG investment gap is in the water and sanitation sector. According to UNCTAD (2023[43]) estimates, the investment gap for SDG 6 (clean water and sanitation) has grown by 70%, or USD 0.2 trillion from 2015 to 2023. This gap encompasses water sources, including new water treatment plants and desalination facilities, as well as sanitation infrastructure and wastewater management. Combined, the energy transition and water and sanitation sectors account for more than 85% of the USD 1.5 trillion increase in the investment gap and nearly 70% of the total investment gap projected for the remaining years until 2030 (UNCTAD, 2023[43]).

The remainder of the overall SDG investment gap is divided among other sectors. To support SDG 9 (industry, innovation and infrastructure), there is a projected combined annual investment gap of USD 400 billion in infrastructure, particularly in transportation and telecommunications and excluding energy infrastructure. The food and agriculture sector is estimated to need an additional USD 300 billion each year to achieve SDG 1 (no poverty) and SDG 2 (zero hunger), primarily for capital investments in agricultural systems, food processing, research and rural infrastructure. Regarding SDG 3 (good health and well-being) and SDG 4 (quality education), the health and education sectors face a gap of USD 100 to USD 600 billion a year, mainly for operational costs related to running hospitals and schools (Zhan et al., 2023[49]).

Additional needs stemming from the multiple crises of recent years are also contributing to the widening SDG financing gap. The investment needs for the SDGs have grown due to external shocks, particularly the COVID-19 pandemic and crises related to food, fuel and finance. These economic disruptions have disproportionately affected developing countries and LDCs. According to the 2024 UN report on financing for sustainable development, the annual financing gap to meet SDG targets in social protection and essential health care has increased by approximately 30% since the onset of the COVID-19 pandemic (UN, 2024[53]). In 2020, the financing gap for implementing a social protection floor for everyone was estimated at USD 1.2 trillion per year, or 3.8% of global GDP (UN, 2024[53]). The annual financing gap is even greater in LMICs and LICs, where it is 5.1% and 15.9% of GDP, respectively (UN, 2024[53]). Investment strategies and financing plans in support of the SDG targets must account for the significant demographic shifts expected over the next three decades. For example, according to some estimates, the world population is projected to increase by 1.9 billion between 2020 and 2050, with all of that growth taking place in EMDCs (except China) – and in all developing regions but especially Africa and South Asia (Bhattacharya et al., 2022[54]).

Concurrent crises have also depleted traditional policy levers

While the SDG financing gap continues to widen, monetary and fiscal policy options have been largely exhausted. While the COVID-19 pandemic contributed to the widening SDG financing gap, the international crisis response that comprised exceptional public expenditures and policy measures left little room for manoeuvre for developing country governments to finance SDG-related investments and expenditures.

Monetary policy measures to tackle inflation in advanced economies led to tighter financing conditions for developing countries. Recent monetary tightening by advanced economies to fight soaring inflation has posed a massive challenge for developing countries. As the ten-year US Treasury yield rose from 1.5% in December 2021 to 4.6% at the end of September 2023, borrowing costs increased for all countries but LICs were altogether cut off from the bond market. At the same time, the number of International Development Association countries issuing sovereign bonds in international bond markets decreased from seven in 2021 to zero in 2023 (Properzi, 2023[55]). Between 2021 and 2022, the amount of public sector bonds outstanding decreased across income groups (Figure 1.9, Panel A), dropping by 5.2% in UMICs, 2.7% in LMICs and 0.3% in LICs.

Steep interest rate increases in developing countries threaten to deter investments in sustainable development. Interest rate increases in the United States and other advanced economies are associated with a greater likelihood of financial crises in developing economies (Arteta, Kamin and Ruch, 2022[56]). For example, the potential for higher interest earnings in advanced economies can encourage capital market investors to re-channel flows by withdrawing investments from developing countries. To counter these risks, central banks in developing countries pursued even faster rate increases than those in developed economies (Figure 1.9, Panel B). High interest rates, however, can deter crucial investments in sustainable development including renewable energy and climate-resilient infrastructure, thereby stalling progress towards the 2030 and climate agendas.

Figure 1.9. Monetary tightening dried up financing for developing countries

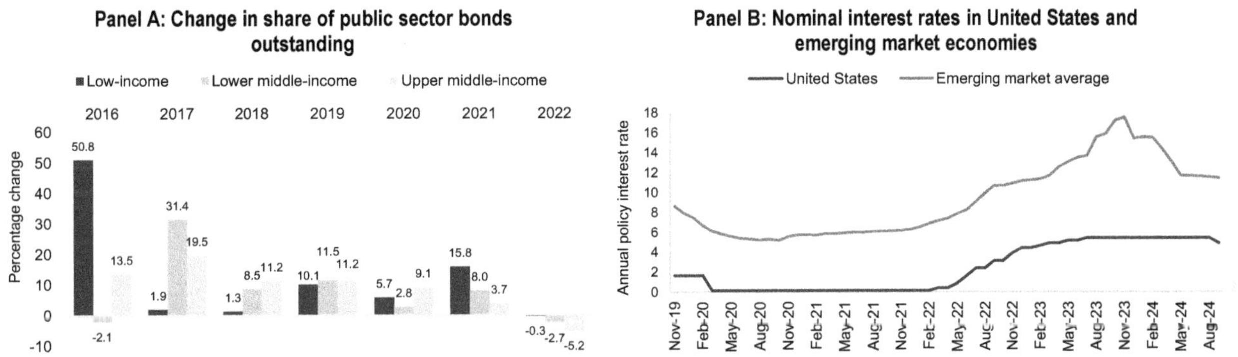

Source: Panel A: Authors' calculations based on World Bank (2023[57]), *Data Bank: International Debt Statistics (database)*, https://databank.worldbank.org/source/international-debt-statistics. Panel B: Bank of International Settlements (2024[58]), *Central Bank Policy Rates* (database), https://data.bis.org/topics/CBPOL.

On the fiscal policy side, the massive expenditures to fight the COVID-19 pandemic have exhausted public budgets. Fiscal support measures to support health systems and provide lifelines to vulnerable households and firms amounted to USD 13.8 trillion globally by the end of 2020 (International Monetary Fund, 2021[59]). Russia's war against Ukraine and climate change-related disasters have further exacerbated the situation, increasing the demand for key public expenditures while revenues were declining. In 2019, developing countries' fiscal deficit reached a peak of 5.3% of GDP before improving to 3.7% in 2021 and 3.1% in 2022 (Figure 1.10, Panel A). Such deficits can strain developing economies, limiting their ability to invest in essential services and infrastructure and making it more difficult to achieve the SDGs (UNCTAD, 2024[60]).

The external debt of developing countries is growing and increasingly costly, crowding out critical investments in sustainable development. Even before the pandemic, many countries were facing rising debt levels and debt service burdens. The pandemic as well as international conflicts and geopolitical tensions worsened these, and debt ratios have consistently exceeded 50% since 2020. The number of countries in debt distress increased from 3 in 2015 to 11 in 2024 while the number at high risk of debt distress rose from 16 to 24 (Figure 1.10, Panel B). In 2023, a record 54 developing countries, 38% of the total, allocated 10% or more of government revenues to interest payments (UNCTAD, 2024[61]). From 2020 to the first quarter of 2024, there were 224 downgrades but only 105 upgrades for EMDCs. There were more upgrades than downgrades in HICs and UMICs in 2023 and the first quarter of 2024, while LICs and LMICs experienced more than twice as many downgrades as upgrades (OECD, forthcoming[62]). In many cases, the fiscal deficit growth also triggered currency devaluations that raised the cost of external debt. Rising interest payments are crowding out critical public expenditures such as for health and education. A total of 3.3 billion people live in countries that spend more on interest payments than on either education or health.

Moreover, interest payments outweigh climate investments, thus slowing efforts towards climate change adaptation and mitigation (UNCTAD, 2024[36]).

Figure 1.10. Expenditures to fight the pandemic and other crises exhausted public budgets in developing countries, plunging some into a debt crisis

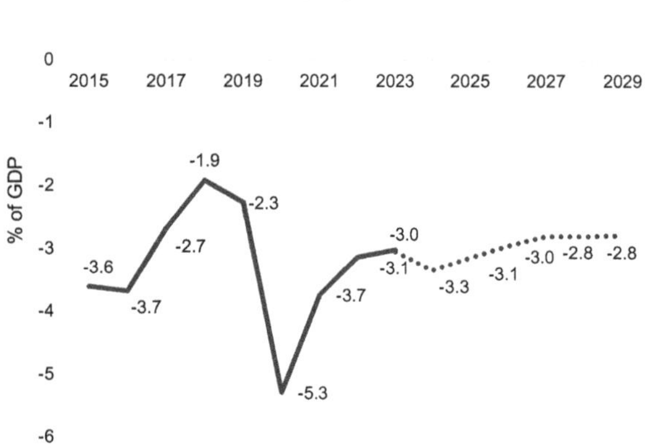

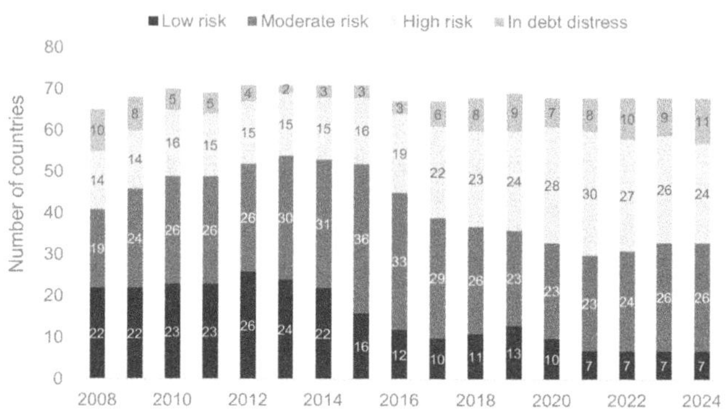

Source: Panel A: Authors' calculations based on International Monetary Fund, (2024[63]), *World Economic Outlook Database: October 2024 Edition*, https://www.imf.org/en/Publications/WEO/weo-database/2024/October. Panel B: World Bank (2024[64]), *Debt Sustainability Analysis (DSA): Latest Publicly Available Debt Sustainability Analyses Under the Joint Bank-Fund Debt Sustainability Framework for Low Income Countries (LIC-DSF)* (database), https://www.worldbank.org/en/programs/debt-toolkit/dsa.

1.3. Walking the crest line towards the global goals

In light of rising geo-economic tensions and growing financing needs, it is crucial to identify a sustainable balance between ambition and practicality to accelerate progress towards the SDGs. Finding this balance requires that a critical equilibrium is maintained between setting ambitious objectives and ensuring that they remain grounded in practical implementation. This approach is essential to avoid unintended negative consequences, particularly in addressing the inherent risks of decoupling. Decoupling refers to growth that simultaneously produces positive economic and social outcomes while avoiding negative environmental ones, such as by reducing carbon dioxide emissions. One such inherent risk of decoupling is that its benefits are distributed unevenly, disproportionately impacting the poorest and most vulnerable populations.

In light of the widening gap between needs and financing, both developed and developing countries must take action to achieve the goals of the 2030 Agenda and Paris Agreement. Failure to act will have far-reaching and costly economic, social and environmental consequences. However, developing countries cannot bear the costs of the upfront investments that are necessary for the SDGs and climate transition. Ensuring policy coherence for sustainable development across sectors and levels of governance will be essential to harmonise efforts and amplify the impact of investments and avoid contradictory measures that undermine progress. Prompt action to close the financing gaps that countries face will be critical if an escalation of costs is to be avoided going forward.

Negative feedback loops need to be closed

Failure to close the gap in financing across the SDGs will generate self-reinforcing and momentum-gaining "feedback loops" that will further amplify the gap. For example, insufficient investment in SDG 16 (peace, justice and strong institutions) leads to heightened conflict and instability, deterring both domestic and foreign investment. This perpetuates cycles of poverty, weakens governance and diverts resources away from critical sectors. Macroeconomic costs of conflict are generally very large and persist for years, with GDP per capita about 28% lower ten years after conflict onset (Novta and Pugacheva, 2021[65]). Similarly, neglect of SDG 4 (quality education) erodes human capital, reducing productivity and economic growth while diminishing the capacity of future generations to address emerging challenges. UNESCO (2024[66]) estimates that the annual global cost of inaction on education is USD 10 trillion, a striking finding that underscores the profound economic impact of skills deficits worldwide. Trade restrictions and barriers, counterproductive to SDG 17 (partnerships for the goals), stifle economic diversification, limit market access for developing countries and exacerbate inequalities in the global economic system. The resulting economic pressures further limit countries' fiscal space to invest in sustainable development, which compounds the negative effects of climate change, conflicts and educational deficits. Investing in key sectors such as electrification, water and sanitation, public transport, and education in developing countries, on the other hand, is a high-return, long-term investment that is crucial for enhancing living standards and yielding economic returns that significantly exceed the cost of capital (Sachs et al., 2023[67]).

Failing to act on climate change will entail considerable economic and social costs in the future. A Climate Policy Initiative study estimates that social and economic costs incurred under business-as-usual warming scenarios will lead to at least USD 1.27 trillion in additional losses due to climate change compared with a warming scenario of 1.5°C (Buchner et al., 2023[48]). Economic losses would result from a reduction in global working hours by 2.2% worldwide by 2030, costing the global economy USD 2.4 trillion (Kjellstrom et al., 2019[68]), as well as climate-related disasters such as hurricanes, floods and wildfires, which have already caused USD 299 billion in economic losses in 2022 alone (Aon, 2023[69]). Climate change impacts will also lead to social costs such as an additional 250 000 deaths per year globally between 2030 and 2050 from malnutrition, malaria, diarrhoea and heat stress alone (WHO, 2024[70]).

The presumed costs of inaction will far exceed the upfront investments necessary for a transition towards a more sustainable development pathway. This makes a compelling case for investment. Climate scenarios from the Network of Central Banks and Supervisors for Greening the Financial System, a group of 127 central banks and financial supervisors working to manage climate risks and boost green investment, suggest that making an orderly transition to net zero by 2050 could result in global GDP being 7% higher than it would be under current policies (Figure 1.11, Panel A) (NGFS, 2024[71]).

Investing in climate transition will not only help avoid losses but also create new local business opportunities in developing countries that promote growth in the long term. Mobilising the investment required to secure clean energy transitions will reshape the entire clean energy supply chain consisting of equipment manufacturers, service providers, developers and engineering, procurement and construction companies. The cumulative market opportunity for manufacturers of wind turbines, solar panels, lithium-ion batteries, electrolysers and fuel cells will amount to USD 27 trillion, if the world gets on track for net zero emissions by 2050, according to the International Energy Agency (2021[72]). Such a shift also offers significant benefits for local industries in developing countries endowed with natural resources needed for the climate transition. However, as highlighted in recent FfD4 discussions it will be crucial that developing countries build local capacities, access technologies and implement industrial standards required to share in the benefits of green industrialisation.

The energy transition could massively boost demand for minerals and metals from developing countries. Renewable technologies such as battery storage systems, low-carbon hydrogen, solar panels and wind turbines, as well as the required expansion of transmission infrastructure, rely on minerals and metals. This growing mineral demand is expected to require an estimated USD 1.7 trillion in global mining investment (World Bank Group, 2022[73]). Many of these resources are held by developing countries. Over two-thirds of the world's known lithium reserves are in the so-called lithium triangle of Argentina, Bolivia and Chile, for example. The Democratic Republic of the Congo holds the world's largest cobalt reserves; bauxite reserves are highly concentrated in Brazil, Guinea, Indonesia and Jamaica (World Bank Group, 2022[73]). Attracting investment in critical minerals could contribute to economic growth, jobs and local development in these countries. At the same time, as highlighted in the FfD4 Zero draft (UN, 2025[74]), global partnerships and regional collaboration; enhanced negotiation and market fairness; and promotion of sustainable commodity practices through innovative financing and technical assistance are essential to ensure critical mineral development that is environmentally and socially responsible and benefits local communities while avoiding harmful impacts (OECD et al., 2024[75]; UN, 2025[74]).

Developing countries are disproportionately affected by climate change and will reap the greatest benefits from an orderly transition. LDCs are particularly vulnerable to the effects of climate change. While they have contributed only about 1% of global emissions, they have seen a fivefold increase in climate-related hazards since the 1970s (UNCTAD, 2022[76]). Thirty-eight LDCs and other LICs – but only six LMICs, five UMICs and no advanced economies – display high climate vulnerability above 0.5 (Figure 1.11, Panel B). The impact of disasters is ten times more costly (as a share of their GDP) for the economies of LDCs than for the economies of the richest countries (UN, 2022[77]). In addition to economic losses, human and social costs are disproportionately high in LDCs. Nearly 70% of deaths caused by climate-related disasters over the last 50 years occurred in LDCs (World Meteorological Organization, 2021[78]).

Other climate impacts, such as biodiversity loss, are more difficult to quantify but make the case for investment in sustainable development more compelling. The World Bank projects up to USD 225 billion in GDP losses by 2030 due to lost ecosystem services such as pollination and the provision of timber and marine stocks (Johnson et al., 2021[79]). The Dasgupta Review of the economics of biodiversity concluded that roughly half the value of global GDP is directly reliant on nature and that damage to nature is costing the global economy roughly USD 2.7 trillion annually (Dasgupta, 2021[80]). Due to their wide variance and the uncertainty around them, these estimates are often excluded from most cost-of-inaction projections. Still, they indicate that failure to make timely investments in biodiversity preservation will add a significant burden to the global economy.

Figure 1.11. Closing the sustainable development finance gap now will generate returns in the form of avoided losses and damages

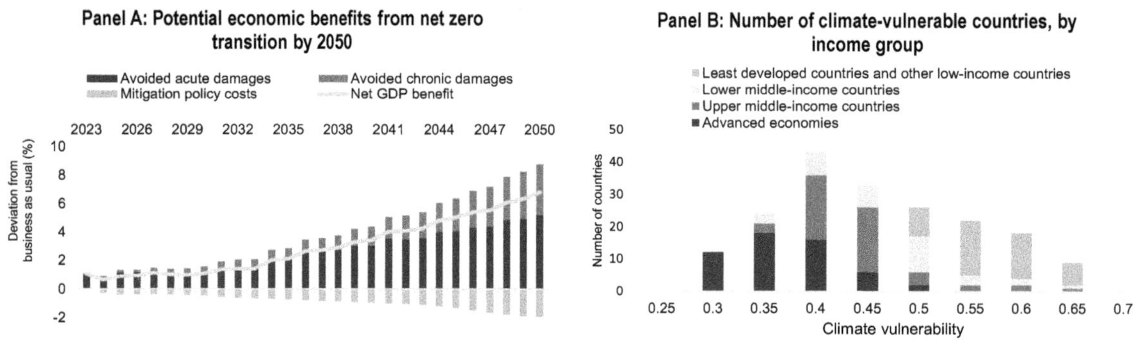

Source: Panel A: Authors' calculations based on the GCAM model of orderly net zero transition in NGFS (2024[71]), *NGFS Climate Scenarios* (database), https://www.ngfs.net/ngfs-scenarios-portal/. Panel B: Authors' calculations based on Notre Dame Global Adaptation Initiative (2022[81]), *ND-GAIN Country Index, Vulnerability and Readiness* (database), https://gain.nd.edu/our-work/country-index/rankings/.

A successful global transition towards sustainability will depend heavily on financing solutions that are tailored to the needs of developing countries. While they have a critical share of the resources and ecosystem services vital to the global economy, developing countries often face severe financial constraints – e.g. high debt levels, limited fiscal space and greater vulnerability to economic shocks – that make the upfront costs of transition unaffordable without external support. Bridging this gap will require mobilising resources including government revenues, official development finance (ODF) and innovative funding mechanisms. The 2025 FfD4 provides an opportunity to develop solutions in support of a truly inclusive transition that leaves no country behind.

The alignment of the trillions can be accelerated

In addition to closing negative feedback loops that will amplify the SDG financing gap, there are opportunities to accelerate alignment of financial flows for a more equitable distribution that responds to vulnerabilities and financing needs. Private sector organisations increasingly manage environmental, social and governance issues, recognising them as financial risks (UN, 2025[74]). However, accelerating the alignment of the global financial system with global goals will require shifting incentives along the investment chain. There are opportunities to do so, including by recalibrating a share of global financial assets and flows to support pathways for mobilising resources at the scale and speed required to meet global challenges.

Insights from the OECD monitoring exercise, presented in subsequent chapters, suggest further options to align the different sources of financing for sustainable development. The exercise looked at progress made on more than 70 SDG targets and many additional proxy indicators that are relevant to the AAAA action areas. Its aim was to contribute to the current financing for development monitoring mechanism, including the UN-led Interagency Task Force on Financing for Development (of which the OECD is a member), whose main monitoring output is the annual Financing for Sustainable Development Report.

There are vast financial resources within the global system that, if better aligned and allocated towards addressing vulnerabilities, could substantially close the SDG and climate financing gaps. Global financial assets total USD 461 trillion, a clear indication that the required funds to support sustainable development already exist (Figure 1.12). However, a mismatch in distribution, high debt servicing costs and other financial leakages limit the effectiveness of these resources in addressing the SDG financing needs (OECD, 2022[26]).

Fixing the incentives within the global financial system is essential to accelerate alignment of resources towards sustainable and equitable transition. Current regulatory frameworks and financial incentives are often out of step with the realities of the required transition, favouring short-term gains and in some cases perpetuating harmful practices such as fossil fuel subsidies. There have been repeated calls to reduce fossil fuel subsidies. For example, G7 countries have committed to phase out inefficient fossil fuel subsidies by 2025. SDG 12 and target 12.c.1 aim to increase the effectiveness of policies that rationalise inefficient fossil fuel subsidies. Despite targets like these, however, global explicit subsidies increased to USD 1.53 trillion globally in 2022, a fivefold increase over 2020, thereby reversing progress towards the net zero transition (UN, 2024[82]). At COP29, countries reaffirmed their commitment to phasing out inefficient fossil fuel subsidies but did not establish a concrete timeline or binding agreements, underscoring the persistent difficulties in achieving substantial progress on this issue. Ensuring policy coherence across ministries will be crucial to harmonise efforts, minimise negative transboundary spillovers and amplify the urgency of reforms. The upcoming FfD4 conference presents an opportunity for nations to discuss and implement solutions that can drive efforts to reshape financial incentives, thus enabling a fair and inclusive transition to sustainable development and climate resilience.

Regulatory adjustments are needed that governments have yet to fully enact. Current regulations often lag in aligning incentives with the SDGs, particularly in subsidies, taxonomies and sustainability reporting, among others. For example, the absence of standardised global frameworks for sustainability taxonomies has resulted in fragmented markets, which dampens investor confidence and slows the alignment of investments with SDG priorities. Similarly, limited progress on integrating double materiality into sustainability reporting leaves gaps in the understanding of the broader social and environmental impacts of private sector activities. Some advances have been made, with regulations on corporate responsible conduct, sustainable sourcing and quality investment standards emerging in the European Union, for instance, and through the Blue Dot Network and other initiatives. The FfD4 zero draft emphasises advancing double materiality disclosure frameworks, standardising SDG fund classifications to prevent greenwashing and creating a global finance taxonomy (UN, 2025[74]). These measures could reshape financial and corporate governance to drive impactful, transparent and sustainable investment strategies.

The financial system's stability and sustainability hinge on robust and adaptive financial regulation. While significant progress has been made in banking regulation since the 2009 financial crisis, non-banking financial regulation remains inadequate, leaving gaps in addressing systemic risks. Mispricing of risks in current financial regulatory frameworks, such as those used in international risk weighting (e.g. Basel III) exacerbates borrowing costs for SDG investments, particularly in LDCs (UN, 2025[74]). Furthermore, environmental sustainability is underrepresented in financial regulations, and climate risk disclosure and transition plans are still at an early stage. Credit rating agencies, pivotal in determining borrowing costs, lack sufficient transparency and long-term alignment with sustainability objectives.

Among the proposals to address these challenges at the upcoming FfD4 are suggestions to review and amend international risk weighting frameworks to ensure accurate risk assessments, including sustainability factors, and to reduce overreliance on credit ratings. A prudential regulation framework tailored for LDCs and less-developed markets is being proposed as well as more transparent, long-term and model-based credit rating systems (UN, 2025[74]). Regular dialogue among regulators, credit rating agencies and stakeholders can ensure appropriate actions during debt swaps and restructurings. Incorporating climate transition plans, stress testing of such plans and exploring global agreements on capital account management and asset management regulation can help create a more resilient and sustainability-aligned financial system.

Global financial assets are concentrated in the private sector, which generally prioritises returns over developmental impact. Non-bank financial institutions account for the largest share (47%), followed by banks (40%) and, with much smaller shares, central banks and public financial institutions (Figure 1.12). There is limited alignment of these sizeable private financial flows with the SDGs as the private sector generally prioritises returns over developmental impact. In this context, public financial institutions, although smaller in asset size, play a critical role by catalysing sustainable investments and supporting public goods. Therefore, enhancing public-private collaboration is essential for creating effective synergies between profitability and positive social impact. Civil society organisations advocate for stronger review of the development impacts of public-private partnerships, blended finance and other private finance instruments to ensure that private finance instruments contribute meaningfully to sustainable development, climate action, gender equality, fiscal stability, labour rights and broader social objectives (Civil Society Financing for Development Mechanism, 2024[83]). The FfD4 can emphasise the importance of aligning blended finance and institutional investments with measurable sustainability impacts by standardising instruments, creating catalytic capital pools, and improving data and impact metrics to drive meaningful development outcomes (UN, 2025[74]).

Figure 1.12. Accelerating alignment of the trillions

Note: NBFIs = non-bank financial institutions. The share of developing countries in the world population is based on the World Bank definition of developing countries. The share of ODA allocated to LDCs is based on 2022 figures, net disbursements, in 2022 constant prices and grant equivalent method. All figures are based on 2022 data except for developing countries' net interest payments on public debt, which are based on 2023 data and global FDI figures which are based data from the first half of 2024.

Source: For global financial assets (except debt stock): Financial Stability Board (2023[84]), *Global Monitoring Report on Non-Bank Financial Intermediation*, https://www.fsb.org/2023/12/global-monitoring-report-on-non-bank-financial-intermediation-2023/. For debt stock: International Monetary Fund (2023[85]), *2023 Global Debt Monitor*, https://www.imf.org/-/media/Files/Conferences/2023/2023-09-2023-global-debt-monitor.ashx. For global government revenues figures: the IMF government revenues; UNCTAD (2024[36]), *A World of Debt: A Growing Burden to Global Prosperity*, https://unctad.org/publication/world-of-debt; OECD (2024[86]), *Global Debt Report 2024: Bond Markets in a High-Debt Environment*, https://doi.org/10.1787/91844ea2-en. For global gross fixed capital formation figures: World Bank (2024[87]), *Data: Gross fixed capital formation (current US$)* (database), https://data.worldbank.org/indicator/NE.GDI.FTOT.CD; OECD (2024[38]), "FDI in figures, October 2024", https://www.oecd.org/en/publications/fdi-in-figures-october-2024_fcdc2fb2-en.html. For global trade figures: World Trade Organization (2023[88]), *Evolution of Trade Under the WTO: Handy Statistics*, https://www.wto.org/english/res_e/statis_e/trade_evolution_e/evolution_trade_wto_e.htm; UN (2024[89]), *About Least Developed Countries* (webpage), https://www.un.org/ohrlls/content/about-least-developed-countries. For illicit financial flows: Gravelle (2022[90]), *Tax Havens: International Tax Avoidance and Evasion*, https://crsreports.congress.gov/product/details?prodcode=R40623. For remittances: World Bank (2024[91]), *World Development Indicators*, https://data.worldbank.org/topic/financial-sector?view=chart.For ODF figures: OECD (2024[30]), *OECD Data Explorer, DAC1: Flows by donor (ODA+OOF+Private) (database)*, http://data-explorer.oecd.org/s/9w; OECD (2024[92]), "Integrating climate action into development finance", https://doi.org/10.1787/41d16c83-en.

Although it is a key source of capital for SDG-related projects, global FDI currently totals only USD 0.8 trillion (OECD, 2024[38]). Gross fixed capital formation (GFCF) and FDI are essential pillars for fostering economic growth, particularly in developing countries where the need for infrastructure and productive capacity is high. GFCF, which represents investments in long-term assets such as infrastructure, machinery and buildings, signals how much capital is being directed towards building a country's economic foundation. By strategically channelling FDI into sectors that increase GFCF in SDG-related and green industries, countries can build resilience, support climate action and foster long-term economic growth. GFCF stood at USD 26 trillion in 2022, driven partly by FDI, which contributed USD 0.8

trillion as a key capital flow (Figure 1.12). FDI also plays a critical and complementary role, enhancing GFCF in developing countries by providing the necessary funds to develop sustainable infrastructure, technology and industries that local capital markets alone might not be able to support. LDCs would have received USD 0.28 trillion in FDI inflows from 2015-23 – an additional USD 0.04 trillion in total – had their inflows increased at the same rate (17%) as FDI inflows in other developing countries over the same period. As noted in 1.2, FDI flows to LDCs have not rebounded following COVID-19 to the same degree as FDI flows to other developing countries due to the disproportionate impacts of food, energy and successive other global crises (UNCTAD, 2023[93]). Among the proposals for the upcoming FfD4 is to scale up and enhance the quality of FDI in developing countries through targeted initiatives such as measuring FDI contributions to the SDGs (i.e. the quality of FDI), creating an investment support centre for LDCs and establishing an infrastructure financing facility for landlocked developing countries (UN, 2024[94]).

Addressing financial leakages is another opportunity to unlock greater financial flows for sustainable development. Remittances, valued at USD 0.5 trillion, are an example. These flows play a crucial role in supporting development in lower-income countries, yet persistently high transfer fees erode their potential. Both the 2030 Agenda and the AAAA called for lowering transfer costs to a target of 3 percentage points, but they remain more than twice as expensive and totalled USD 0.03 trillion in 2022. Meeting the target could have mobilised an additional USD 0.02 trillion per year in support of developing country households in 2022 (Chapter 3). The FfD4 could aim to lower transfer costs to 3 percentage points by 2030 through digital technologies, enhanced competition among money transfer operators, increased fee transparency and proportionate regulatory frameworks for private money flows (UN, 2025[74]).

Criminal and illicit economies are another major source of financial leakage in developing countries, and in some countries illicit financial flows (IFFs) may exceed both ODA and FDI inflows (Spanjers and Foss, 2015[95]). While there is no internationally agreed definition of IFFs, they are traditionally considered to include money laundering, bribery and tax evasion by international companies, and trade mispricing (OECD, 2014[96]). IFFs threaten the strategic, political and economic interests of countries and undermine public trust in government and the financial system. Over 2018-22, 22 countries piloted estimates of IFFs. While incomplete data and the risk of double counting make it difficult to sum up these estimates, UNCTAD used feedback from the pilots to release a refined methodological guidance on the tracking of IFFs (Chapter 2) (UNCTAD, 2024[97]). Key challenges in addressing IFFs remain, however, and include insufficient exchange of information, limited capacity to utilise financial data, and weak anti-corruption and anti-money laundering measures. Additionally, the lack of standardised regulations for professional service providers (e.g. lawyers, accountants, real estate agents, etc.) may enable or facilitate IFFs. Proposed solutions for the FfD4 emphasise fostering global financial transparency through strengthened international co-operation, national regulation of professional service providers and implementation of international anti-corruption standards. Enhancing asset recovery practices and reinforcing anti-money laundering measures are also needed to address IFFs and reduce financial leakages that divert resources that could support sustainable development.

A huge portion of financial resources are tied up in public and private debt stocks, which amount to USD 235 trillion, and in debt servicing costs in developing countries, which reached USD .847 trillion in 2023. Successive global shocks, rising debt vulnerabilities and limited fiscal space exacerbate developing countries' debt challenges, undermining their ability to invest in the SDGs and climate resilience. There is an urgent need to manage debt burdens more effectively to free up capital for developmental priorities. The zero draft outcome document published ahead of the FfD4 conference calls for the creation of a more equitable debt architecture to address these systemic barriers, including a recommendation to establish globally endorsed principles for responsible borrowing and lending alongside tools to monitor and implement these principles across all stages of the debt cycle. The zero draft also centres on the need for greater transparency, with a call to create a global central debt data registry to harmonise reporting, improve creditor-borrower trust and enhance decision making (UN, 2025[74]).

If effectively mobilised, global government revenues, estimated at USD 31 trillion, are an essential resource to support SDG financing. Strengthening tax collection mechanisms, particularly in developing countries, could significantly boost domestic public resources. According to International Monetary Fund (IMF) estimates, low-income developing countries could increase their tax-to-GDP ratio by 9 percentage points on average through a combination of tax and institutional reforms (International Monetary Fund, 2024[98]). LICs could mobilise an additional USD 0.28 trillion per year in tax revenues by raising the ratio to a level equivalent to that of other developing countries (Chapter 2). This would require increased revenues from a range of taxes, with taxes on goods and services and personal income taxes having the most potential. While there is scope for some increase in revenues from corporate income tax, this is limited in light of the scale of resources needed. FfD4 proposals support the implementation of the OECD/G20 BEPS Two Pillar framework, emphasising the importance of ensuring that its outcomes benefit developing countries. Recommendations include increasing the second pillar on the global minimum corporate tax rate and providing capacity-building support to help developing countries analyse and implement the framework effectively (UN, 2024[94]). Strengthening country-by-country reporting and improving ownership transparency through global registries are also critical steps to ensure tax compliance. These measures aim to establish a fairer international tax system, thus empowering developing countries to safeguard their tax bases and mobilise sufficient revenues for sustainable development investments.

Aligning trade policies with sustainability targets would give developing countries an important opportunity to enhance their economic resilience and capture more value from global trade flows. Global trade in goods and services, valued at USD 25 trillion in 2022, is a key component of public financial resources that can be leveraged to support sustainable development (Figure 1.12). By incorporating sustainable practices into trade agreements and national policies, countries can foster inclusive growth and long-term economic stability. For example, LDCs account for 14% of the world's population but only 1% of global trade. Doubling their share of global trade to 2% could add USD 0.23 trillion per year to their economies, contributing to poverty reduction and economic diversification (Chapter 5). The zero draft in the FfD4 context calls for stepping up aid for trade infrastructure and facilitation with the objective of doubling aid for trade to LDCs by 2031 and with at least 50% of such aid dedicated to building productive capacities (UN, 2025[74]). The African Continental Free Trade Area, for instance, is expected to boost African countries' trade income by USD 450 billion by 2035, with a projected 81% increase in intra-African trade. These examples underscore the potential of well-aligned trade policies to drive sustainable growth, particularly when targeted towards regions and countries with greatest needs.

While ODF from bilateral and multilateral providers accounts for just USD 0.3 trillion of total SDG financing, it is a critical resource, especially in countries most in need. Although ODF alone cannot close the financing gap, it plays an essential role in areas where private investment is limited such as fragile or high-risk regions. Redoubling ODA commitments and improving ODA effectiveness in catalysing other financial flows will be essential in ensuring that development financing reaches the most vulnerable. DAC members would have mobilised an additional USD 0.2 trillion in 2023 had they agreed to and met the spending target of 0.7% of gross national income (GNI) to ODA. Over 2015-22, however, ODA from DAC members to the most vulnerable countries did not keep pace with the total increase, growing by only 28%, while total ODA increased by 48% (Chapter 4). Proposals to address these challenges include achieving more ambitious time frames for ODA targets; increasing the commitment to LDCs from the current 0.15-0.20% to 0.20% of GNI to ODA; increasing the share of ODA in support of strengthening core capacities and institutions in developing countries (e.g. country programmable aid, budget support); and enhancing transparency and accountability of all development co-operation providers, including South-South and triangular co-operation providers (UN, 2025[74]).

Encouraging private sector involvement through blended finance, coupled with robust monitoring, could facilitate substantial investment flows into sectors critical to sustainable development. Tools such as blended finance, impact investing and green bonds can also attract private investors by reducing risk through partial public guarantees. Innovative financial mechanisms and increasing the catalytic effects of ODA will also play a role in unlocking resources for critical SDG investments, enabling a more equitable distribution of global wealth in support of inclusive and sustainable growth. However, for innovative finance to make a meaningful impact, a supportive regulatory framework and clear metrics are needed to ensure that these mechanisms genuinely contribute to SDG outcomes.

Multilateral development banks (MDBs) face challenges in scaling their financial capacity, aligning incentives with development impact and expanding access to concessional finance. At the same time, they must navigate a landscape of fragmented co-ordination and rising demands for sustainable and inclusive investments. Ongoing reforms of MDBs aim to triple total lending volumes by 2030 to reach USD 400 billion per year. Yet, even under the most optimistic scenario, additional MDB lending would amount to USD 40 billion per year – substantially less than the target set by the G20 Independent Expert Group of an additional USD 260 billion a year (OECD, 2024[99]). The FfD4 zero draft proposals to address these challenges include implementing capital adequacy reforms, increasing concessional financing, aligning incentives with sustainable development impact, enhancing local currency lending, and fostering collaboration to streamline operations and maximise resource mobilisation (UN, 2025[74]).

New levers for transition can be identified

Transitioning to a sustainable and inclusive global economy requires co-ordinated and differentiated efforts to implement policy levers that integrate the interlinked goals of poverty eradication, economic growth and climate action. Such efforts must be tailored to the varying needs and capacities of countries at different stages of development. LICs, which have low emissions and low GDP per capita, should focus on poverty eradication through investments in human, physical and financial capital. MICs, especially LMICs, should prioritise income growth while reducing vulnerability and leveraging synergies, such as by cutting air pollution. HICs, which are responsible for the majority of global emissions, must lead in climate mitigation while managing the costs of transition (World Bank Group, 2024[100]).

New policy levers can promote long-term benefits for social equity, financial stability and sustainability. The traditional monetary and fiscal policy levers deployed following the COVID-19 crisis have largely been exhausted. To avoid unintended negative consequences, particularly in addressing the inherent risks of decoupling, a range of public economic levers including new regulatory frameworks, just transition policies and financial instruments are needed to unlock fresh opportunities to boost finance and revenues and achieve global climate and sustainable development goals. Figure 1.13 provides an overview of these opportunities and the variety of benefits they can promote, including tax and subsidy reform, market creation (e.g. carbon), strengthened regulatory frameworks, valorisation of natural assets (e.g. ocean and bioeconomy), and just transition policies. These benefits have varying potential to be scaled up in different country contexts.

Figure 1.13. New levers for transition

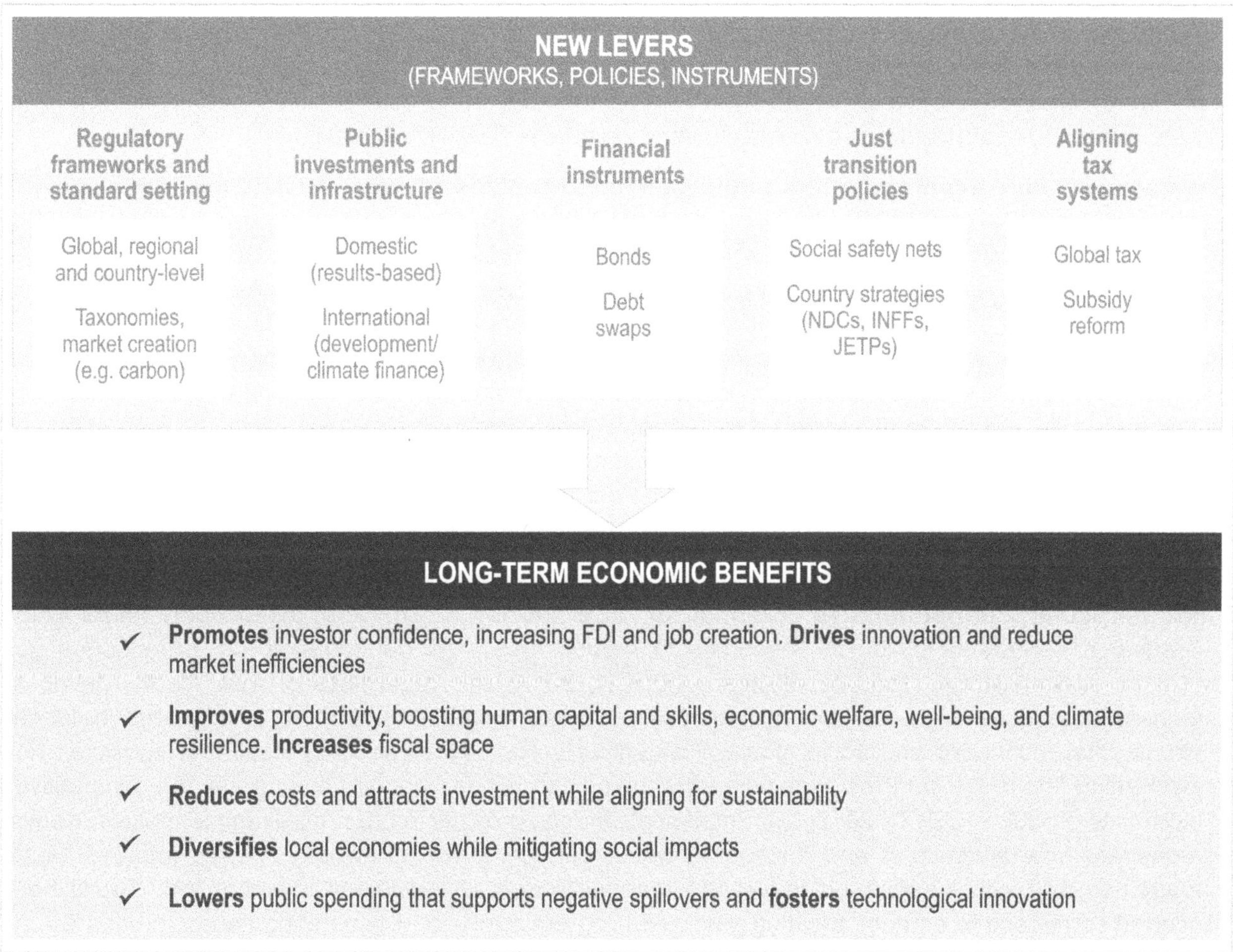

Note: NDCs = nationally determined contributions; INFFs = integrated national financing frameworks; JETPS = Just Energy Transition Partnerships.

While challenging, repurposing fossil fuel subsidies is critical for all countries, though its priority level differs for countries at different income levels. Balancing fiscal and environmental goals with social equity is a challenge for all countries regardless of income level. At COP28, a coalition of nations from varying income groups pledged to end fossil fuel subsidies by promoting transparency, addressing international barriers and fostering national strategies to phase out subsidies while also minimising carbon leakage and maintaining a level playing field (International Institute for Sustainable Development, 2024[101]). Redirecting subsidies from carbon-intensive activities to renewable energy projects can significantly reduce emissions and create pathways for green innovation. In lower-income countries, priorities often centre on minimising social and economic disruptions by using these resources to expand energy access, support social safety nets and foster inclusive development. These resources can be redirected to address pressing development needs such as access to clean energy, infrastructure and poverty alleviation. A notable example is Indonesia, which has gradually restructured fossil fuel subsidies while investing in renewable energy and direct cash transfers to support vulnerable populations (Laan and Sharma, 2024[102]). Effective policy levers require robust social safety nets, clear communication and stakeholder engagement to ensure political and social acceptability (Alers and Jones, 2021[103]).

Carbon markets hold potential as supplementary policy levers but require significant reform to benefit lower-income countries. The COP29 outcome on carbon markets highlighted the lack of robust safeguards to ensure equitable access for developing countries and insufficient measures to prevent greenwashing. Developing countries will require support for carbon trading that aligns with their national development goals, clarifies revenue-sharing rules and integrates carbon market projects with broader economic policies. Development partners can strengthen the institutional and technical capacity of these countries to ensure effective participation in carbon markets while differentiating carbon finance from climate finance to avoid duplicative or misallocated resources (UNCTAD, 2024[104]).

The ocean or blue economy offers significant opportunities to drive sustainable development, particularly in LICs and SIDS where ocean-based industries are vital economic pillars (OECD, 2024[105]). LICs rely on ocean-based industries, which contribute over 11% of their GDP, much more than OECD countries, where such activities account for 2% of GDP. For example, tourism, including marine and coastal tourism, plays a central role in livelihoods and economic resilience in Cabo Verde, Seychelles and Maldives, where it accounts for more than 50% of GDP. ODA for the ocean economy totalled USD 3.5 billion in 2022, a 45% increase over 2021, but it still represented only 1% of total ODA (OECD, 2024[105]). Of this total, USD 2.4 billion (69%) was directed towards enhancing the sustainability of ocean economy sectors or conserving ocean resources. These investments underscore the potential of the blue economy to foster inclusive growth and address environmental challenges, provided that policies and financial mechanisms continue to align with sustainability and resilience goals.

With the right policy levers in place, the bioeconomy presents opportunities for all countries but offers particularly transformative potential for LICs and MICs. The term bioeconomy refers to the leveraging of renewable biological resources to reduce fossil fuel dependency, cut greenhouse gas emissions and maximise resource efficiency (OECD, 2018[106]). Regardless of their income level, all countries must collaborate to ensure biomass is used sustainably and in a way that balances environmental, economic and social goals. Policy levers such as eliminating fossil fuel subsidies and implementing financial incentives such as carbon taxes can act as enablers to increase the competitivity of bio-based products (OECD, 2018[106]). Small-scale biogas projects in LICs, for example those in Kenya, demonstrate how agricultural and household waste can generate renewable energy, improve waste management and reduce deforestation (World Economic Forum, 2024[107]). MICs, among them Brazil, have converted sugarcane to ethanol, creating jobs, reducing emissions and generating carbon credits (World Economic Forum, 2024[107]).

Ensuring a sustainable and inclusive global response at all income levels can also include solidarity levies aimed at raising significant new resources for climate and development goals. The Global Solidarity Levies Task Force (2024[108]), for instance, highlights a range of opportunities to introduce levies on high-emission and resource-intensive sectors in a progress report released at COP29. Among the options presented are solidarity levies targeting fossil fuels, aviation, maritime fuel, carbon pricing and financial transactions as well as proposals for a fossil fuel extraction levy and a financial transaction tax that could raise between EUR 156 and EUR 260 billion per year, with significant portions allocated to developing countries. HICs are encouraged to lead by implementing demand-side incentives such as public procurement mandates. In 2022, 92% of the surveyed OECD countries (35 out of 38) reported they had adopted a national green public policy or policy framework and 29 reported that they refer to such a policy or to public procurement in their national environmental commitments as a tool in pursuit of sustainability goals (OECD, 2024[109]). At the same time, MICs can focus on industrial collaboration and LICs can integrate renewable carbon projects into national strategies with support from concessional finance and technology transfers.

Debt can be a powerful policy lever for development when aligned with SDG objectives, ensuring effective use of and high returns on investment. In advance of the FfD4, a range of proposals have already been made to tackle the debt crisis while also fostering sustainable and inclusive growth (UN, 2024[94]). For example, scaling up and simplifying debt swaps for climate and nature could channel resources into sustainable development and also reduce transaction costs. Innovative solutions including debt-for-climate and debt-for-nature swaps could help redirect an estimated USD 100 billion of debt towards nature restoration and climate adaptation in developing nations. Climate-resilient debt clauses, which allow for temporary suspension or restructuring of payments during climate-related disasters, are increasingly integrated into financial instruments, providing much-needed fiscal space for vulnerable nations. Additionally, up to USD 80 billion could be unlocked through the rechannelling of special drawing rights via MDBs to enable greater investments in climate resilience and sustainable development. Chapter 6 on debt and debt sustainability notes drawbacks and other considerations relating to such arrangements. Complementary proposals call for a new mechanism to co-ordinate liquidity support, technical assistance and legal advice to debtor nations that would enable them to manage debt sustainably without triggering defaults. Reforms to the G20 Common Framework aim to ensure fairer and more effective resolutions by expanding eligibility, standardising debt service suspension during negotiations and accelerating timelines for debt treatments. National governments and advocacy groups are also pushing for domestic legislative reforms to prevent disruptions from holdout creditors and to refine debt contracts. In addition, there are calls for updated debt sustainability assessments to account for SDG spending needs, climate risks and the long-term growth impacts of sustainable investments that would provide a foundation for debt strategies that align with development and resilience goals.

Finally, strengthening nationally owned financing for development strategies in lower-income countries is essential to align international co-operation and global financial flows with a just transition. Country-owned SDG and climate financing strategies such as Integrated national financing frameworks (INFFs), nationally determined contributions (NDCs) and Just Energy Transition Partnerships (JETPs) play a critical role in embedding SDGs within national budgets and economic planning. For example, NDCs are a policy lever that countries put into place and detail how they will contribute to the global temperature goals outlined under the Paris Agreement. Supporting these strategies requires concessional funding, technical assistance and capacity building to strengthen public financial management systems, enhance alignment with SDG targets and integrate climate resilience into national development frameworks. Climate finance must complement, not replace, development finance, ensuring that progress on climate action aligns with poverty eradication and inclusive growth. The FfD4 can seize opportunities to align development efforts with NDCs, utilising integrated frameworks to guide planning and decision making, and fostering stable, multi-year co-operation agreements (UN, 2024[94]). Enhanced international dialogue is also proposed as a means of ensuring coherence in financing development, climate and humanitarian needs while rationalising national-level architectures to place developing countries at the centre of their own co-ordination and decision making. International co-operation should also prioritise the harmonisation of donor strategies with these country-led plans to promote ownership, coherence and long-term impact.

Looking ahead, the FfD4 will offer a critical opportunity to develop a framework to advance collective and individual efforts to align financing flows, policies and strategies in favour of a sustainable transition. To promote adoption of new policy levers aligned to countries' unique circumstances and income levels, the global community can foster convergence on global financing priorities, addressing systemic barriers and enabling policy coherence. The FfD4 can provide the necessary impetus for scaling up investments in sustainable development, aligning financial flows with the SDGs, and ensuring no country is left behind in the transition to a resilient and inclusive future.

1.4. Preparing for the Fourth International Conference on Financing for Development and the post-2025 era

The renewal of the AAAA, which has served as the framework for financing sustainable development, is an opportunity to support a more sustainable and equitable financing architecture in 2025. Since its adoption in 2015, the AAAA has catalysed a range of initiatives that strengthen international tax co-operation, integrate financing frameworks and establish innovative financial mechanisms, among others. However, the COVID-19 pandemic, climate change, shrinking fiscal space and other challenges have shifted financing needs and priorities. The aim of the FfD4 in Seville, Spain, in 2025 is to evaluate progress on previous commitments, address emerging challenges to accelerate progress towards the 2030 Agenda and advocate for reforms in the international financial architecture to better support sustainable development (UN, 2024[110]).

Recent major international agreements underscore the magnitude of the financing challenge, while raising the stakes for the FfD4. Key initiatives such as the Bridgetown Initiative; the UN SDG Stimulus; the High-level Working Group of African ministers of finance, planning and economic development; the Vulnerable Twenty Group, or the V20; and the Paris Pact for People and Planet, among others, collectively aim to address global financial inequalities and support sustainable development. Reform has never been more essential or more challenging to achieve. Expectations are high and demand a comprehensive and cohesive strategy to foster both just and sustainable growth. The SDG Stimulus call for USD 500 billion annually remains unfulfilled, highlighting the gap between ambition and implementation (UN, 2023[111]). Recent major agreements led by the UN such as the Pact for the Future, COP29 and the Biodiversity COP have not delivered the necessary breakthroughs on financing, deferring critical decisions to the FfD4 and raising the stakes for the conference.

How can negotiators make the most of the opportunity afforded by the FfD4? Three considerations should guide them. First, aim for a meaningful and politically feasible outcome while building trust. Second, ensure that the FfD4 framework is fit for purpose in the post-2025 era. And third, reinforce the FfD4 monitoring mechanism to ensure its implementation. New challenges and a new context have emerged in the ten years since the AAAA was agreed, requiring that it be updated to remain relevant in the post-2025 period. The FfD4 could help the international community walk the crest line between the need for ambition and the risks of geo-economic fragmentation.[10]

Aim for a meaningful and politically feasible outcome

In light of geo-economic tensions and the risks of economic decoupling outlined in this chapter, the priority should be to restore trust between actors. The erosion of trust between nations makes it challenging to agree the renewal of the existing financing framework. This was apparent during the COVID-19 pandemic, when disparities in vaccine distribution revealed deep cracks in global solidarity, reinforcing perceptions of inequity and undermining trust. More equitable governance structures can help prevent the fragmentation of global trade, investment and financial systems (UN, 2024[94]). Further modernising of governance structures in institutions like the IMF and World Bank and in debt negotiation processes (e.g. those carried out by the Paris Club) could increase the voice and influence of developing countries in decision making. Developing countries hold 37% of the voting rights at the IMF and 39% at the World Bank though they constitute 75% of the membership in these institutions[11] (UN, 2023[112]) (see also Chapter 7 on systemic issues).

Restoring trust should start with greater policy coherence for sustainable development (PCSD).[12] In a 2023 survey by the OECD, 73% of responding countries identified lack of data and analysis on the transboundary impacts of policies as a key barrier to progress on PCSD (OECD, 2024[113]). Addressing contradictions and promoting integrated efforts will prevent negative feedback loops such as conflicts, underinvestment in education and climate change, among others, that exacerbate global inequalities (see section 1.3). Aligning global financial flows with the SDG and Paris Agreement targets requires significant reforms in OECD countries, including adjustments to fiscal policies, tax systems, subsidies and institutional governance. By prioritising PCSD, the FfD4 can promote more integrated and transparent policy approaches, fostering mutual trust among nations.

At the FfD4 conference, embedding inclusive practices and calling on existing platforms to work together will be pivotal to crafting actionable and equitable outcomes that resonate and build trust

among all partners. The OECD DAC has undergone adjustments to incorporate broader perspectives from non-members, civil society organisations and emerging South-South and triangular co-operation providers. Likewise, the transition of the Total official support for sustainable development (TOSSD) project to an independent international forum in 2024 reflects the evolution of the TOSSD measure towards becoming a global standard for tracking sustainable development finance in ways that ensure transparency, accountability and local ownership. Initially developed under the DAC and the AAAA, TOSSD has expanded to include South-South co-operation, triangular partnerships and financing for global public goods, an evolution that required a governance structure beyond the OECD (Chapter 4). These efforts reflect the growing recognition that inclusive governance that ensures a voice for all developed and developing countries, MDBs, private sector actors and grassroots organisations is essential to align development finance with diverse needs and priorities. Strengthening consultations with all relevant stakeholders not only enhances the legitimacy of international frameworks but also ensures that financing solutions are grounded in local realities.

The reform of the financial architecture at the FfD4 should not dismantle nor duplicate existing structures, it should accelerate the transformation of established platforms. Calls to centralise decision making within the UN to achieve global consensus could lead to duplicating efforts and polarising debates through bloc voting, which may hinder progress and dilute existing agreements (e.g. the definition of and commitment to ODA). Instead, leveraging the value-added contributions of existing regional and like-minded platforms can enhance effectiveness by promoting data-driven, evidence-based approaches; setting global standards; and fostering peer reviews and benchmarking to guide best practices. Efforts should prioritise refining the definition and ringfencing of ODA to maintain its integrity. Collaboration among institutions remains essential to ensuring a balanced and effective governance framework. A harmonised approach that capitalises on these complementary strengths can bolster global governance and promote greater coherence towards sustainable development objectives.

The focus on quantitative targets has its virtues but comes at a price, as missed targets risk further contributing to the trust deficit. New commitments to finance sustainable development must avoid overpromising, and address gaps in capital needs for a just and green transition. Some areas of the AAAA, such as *domestic and international private business and finance*, are dense with commitments targeting specific outcomes – among them, mobilisation of USD 100 billion annually in climate finance by 2020, full and equal access to financial services by 2030, and a reduction of the transfer cost of remittances to 3% – though only one of the commitments was met and then only past the deadline. Other AAAA areas also include long-standing targets that continue to fuel the trust deficit. For instance, through UN General Assembly Resolution 2626 (XXV) adopted in 1970, developed countries committed to devote 0.7% of their GNI in ODA to developing countries. However, there is no international agreement that specifies which developed countries the target applies to, nor the time frame they have for reaching the target (Chapter 4). More recently, ambiguous pledges such as the USD 1.3 trillion commitment made at COP29 continue to highlight challenges in enforcement of financing targets and the risk of fragmenting resources (COP29, 2024[114]). Aligned priorities and clearer frameworks with timelines and transparency for stronger accountability are crucial to bridge these gaps effectively.

Beyond the volume of financing mobilised, the quality of resources and their alignment with effectiveness principles are critical to achieving sustainable development outcomes. These require the reaffirmation of core principles such as country ownership, better co-ordination among stakeholders, a focus on measurable results and mutual accountability. The updated Global Partnership for Effective Development Co-operation (GPEDC) monitoring framework provides a valuable tool for measuring and advancing these principles by emphasising inclusivity, transparency and alignment with country systems. Empowering recipient countries to take the lead in designing and implementing development strategies ensures that financing is responsive to their specific needs and priorities. Enhanced co-ordination among donors, governments and other partners can reduce fragmentation and improve the efficiency of resource allocation. Such approaches can place countries in the driver's seat while ensuring a cohesive, results-oriented framework for financing.

National strategies should be placed at the core of the system and all other financial levers designed to support and enhance these strategies. INFFs offer a practical tool for aligning financial flows with national development priorities, enabling governments to leverage public, private, domestic and international resources more effectively. Similarly, country-specific platforms such as the JETPs demonstrate how international collaboration can be tailored to specific national needs and ensure alignment with global goals. Dual approaches such as these – anchored in the development strategies of LICs and MICs and complemented by the SDG financing strategies of the OECD and HICs – reflect a shared responsibility. For example, financing mechanisms such as blended finance initiatives can de-risk private investments in renewable energy projects in Africa while directly contributing to the host countries' climate strategies. Progress on the SDGs requires that a substantial portion of financing efforts by OECD members and other HICs directly supports sustainable development in developing regions, which will foster a more equitable and results-oriented approach to global development.

Incorporating broader measures of well-being and environmental sustainability into decision-making processes –following the so-called *beyond GDP* guidelines-- supports transitions towards more inclusive and sustainable development. While GNI per capita remains the key metric for determining the ODA eligibility of countries (including low- and middle-income countries as defined by the World Bank), GNI per capita is not the only measure of how concessional finance is allocated. Applying multidimensional vulnerability indices and other tailored financial tools that consider the unique vulnerabilities of debt-distressed and climate-affected countries can help allocate scarce ODA more equitably. These tools, alongside country-specific INFFs and smooth transition strategies, can also help vulnerable countries attract more external public and private resources while ensuring that financing strategies are country owned and responsive to individual countries' challenges and capacities.

Update the FfD4 framework for relevance in a post-2025 era

The AAAA remains a foundational reference for financing sustainable development, but its framework must be updated to tackle new challenges and promote innovative solutions. Addressing gaps in areas such as climate and biodiversity, health systems, and other systemic issues is essential to help the global community walk the crest line towards the SDGs. This requires closing negative financing loops, aligning financial flows with SDGs and deploying innovative mechanisms that mobilise resources more effectively. By fostering a just climate transition, for instance, an updated framework for financing sustainable development can help reduce vulnerabilities across regions and income levels while driving equitable progress.

Several of the updates under discussion, including the differentiation of climate and development finance, will be challenging to achieve and may not be resolved. The Pact for the Future, adopted at the 2024 UN Summit of the Future, reinforces commitments to mobilise more climate finance, particularly for adaptation and renewable energy projects. The issue of clarifying the additionality of climate finance to existing development finance commitments was left unresolved. This ambiguity is critical given that climate is a cross-cutting theme. Ensuring sufficient financing is important to help mitigate risks of negative impacts and unlock greater resource mobilisation across sectors. While climate is recognised as a cross-cutting theme in the AAAA, there can be further emphasis across the action areas on the risks of negative impacts and the potential to scale up resources. For example, trade is a driver of the triple transition (digital, environmental and social) and has an important role to play in sustainable development (Chapter 5). Environmentally related taxation can advance sustainable development by simultaneously addressing environmental challenges and supporting economic growth (Chapter 2). Renewable energy and climate technologies can help developing countries transition towards more circular and greener economies (Chapter 8).

The scope of systemic risks now includes complex financial and non-financial challenges that require a better global financial safety net, among them the challenges of climate change and biodiversity loss, health and pandemics, AI, and cybersecurity vulnerabilities. The FfD4 conference can support an expansion of IMF resources and facilities, for instance by creating a multilateral swap line, ensuring emergency financing is based on need, and scaling up concessional lending through mechanisms such as the Resilience and Sustainability Trust. Issuing new special drawing rights with streamlined rechannelling to vulnerable countries and supporting regional arrangements, particularly in Africa and other underrepresented regions, would enhance the coverage, reliability and responsiveness of the safety net (Chapter 7). Expanding the scope and accessibility of these mechanisms to address climate, health and other systemic shocks will also enhance global preparedness, protect vulnerable economies and ensure a more resilient response to future crises.

While the AAAA emphasises the need for clear guidelines on the responsibilities of creditors and debtors, progress to co-ordinate actors in support of debt sustainability remains fragmented and debt transparency remains low. Sovereign debt restructuring has grown significantly more complex, driven by an increase in defaulted debt and a more diverse creditor base that includes the private sector, China and Gulf states (Chapter 6). To prevent debtors from selectively favouring certain creditors over others, the FfD4 should encourage the participation of a broader range of creditors through the co-ordinated use of tools such as guarantees, credit enhancements and debt swaps alongside strengthened contractual provisions such as most-favoured creditor clauses. Engagement with credit rating agencies can further help increase the transparency of risk assessments. The conference should also promote loss reinstatement features that protect creditors against risks associated with the potential reversal of debt restructuring agreements, and support the work of the G20 Common Framework to track debt treatment and fiscal space for sustainable development spending. Strengthening debt transparency, including full disclosure of debt terms and obligations, is critical to ensuring accountability and fostering trust among all stakeholders, and thus to enabling more effective debt restructuring and sustainable development outcomes.

Efforts must prioritise those that have benefited the least from resource mobilisation since the adoption of the AAAA, such as LDCs and underfunded social sectors. As discussed, LDCs and other LICs face challenges in attracting private investment. A cohesive and comprehensive strategy is thus essential to foster both just and sustainable growth, address long-standing inequities, and ensure no one is left behind. In addition, the FfD4 should encourage the removal of bottlenecks hindering the expansion of private business and finance in these countries. For example, the FfD4 should promote innovative financial instruments, enhance risk mitigation strategies and improve data transparency to attract private investment to LDCs and other LICs. Global efforts to strengthen financing for health and education in developing countries are also crucial as these sectors remain significantly underfunded. As discussed in section 1.2, external debt service diverting public resources away from essential services like healthcare and education is another negative feedback loop. This financial strain exacerbates existing challenges such as shortages of healthcare professionals and limited access to quality education in developing countries. To achieve sustainable progress, the FfD4 must focus more on investment from both domestic governments and international donors in equitable access to these critical services.

Reinforce the FfD monitoring framework for heightened accountability

To support the development of a robust global FfD monitoring framework in 2025, the OECD monitoring exercise of the AAAA identifies at least 70 relevant SDG targets and many additional proxy indicators. The aim of that exercise is to contribute to the current mechanism that monitors financing for development, including the UN-led Interagency Task Force on Financing for Development (of which the OECD is a member), whose main monitoring output is the annual Financing for Sustainable Development Report. As part of this process, Chapters 2 through 8 of the *2025 Global Outlook on Financing for Sustainable Development* were submitted in draft form as inputs to the FfD4 Elements paper

(OECD, 2024[115]) and updated following comments and consultations for this report to provide an in-depth review of ten years of implementation of the AAAA. The insights across the seven action areas are covered in the following chapters: domestic public resources (Chapter 2); domestic and international private business and finance (Chapter 3); international development co-operation (Chapter 4); international trade as an engine for development (Chapter 5); debt and debt sustainability (Chapter 6); addressing systemic issues (Chapter 7); and science, technology, innovation and capacity building (Chapter 8). For each AAAA action area, the respective chapters take stock of where progress has been made, where progress has lagged, and where new challenges or solutions have emerged that require adjustments to the AAAA. The chapters are accompanied by statistical annexes that, together with the stocktake, provide the basis of a reinforced monitoring framework that measures progress against quantifiable or qualitative targets in line with the SDGs.

The FfD4 agreement should define clear and actionable deliverables, complemented by well-defined targets for broader commitments and rigorous impact assessment mechanisms to evaluate progress against social, economic and environmental indicators. Focusing on measurable outcomes aligned with the SDGs can maximise the impact of all sources of financing for development. For example, SDG 17.3.1, which tracks FDI, remittances and other financial flows to developing countries, is critical to ensuring sufficient resources are mobilised to meet development needs and fill financing gaps. But many other SDG targets, indicators and additional proxies are important to ensure a comprehensive monitoring framework across action areas. The OECD monitoring exercise demonstrates the potential of new metrics and safeguards to ensure equitable resource allocation, enhance accountability and effectively track contributions towards achieving SDGs:

- International development co-operation: A consolidation of efforts, based on the strengths of existing mechanisms within and beyond the UN, is needed to shift to a new era. The FfD4 should strengthen the quality, impact and effectiveness of all types of development co-operation while the GPEDC continues generating data – for instance regarding SDG indicator 17.15.1 (extent of use of country-owned results frameworks and planning tools by providers of development co-operation) – supporting policy dialogue and learning, and promoting accountability and progress on development effectiveness (GPEDC, 2024[116]).
- Debt and debt sustainability: Monitoring frameworks need to incorporate additional indicators, such as those from the G20 Common Framework, to track debt treatment and fiscal space for sustainable development spending. Only SDG indicator 17.4 (assist developing countries in attaining long-term debt sustainability through co-ordinated policies aimed at fostering debt financing) directly addresses debt sustainability by measuring debt service as a share of exports. Expanding these metrics could ensure a unified approach to monitoring progress of international debt management arrangements, enabling more effective debt management aligned with sustainable development objectives.
- Addressing systemic issues: Establishing clear, quantifiable targets for addressing systemic risks would enhance the ability to mitigate interconnected impacts on sustainable financing. Statistical proxies, such as financing for global health or indicators for climate risk disclosure, could expand monitoring efforts and better align with the needs of a more interdependent global system.

Key actors could make tailored commitments to support FfD4 monitoring, aligned with their capacities and roles. The FfD4 monitoring framework could be accompanied by a *roadmap* or *package* of supporting actions pledged by different actors such as the OECD DAC, the Finance in Common Summit, the GPEDC, the UN-led Global Investors for Sustainable Development Alliance and philanthropies, among others. Implementation of the actions could be continuously monitored and progress reported to the UN on a regular basis, with the possibility to adjust the roadmap as actors fulfil their reform pledges. Multilateral organisations could provide systematic data on concessional finance, debt sustainability measures and innovative financial instruments, while regional organisations could focus on region-specific financing gaps and solutions. Networks of DFIs could offer insights on private sector mobilisation and blended finance projects. Civil society organisations could play a critical role in tracking transparency, inclusivity and the social impact of financing commitments, ensuring accountability for underserved communities. Bilateral providers might align their reporting to the SDG targets by offering sector-specific financing data, and providers of South-South and triangular co-operation could share their experiences in financing as well as capacity building, technology transfer and regional partnerships. To facilitate coherence, the DAC should reinforce commitments to FfD monitoring by establishing reporting standards and encouraging participation, including building on the methodology developed by the DAC peer review monitoring of financing for sustainable development. The collective efforts of these actors would ensure that voluntary FfD reporting is robust, inclusive, and capable of driving progress on financing SDGs.

While impact measurement has inherent limitations, the FfD4 should nevertheless leverage existing platforms to monitor development impacts across the action areas. Many of these platforms were identified and proposed ahead of the FfD4 negotiations. One is a proposal to review how prudential regulations impact access to financing for small and medium-sized enterprises in developing countries, to ensure that blended finance initiatives are aligned with national priorities. Several other proposals call on diverse actors to step up impact monitoring. For example, development banks could better integrate methodologies that value externalities into financial models and transactions. MDBs can align their impact frameworks with the SDGs, capturing both positive and negative effects. Finally, promoting leadership by developing countries and fostering coherence and accountability among development partners can help embed sustainable development impacts into decisions on funding allocation and co-operation modalities.

By linking commitments to concrete outcomes, the new FfD framework can be a dynamic tool for adaptive learning, driving continuous improvements in how financing contributes to the SDGs. Reporting should draw from existing processes such as the SDG voluntary national reviews (VNRs), NDCs and INFFs reporting. Some countries have already made strides in this area. For instance, Mexico integrates financing for development reporting into its national budget planning processes, linking financing flows to specific SDG outcomes (Government of Mexico, 2024[117]). Costa Rica conducts detailed assessments of climate finance impacts on biodiversity conservation and carbon reduction targets (UN, 2023[118]). Rwanda uses its sustainable finance framework to align financing strategies with measurable development outcomes, providing detailed reporting on resource allocations and their impacts (Rwanda Ministry of Finance and Economic Planning, 2024[119]). Since the initiation of VNRs in 2016, the number of countries participating has increased from the initial 22 to 39 by 2023 (UNDP, 2023[120]). These assessments should be further encouraged so that stakeholders are able to measure the real-world effects of initiatives, which can foster accountability and refine strategies to maximise impact. Under the Paris Agreement, countries must submit new NDCs every five years, progressively strengthening their commitments to reflect their "highest possible ambition" and the latest climate science (UN, 2015[121]). By June 2024, most countries had submitted updated NDCs with 2030 targets; the next round, covering 2035 targets, is due by early 2025. The FfD4 conference can encourage countries to improve both their reporting systems and their support to developing countries to enhance their capacity for data-driven decision making. Technical assistance for statistical systems and capacity building for tracking progress against SDG-aligned targets will further strengthen global monitoring efforts.

The next chapters provide a detailed evaluation of the AAAA commitments as well as progress made to date, ongoing challenges and gaps, and areas emerging since 2015. They also highlight critical areas for updates of the financing framework.

References

Abdel-Latif, H. et al. (2023), "China's Slowing Economy Will Hit Sub-Saharan Africa's Growth", https://www.imf.org/en/News/Articles/2023/11/09/cf-chinas-slowing-economy-will-hit-sub-saharan-africas-growth. [24]

Aiyar, S. et al. (2023), "Geoeconomic fragmentation and the future of multilateralism", *IMF Staff Discussion Notes*, No. SDN/ 2023/001, International Monetary Fund, Washington, DC, https://www.imf.org/en/Publications/Staff-Discussion-Notes/Issues/2023/01/11/Geo-Economic-Fragmentation-and-the-Future-of-Multilateralism-527266. [7]

Alers, M. and B. Jones (2021), *Fossil Fuel Subsidy Reforms: Lessons and Opportunities*, United Nations Development Programme, New York, https://www.undp.org/publications/fossil-fuel-subsidy-reform-lessons-and-opportunities. [103]

Aon (2023), *2023 Weather, Climate and Catastrophe Insight*, https://www.aon.com/weather-climate-catastrophe/index.aspx. [69]

Arteta, C., S. Kamin and F. Ruch (2022), "How do rising U.S. interest rates affect emergine and developing economies? It depends", *Policy Research Working Paper*, No. 10258, World Bank Group, Washington, DC, https://documents1.worldbank.org/curated/en/099036212082239238/pdf/IDU032d1feef0db0d0480e0b3190f92d87c50de8.pdf. [56]

Bank of International Settlements (2024), *Central bank policy rates (database)*, https://data.bis.org/topics/CBPOL (accessed on 15 November 2024). [58]

Bhattacharya, A. et al. (2022), *Financing a Big Investment Push in Emerging Markets and Developing Countries for Sustainable, Resilient and Inclusive Recovery and Growth*, Grantham Research Institute on Climate Change and the Environment, London School of Economics and Political Science, London, and Brookings, Washington, DC, https://www.lse.ac.uk/granthaminstitute/wp-content/uploads/2022/05/Financing-the-big-investment-push-in-emerging-markets-and-developing-economies-for-sustainable-resilient-and-inclusive-recovery-and-growth-1.pdf. [54]

Bhattacharya, A. et al. (2023), *A Climate Finance Framework: Decisive Action to Deliver on the Paris Agreement – Summary*, Grantham Research Institute on Climate Change and the Environment and London School of Economics and Political Science, London, https://www.lse.ac.uk/granthaminstitute/wp-content/uploads/2023/11/A-Climate-Finance-Framework-IHLEG-Report-2-SUMMARY.pdf. [45]

Bolhuis, M., J. Chen and B. Kett (2023), "Fragmentation in global trade: Accounting for commodities", *IMF Working Papers*, No. WP/23/73, International Monetary Fund, Washington, DC, https://www.imf.org/en/Publications/WP/Issues/2023/03/24/Fragmentation-in-Global-Trade-Accounting-for-Commodities-531327. [19]

Buchner, B. et al. (2023), *Global Landscape of Climate Finance 2023*, Climate Policy Initiative, San Francisco, https://www.climatepolicyinitiative.org/publication/global-landscape-of-climate-finance-2023/. [48]

Carluccio, J. et al. (2024), *Tracking Fragmentation in World Trade*, Banque de France, https://www.banque-france.fr/system/files/2024-07/slide_2024_07.pdf. [10]

Cazzaniga, M. et al. (2024), “Gen-AI: Artificial intelligence and the future of work”, *Staff Discussion Note*, No. SDN/2024/001, International Monetary Fund, Washington, DC, https://www.imf.org/en/Publications/Staff-Discussion-Notes/Issues/2024/01/14/Gen-AI-Artificial-Intelligence-and-the-Future-of-Work-542379. [20]

Chakrabarty, M. (2024), *Shrinking Chinese demand, loan volumes weaken Africa’s growth prospects*, Observer Research Foundation, https://www.orfonline.org/expert-speak/shrinking-chinese-demand-loan-volumes-weaken-africa-s-growth-prospects. [21]

Chen, W., M. Fornino and H. Rawlings (2024), “Navigating the Evolving Landscape between China and Africa’s Economic Engagements”, https://www.imf.org/en/Publications/WP/Issues/2024/02/23/Navigating-the-Evolving-Landscape-between-China-and-Africas-Economic-Engagements-545104. [22]

Cho, W. et al. (2024), “Diagnosis and policy action for sustainable and inclusive productivity growth”, *OECD Science, Technology and Industry Working Papers*, No. 2024/07, OECD Publishing, Paris, https://doi.org/10.1787/1668f250-en. [3]

Civil Society Financing for Development Mechanism (2024), “Civil society FfD mechanism submission to FfD4 elements paper”, https://csoforffd.org/resources/civil-society-ffd-mechanism-submission-to-ffd4-elements-paper/. [83]

COP29 (2024), *Breakthrough in Baku delivers $1.3 trillion ’Baku Finance Goal’ with new core finance goal of $300 billion*, https://cop29.az/en/media-hub/news/breakthrough-in-baku-delivers-13tn-baku-finance-goal (accessed on 10 December 2024). [114]

Dasgupta, P. (2021), *The Economics of Biodiversity: The Dasgupta Review*, HM Treasury, London, https://www.gov.uk/government/publications/final-report-the-economics-of-biodiversity-the-dasgupta-review. [80]

D’Orazio, A., F. Ferriani and A. Gazzani (2024), *Geoeconomic fragmentation and firms’ financial performance*, Centre for Economic Policy Research, London, https://cepr.org/voxeu/columns/geoeconomic-fragmentation-and-firms-financial-performance. [9]

Felbermayr, G. et al. (2020), “The global sanctions data base”, *European Economic Review*, Vol. 129, https://doi.org/10.1016/j.euroecorev.2020.103561. [17]

Financial Action Task Force (2021), *High-Level Synopsis of the Stocktake of the Unintended Consequences of the FATF Standard*, https://www.fatf-gafi.org/content/dam/fatf-gafi/reports/Unintended-Consequences.pdf. [13]

Financial Stability Board (2023), *Global Monitoring Report on Non-Bank Financial Intermediation*, https://www.fsb.org/2023/12/global-monitoring-report-on-non-bank-financial-intermediation-2023/. [84]

Food and Agriculture Organization (2024), *World Food Situation: FAO Food Price Index*, https://www.fao.org/worldfoodsituation/foodpricesindex/en. [5]

G20 Independent Experts Group (2023), *Strengthening Multilateral Development Banks: The Triple Agenda - Volume 1*, https://www.gihub.org/resources/publications/strengthening-multilateral-development-banks-the-triple-agenda-report-of-the-g20-independent-experts-group/. [44]

Global Development Policy Center (2024), *Chinse Loans to Africa Database*, https://www.bu.edu/gdp/chinese-loans-to-africa-database/ (accessed on 11 December 2024). [23]

Global Solidarity Levies Tax Force (2024), *Scaling Solidarity: Progress on Global Solidarity Levies*, https://globalsolidaritylevies.org/app/uploads/2024/11/GSLTF-Scaling-Solidarity-Progress-on-Global-Solidarity-Levies-report.pdf. [108]

Global Trade Alert (2024), *Data Center (database)*, https://data.globaltradealert.org/ (accessed on 10 November 2024). [15]

Góes, C. and E. Bekkers (2022), "The impact of geopolitical conflicts on trade, growth, and innovation", *Staff Working Paper*, No. ERSD-2022-09, World Trade Organization, Geneva, https://www.wto.org/english/res_e/reser_e/ersd202209_e.htm. [11]

Government of Mexico (2024), *Allocation and Impact Report 2024: Mexico's SDG Bonds*, https://www.finanzaspublicas.hacienda.gob.mx/work/models/Finanzas_Publicas/docs/ori/Ingles/SDG/Mexicos_SDG_Bond_Allocation_and_Impact_Report_2024.pdf. [117]

GPEDC (2024), *GPEDC Inputs to the FfD4 Elements Paper*, https://www.effectivecooperation.org/system/files/2024-10/GPEDC%20Inputs%20to%20the%20FfD4%20Elements%20Paper.pdf. [116]

Gravelle, J. (2022), *Tax Havens: International Tax Avoidance and Evasion*, Congressional Research Service, Washington, DC, https://crsreports.congress.gov/product/details?prodcode=R40623. [90]

Institute for Economics & Peace (2024), *Global Peace Index 2024: Measuring Peace in a Complex World*, https://www.economicsandpeace.org/wp-content/uploads/2024/06/GPI-2024-web.pdf (accessed on 1 October 2024). [8]

International Energy Agency (2021), *World Energy Outlook 2021*, IEA, Paris, https://www.iea.org/reports/world-energy-outlook-2021. [72]

International Institute for Sustainable Development (2024), *The United Kingdom, New Zealand, and Colombia Join Coalition to Phase Out Fossil Fuel Subsidies*, https://www.iisd.org/articles/press-release/united-kingdom-new-zealand-colombia-join-coffis. [101]

International Monetary Fund (2024), *G-20 Note on Alternative Options for Revenue Mobilization*, https://www.imf.org/external/np/g20/062424.htm. [98]

International Monetary Fund (2024), *World Economic Outlook Database: October 2024 Edition*, https://www.imf.org/en/Publications/WEO/weo-database/2024/October. [63]

International Monetary Fund (2024), *World Economic Outlook, April 2024: Resilience Amid Divergence*, https://www.imf.org/en/Publications/WEO/Issues/2024/04/16/world-economic-outlook-april-2024. [4]

International Monetary Fund (2023), *2023 Global Debt Monitor*, https://www.imf.org/-/media/Files/Conferences/2023/2023-09-2023-global-debt-monitor.ashx. [85]

International Monetary Fund (2021), *Policy Responses to COVID-19 (webpage)*, https://www.imf.org/en/Topics/imf-and-covid19/Policy-Responses-to-COVID-19 (accessed on 1 December 2024). [59]

International Monetary Fund (2020), *World Economic Outlook, January 2020: Tentative Stabilization, Sluggish Recovery?*, https://www.imf.org/en/Publications/WEO/Issues/2024/10/22/world-economic-outlook-october-2024. [1]

Johnson, J. et al. (2021), *The Economic Case for Nature: A Global Earth-Economy Model to Assess Development Policy Pathways*, World Bank, Washington, DC, https://openknowledge.worldbank.org/entities/publication/fcc11682-c752-51c4-a59f-0ab5cd40dc6f. [79]

Kida, M. and S. Paetzold (2021), "The Impact of Gray-Listing on Capital Flows: An Analysis Using Machine Learning", *Working Paper*, No. 2021/153, IMF, https://www.imf.org/en/Publications/WP/Issues/2021/05/27/The-Impact-of-Gray-Listing-on-Capital-Flows-An-Analysis-Using-Machine-Learning-50289. [14]

Kirilakha, A. et al. (2021), "The global sanctions data base: An update that includes the years of the Trump presidency", in van Bergeijk, P. (ed.), *The Research Handbook on Economic Sanctions*, Edward Elgar Publishing Limited, Cheltenham, UK, https://doi.org/10.4337/9781839102721. [18]

Kjellstrom, T. et al. (2019), *Working On a Warmer Planet: The Effect of Heat Stress on Productivity and Decent Work*, International Labor Organization, Geneva, https://www.ilo.org/publications/major-publications/working-warmer-planet-effect-heat-stress-productivity-and-decent-work. [68]

Laan, T. and S. Sharma (2024), "Pro-poor fossil fuel subsidy reform", in *Development Co-operation Report 2024: Tackling Poverty and Inequalities through the Green Transition*, OECD Publishing, Paris, https://doi.org/10.1787/357b63f7-en. [102]

Migration Data Portal (2024), *Migration & Development: Remittances (webpage)*, https://www.migrationdataportal.org/themes/remittances (accessed on 10 November 2024). [37]

NGFS (2024), *NGFS Climate Scenarios (database)*, Network of Central Banks and Supervisors for Greening the Financial System (NGFS), Paris, https://www.ngfs.net/ngfs-scenarios-portal/ (accessed on 1 December 2024). [71]

Notre Dame Global Adaptation Initiative (2022), *ND-GAIN Country Index, Vulnerability and Readiness (database)*, https://gain.nd.edu/our-work/country-index/rankings/. [81]

Novta, N. and E. Pugacheva (2021), "The macroeconomic costs of conflict", *Journal of Macroeconomics*, Vol. 68, p. 103286, https://doi.org/10.1016/j.jmacro.2021.103286. [65]

OECD (2024), *Climate Finance Provided and Mobilised by Developed Countries in 2013-2022*, Climate Finance and the USD 100 Billion Goal, OECD Publishing, Paris, https://doi.org/10.1787/19150727-en. [52]

OECD (2024), *DAC1: Flows by donor (ODA+OOF+Private) (database)*, http://data-explorer.oecd.org/s/9w (accessed on 24 November 2024). [30]

OECD (2024), *Development Co-operation for a Sustainable Ocean Economy in 2022: A Snapshot*, ONE Members and Partners, https://one.oecd.org/document/DCD(2024)21/en/pdf (accessed on 5 November 2024). [105]

OECD (2024), “FDI in Figures, October 2024”, OECD Publishing, Paris, https://www.oecd.org/en/publications/fdi-in-figures-october-2024_fcdc2fb2-en.html. [38]

OECD (2024), *Financing for Development 2025 Draft Fact Sheets and Statistical Annexes*, ONE Members and Partners, https://one.oecd.org/document/DCD(2024)29/en/pdf. [115]

OECD (2024), *Global Debt Report 2024: Bond Markets in a High-Debt Environment*, OECD Publishing, Paris, https://doi.org/10.1787/91844ea2-en. [86]

OECD (2024), *Harnessing Public Procurement for the Green Transition: Good Practices in OECD Countries*, OECD Public Governance Reviews, OECD Publishing, Paris, https://doi.org/10.1787/e551f448-en. [109]

OECD (2024), *Integrating climate action into development finance*, OECD Publishing, Paris, https://doi.org/10.1787/41d16c83-en. [92]

OECD (2024), *International aid rises in 2023 with increased support to Ukraine and humanitarian needs*, https://www.oecd.org/en/about/news/press-releases/2024/04/international-aid-rises-in-2023-with-increased-support-to-ukraine-and-humanitarian-needs.html (accessed on 1 November 2024). [39]

OECD (2024), *Multilateral Development Finance 2024*, OECD Publishing, Paris, https://doi.org/10.1787/8f1e2b9b-en. [99]

OECD (2024), *OECD Data Explorer: Private Philanthropy for Development (database)*, http://data-explorer.oecd.org/s/11v. [40]

OECD (2024), *OECD Economic Outlook, Interim Report September 2024: Turning the Corner*, OECD Publishing, Paris, https://doi.org/10.1787/1517c196-en. [2]

OECD (2024), *Unleashing Policy Coherence to Achieve the SDGs: An Assessment of Governance Mechanisms*, OECD Publishing, Paris, https://doi.org/10.1787/a1c8dbf8-en. [113]

OECD (2023), *Revenue Statistics 2023: Tax Revenue Buoyancy in OECD Countries*, OECD Publishing, Paris, https://doi.org/10.1787/9d0453d5-en. [35]

OECD (2022), *Global Outlook on Financing for Sustainable Development 2023: No Sustainability Without Equity*, OECD Publishing, Paris, https://doi.org/10.1787/fcbe6ce9-en. [26]

OECD (2020), *Global Outlook on Financing for Sustainable Development 2021: A New Way to Invest for People and Planet*, OECD Publishing, Paris, https://doi.org/10.1787/e3c30a9a-en. [27]

OECD (2018), “The bioeconomy concept: Then and now”, in *Meeting Policy Challenges for a Sustainable Bioeconomy*, OECD Publishing, Paris, https://doi.org/10.1787/9789264292345-en. [106]

OECD (2014), *Illicit Financial Flows from Developing Countries: Measuring OECD Responses*, OECD Publishing, Paris, https://doi.org/10.1787/9789264203501-en. [96]

OECD (forthcoming), *Global Debt Report 2025*, OECD Publishing, Paris. [62]

OECD DAC Network on Governance (forthcoming), *ACTT Programme of Work on Illicit Financial Flows (IFFs), De-risking and Financial Exclusion: Synthesis Report*. [12]

OECD et al. (2024), *The Role of the G20 in Promoting Green and Just Transitions*, OECD Publishing, Paris, https://doi.org/10.1787/548e71cd-en. [75]

ONE Campaign (2024), *The Trillions Tracker (webpage)*, https://data.one.org/trillionstracker/ (accessed on 19 November 2024). [46]

Properzi, E. (2023), *Closing the spigots: the rise and collapse of bond markets for developing countries*, Finance for Development Lab, Paris, https://findevlab.org/closing-the-spigots-the-rise-and-collapse-of-bond-markets-for-developing-countries/. [55]

Rwanda Ministry of Finance and Economic Planning (2024), *Rwanda's Sustainable Finance Framework*, https://www.afdb.org/sites/default/files/esg_minecofin_rwanda_executed_version_sp_spo_approval_27-03-2024.pdf. [119]

Sachs, J. et al. (2023), "The case for long-term SDG financing", *Reflection Paper*, United Nations Sustainable Development Solutions Network, Paris, https://www.unsdsn.org/resources/the-case-for-long-term-sdg-financing/. [67]

Sachs, J., G. Lafortune and G. Fuller (2024), *Sustainable Development Report 2024: The SDGs and the UN Summit of the Future*, Sustainable Development Solutions Network, Paris/Dublin University Press, Dublin, https://sdgtransformationcenter.org/reports/sustainable-development-report-2024. [25]

Spanjers, J. and H. Foss (2015), *Illicit Financial Flows and Development Indices: 2008–2012*, Global Financial Integrity, Washington, DC, https://gfintegrity.org/report/illicit-financial-flows-development-indices-2008-2012/. [95]

Syropoulos, C. et al. (2024), "The global sanctions data base–Release 3: COVID-19, Russia, and multilateral sanctions", *Review of International Economics*, Vol. 32/1, pp. 12-48, https://doi.org/10.1111/roie.12691. [16]

UN (2025), *Zero draft: Outcome document of the Fourth International Conference on Financing for Development*, Financing for Sustainable Development Office, United Nations Department of Economic and Social Affairs, New York, https://financing.desa.un.org/sites/default/files/2025-01/FfD4%20Outcome%20Zero%20Draft.pdf. [74]

UN (2024), *About Least Developed Countries (webpage)*, https://www.un.org/ohrlls/content/about-least-developed-countries (accessed on 5 November 2024). [89]

UN (2024), "Elements paper for the outcome document of the Fourth International Conference on Financing for Development", Financing for Sustainable Development Office, United Nations Department of Economic and Social Affairs, New York, https://financing.desa.un.org/sites/default/files/2024-11/FfD4%20Elements%20paper_Nov%2022.pdf. [94]

UN (2024), *Financing for Sustainable Development Report 2024: Financing for Development at a Crossroads*, UN Inter-agency Task Force on Financing for Development and Department of Economic and Social Affairs, New YOrk, https://desapublications.un.org/publications/financing-sustainable-development-report-2024 (accessed on 20 November 2024). [53]

UN (2024), *The 4th International Conference on Financing for Development (webpage)*, https://financing.desa.un.org/ffd4 (accessed on 2 December 2024). [110]

UN (2024), *The Sustainable Development Goals Extended Report 2024 - Goal 12 Responsible Consumption and Production*, United Nations Statistics Division, New York, https://unstats.un.org/sdgs/report/2024/extended-report/Extended-Report_Goal-12.pdf. [82]

UN (2024), *The Sustainable Development Goals Extended Report 2024 - Goal 17 Partnership for the Goals*, United Nations Statistics Division, New York, https://unstats.un.org/sdgs/report/2024/extended-report/Extended-Report_Goal-17.pdf. [33]

UN (2023), *Payments for Environmental Services Program – Costa Rica (webpage)*, https://unfccc.int/climate-action/momentum-for-change/financing-for-climate-friendly-investment/payments-for-environmental-services-program (accessed on 3 October 2024). [118]

UN (2023), *Progress Towards the Sustainable Development Goals - Report of the Secretary-General: Statistical Annex*, United Nations Economic and Social Council, New York, https://unstats.un.org/sdgs/files/report/2023/E_2023_64_Statistical_Annex_I_and_II.pdf. [112]

UN (2023), "Time to scale up creative solutions to bridge the SDG funding gap", *UN DESA Voices*, Vol. 27/9, https://desapublications.un.org/un-desa-voice/expert-voices/september-2023/time-scale-creative-solutions-bridge-sdg-funding-gap (accessed on 18 November 2024). [42]

UN (2023), *United Nations Secretary-General's SDG Stimulus to Deliver Agenda 2030*, https://www.un.org/sustainabledevelopment/wp-content/uploads/2023/02/SDG-Stimulus-to-Deliver-Agenda-2030.pdf. [111]

UN (2022), *Global Assessment Report on Disaster Risk Reduction (GAR): Transforming Governance for a Resilient Future*, United Nations Office of Disaster Risk Reduction, New York, https://www.undrr.org/gar/gar2022-our-world-risk-gar. [77]

UN (2015), *Key Aspects of the Paris Agreement*, https://unfccc.int/most-requested/key-aspects-of-the-paris-agreement. [121]

UNCTAD (2024), *A drop in the ocean: Carbon markets have provided limited finance for least developed countries*, https://unctad.org/news/drop-ocean-carbon-markets-have-provided-limited-finance-least-developed-countries. [104]

UNCTAD (2024), *A World of Debt: A Growing Burden to Global Prosperity*, UN Trade and Development, Geneva, https://unctad.org/publication/world-of-debt. [36]

UNCTAD (2024), *Efforts to track illicit financial flows need scaling up*, UN Trade and Development, Geneva, https://sdgpulse.unctad.org/illicit-financial-flows/. [97]

UNCTAD (2024), *Foreign direct investment: Inward and outward flows and stock, annual (database)*, https://unctadstat.unctad.org/datacentre/dataviewer/US.FdiFlowsStock (accessed on 9 November 2024). [31]

UNCTAD (2024), "Mounting fiscal deficits and debt in least developed countries require urgent international action", https://unctad.org/news/mounting-fiscal-deficits-and-debt-least-developed-countries-require-urgent-international. [61]

UNCTAD (2024), *Mounting fiscal deficits and debt in least developed countries require urgent international action*, https://unctad.org/news/mounting-fiscal-deficits-and-debt-least-developed-countries-require-urgent-international. [60]

UNCTAD (2023), "Investment flows to least developed countries affected disproportionately by global crises", *Investment Trends Monitor*, UN Trade and Development, Geneva, https://unctad.org/publication/investment-flows-least-developed-countries-affected-disproportionally-global-crises. [93]

UNCTAD (2023), "SDG investment is growing, but too slowly: The investment gap is now $4 trillion, up from $2.5 in 2015", *SDG Investment Trends Monitor*, UN Trade and Development, Geneva, https://unctad.org/publication/sdg-investment-trends-monitor-issue-4 (accessed on 19 November 2024). [43]

UNCTAD (2023), *World Investment Report 2023: Investing in Sustainable Energy for All*, UN Trade and Development, Geneva, https://unctad.org/publication/world-investment-report-2023. [47]

UNCTAD (2022), *The Least Developed Countries Report 2022: The Low-carbon Transition and its Daunting Implications for Structural Transformation*, UN Trade and Development, Geneva, https://unctad.org/publication/least-developed-countries-report-2022. [76]

UNCTAD (2014), *World Investment Report 2014: Investing in the SDGs - An Action Plan*, UN Trade and Development, Geneva, https://unctad.org/publication/world-investment-report-2014 (accessed on 20 November 2024). [41]

UNDP (2023), *2023 Voluntary National Reviews through the Lens of Peaceful, Just and Strong Institutions*, United Nations Development Programme (UNDP), New York, https://www.undp.org/publications/2023-voluntary-national-reviews-through-lens-peaceful-just-and-strong-institutions. [120]

UNESCO (2024), *The Price of Inaction: The Global Fiscal and Social Costs of Children and Youth Not Learning*, United Nations Educational, Scientific and Cultural Organization (UNESCO), Paris, https://unesdoc.unesco.org/ark:/48223/pf0000390193. [66]

United Nations Environment Programme (2023), *Adaptation Gap Report 2023: Underfinanced. Underprepared. Inadequate Investment and Planning on Climate Adaptation Leaves World Exposed*, https://www.unep.org/adaptation-gap-report-2023. [51]

UNU-WIDER (2023), "Tax revenues as a share of GDP (dataset)", *UNU-WIDER Government Revenue Dataset (with major processing by Our World in Data)*, Our World in Data, Global Change Data Lab, https://ourworldindata.org/grapher/tax-revenues-as-a-share-of-gdp-unu-wider. [34]

van Tilburg, R., A. Simić and S. Murawski (2024), *The Climate Trillions We Need: Proposals for a New Global Financial Architecture to End Poverty and Save the Planet*, Sustainable Finance Lab, Utrecht, Netherlands, https://sustainablefinancelab.nl/wp-content/uploads/sites/334/2023/11/The-climate-trillions-we-need-5.pdf (accessed on 20 November 2024). [50]

WHO (2024), *Public Health and the Climate Crisis (video presentation)*, World Health Organization (WHO), Geneva, https://www.who.int/publications/m/item/public-health-and-the-climate-crisis. [70]

World Bank (2024), *Data: Gross fixed capital formation (current US$) (database)*, https://data.worldbank.org/indicator/NE.GDI.FTOT.CD (accessed on 10 November 2024). [87]

World Bank (2024), *Debt Sustainability Analysis (DSA): Latest Publicly Available Debt Sustainability Analyses Under the Joint Bank-Fund Debt Sustainability Framework for Low Income Countries (LIC-DSF) (database)*, https://www.worldbank.org/en/programs/debt-toolkit/dsa. [64]

World Bank (2024), *International Debt Report 2024*, http://hdl.handle.net/10986/42444. [29]

World Bank (2024), *World Development Indicators (database): Financial Sector*, https://data.worldbank.org/topic/financial-sector?view=chart (accessed on 10 December 2024). [91]

World Bank (2023), *Data Bank: International Debt Statistics (database)*, https://databank.worldbank.org/source/international-debt-statistics. (accessed on 4 November 2024). [57]

World Bank Group (2024), *Data Bank: International Debt Statistics (database)*, https://databank.worldbank.org/source/international-debt-statistics (accessed on 10 November 2024). [28]

World Bank Group (2024), *Data: Personal remittances, received (current US$) (database)*, https://data.worldbank.org/indicator/BX.TRF.PWKR.CD.DT (accessed on 5 November 2024). [32]

World Bank Group (2024), *Data: World Development Indicators (database)*, https://databank.worldbank.org/source/world-development-indicators (accessed on 7 November 2024). [6]

World Bank Group (2024), *Poverty, Prosperity, and Planet Report 2024: Pathways ouf of the Polycrisis*, https://www.worldbank.org/en/publication/poverty-prosperity-and-planet. [100]

World Bank Group (2022), *Mineral-rich developing countries can drive a net-zero future*, https://www.worldbank.org/en/news/feature/2022/06/06/mineral-rich-developing-countries-can-drive-a-net-zero-future. [73]

World Economic Forum (2024), *What is the bioeconomy and how can it drive sustainable development?*, https://www.weforum.org/stories/2024/07/bioeconomy-sustainable-development/. [107]

World Meteorological Organization (2021), *State of the Global Climate 2020*, https://wmo.int/publication-series/state-of-global-climate-2020. [78]

World Trade Organization (2023), *Evolution of Trade Under the WTO: Handy Statistics*, https://www.wto.org/english/res_e/statis_e/trade_evolution_e/evolution_trade_wto_e.htm. [88]

Zhan, J. et al. (2023), “Why trillions are needed to bridge the SDG financing gap”, *World Economic Forum*, https://www.weforum.org/stories/2023/09/why-trillions-more-are-needed-to-bridge-the-sdg-financing-gap/ (accessed on 20 November 2024). [49]

Notes

[1] This represents an increase of 0.3 percentage points over the 2023 forecasts of 2.9%.

[2] Global headline inflation has steadily declined from its peak of 8.7% in 2022 (annual average) to 6.9% in 2023 and is expected to further decrease to 5.8% in 2024. See https://www.imf.org/en/Publications/WEO/Issues/2024/10/22/world-economic-outlook-october-2024.

[3] In comparison, the medium growth forecast before the onset of the pandemic stood at 3.6% in 2020 (see https://www.imf.org/en/Publications/WEO/Issues/2024/10/22/world-economic-outlook-october-2024) and at 4.9% before the global financial crisis in 2008 (see https://www.imf.org/en/Publications/WEO/Issues/2016/12/31/Housing-and-the-Business-Cycle), while the actual annual average from 2000-19 was 3.8%.

[4] According to a 2024 International Monetary Fund staff discussion note, AI will affect about 60% of workers in advanced economies, with about half of those achieving higher productivity and earning higher incomes and half seeing lower demand for their labour and lower wages. In comparison, AI will affect only an estimated 40% of jobs in emerging market economies and 26% of jobs in LICs as a smaller share of their workforce is active in knowledge-intensive sectors. In these countries, less labour market disruption in the short term will also translate to less scope for related productivity improvements. See https://www.imf.org/-/media/Files/Publications/SDN/2024/English/SDNEA2024001.ashx.

[5] These calculations exclude social security contributions.

[6] These calculations include social security contributions.

[7] Official donors include OECD DAC countries, non-DAC countries and multilateral organisations. Calculations are based on grant equivalents and 2015 constant prices.

[8] Loss and damage are the financing needs to assist developing countries in recovering from climate-related disasters where adaptation has been insufficient or where adaptation limits have been exceeded. For more detail, see https://www.lse.ac.uk/granthaminstitute/publication/a-climate-finance-framework-decisive-action-to-deliver-on-the-paris-agreement-summary/.

[9] A just transition refers to a transition that addresses the needs of individuals and regions negatively impacted by the shift away from high-carbon activities and ensures that they are not left to bear the costs without support. The concept also involves recognising that countries and communities that have contributed little to climate change should not bear the disproportionate burden of mitigating its impacts and emphasises the importance of acting to reduce emissions to protect the well-being of future generations. For more detail, see https://www.lse.ac.uk/granthaminstitute/publication/a-climate-finance-framework-decisive-action-to-deliver-on-the-paris-agreement-summary/.

[10] The remainder of this chapter builds on the findings from an OECD monitoring exercise carried out in 2024 to explore how a renewed agenda could shape priorities for financing for sustainable development in the post-2025 period. A whole-of-OECD task force prepared fact sheets and statistical annexes to monitor progress on the seven action areas of the AAAA with critical analysis and key data points. These were submitted to the UN and member states to inform preparations for the FfD4 Elements paper. They align with international processes and are presented in this report as Chapters 2 through 8.

[11] There has, however, been progress. For example, as of 1 November 2024, the IMF has included sub-Saharan Africa on its executive board by extending a third seat For more detail, see: https://www.imf.org/en/News/Articles/2024/11/01/pr-24403-imf-expands-executive-board-with-addition-of-25th-chair.

[12] The OECD defines policy coherence for sustainable development as "an approach to integrate the dimensions of sustainable development throughout domestic and international policy-making" with the objective of "advancing the integrated implementation of the 2030 Agenda [by] (i) fostering synergies and maximising benefits across economic, social and environmental policy areas; (ii) balancing domestic policy objectives with internationally recognised sustainable development goals; and (iii) addressing the transboundary and long-term impacts of policies, including those likely to affect developing countries". For the full Recommendation, see https://legalinstruments.oecd.org/en/instruments/oecd-legal-0381.

2 Domestic Public Resources

This chapter reviews the Domestic Public Resources action area of the Addis Ababa Action Agenda (AAAA) including progress, persistent challenges, and emerging areas as the international community prepares for the Fourth International Conference on Financing for Development (FfD4). It examines global trends in revenue mobilisation, emphasising the role of tax and non-tax revenues in sustainable development and bridging financing gaps. Progress includes rising tax-to-GDP ratios, strengthened international tax frameworks, and adoption of innovative measures like digital tax systems and environmental taxation. Persistent challenges remain, such as narrow revenue bases, insufficient oversight of tax incentives, and financing gaps for essential services in low- and middle-income countries. Emerging opportunities lie in digitalising tax administration, implementing a global minimum tax, and aligning tax policy with Sustainable Development Goals, offering transformative potential to enhance resource mobilisation and foster equitable economic growth.

2.1. Data Dashboard

Key Trends

Tax-to-GDP ratios in a majority of countries worldwide rebounded despite the negative impact of the COVID-19 pandemic on revenues.

From 2015 to 2022, tax revenue as a percentage of gross domestic product (GDP) increased from 16.5% to 17.1% on average in developing countries (UN, 2024[1]). The tax-to-GDP ratio increased in both low-income countries (LICs) (+4%) and lower middle-income countries (LMICs) (+2%) or from 11% to 11.4% and from 15.4% to 15.7%, respectively, over the period. Despite this growth, the tax-to-GDP ratio in LICs remains below the effective 15% threshold (11.44% in 2022). The tax-to-GDP decreased (-3%) in upper middle-income countries (UMICs) or from 19.2% in 2015 to 18.3% in 2022 (Our World in Data, 2023[2]).

Between 2015 and 2021, tax-to-GDP ratios increased in three-fifths of the 130 economies included in the OECD Global Revenue Statistics database. However, in 86% of LICs and 43% of LMICs, revenues remain below the level required to finance critical social services and to invest in economic development (15% of GDP) (Benitez et al., 2023[3]; Choudhary, Ruch and Skrok, 2024[4]).

While tax revenues (excluding social security contributions) are the primary source of government revenue, non-tax revenues represent a significant share in all countries. According to International Monetary Fund (2024[5]) data, non-tax revenues make up one-third of government revenues in developed countries but nearly half of government revenues in developing countries.

Between 2015-22, total tax and non-tax government revenue in developing countries rose 20%, or 2% annually, from USD 3.15 trillion a record high of USD 3.79 trillion in 2022 (constant 2015 prices).

Figure 2.1. Tax-to-GDP

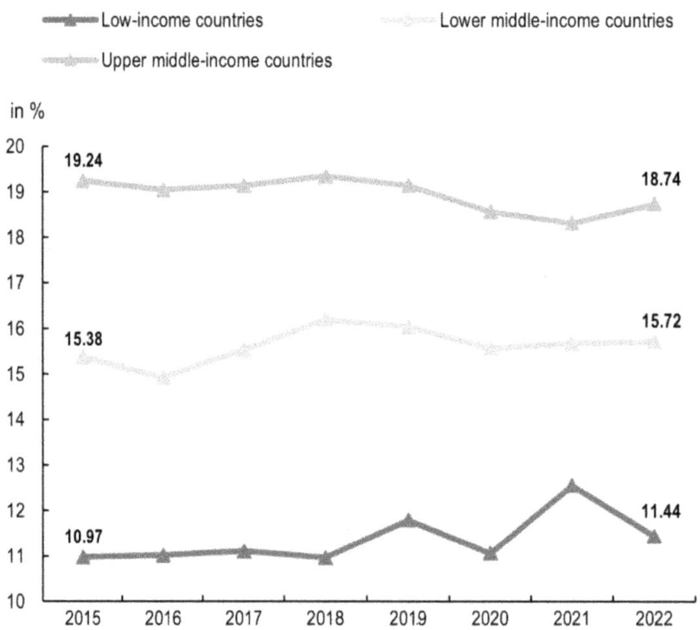

Note: Figures exclude social security contributions.
Source: Authors' calculations based on Our World in Data (2023[2]), *Tax revenues as a share of GDP (UNU-WIDER Government Revenue Dataset)*, https://ourworldindata.org/grapher/tax-revenues-as-a-share-of-gdp-unu-wider.

The tax structure, – or tax mix – varies significantly between countries and has evolved since 2015.

The tax mix, or share of tax revenues from various tax types, is different in developing and developed economies. Taxes on good and services account for about half of tax revenues in developing countries, while taxes on income and profits and social security contributions make up a much larger share of the tax mix in developed economies. In most regions and income groups, income taxes and social security contributions increased as a share of the tax mix between 2015 and 2021 while the share of taxes on goods and services declined. In Africa specifically, value added tax as a share of revenues decreased while the share of other consumption taxes increased by a similar proportion. On average, LICs experienced the largest shift in their tax mix between 2015 and 2021 with taxes on goods and services playing a smaller role and corporate income tax and social security contributions a larger one.

Other sources of public revenues beyond taxes can provide additional resources for development. Governments of countries with exploitable natural resources, for example, can raise revenues through non-tax instruments such as royalties or interest and dividends. The mandatory, privately managed social security arrangements in some countries offer another revenue source. In 2021, non-tax revenues from natural resources and private social security contributions amounted to 1.7% of GDP on average in Latin America and the Caribbean (LAC) and in some economies, among them Chile and Mexico, these represented more than 5% of GDP (OECD et al., 2023[6]).

Figure 2.2. Changes in tax mix in Africa (33), Asia-Pacific (36), LAC, and OECD and developing economies, 2015-21

Percentage points as % of total tax revenue

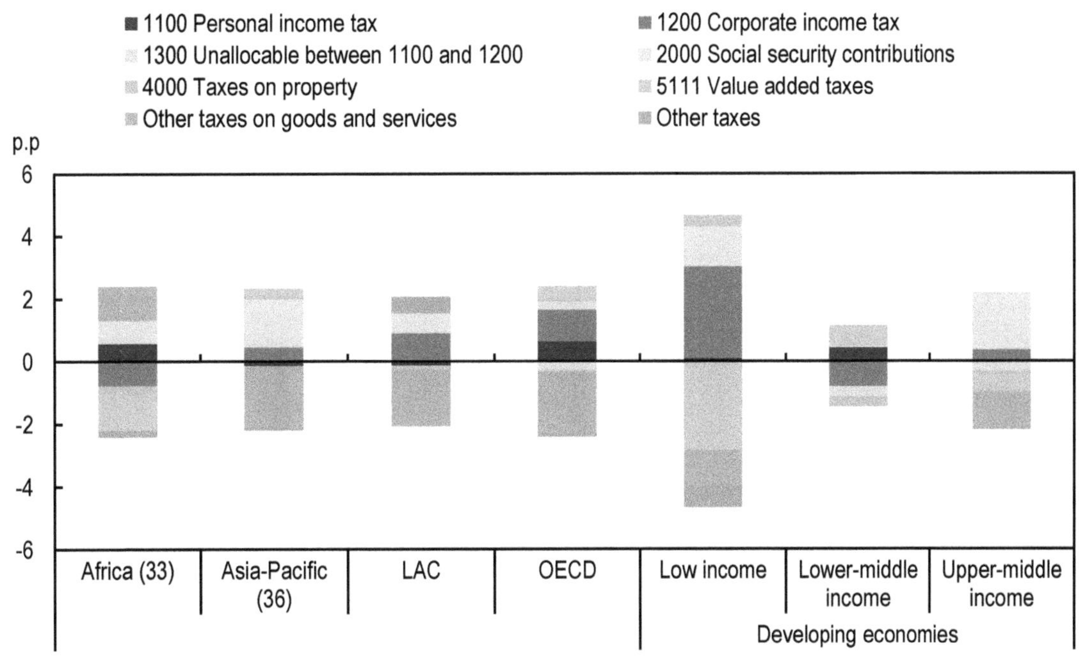

Note: Developing economies (80) include those in the Global Revenue Statistics Database defined as low income (11), lower middle-income (35) and upper middle-income (34) economies by the World Bank.
Source: Authors' calculations based on OECD (2023[7]), *Global Revenue Statistics Database*, https://www.oecd.org/en/data/datasets/global-revenue-statistics-database.html.

Total ODA in support of domestic revenue mobilisation has increased since 2015.

Total official development assistance (ODA) in support of domestic revenue mobilisation (DRM) has increased significantly since 2015, rising from USD 219.7 million in 2015 to USD 748.7 million in 2022 though this was a decline from the peak of USD 1.1 billion in 2020. Loans provided by the multilateral system accounted for much of the increase, with countries that are not least developed countries (LDCs) receiving a significant portion.

Development partners that are members of the Addis Tax Initiative collectively committed to doubling their assistance on tax to USD 441.1 million by 2020 and maintaining or surpassing this level thereafter. While this target has been missed, assistance on tax has increased significantly.

Launched in 2022, the OECD's Tax Treatment of Official Development Assistance Hub is the first public resource to improve the transparency around the taxation of aid. The Hub presents approaches taken by 22 of 30 DAC members that participated in the survey, representing over 80% of total bilateral ODA in 2020. Of these 22, 13 donors on the Hub reported having reviewed their policy since 2015. Of these, four reported they never or rarely request exemptions; three sometimes request exemptions; nine generally request exemptions and six have no general policy on the issue.

The United Nations (UN) through the Subcommittee on the Tax Treatment of ODA Projects produced guidelines on the tax treatment of government-to-government aid projects. The UN Tax Committee also adopted a recommendation on the public disclosure of provisions concerning the tax treatment of government-to-government aid projects.

Figure 2.3. ODA in support of domestic resource mobilisation

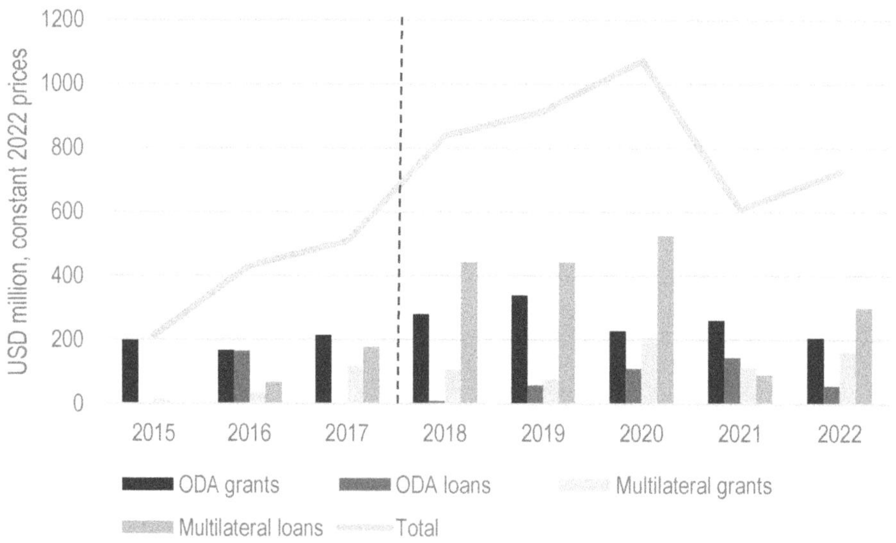

Note: Figures prior to 2018 are calculated using the cash flow method. Figures from 2018 onward are based on the grant equivalent method.
Source: Authors' calculations based on OECD (2024[8]), *Creditor Reporting System* (database), http://data-explorer.oecd.org/s/c.

Key performance indicators

↑	Since 2015, the average tax revenue as a percent of GDP increased from 16.8% to 17.5% in 2022 in developing countries. Despite this growth, the tax-to-GDP ratio in LICs remains below the effective 15% threshold (11.44% in 2022).
↓	Globally, explicit fossil fuel subsidies increased threefold from USD 503.3 billion in 2015 to USD 1.53 trillion in 2022. The increase in subsidies for all regions ranged from 36% to 58% from 2021 to 2022 except for Oceania (+22%) and Australia and New Zealand (+6%) (UN, 2024[9]).
↔	While ODA from Addis Tax Initiative members in support of DRM increased from USD 220 million in 2015 to USD 345 million in 2022, the increase still falls short of the commitment to double volumes to USD 441.1 million by 2020 (Addis Tax Initiative, 2024[10]).

↓ Slight setback	↓ Setback	↔ No change, neutral	↔ Stagnant, possible issue	↑ Major progress	↑ Minimal progress
↓ Minimal setback	↓ Major setback	↔ Holding steady, slight concern	↔ Negative stagnation, concerning	↑ Progress	↑ Negligible progress or progress contested

Note: Selected quantifiable commitments. Annex Table 2.A.1 contains the full list of indicators.

Resource mobilisation potential

- By increasing the tax-to-GDP ratio to a level equivalent to that of other developing countries, LICs could mobilise an additional 4.3 percentage points of tax-to-GDP, equivalent to USD 27.8 billion per year in tax revenues.[1]
- Achieving this mobilisation would require an increase in revenues from a range of taxes, of which taxes on goods and services and personal income taxes offer the greatest potential. While there is scope for some increase in revenues from corporate income tax, the gain would be limited compared to the scale of resources needed.
- Globally, carbon pricing scenarios could generate roughly USD 1.4 trillion annually by 2030, or 1.1% of global GDP (IMF, 2024[11]).
- Estimates of illicit financial flows vary widely due to the lack of a commonly agreed definition and statistical challenges (OECD, 2022[12]). However, progress is being made to harmonise and clarify approaches, particularly on a country-by-country basis.

2.2. Key areas of progress

International tax co-operation has expanded significantly in recent years

Through the work of the Global Forum on Transparency and Exchange of Information for Tax Purposes (the Global Forum) and its 171 members, 55% of which are developing countries, bank secrecy has been effectively eliminated and over EUR 130 billion in additional revenues and penalties have been identified, including more than EUR 45 billion identified by developing countries. In addition, 147 jurisdictions participate in the Multilateral Convention on Mutual Administrative Assistance in Tax Matters, which facilitates exchange of information between countries, Of these, 126 jurisdictions have committed to automatic exchange of financial account information. To date, 108 jurisdictions of them are already exchanging information automatically; 51 of these are developing countries including several LDCs.

International co-operation has also expanded in efforts to effectively tax multinational enterprises (MNEs). Laws are in place to allow tax authorities to share key country information in 102 jurisdictions, and as of November 2024, 104 jurisdictions signed the Multilateral Convention to Implement Tax Treaty Related Measures to Prevent Base Erosion and Profit Shifting (BEPS) to modify their bilateral tax treaties and close loopholes (OECD, 2024[13]). The 147 members of the Inclusive Framework on BEPS, half of which are developing countries, have agreed on rules to establish a global minimum tax with a minimum effective tax rate of 15%, and implementation of the agreement has begun. The Inclusive Framework has also negotiated a simplified and streamlined approach to the application of the arm's length principle for certain activities of MNEs. In a recent report, the OECD (2024[14]) predicted that this approach will reduce transfer pricing disputes and compliance costs; enhance tax certainty for both tax administrations and taxpayers; and benefit low-capacity jurisdictions facing limited resources and data availability in particular.

Despite the enhanced international tax co-operation, not all countries have yet been able to benefit, especially LDCs.

Regional and international support to build taxation capacity is delivering results and in high demand

Increased international funding, technical support and training are boosting taxation capacity in developing countries, particularly with respect to international taxation. The joint OECD-UNDP Tax Inspectors Without Borders (TIWB) initiative, launched at the Third International Conference on Financing for Development in Addis Ababa in 2015, deploys experts to work alongside tax administrators in developing countries on live audit cases and related international tax issues. To date, TIWB programmes, including those jointly delivered with the African Tax Administration Forum (ATAF), have generated over USD 2.30 billion in additional tax revenues and USD 6.05 billion in additional tax assessments across 62 jurisdictions (OECD/UNDP, 2024[15]). The OECD and the Global Forum are expanding capacity-building support to meet increasing demand from developing countries that seek to implement the evolving international standards on taxation. The Global Forum, for instance, provided support to 91 jurisdictions in 2023 that ranged from induction programmes for new members and bilateral programmes as well as trainings, e-learning, toolkits and guidance, and much of the capacity-building activities were conducted in partnership with international and regional tax organisations (OECD, 2024[16]).

Collaboration with regional tax organisations has become increasingly important. The ATAF plays a leading role in building tax capacity across Africa, providing technical assistance missions to 35 countries in 2023. Thanks to these initiatives, ATAF members issued new tax assessments of USD 1.41 billion, of which USD 620 million was collected through audits. Since 2016, cumulative efforts by the ATAF and joint ATAF-TIWB programmes brought total tax collections to USD 1.92 billion (African Tax Administration Forum, 2024[17]). Another example is the Platform for Collaboration on Tax, established in 2016, that brings together the secretariats of the IMF, OECD, UN and World Bank Group to strengthen collaboration on DRM (Platform for Collaboration on Tax, 2024[18]). Separately, the OECD Academy for Tax and Financial Crime Investigation has provided training to more than 3 000 government officials from 167 jurisdictions to better detect and investigate tax and other financial crimes, helping countries in their efforts to stamp out illicit financial flows (IFFs).

Public development banks (PDBs) are increasingly mobilising finance for sustainable development in developing countries

PDBs are playing a crucial role in aligning investments with global goals such as the Sustainable Development Goals (SDGs), the Paris Agreement and the Kunming-Montreal Biodiversity Framework. Of the 127 PDBs and development finance institutions established since 2006, 72% were established in low- and middle-income countries, with 37.8% now domiciled in LMICs and 23.5% in UMICs but just 3.6% in LICs[2] (Peking University and Agence Française de Développement, 2024[19]). PDBs are increasingly mobilising finance for climate adaptation, biodiversity and social investments and exploring the use of sustainability-linked bonds, debt swaps and other innovative financial tools. Many PDBs have adopted green goals but green assets account for a relatively small share of their portfolios of just 14% on average (OECD et al., 2023[6]). For instance, only 19% of the instruments offered by PDBs in the Latin America and

Caribbean region address digital, gender or green goals (OECD et al., 2023[6]). Finance in Common supports PDBs by promoting research, dialogue and peer learning to enhance their strategies and operations. The network also works to foster global co-operation among stakeholders with the aim of streamlining financial frameworks to support sustainability goals, including recent efforts activities to strengthen alliances, enhance technical assistance and address currency mismatch challenges to boost cross-border capital flows.

2.3. Persistent challenges

A narrow focus on specific taxes undermines the potential to provide the revenues required

No single revenue type can generate the amount of revenue needed to achieve the SDGs. Yet, efforts to increase DRM are often narrowly focused on international corporate income tax, which is important, including for ensuring a level playing field and maintaining trust in the tax system, but cannot provide the level of domestic public revenues that many countries require. It is therefore important to look across the tax system as a whole to identify revenue-generating opportunities. Developing Medium-term revenue strategies can be a useful approach to align revenue goals with tax system reform (Platform for Collaboration on Tax, 2021[20]; Platform for Collaboration on Tax, 2023[21])More than 25 countries are already exploring this. When developed in consultation with and support from society as a whole, such strategies can be a useful complement to integrated national financing frameworks. The revenue strategy approach can also build durable political momentum for tax reform. This is critical since political economy constraints are frequently cited as a major challenge to achieving and maintaining DRM reforms (Independent Evaluation Group, 2023[22]).

Economic growth does not always translate into increased tax revenues

Low- and middle-income countries require economic growth in order to develop a well-functioning state that provides good quality public services, an education system and a social protection system. The tax system should contribute to an environment that is conducive to economic growth. However, economic growth must also produce higher tax revenues. When tax revenues increase in parallel with economic growth, countries can avoid having to increase statutory tax rates that would result in economic distortions. Broad tax bases, the avoidance of generous income-based tax incentives, and progressive tax systems can amplify the contribution of growth to higher revenues.

Tax incentives including fossil fuel subsidies still lack effective oversight

Tax incentives are increasing popular and generous in much of the world (OECD, 2022[23]). While tax incentives can play a valuable role in development, the foregone revenues can be significant. Corporate income tax (CIT) incentives cost on average 0.2% and 0.3% of GDP in Africa and Asia and almost double that in a quarter of countries in each region (OECD, 2022[23]). Almost 90% of developing countries have an income-based tax incentive that means in-scope firms pay zero CIT rates on their profits. The evidence on the effectiveness of tax incentives is mixed as most lack effective monitoring and analysis to determine value for money. A more comprehensive review of tax expenditures, including and beyond tax incentives for the largest multinational enterprises, is needed in many countries. Such reforms should ensure that incentives are well designed, well targeted and based on clear eligibility criteria and are transparent in granting, administration and evaluation (IMF, OECD, UN, WBG, 2015[24]).

Fossil fuel subsidies, which remain widespread globally, significantly hinder environmental sustainability and economic efficiency by encouraging the overconsumption of carbon-intensive energy sources. The fiscal cost of such subsidies, including those provided through tax expenditures, is substantial; in 2022, government support for fossil fuels surged to over USD 1.4 trillion across 48 OECD and partner countries, nearly doubling from the 2021 level as a result of initiatives aimed at mitigating high energy costs (OECD, 2023[25]). The trend shows an alarming increase in these subsidies despite growing awareness of their adverse impacts and complicating efforts to meet climate commitments and increasing fiscal costs. Phasing out fossil fuel subsidies can alleviate fiscal burdens, freeing up resources for more productive investments in renewable energy, education and healthcare while also aligning market signals with climate policy objectives. It is important to offset the potential regressive pricing of fossil fuels by ensuring that savings are redirected to targeted programmes for vulnerable populations, though this may be challenging in some countries.

Addressing tax crimes, corruption and illicit financial flows requires cross-government co-operation, which is often lacking

IFFs can be defined as activities such as money laundering, bribery, tax fraud and evasion and trade invoice mispricing, which aim to move resources from one country to another infringing the law (OECD, 2014[26]). These illicit flows contribute to the weakening of public institutions, foreign bribery and corruption, which inflict widespread harm and financial losses.

IFFs threaten the strategic, political and economic interests of countries and undermine public trust in governments and the financial system. IFFs can nullify legitimate financial inflows and reduce domestic investment capacity. Illicit financial outflows in some countries may exceed both ODA and foreign direct investment (FDI) inflows, making the fight against IFFs a key issue for policy coherence for sustainable development (Global Financial Integrity, 2015[27]; OECD, 2024[28]).

While there has been some success with the Stolen Asset Recovery Initiative, a partnership by the World Bank and the UN Office on Drugs and Crime that facilitated the recovery of about USD 1.9 billion in stolen assets, it is estimated that only 1% of crime proceeds are typically recovered. Detecting risks and emerging trends in tax criminality can improve performance as can improved inter-agency co-ordination and national strategies to tackle tax crime and foster a whole-of-government approach to combat IFFs.[3]

International co-operation is essential, and ODA can support by targeting non-tax revenue sectors such as energy and transport, strengthening key domestic institutions such as central banks and revenue collection authorities, and engaging with the private sector to enhance risk management, due diligence and responsible FDI. All this entails building technical expertise on IFFs. Efforts should focus on supporting developing countries in implementing Financial Action Task Force (FATF) standards to strengthen market and investor confidence, deter de-risking, and ensure sustained access to financial markets and cross-border payment systems.[4]

Knowledge of beneficial ownership information needs further improvement

Knowledge of beneficial ownership information is the cornerstone of the fight against tax evasion and other IFFs. Building on the work of the Global Forum and the synergies with the FATF process, jurisdictions took concrete steps in recent years to boost transparency of beneficial ownership information and foster compliance of domestic and foreign stakeholders. These steps included enacting legislation and creating tools to bridge information gaps, investigate tax and financial crimes effectively, and increase DRM. However, only 53% of the 118 jurisdictions reviewed by the Global Forum as of June 2024 have received a satisfactory rating on beneficial ownership, mostly because of implementation issues. Further progress is needed regarding practical administration of the adopted reforms and in terms of the resources that administrations must devote to this. Strategies to combat IFFs should centre on establishing beneficial ownership registers, whose set-up, administration and supervision are complex for both developed and developing countries.

Subnational and urban actors continue to lack access to finance

Some 65% of the 169 SDG targets cannot be achieved without involving subnational governments, including city governments. In a recent survey jointly conducted by the OECD, the Sustainable Development Solutions Network and the European Committee of the Regions, two-thirds of subnational governments cited the lack of financial resources as their main challenge in achieving the SDGs (OECD, 2024[29]). Their responses highlight the need for decentralisation, especially in some African countries, to allow local governments to raise their own revenues, for instance via property (Cities Alliance, 2021[30]). Regional and local governments play a key role in achieving climate and environmental objectives and are responsible for most of the public spending on climate change adaptation and mitigation. Yet, at current levels of investment, there is an annual financing shortfall of USD 350 billion in cities to meet climate targets in emerging economies per year (Birch, Rodas and Drumm, 2023[31]). International co-operation can play a critical role in bolstering subnational governments and urban finance. Guarantees, for instance, have potential to mobilise financing for sustainable development, as highlighted in discussions around multilateral development bank reform and by the G20 Independent Experts Group (2023[32]); harnessing this potential for cities can provide them with greater access to finance to address the impacts of climate change. As of 2024, The Multilateral Investment Guarantee Agency has issued USD 84.5 billion in guarantees since 1988, with only 11 claims paid (Multilateral Investment Guarantee Agency, 2024[33]). Most of its activities have focused on UMICs, though insurance in LICs accounted for more than 10% of new issuance volume for the first time in FY2022 (Mathiasen and Aboneaaj, 2023[34]).

Gender-responsive budgeting is needed to close gender gaps

Adequate and effective financing is essential to achieve gender equality and empower all women and girls. Gender-responsive budgeting can help address gender biases from government processes and tools and ensure that they are advancing gender equality efforts in areas such as equal pay and equal access to labour markets. Gender budgeting is increasingly practiced in OECD countries (OECD, 2024[35]). Partner countries are currently assessing whether they have systems in place to track budget allocations to gender equality as part of the 2023-26 monitoring round of the Global Partnership for Effective Development Co-operation (2024[36]).

2.4. New and emerging areas

Digitalisation of tax administration can have multiple benefits including and beyond revenue gains

The digitalisation of tax administration is linked with multiple benefits including improved revenues – for instance, increasing e-filing adoption by half of total tax filing could increase revenues by 1.6% of GDP (Nose and Mengistu, 2023[37]). It also is associated with greater public trust of tax officials and a lower perception of corruption (IMF, 2022[38]). While developing countries have been making progress, there remains significant scope for action. A combination of policies and complementary human resources are key to successful digitalisation (Nose and Mengistu, 2023[37]). There is a growing range of support available from different actors including TIWB programmes and self-assessment maturity models (OECD, 2022[39]).

Implementation of the global minimum tax for multinational enterprises can generate significant revenue gains

The global minimum tax ensures that large MNEs pay a minimum level of tax (at an effective rate of 15%) on their income in each jurisdiction where they operate, thereby reducing the incentive for profit shifting, placing a floor under tax competition and bringing an end to the race to the bottom on corporate tax rates.

To date, roughly 45 jurisdictions have already implemented or are planning to implement the global minimum tax in their domestic law. The revenue gains are estimated at between USD 155 and USD192 billion a year, or 6.5%-8.1% of global CIT revenues (OECD, 2024[40]). While gains would potentially be shared widely among jurisdictions, they would be higher for jurisdictions that implement some component of the global minimum tax. Those that do not implement the minimum level of tax risk foregoing revenues they could otherwise collect. The minimum tax will also provide an opportunity for jurisdictions to reassess their tax incentives and move towards incentive designs that offer better value for money in terms of investment generated per US dollar of revenue foregone.

Increasing the link between tax and the SDGs

While tax is primarily seen as a tool to raise revenues to deliver development goals, tax policy can also be used more directly to influence development outcomes. This potential has not been fully utilised to date. The development potential is especially substantial in the areas of inequality reduction, the environment and health.

Tax policy can strengthen progressivity and help combat global income and wealth inequalities

Global wealth concentration has increased at the top of the distribution. The estimated share of wealth held by the wealthiest 0.001% of the world population more than doubled between 1995 and 2022 from 3.3% to 6.9% (OECD, 2024[41]). Effective tax rates on high net worth individuals are often substantially lower than rates on persons with lower incomes[5] (OECD, 2024[41]).In terms of DRM, the primary limitation of individual income tax is the ability of wealthy individuals to minimise taxable income through deferred capital gains and strategic use of holding companies.

Policies can help broaden tax bases and achieve greater neutrality between taxation of different types of income and assets. In countries where level of tax expenditures is high, reforming regressive tax expenditures would increase the progressivity of the tax system. Countries need annual tax expenditure reports that not only measure the tax revenue foregone but also analyse the distributional impact. There is also a need to develop coherent strategies to strengthen the formal economy and bring informal businesses and their workers within the tax net. This will require tax and benefits reform. Many countries have informal sector businesses and workers that do have the capacity to make tax and social security contributions. A well-designed presumptive tax regime incentivises formalisation and does not constrain business growth.

Environment-related taxation can advance sustainable development by simultaneously addressing environmental challenges and supporting economic growth

Revenues from carbon taxes and emissions trading systems increased to a record high of USD 104 billion in 2023 (World Bank Group, 2023[42]). The global coverage of explicit carbon pricing policies is expanding, with nearly a quarter of global greenhouse gas (GHG) emissions now subject to a carbon tax or emissions trading system. When implicit carbon pricing via fuel excise taxes is included, coverage of explicit and implicit carbon pricing policies increases to 42% of global GHG emissions (OECD, 2023[43]). These taxes can generate significant revenue that can be allocated to essential public services and help dampen adverse distributional impacts. Their primary role is to incentivise the reduction of environmental damage, promote innovation in green technologies and improve public health outcomes by lowering pollution-related risks. Though environmental taxes may have regressive effects, they can be designed to incorporate compensatory measures such as tax credits or social transfers to mitigate impacts on vulnerable households and ensure an equitable distribution of benefits. Such an approach fosters both environmental and economic resilience, contributing to long-term sustainable development.

A recent declaration by the G20 on implementing a 2% minimum tax on the wealth of the world's billionaires as well as the Global Solidarity Levies Task Force advocate introducing levies on high-emission and resource-intensive sectors. Proposals include a fossil fuel extraction levy and a financial transaction tax, with significant portions of the revenues to be allocated to developing countries.

Increased fiscal space and external resources are needed to narrow the financing gaps for social protection and essential health care in developing countries

Despite initial progress in expanding essential health services coverage since 2000, the pace of improvements has stagnated globally since 2015, and 4.5 billion people lacked coverage in 2021. Financial hardship due to out-of-pocket health spending affected 2 billion people in 2019, with 1 billion people facing catastrophic costs and 344 million pushed into extreme poverty. The proportion of people spending over 10% of their household budget on health increased from 12.6% in 2015 to 13.5% in 2019 (UN, 2024[44]).

The COVID-19 pandemic exacerbated the financing gap for social protection and essential health care in many countries. In addition, many developing countries with large informal economies especially struggle to fund critical services. LICs would need to invest an additional 15.9% and LIMICs 5.1% of their GDP to finance a social protection floor. Put another way, many LICs would have to spend more than 75% of their tax revenues on social protection to close the gap – more than the expenditures of OECD member countries with a much larger tax revenue base (OECD, 2024[45]). In sub-Saharan Africa, public spending on health was only about 5.2% of GDP in 2019 compared with the global average of 9.8% of GDP (Piatti-Fünfkirchen, Lindelow and Yoo, 2018[46]).

Creating fiscal space – increasing tax revenues, expanding social security coverage, managing debt and reallocating public expenditures, among other approaches – would narrow the financing gap. But in most countries, health taxes are underutilised: According to the World Health Organization (2021[47]), the total number of countries that raised tobacco taxes to a level at or above 75% of the price of the most sold brand of cigarettes was 40 as of 2020. Taxes on tobacco and alcohol, and to a lesser extent taxes on sugar and sugar-sweetened beverages, have significant tax revenue potential and the added benefit of incentivising people to live a healthier lifestyle, which would significantly reduce the health, economic and social costs for society. Countries have opportunities to levy social security payments to finance social protection in ways that are aligned with the productivity of the workforce and lessen the possibility that the tax and social security system will push workers into informality.

Annex 2.A. Domestic Public Resources

Annex Table 2.A.1. Assessment of the action area: Domestic public resources

AAAA paragraph	Commitment	Specific target or objective (quantifiable/ timebound)	Matching SDG target (where available)	State of implementation or progress made since 2015, using SDG or other relevant indicator (proxy)
20	Strengthen domestic enabling environments, including the rule of law, and combat corruption at all levels and in all its forms.	No	Target 16.3 Promote the rule of law at the national and international levels and ensure equal access to justice for all. Target 16.5 Substantially reduce corruption and bribery in all their forms. Target 16.10 Ensure public access to information and protect fundamental freedoms in accordance with national legislation and international agreements.	See also paras. 22-25. *Other targets and indicators not listed in this annex are also relevant. For more information, see https://www.sdg16hub.org/home and https://unstats.un.org/sdgs/report/2023/extended-report/Extended-Report_Goal-16.pdf.* SDG indicator 16.3.1 Proportion of victims of (a) physical, (b) psychological and/or (c) sexual violence in the previous 12 months who reported their victimisation to competent authorities or other officially recognised conflict resolution mechanisms. As of early 2024, only 53 countries have at least one data point on the reporting of any type of violence covered by indicator 16.3.1 since 2010 (UN, 2024[48]). SDG indicator 16.5.1 Proportion of persons who had at least one contact with a public official and who paid a bribe to a public official or were asked for a bribe by those public officials, during the previous 12 months. In 2022, the average prevalence of bribery was higher in lower-income countries. For example, the average prevalence in low-income countries (LICs) is 31.6%, 26.2% in lower middle-income countries (LMICs), 17.1% in upper middle-income countries (UMICs) and 8.9% in high-income countries (UN, 2024[48]). Transparency International Corruption Perception Index (CPI) Since 2011, 28 of the 180 countries measured by the CPI improved their corruption scores and the scores of 34 countries deteriorated significantly. In sub-Saharan

AAAA paragraph	Commitment	Specific target or objective (quantifiable/ timebound)	Matching SDG target (where available)	State of implementation or progress made since 2015, using SDG or other relevant indicator (proxy)
				Africa, over 90% of countries scored below 50 (Transparency International, 2024[49]). OECD Government at a Glance indicators, anti-bribery convention reports, trust in government indicators Data available for OECD countries show that progress has been made since 2015 to increase public access to budgetary documents and to increase the number of countries with active enforcement of anti-bribery laws (OECD, 2023[50]).
21	Commit to promoting social inclusion in domestic policies. Promote and enforce non-discriminatory laws, social infrastructure and policies for sustainable development. Enable women's full and equal participation in the economy and ensure their equal access to decision-making processes and leadership.	No	Target 5.5 Ensure women's full and effective participation and equal opportunities for leadership at all levels of decision making in political, economic and public life. Target 10.2 By 2030, empower and promote the social, economic and political inclusion of all, irrespective of age, sex, disability, race, ethnicity, origin, religion, or economic or other status. Target 10.3 Ensure equal opportunity and reduce inequalities of outcome, including by eliminating discriminatory laws, policies and practices and promoting appropriate legislation, policies and action in this regard. Target 16.b Promote and enforce non-discriminatory laws and policies for sustainable development.	SDG indicator 5.5.1 Proportion of seats held by women in (a) national parliaments and (b) local governments. In 2024, women held 26.9% of seats in national parliaments worldwide (single and lower chambers), up from 22.3% in 2015. In least developed countries (LDCs), their share rose to 26.8% in 2024 compared with 21.7% in 2015. Additionally, women held 35.5% of elected seats in local government deliberative bodies globally in 2023; in LDCs, the proportion was 27% (UN, 2019[51]). SDG indicator 10.2.1 Proportion of people living below 50% of median income, by age, sex and persons with disabilities. Since 2000, two-thirds of countries have reduced the share of their population living on less than half the median income. More than 12% of people in these countries, however, still live on less than half the median (UN, 2019[51]). SDG indicators 10.3.1 and 16.b.1 Proportion of the population reporting having personally felt discriminated against or harassed in the previous 12 months on the basis of a ground of discrimination prohibited under international human rights law. According to data from 2015-23, one in six persons encountered discrimination over a 12-month period. Discrimination by colour or ethnic background continues to affect large population groups. Discrimination based on age, gender, religion or belief is also pervasive (UN, 2019[51]). Global Gender Gap Report, World Economic Forum In 2023, according to the World Economic Forum, the largest gender gap is in political empowerment of women, with 22.1% of the gap closed. Only 12 countries out of the 146 covered in the 2023 Global Gender Report scored above the 50%

AAAA paragraph	Commitment	Specific target or objective (quantifiable/ timebound)	Matching SDG target (where available)	State of implementation or progress made since 2015, using SDG or other relevant indicator (proxy)
				parity score in 2023, and in 75 countries women hold 20% or fewer ministerial posts (World Economic Forum, 2023[52]). OECD Social Institutions and Gender Index (SIGI) According to the 2019 OECD SIGI, on average, sub-Saharan Africa and South Asia countries had the highest levels of gender-based discrimination in social institutions (OECD, 2019[53]).
22	Work to improve the fairness, transparency, efficiency and effectiveness of tax systems, including by broadening the tax base and integrating the informal sector into the formal economy in line with country circumstances. Welcome efforts by countries to set nationally defined domestic targets and timelines for enhancing domestic revenue as part of their national sustainable development strategies. Support developing countries in need in reaching these targets. Commit to enhancing revenue administration through modernised and progressive tax systems, improved tax policy, and more efficient tax collection. Strengthen international co-operation to support efforts to build capacity in developing countries, including through enhanced official development assistance (ODA).	No	Target 8.3 Promote development-oriented policies that support productive activities, decent job creation, entrepreneurship, creativity and innovation and encourage the formalisation and growth of micro, small and medium-sized enterprises, including through access to financial services. Target 10.4 Adopt policies, especially fiscal, wage and social protection policies, and progressively achieve greater equality. Target 17.1 Strengthen domestic resource mobilisation, including through international support to developing countries, to improve domestic capacity for tax and other revenue collection.	SDG indicator 8.3.1 Proportion of informal employment in total employment, by sector and sex. The informality rate globally has declined by less than a percentage point since 2015. Although the global informality rate is at its lowest level, the number of informal workers is at its highest (ILO, 2024[54]). Over 90% of employed women in LDCs and nearly 90% in sub-Saharan Africa and in Central and Southern Asia were informally employed, with little improvement since 2015 (UN, 2024[55]). SDG indicator 10.4.2 Redistributive impact of fiscal policy. No SDG data are available for indicator 10.4.2 on the redistributive impact of fiscal policy. SDG indicator 17.1.1 Total government revenue as a proportion of gross domestic product (GDP), by source. This indicator directly measures the effectiveness of tax systems and their ability to broaden the tax base. Total government revenue (tax and non-tax) as a percent of GDP remained constant in developing countries, increasing only slightly from 28.2% to 28.3% over the 2015-22 period (IMF, 2023[56]). Since 2015, tax revenue as a percent of GDP increased from 16.8% to 17.5% in 2022 in developing countries, declining 16.1% in 2020 due to COVID-19. Developed countries have increased their tax revenue to GDP ratio at a faster pace: the ratio rose from 24.8% in 2015 to 26% in 2022 and the COVID-19 crisis had less of an impact, with tax revenue declining to only 24.7% of GDP in 2020 (IMF, 2023[56]).

AAAA paragraph	Commitment	Specific target or objective (quantifiable/ timebound)	Matching SDG target (where available)	State of implementation or progress made since 2015, using SDG or other relevant indicator (proxy)
				SDG indicator 17.1.2 Proportion of domestic budget funded by domestic taxes. The indicator reflects the effectiveness of tax collection systems and integration of informal sectors into the formal economy. The proportion of domestic budget funded by domestic taxes declined globally since 2000 from 63.5% to 59.0% in 2022 (UN, 2019[51]). OECD Global Revenue Statistics Database Between 2010 and 2021, over two-thirds of countries included in the OECD Global Revenue Statistics Database increased their tax-to-GDP ratio despite the impact of the COVID-19 pandemic on public revenues (OECD, 2024[57]). Tax-to-GDP ratio The tax-to-GDP ratio remains below the 15% threshold for 86% of LICs and 43% of LMICs. In countries affected by fragility, conflict and violence, the average tax-to-GDP ratio was as low as 12.6% in 2023, and the gap between developing and OECD country levels generally widened over 2010-21 (OECD, 2024[58]; World Bank, 2024[59]). Better tax design and stronger institutions could raise the tax-to-GDP ratio by 9 and 5 percentage points on average in LICs and emerging economies, respectively (IMF, 2023[60]). Proportion of government expenditure funded by taxes In 2020, the first year of the pandemic, the proportion of government expenditure funded by taxes declined by roughly 10% from 2019 in both developed and developing countries due in part to an increase in expenditure on policy measures as well as a decrease in tax revenues. The share of expenditure funded by taxes had not recovered to pre-pandemic level as of 2022 (UN, 2024[1]). Addis Tax Initiative (ATI) commitment to double ODA to domestic revenue mobilisation (DRM) in relation to 2020 levels ATI development partners collectively commit to maintain or surpass the 2020 global target level of USD 441.1 million for DRM co-operation supporting country-owned tax reforms (ATI, 2024[61]). Total ODA in support of DRM including and beyond ATI

AAAA paragraph	Commitment	Specific target or objective (quantifiable/ timebound)	Matching SDG target (where available)	State of implementation or progress made since 2015, using SDG or other relevant indicator (proxy)
				development partners reached USD 749 million in 2022 and is increasingly being channelled through the multilateral system. Twenty-five countries are actively involved in formulating and implementing Medium-Term Revenue Strategies with significant support from Platform for Collaboration on Tax partners, especially the IMF and World Bank. These efforts build on existing domestic tax reforms in law, policy and administration that are aligned with development spending needs. Some reforms are funded through the IMF Revenue Mobilization Thematic Fund, the World Bank Global Tax Program and similar initiatives. The UN, OECD and programmes including Tax Inspectors Without Borders (TIWB) provide additional support to link such strategies to global development goals (IMF; OECD; UN; WBG, 2021[62]).
23	Redouble efforts to substantially reduce illicit financial flows (IFFs) by 2030 with a view to eventually eliminating them. Combat tax evasion and corruption through strengthened national regulation and increased international co-operation. Enhance transparency in financial transactions between governments and companies, ensuring all companies, including multinationals, pay taxes where economic activity occurs and value is created, in line with national and international laws.	No	Target 16.4 By 2030, significantly reduce illicit financial and arms flows, strengthen the recovery and return of stolen assets and combat all forms of organised crime. See paras. 20, 24 and 25.	See paras, 20, 24 and 25. SDG indicator 16.4.1 Total value of inward and outward IFFs (in current US dollars). In 2023, nine countries joined new efforts to develop the first total estimates of IFFs, which will bring together estimates of IFFs from criminal, tax and commercial activities (UNCTAD, 2024[63]). Number of countries implementing base erosion and profit shifting (BEPS) actions and compliance levels among multinational enterprises (MNEs). The 15 BEPS Actions provide new tools for countries to address base erosion and profit shifting. These include both unilateral and multilateral actions. Under BEPS Action 5, countries exchange information on tax rulings and peer review regimes. Prior to agreement on Action 5 in 2015, there was almost no exchange of information on tax rulings, but by 2024, over 54 000 exchanges had taken place and 322 regimes have been reviewed, with almost all now in line with the standard (OECD, 2024[64]). BEPS Action 6 is focused on strengthening treaty anti-abuse positions and is facilitated through a multilateral instrument (MLI) that implements treaty-related BEPS measures. To date, 104 jurisdictions have signed the BEPS MLI and over 1 400 existing treaties have been amended (OECD, 2024[64]). Under BEPS Action 13, MNEs are mandated to prepare a country-by-country (CbC)

AAAA paragraph	Commitment	Specific target or objective (quantifiable/ timebound)	Matching SDG target (where available)	State of implementation or progress made since 2015, using SDG or other relevant indicator (proxy)
				report that provides an overview of their global income, profit, taxes paid and economic activity across different jurisdictions. Over 115 jurisdictions have introduced CbC reporting (OECD, 2024[64]), an increase from 49 to 2016 (OECD, 2025[65]), meaning that substantially all MNEs with a turnover above EUR 750 million are now covered by a CbC reporting obligation (OECD, 2024[64]). Number of jurisdictions participating in Automatic Exchange of Information (AEOI) and volumes of information exchanged The Global Forum includes 171 jurisdictions and is focused on implementing two international standards: the standard on transparency and exchange of information on request (EOIR) and the standards on AEOI (financial account information and Crypto-Assets). Between 2009 and 2022, Global Forum members reported making over 306 000 requests for information and nearly 90% of the jurisdictions achieved a satisfactory level of compliance with the EOIR standard. As of 2024, 126 countries have committed to implementing the standard on AEOI of financial accounts and 108 jurisdictions have exchanged information. Information on over 134 million financial accounts was exchanged automatically in 2023, covering total assets of nearly USD 12 trillion (OECD, 2024[66]). These exchanges are made possible by participation to the Multilateral Convention on Mutual Administrative Assistance in Tax Matters, which now counts 147 jurisdictions. The AEOI standard and the Creditor Reporting System were endorsed by ECOSOC as part of the UN code of conduct on co-operation in combating international tax evasion (OECD, 2024[66]). In addition, 59 jurisdictions have committed to start AEOI on Crypto-Assets in 2027 Number of jurisdictions implementing the OECD/G20 Inclusive Framework on BEPS two-pillar solution The 147 member OECD/G20 Inclusive Framework on BEPS has led to the development of a two-pillar solution addressing the challenges posed to the traditional international tax system by digitalisation of the economy. Pillar One aims to allocate taxing rights more fairly among countries by ensuring that MNEs, particularly those in the digital economy, pay taxes where their users and customers are located regardless of where the enterprise is domiciled. Pillar One also includes measures to simplify transfer pricing to provide a simplified and streamlined approach to the arm's length principle for certain transactions (the first phase of this has been adopted). While optional, Inclusive Framework members have committed to respect the use of Amount B by developing countries. Pillar Two introduces a global minimum corporate

AAAA paragraph	Commitment	Specific target or objective (quantifiable/ timebound)	Matching SDG target (where available)	State of implementation or progress made since 2015, using SDG or other relevant indicator (proxy)
				tax rate of 15% aimed at curbing tax competition and ensuring that MNEs pay a minimum level of tax on their global income. Approximately 45 jurisdictions are already taking steps to implement the global minimum tax for MNEs and about 90% of in-scope MNEs are expected to be subject to the global minimum tax by 2025.
24	Identify, assess and act on money laundering risks by effectively implementing Financial Action Task Force (FATF) standards on anti-money laundering and counter-terrorism financing. Encourage information sharing among financial institutions. (Calls on the International Monetary Fund, the World Bank and the UN)	No	**See paras. 20, 23 and 25.** Target 16.4 By 2030, significantly reduce illicit financial and arms flows, strengthen the recovery and return of stolen assets, and combat all forms of organised crime.	See paras. 20, 23 and 25. Progress on implementing FATF standards The FATF Global Network, which consists of the FATF and nine regional bodies as associate members (FATF-style regional bodies) as well as observers, brings together 206 countries and jurisdictions committed to implement the FATF Recommendation (FATF, 2023[67]). See 2022-23 FATF annual report, https://www.fatf-gafi.org/en/publications/Fatfgeneral/FATF-Annual-report-2022-2023.html. IMF anti-money laundering and combating the financing of terrorism (AML/CFT) assessments. The national AML/CFT frameworks of 89% of FATF members have now been assessed in the current fourth round of evaluations (FATF, 2023[67]).
25	Urge all countries that have not yet done so to ratify and accede to the United Nations Convention against Corruption (UNCAC) and encourage parties to review its implementation. (ref to UNCAC). Strengthen international co-operation and national institutions to combat money laundering and the financing of terrorism. Encourages international community to support return of assets. (reference to Stolen Asset Recovery Initiative)	Yes All countries to ratify and accede to the UNCAC.	See paras 20, 23 and 24.	See paras. 20, 23 and 24. Number of countries that ratify and accede to the UNCAC The UNCAC is the only legally binding universal anti-corruption instrument. As of 7 August 2024, there were 140 signatories and 191 parties to the UNCAC (UNODC, 2024[68]). Progress by the Stolen Asset Recovery Initiative (StAR) Established in 2007, StAR has helped over 50 countries build their capacity to trace, seize and recover stolen assets and supports the implementation of Chapter V of the UNCAC (World Bank / UNODC, 2024[69]; World Bank / UNODC, 2023[70]). Through the initiative, 141 jurisdictions were involved in international asset recovery cases leading to USD 10 billion of assets being returned internationally; USD 16.5 billion of assets being either frozen, confiscated or returned' and 563 asset recovery cases

AAAA paragraph	Commitment	Specific target or objective (quantifiable/ timebound)	Matching SDG target (where available)	State of implementation or progress made since 2015, using SDG or other relevant indicator (proxy)
				documented (World Bank / UNODC, n.d.[71]). Number of countries that ratify the OECD Anti-Bribery Convention The OECD Anti-Bribery Convention currently counts 46 countries (referred to as Parties) that have committed to the fight against bribery in international business transactions (OECD, 2025[72]).
26	Encourage investment in value addition and diversification of natural resources while addressing excessive tax incentives, especially in extractive industries. Promote transparency, including initiatives such as the Extractive Industries Transparency Initiative (EITI). Support sharing best practices, peer learning and capacity building for fair and transparent contract negotiations and monitoring of agreements. (ref to EITI)	No	Target 8.2 Achieve higher levels of economic productivity through diversification, technological upgrading and innovation.	SDG indicator 8.2.1 Annual growth rate of real GDP per employed person. Productivity growth, or the growth rate of real GDP per employed person, stagnated in both 2022 and 2023, with growth rates below 0.5%. From 2015 to 2019, the average growth rate exceeded 1.5% (UN, 2019[51]). Number of commodity-dependent countries. (IMF) In 2015, approximately 91 countries were classified as commodity dependent, meaning that more than 60% of their total merchandise exports were made up of commodities. In 2019-21, the number of commodity-dependent countries slightly increased to 101 (UNCTAD, 2023[73]). The International Monetary Fund finds that excessive tax incentives can lead to revenue losses ranging from 5%-10% of GDP in countries that rely on oil, gas and/or mining. The OECD tax incentives database shows that approximately 90% of developing countries covered have a tax incentive that allows the MNE to be exempt from corporate taxation on the affected income entirely. Progress by the EITI The number of countries implementing the EITI Standard increased from 48 in 2015 to over 50 in 2023. As of 2023, nearly 60 countries have published data in an open and standardised format in accordance with the EITI open data policy. Since 2015, USD 2.97 trillion in revenues have been reported through the EITI (Extractive Industries Transparency Initiative, 2023[74]).
27	Commit to scaling up international tax co-operation. Encourage countries to strengthen transparency and adopt	No		See paras. 22, 23 and 28 (MNE reporting CbC, automatic exchange of tax information and ODA to developing countries).

AAAA paragraph	Commitment	Specific target or objective (quantifiable/ timebound)	Matching SDG target (where available)	State of implementation or progress made since 2015, using SDG or other relevant indicator (proxy)
	appropriate policies, e.g. for MNEs to report CbC to tax authorities where they operate; strengthen access to beneficial ownership information for competent authorities; and progressively advance towards automatic exchange of tax information among tax authorities as appropriate, with assistance to developing countries and especially the LDCs as needed.			
28	Calls for universal participation in international tax co-operation, particularly LDCs, small island developing states (SIDS), landlocked developing countries (LLDCs) and African countries (reference to Global Forum on Transparency and Exchange of Information for Tax Purposes, OECD G20 on BEPS). Recognises the need for technical assistance and capacity building (reference to OECD/UNDP TIWB initiative).	No		See para. 23. Participation particularly by LDCs, SIDS, LLDCs and African countries in Exchange of Information for Tax Purposes and OECD/ G20 Inclusive Framework on BEPS The OECD/G20 Inclusive Framework on BEPS was established in 2016 to allow interested countries to work together to address BEPS issues. Membership has grown from 82 jurisdictions at its launch to 143 in September 2024, and other countries are still welcome to join. The steering group is comprised of 25 countries with broad geographic and developmental representation. In 2022, the governance was modified to provide for two co-chairs to increase representation (the current co-chairs are from the United Kingdom and Jamaica) (OECD, 2025[75]). Participation of countries, particularly LDCs, SIDS, LLDCs and African countries, in the Global Forum The Global Forum includes 171 jurisdictions and is focused on implementing two international standards: the standard on transparency and EOIR and the standard on AEOI (financial account information and Crypto-Assets). Between 2009 and 2022, Global Forum members reported making over 306 000 requests for information and nearly 90% of the jurisdictions achieved a satisfactory level of compliance with the EOIR standard. On AEOI, as of 2024, 126 countries have committed to implementing the standard on AEOI of financial accounts and 108 jurisdictions have exchanged information. Information on over 134 million financial accounts was exchanged automatically in 2023, covering total assets of nearly USD 12 trillion (OECD, 2024[66]). These exchanges are made possible by participation to the Multilateral Convention

AAAA paragraph	Commitment	Specific target or objective (quantifiable/ timebound)	Matching SDG target (where available)	State of implementation or progress made since 2015, using SDG or other relevant indicator (proxy)
				on Mutual Administrative Assistance in Tax Matters, which now counts 147 jurisdictions. The AEOI standard and the Creditor Reporting System were endorsed by the UN Economic and Social Council as part of the UN code of conduct on co-operation in combating international tax evasion (UN, 2017[76]). In addition, 59 jurisdictions have committed to start AEOI on Crypto-Assets in 2027. Support provided by TIWB (OECD and UNDP) TIWB includes a portfolio of 59 ongoing (current) and 71 completed programmes, including 25 South-South collaborations. Since 2015, TIWB assistance has helped tax administrations in developing countries generate an additional USD 2.30 billion in tax revenues and USD 6.05 billion in tax assessments across 62 jurisdictions in Africa, Asia and the Pacific, Eastern Europe, and LAC (OECD/UNDP, 2024[15]). Participation in various multilateral instruments to facilitate international tax co-operation including the Multilateral Convention on Mutual Administrative Assistance in Tax Matters, Multilateral Competent Authority Agreement on automatic exchange of financial account information, Multilateral Competent Authority Agreement on the exchange of country-by-country reports and the Multilateral Convention to Implement Tax Treaty Related Measures to Prevent Base Erosion and Profit Shifting. See Chapter 3 for more information.
29	Welcome the work of the Committee of Experts on International Cooperation in Tax Matters and its subcommittees. Decide to work on enhancing its resources to strengthen its effectiveness and operational capacity.	No		Resources provided to the Committee of Experts on International Cooperation in Tax Matters A proposal for Draft Terms of Reference for a United Nations Framework Convention on International Tax Cooperation was released on 19 July 2024 (UN, 2024[77]).
30	Strengthen national control mechanisms such as supreme audit institutions and other independent oversight bodies. Increase transparency and equal participation in the budgeting process, promote gender-responsive budgeting and	No	Target 5.c Adopt and strengthen sound policies and enforceable legislation for the promotion of gender equality and the empowerment of all women and girls at all levels.	See para. 20. SDG indicator 5.c.1 Proportion of countries with systems to track and make public allocations for gender equality and women's empowerment. According to data from 105 countries and areas for the period 2018-21, 26% of countries have comprehensive systems to track and make public allocations for

AAAA paragraph	Commitment	Specific target or objective (quantifiable/ timebound)	Matching SDG target (where available)	State of implementation or progress made since 2015, using SDG or other relevant indicator (proxy)
	tracking, and establish transparent public procurement frameworks to support sustainable development. (reference to Open Government Partnership).		Target 16.6 Develop effective, accountable and transparent institutions at all levels.	gender equality, 59% have some features of a system, and 15% do not have minimum elements of these systems (UN, 2019[51]). SDG indicator 16.6.1 Primary government expenditures as a proportion of the original approved budget, by sector (or by budget codes or similar). Budget reliability improved in 2021 and 2022 compared with 2020 but remained weaker than prior to the pandemic. Budget reliability was lower in the 2021-22 post-pandemic period than in the 2015-19 pre-COVID period in most regions except Latin America and the Caribbean and sub-Saharan Africa (UN, 2024[48]). International Organization of Supreme Audit Institutions (INTOSAI) and World Bank survey on supreme audit institutions Nearly all developing countries now have operational supreme audit institutions with support from the World Bank and the INTOSAI. However, the independence and effectiveness of these institutions vary widely across regions (International Bank for Reconstruction and Development / The World Bank, 2021[78]). Open Budget Survey (OBS) The 77 countries included in the 2023 OBS will only reach an adequate level of budget transparency in about two decades (International Budget Partnership, 2023[79]). Public Expenditure and Financial Accountability (PEFA) Since they were created in 2001, PEFA assessments have been conducted in more than 150 countries and territories, including both developed and developing nations. A supplementary framework for assessing gender responsive public financial management includes nine indicators distributed across the budget cycle and can be applied at both national and subnational levels (PEFA, 2020[80]).
31	Reaffirms the commitment to rationalise inefficient fossil fuel subsidies that encourage wasteful consumption by removing market distortions.	Yes Recommits to previous pledges to end inefficient fossil	Target 12.c Rationalise inefficient fossil fuel subsidies.	SDG indicator 12.c.1 Amount of fossil fuel subsidies (production and consumption) per unit of GDP. Explicit subsidies to fossil fuels (undercharging for supply costs) have more than doubled since 2020 and reached a record high of USD 1.53 trillion globally in 2022. Subsidies increased in all regions by 36%-58% between 2021 and 2022. The most

AAAA paragraph	Commitment	Specific target or objective (quantifiable/ timebound)	Matching SDG target (where available)	State of implementation or progress made since 2015, using SDG or other relevant indicator (proxy)
		fuel subsidies.		recent call to phase out inefficient fossil fuel subsidies was made in 2021 at COP26 in Glasgow (UN, 2024[9]). Explicit subsidies in 2021 were almost five times higher than the levels recorded in 2020 due to the global energy crisis triggered by Russia's invasion of Ukraine (IEA, 2023[81]). Implicit fossil fuel subsidies reached USD 7 trillion in 2022 or 7.1% of global GDP. Differences between efficient prices and retail fuel prices are large and pervasive. For example, 80% of global coal consumption was priced at below half of its efficient level in 2022 (IMF, 2023[82]). Full fossil fuel price reform could reduce global carbon dioxide emissions to an estimated 43% below baseline levels in 2030 (in line with keeping global warming to 1.5-2°C) while also raising revenues worth 3.6% of global GDP (IMF, 2023[82]).
32	Notes the burden and costs that noncommunicable diseases place on developed and developing countries. Recognises that a comprehensive strategy of prevention and control and price and tax measures on tobacco can be an effective and important means to reduce tobacco consumption and healthcare costs and represent a revenue stream for financing development.	No	Target 3.a Strengthen the implementation of the World Health Organization Framework Convention on Tobacco Control in all countries, as appropriate. Target 3.4 By 2030, reduce by one third premature mortality from noncommunicable diseases through prevention and treatment and promote mental health and well-being.	SDG indicator 3.a.1 Age-standardised prevalence of current tobacco use among persons ages 15 years and older. Worldwide, the total economic damage of smoking (including productivity losses from death and disability) has been estimated at more than USD 1.4 trillion per year, equivalent to 1.8% of the world's annual GDP. More than 80% of the world's smokers live in LMICs. Economic modelling carried out by the World Bank shows that raising cigarette excise tax rates in all developing countries by the equivalent of USD 0.25 per pack would generate an extra USD 41 billion in government tobacco excise revenue for LMICs (World Bank Group, 2017[83]). In 2022, the global prevalence of current tobacco use among the population aged 15 years and older was estimated at 20.9% (34.4% among men and 7.4% among women), which translates to roughly 1.25 billion adult tobacco users in the world. The prevalence has declined since 2015, when it was 23.9%, and the number of users has decreased by 50 million. By investing in proven tobacco control measures, global smoking prevalence could decline by over half in 15 years, which would save 42.8 million lives and generate USD 6.2 trillion in social and economic benefits, including USD 2.3 trillion in direct healthcare savings (UN, 2024[44]). There are now 182 countries that are Parties to the WHO Framework Convention on Tobacco Control (WHO FCTC), demonstrating strong political will to reduce both the demand for and

AAAA paragraph	Commitment	Specific target or objective (quantifiable/ timebound)	Matching SDG target (where available)	State of implementation or progress made since 2015, using SDG or other relevant indicator (proxy)
				supply of tobacco products (UN, 2024[44]). SDG indicator 3.4.1 Mortality rate attributed to cardiovascular disease, cancer, diabetes or chronic respiratory disease. In 2019, a 30-year-old person had a 17.8% chance of dying from one of the four major noncommunicable diseases (NCDs) (cardiovascular diseases, cancer, chronic respiratory diseases, or diabetes) before the age of 70. This is a slight decline from the 18.5% risk in 2015. Men had a higher probability of premature death from NCDs than women globally (UN, 2019[51]). A majority (77%) of NCD deaths occur in low- and middle-income countries. Cardiovascular diseases account for most NCD deaths (17.9 million people annually), followed by cancers (9.3 million), chronic respiratory diseases (4.1 million), and diabetes (2.0 million including kidney disease deaths caused by diabetes). These four groups of diseases account for over 80% of all premature NCD deaths (WHO, 2023[84]).
33	Call on national and regional development banks to expand their contributions to sustainable infrastructure, energy, etc., especially during financial crises, and urge relevant international public and private actors to support such banks in developing countries.	No	n.a.	For more information on public development bank (PDB) and development finance institution (DFI) activities, see the Peking University and Agence Française de Développement (AFD) database at http://www.dfidatabase.pku.cn and International Development Finance Club (IDFC, n.d.[85]). SDG alignment of public development banks (and development finance institutions activities) The accumulated assets of over 500 PDBs totalled about USD 23 trillion in 2022, representing 10% of global investment. These include ten mega banks that hold 70% of the total. The China Development Bank stands out as the largest general mandate public development bank, with approximately USD 2.6 trillion in assets (Finance in Common, 2022[86]). Only 3.6% of global DFIs and PDBs are in LICs (Finance in Common, 2022[86]). A survey of the largest national development banks found that more than 80% of those responding have adopted green goals though the share of green assets in their

AAAA paragraph	Commitment	Specific target or objective (quantifiable/ timebound)	Matching SDG target (where available)	State of implementation or progress made since 2015, using SDG or other relevant indicator (proxy)
				portfolios remains low, with average levels at just 14% (Dalhuijsen et al., 2023[87]).
34	Commit to scaling up international co-operation to enhance the capacities of municipalities and local authorities, especially in LDCs and SIDS. Enhance inclusive and sustainable urbanisation and strengthen economic, social and environmental links between urban, peri-urban and rural areas through improved national and regional development planning. Strengthen debt management, support the establishment of municipal bond markets, and promote lending from financial institutions and development banks, including risk mitigation mechanisms. (reference to MIGA). By 2020, increase the number of cities and human settlements adopting and implementing integrated policies and plans for inclusion, resource efficiency, climate change mitigation and adaptation, and disaster resilience. Develop and implement holistic disaster risk management at all levels in alignment with the Sendai.	No	Target 11.3 By 2030, enhance inclusive and sustainable urbanisation and capacities for participatory, integrated and sustainable human settlement planning and management in all countries. Target 11.a Support positive economic, social and environmental links between urban, peri-urban and rural areas by strengthening national and regional development planning. Target 13.1 Strengthen resilience and adaptive capacity to climate-related hazards and natural disasters in all countries	SDG indicator 11.3.1 Ratio of land consumption rate to population growth rate. A sample of 1 217 cities indicates that over 2000-20 the rate at which cities sprawled was up to 3.7 faster than the rates of their densification (UN, 2024[88]). SDG indicator 11.a.1 Number of countries that have national urban policies or regional development plans that (a) respond to population dynamics; (b) ensure balanced territorial development; and (c) increase local fiscal space. In 2021, 55 out of 58 national urban policies (95%) fulfilled the first criteria on "responding to population dynamics", 54 (93%) fulfilled the second criteria on "ensuring balanced territorial development" and only 26 (45%) met the third criteria on making considerations for "increased local fiscal space" (UN, 2019[51]). SDG indicator 13.1.2 Number of countries that adopt and implement national disaster risk reduction strategies in line with the Sendai Framework for Disaster Risk Reduction 2015-30. In 2023, 129 countries reported having a national disaster risk reduction (DRR) strategy that is aligned to the Sendai Framework, a substantial increase compared to 55 countries in 2015. Of the 129, 122 countries indicated that "promoting policy coherence and alignment with the SDGs and the Paris Agreement" is a central component of their DRR strategy, highlighting the importance of incorporating climate resilience and sustainable development (UN, 2019[51]; UN, 2024[89]). SDG indicator 13.1.3 Proportion of local governments that adopt and implement local disaster risk reduction strategies in line with national disaster risk reduction strategies Most (82%) countries with a DRR strategy also have corresponding local DRR strategies aligned with their national plans. Local-level risk governance has progressed in recent years, and 106 countries reported the implementation of local DRR strategies consistent with national frameworks by 2023. On average, 72% of local governments in these reporting countries indicate they have local DRR strategies in place (UN, 2024[89]). Share of the world and developing countries' population living in cities

AAAA paragraph	Commitment	Specific target or objective (quantifiable/ timebound)	Matching SDG target (where available)	State of implementation or progress made since 2015, using SDG or other relevant indicator (proxy)
				By 2030, almost 60% of the total population living in the developing world will live in cities. In 2023, about 75% of the world's population lived in small cities of less than 500 000 people (UN-HABITAT, 2023[90]). In 2020, Africa's urban population was 716 million people, and it will double to 1.4 billion people living in cities by 2050, according to OECD- Sahel and West Africa Club projections (Africapolis, 2023[91]). In 2050, approximately 60% of these urban residents will live in large cities (i.e. more than 1 million habitants). Larger African cities (especially those above 4 million) are already more compact (meaning less distance between buildings) than cities of less than 4 million (Anderson, Prieto Curiel and Patiño Quinchía, 2023[92]). While infill reduces outward expansion, trade-offs emerge in these cities such as loss of green space (Anderson, Patiño Quinchía and Prieto Curiel, 2022[93]). Urban infrastructure gap The annual urban public infrastructure gap in developing countries is estimated at USD 1.3 trillion of investment (UN-HABITAT, 2024[94]). To meet climate targets, USD 29.4 trillion will be needed in cities in emerging economies between 2018 and 2030. At current levels of investment, the shortfall is USD 350 billion per year (SDG Action, 2023[95]). Without involving subnational governments, including cities, 65% of the 169 SDG targets cannot be achieved (OECD, 2025[96]). Municipal green bonds Municipal green bonds are debt securities issued by subnational governmental entities that are labelled green to signal to the financial market a climate- and environment-related investment. Their issuance is concentrated in the United States, with issuances also in Europe and China. In Africa and Latin America, nine municipal green bonds were issued by local governments over the 2014-23 period, including governments of cities and provinces in Argentina, Mexico, Morocco and South Africa (Herrera, 2024[97]). Risk insurance in developing countries. The World Bank Multilateral Investment Guarantee Agency (MIGA) provides political

AAAA paragraph	Commitment	Specific target or objective (quantifiable/ timebound)	Matching SDG target (where available)	State of implementation or progress made since 2015, using SDG or other relevant indicator (proxy)
				risk insurance covering 90%-95% of investments or loans against non-commercial risks. Over 35 years, MIGA has issued USD 70 billion in guarantees, with only 11 claims paid, and operates with a 76:1 leverage ratio without having had a capital infusion since 1988. However, most activities focus on UMICs, with FY2022 marking the first time that insurance in LICs exceeded 10% of new issuance volume (Mathiasen and Aboneaaj, 2023[34]).

Notes: The data points are mainly drawn from the UN's Sustainable Development Goals Extended Report 2024 and its statistical annexes. Trend data in are in constant USD 2015 prices unless otherwise indicated.

References

Addis Tax Initiative (2024), *ATI Matchmaking (webpage)*, https://www.addistaxinitiative.net/sites/default/files/resources/2021-22%20%20ATI%20Monitoring%20Brief.pdf (accessed on 18 October 2024). [10]

African Tax Administration Forum (2024), "ATAF unveils 2023 annual report highlighting significant achievements", https://www.ataftax.org/press-release-ataf-release-2023-annual-report. [17]

Africapolis (2023), *Visualise urbanisation in Africa*, https://africapolis.org/en (accessed on 24 January 2025). [91]

Anderson, B., J. Patiño Quinchía and R. Prieto Curiel (2022), "Boosting African cities' resilience to climate change: The role of green spaces", *West African Papers*, No. 37, OECD Publishing, Paris, https://doi.org/10.1787/3303cfb3-en. [93]

Anderson, B., R. Prieto Curiel and J. Patiño Quinchía (2023), "City shapes and climate change in Africa", *West African Papers*, No. 40, OECD Publishing, Paris, https://doi.org/10.1787/a944a930-en. [92]

ATI (2024), *Commitments & Principles*, Addis Tax Initiative, https://www.addistaxinitiative.net/fr/engagements-et-principes. [61]

Benitez, J. et al. (2023), "Building tax capacity in developing countries", *Staff Discussion Notes*, No. 2023/006, International Monetary Fund, Washington, DC, https://www.imf.org/en/Publications/Staff-Discussion-Notes/Issues/2023/09/15/Building-Tax-Capacity-in-Developing-Countries-535449. [3]

Birch, E., M. Rodas and E. Drumm (2023), "Bridging the SDG funding gap in cities", *SDG Action*, https://sdg-action.org/bridging-the-sdg-funding-gap-in-cities/. [31]

Choudhary, R., F. Ruch and E. Skrok (2024), *Taxing for Growth: Revisiting the 15 Percent Threshold*, World Bank, Washington, DC, https://documents.worldbank.org/pt/publication/documents-reports/documentdetail/099062724151523023/p1778861e0c40b081186a61ced16cac6cde. [4]

Cities Alliance (2021), *Assessing the Institutional Environment of Cities and Subnational Governments in Africa*, https://www.citiesalliance.org/sites/default/files/2022-05/CitiesAlliance_Assessing%20Inst.%20Environment%20of%20Cities%20and%20Subnal.%20Govs%20in%20Africa_EN.pdf. [30]

Dalhuijsen, E. et al. (2023), *Greening National Development Financial Institutions: Trends, Lessons Learned, and Ways Forward (Overview)*, Washington, DC: World Bank, https://doi.org/10.1596/978-1-4648-2031-1. [87]

Extractive Industries Transparency Initiative (2023), *EITI Anniversary Report 2023: twenty years of extractives transparency*, https://eiti.org/sites/default/files/2023-06/EITI%2020th%20Anniversary%20Report-%20web.pdf. [74]

FATF (2023), *FATF Annual Report 2022-2023*, https://www.fatf-gafi.org/en/publications/Fatfgeneral/FATF-Annual-report-2022-2023.html. [67]

Finance in Common (2022), *FICS Progress Report 2022*, https://financeincommon.org/sites/default/files/2022-10/Finance%20in%20Common%20Progress%20Report%202022.pdf. [86]

G20 Independent Experts Group (2023), *Strengthening Multilateral Development Banks: The Triple Agenda - Volume 1*, https://www.gihub.org/resources/publications/strengthening-multilateral-development-banks-the-triple-agenda-report-of-the-g20-independent-experts-group/. [32]

Global Financial Integrity (2015), *Illicit Financial Flows and Development Indices: 2008-2012*, Global Financial Integrity, Washington, DC, https://gfintegrity.org/report/illicit-financial-flows-development-indices-2008-2012/. [27]

Global Partnership for Effective Development Co-operation (2024), *Global Dashboard (database)*, https://www.effectivecooperation.org/GlobalEDCDashboard (accessed on 11 December 2024). [36]

Herrera, H. (2024), "The proliferation of municipal green bonds in Africa and Latin America: the need for a climate justice approach", *Environment and Urbanization*, Vol. 36/1, pp. 147-172, https://doi.org/10.1177/09562478241230290. [97]

IDFC (n.d.), *Working together to implement the Sustainable Development Goals*, International Development Finance Club, https://www.idfc.org/. [85]

IEA (2023), *Tracking the impact of government support: Fossil Fuel Subsidies*, https://www.iea.org/topics/fossil-fuel-subsidies. [81]

ILO (2024), *World Employment and Social Outlook: May 2024 Update*, International Labour Organization, https://www.ilo.org/sites/default/files/2024-06/WESO_May2024%20-%20Final_30-05-24_2.pdf. [54]

IMF (2024), *G-20 Note on Alternative Options for Revenue Mobilization*, International Monetary Fund (IMF), Washington, DC, https://www.imf.org/external/np/g20/pdf/2024/062424.pdf. [11]

IMF (2024), *World Revenue Longitudinal Database: Tracking Domestic Revenue Mobilization and Changes in Government Revenue Structures*, International Monetary Fund (IMF), Washington, DC, https://www.imf.org/en/Topics/fiscal-policies/world-revenue-longitudinal-database. [5]

IMF (2023), *Countries Can Tap Tax Potential to Finance Development Goals*, International Monetary Fund, https://www.imf.org/en/Blogs/Articles/2023/09/19/countries-can-tap-tax-potential-to-finance-development-goals. [60]

IMF (2023), *Government Finance Statistics (database)*, International Monterary Fund, https://data.imf.org/?sk=a0867067-d23c-4ebc-ad23-d3b015045405 (accessed on 15 September 2024). [56]

IMF (2023), *IMF Fossil Fuel Subsidies Data: 2023 Update*, International Monetary Fund, Washington, DC, https://www.imf.org/en/Publications/WP/Issues/2023/08/22/IMF-Fossil-Fuel-Subsidies-Data-2023-Update-537281. [82]

IMF, OECD, UN, WBG (2015), *Options for Low Income Countries' Effective and Efficient Use of Tax Incentives for Investment*, https://www.tax-platform.org/sites/pct/files/publications/100756-Tax-incentives-Main-report-options-PUBLIC_0.pdf. [24]

IMF; OECD; UN; WBG (2021), *Platform for Collaboration on Tax: Medium-Term Revenue Strategy (MTRS)*, https://www.tax-platform.org/medium-term-revenue-strategy (accessed on 20 January 2024). [62]

Independent Evaluation Group (2023), "Domestic revenue mobilization", *Evaluation Insight Note*, World Bank Group, Washington, DC, https://ieg.worldbankgroup.org/evaluations/evaluation-insight-note-domestic-revenue-mobilization. [22]

International Bank for Reconstruction and Development / The World Bank (2021), *Supreme Audit Institutions Independence Index: 2021 Global Synthesis Report. EFI Insight-Governance.*, World Bank, Washington DC, https://insai.worldbank.org/sites/default/files/2021-07/InSAI%202021%20Final%20Report_1.pdf. [78]

International Budget Partnership (2023), *Open Budget Survey 2023*, https://internationalbudget.org/wp-content/uploads/IBP-OBS-Global-Report-2023-v4-Final-Artwork.pdf. [79]

Mathiasen, K. and R. Aboneaaj (2023), "MIGA: The little engine that should", *CGD Policy Paper*, No. 309, Center for Global Development, Washington, DC, https://www.cgdev.org/sites/default/files/miga-little-engine-should.pdf. [34]

Multilateral Investment Guarantee Agency (2024), *Management's Discussion & Analysis and Financial Statements*, https://www.miga.org/sites/default/files/2024-08/MIGA%20MD%20%26A%20and%20Financial%20Statement%20June%2030%202024.pdf. [33]

Newiak, M., A. Segura-Ubiergo and A. Wane (eds.) (2022), *Digitalization, corruption, and trust in tax officials in Africa*, International Monetary Fund, Washington, DC, https://www.elibrary.imf.org/display/book/9781513584058/CH015.xml. [38]

Nose, M. and A. Mengistu (2023), "Exploring the adoption of selected digital technologies in tax administration", *IMF Notes*, No. 2023/008, International Monetary Fund, Washington, DC, https://www.imf.org/en/Publications/IMF-Notes/Issues/2023/12/11/Exploring-the-Adoption-of-Selected-Digital-Technologies-in-Tax-Administration-A-Cross-541094. [37]

OECD (2025), *Base erosion and profit shifting (BEPS) (webpage)*, https://www.oecd.org/en/topics/policy-issues/base-erosion-and-profit-shifting-beps.html (accessed on 20 January 2025). [75]

OECD (2025), *Country-by-country reporting for tax purposes (webpage)*, https://www.oecd.org/en/topics/sub-issues/country-by-country-reporting-for-tax-purposes.html (accessed on 20 January 2025). [65]

OECD (2025), *Global engagement on anti-corruption and anti-bribery (webpage)*, https://www.oecd.org/en/networks/global-engagement-on-anti-corruption-and-anti-bribery.html (accessed on 20 January 2025). [72]

OECD (2025), *OECD Programme on A Territorial Approach to the SDGs*, https://www.oecd.org/en/about/programmes/oecd-programme-on-a-territorial-approach-to-the-sdgs.html (accessed on 20 January 2025). [96]

OECD (2024), *BEPS Multilateral Instrument (webpage)*, OECD Publishing, Paris, https://www.oecd.org/en/topics/sub-issues/beps-multilateral-instrument.html (accessed on 11 December 2024). [13]

OECD (2024), *Breaking the Vicious Circles of Informal Employment and Low-Paying Work*, OECD Publishing, Paris, https://doi.org/10.1787/f95c5a74-en. [45]

OECD (2024), *Compare your country - Tax co-operation*, https://www.compareyourcountry.org/tax-cooperation/en/1/category/ (accessed on 20 January 2025). [66]

OECD (2024), *Convention on Combating Bribery of Foreign Public Officials in International Business Transactions and Commentaries to the Convention*, OECD Publishing, Paris, https://www.oecd.org/content/dam/oecd/en/topics/policy-sub-issues/fighting-foreign-bribery/Convention%20and%20commentaries%20booklet%202024.pdf. [28]

OECD (2024), *Creditor Reporting System (database)*, http://data-explorer.oecd.org/s/c (accessed on 20 January 2025). [8]

OECD (2024), *Events: Update of the economic impact assessment of the Global Minimum Tax (webinar)*, https://www.oecd.org/en/events/2024/01/update-of-the-economic-impact-assessment-of-the-global-minimum-tax.html (accessed on 12 December 2024). [40]

OECD (2024), *Gender budgeting (webpage)*, https://www.oecd.org/en/topics/gender-budgeting.html (accessed on 2 December 2024). [35]

OECD (2024), "Localising the SDGs in a changing landscape", *OECD Regional Development Papers*, No. 68, OECD Publishing, Paris, https://doi.org/10.1787/a76810d7-en. [29]

OECD (2024), *OECD Secretary-General Tax Report to G20 Finance Ministers and Central Bank Governors (G20 Brazil, July 2024)*, OECD Publishing, Paris, https://doi.org/10.1787/3bacc6e8-en. [64]

OECD (2024), *Pillar One - Amount B: Inclusive Framework on BEPS*, OECD/G20 Base Erosion and Profit Shifting Project, OECD Publishing, Paris, https://doi.org/10.1787/21ea168b-en. [14]

OECD (2024), *Tax and development (webpage)*, https://www.oecd.org/en/topics/policy-issues/tax-and-development.html (accessed on 2 December 2024). [58]

OECD (2024), *Tax and Development at the OECD: A Retrospective (2009-2024)*, OECD Publishing, Paris, https://doi.org/10.1787/9db734bc-en. [16]

OECD (2024), *Taxation and Inequality: OECD Report to G20 Finance Ministers and Central Bank Governors*, OECD Publishing, Paris, https://doi.org/10.1787/8dbf9a62-en. [41]

OECD (2024), *The Global Revenue Statistics Database 2024 (Brochure)*, https://www.oecd.org/content/dam/oecd/en/topics/policy-sub-issues/global-tax-revenues/brochure-global-revenue-statistics-database.pdf. [57]

OECD (2023), *Effective Carbon Rates 2023: Pricing Greenhouse Gas Emissions through Taxes and Emissions Trading*, OECD Series on Carbon Pricing and Energy Taxation, OECD Publishing, Paris, https://doi.org/10.1787/b84d5b36-e. [43]

OECD (2023), *Global Revenue Statistics Database*, https://www.oecd.org/en/data/datasets/global-revenue-statistics-database.html (accessed on 12 December 2024). [7]

OECD (2023), *Government at a Glance 2023*, OECD Publishing, Paris, https://doi.org/10.1787/3d5c5d31-en. [50]

OECD (2023), *OECD Inventory of Support Measures for Fossil Fuels 2023*, OECD Publishing, Paris, https://doi.org/10.1787/87dc4a55-en. [25]

OECD (2022), *Assessing Tax Compliance and Illicit Financial Flows in South Africa*, OECD Publishing, Paris, https://doi.org/10.1787/e8c9ff5b-en. [12]

OECD (2022), *Digital Transformation Maturity Model*, OECD Tax Administration Maturity Model Series, OECD Publishing, Paris, https://www.oecd.org/content/dam/oecd/en/topics/policy-issues/tax-administration/digital-transformation-maturity-model.pdf. [39]

OECD (2022), *Tax Incentives and the Global Minimum Corporate Tax: Reconsidering Tax Incentives after the GloBE Rules*, OECD Publishing, Paris, https://doi.org/10.1787/25d30b96-en. [23]

OECD (2019), *SIGI 2019 Global Report: Transforming Challenges into Opportunities*, Social Institutions and Gender Index, OECD Publishing, Paris, https://doi.org/10.1787/bc56d212-en. [53]

OECD (2014), *Illicit Financial Flows from Developing Countries: Measuring OECD Responses*, OECD Publishing, Paris, https://doi.org/10.1787/9789264203501-en. [26]

OECD et al. (2023), *Latin American Economic Outlook 2023: Investing in Sustainable Development*, OECD Publishing, Paris, https://doi.org/10.1787/8c93ff6e-en. [6]

OECD/UNDP (2024), *Tax Inspectors Without Borders Annual Report 2024*, OECD Publishing, Paris, https://doi.org/10.1787/8968125d-en. [15]

Our World in Data (2023), *Tax revenues as a share of GDP (UNU-WIDER Government Revenue Dataset)*, https://ourworldindata.org/grapher/tax-revenues-as-a-share-of-gdp-unu-wider (accessed on 12 December 2024). [2]

PEFA (2020), *Supplementary Framework for Assessing Gender Responsive Public Financial Management*, PEFA Secretariat, Washington DC, https://www.pefa.org/resources/supplementary-framework-assessing-gender-responsive-public-financial-management-0. [80]

Peking University and Agence Française de Développement (2024), *Public Development Banks and Development Financing Institutions Database*, http://www.dfidatabase.pku.edu.cn/DataVisualization/index.htm (accessed on 2 December 2024). [19]

Piatti-Fünfkirchen, M., M. Lindelow and K. Yoo (2018), “What are governments spending on health in east and Southern Africa?”, *Health Systems & Reform*, Vol. 4/4, pp. 284-299, https://doi.org/10.1080/23288604.2018.1510287. [46]

Platform for Collaboration on Tax (2024), *Who We Are (webpage)*, https://www.tax-platform.org/ (accessed on 18 October 2024). [18]

Platform for Collaboration on Tax (2023), *PCT Progress Report 2023*, International Monetary Fund, World Bank Group, OECD, United Nations/Washington, DC, Paris, New York, https://www.tax-platform.org/sites/pct/files/publications/PCT-Progress-Report-2023.pdf. [21]

Platform for Collaboration on Tax (2021), *MTRS (webpage)*, https://www.tax-platform.org/publications/mtrs (accessed on 2 December 2024). [20]

SDG Action (2023), *Bridging the SDG funding gap in cities*, https://sdg-action.org/bridging-the-sdg-funding-gap-in-cities/ (accessed on 2 December 2024). [95]

Transparency International (2024), *Corruption Perceptions Index*, https://www.transparency.org/en/cpi/2023. [49]

UN (2024), *Goal 8: Decent work and economic growth*, United Nations, https://mdgs.un.org/sdgs/report/2024/goal-08/?utm_source=chatgpt.com. [55]

UN (2024), *Introductory Note to the Bureau's Proposal for the Revised Draft Terms of Reference for a United Nations Framework Convention on International Tax Cooperation by the Chair of the Ad Hoc Committee, Mr. Ramy M. Youssef, 18 July 2024*, United Nations, https://financing.desa.un.org/sites/default/files/2024-07/Revised%20draft%20ToR_18%20July%202024.pdf. [77]

UN (2024), *The Sustainable Development Goals Extended Report 2024: Goal 11*, United Nations Statistical Commission, New York, https://unstats.un.org/sdgs/report/2024/extended-report/Extended-Report_Goal-11.pdf. [88]

UN (2024), *The Sustainable Development Goals Extended Report 2024: Goal 12 Responsible Consumption and Production*, United Nations Statistics Division, New York, https://unstats.un.org/sdgs/report/2024/extended-report/Extended-Report_Goal-12.pdf. [9]

UN (2024), *The Sustainable Development Goals Extended Report 2024: Goal 13*, United Nations Statistical Commission, New York, https://unstats.un.org/sdgs/report/2024/extended-report/Extended-Report_Goal-13.pdf. [89]

UN (2024), *The Sustainable Development Goals Extended Report 2024: Goal 16*, United Nations Statistical Commission, New York, https://unstats.un.org/sdgs/report/2024/extended-report/Extended-Report_Goal-16.pdf. [48]

UN (2024), *The Sustainable Development Goals Extended Report 2024: Goal 17*, United Nations Statistics Division, New York, https://unstats.un.org/sdgs/report/2024/extended-report/Extended-Report_Goal-17.pdf. [1]

UN (2024), *The Sustainable Development Goals Extended Report 2024: Goal 3*, United Nations Statistics Division, New York, https://unstats.un.org/sdgs/report/2024/extended-report/Extended-Report_Goal-3.pdf. [44]

UN (2019), *Progress Towards the Sustainable Development Goals - Report of the Secretary-General: Statistical Annex*, United Nations Economic and Social Council, New York, https://digitallibrary.un.org/record/3810131?ln=en&v=pdf. [51]

UN (2017), *Resolution adopted by the Economic and Social Council on 20 April 2017*, United Nations, https://documents.un.org/doc/undoc/gen/n17/184/54/pdf/n1718454.pdf. [76]

UNCTAD (2024), *Efforts to track illicit financial flows need scaling up*, https://sdgpulse.unctad.org/illicit-financial-flows/. [63]

UNCTAD (2023), *State of Commodity Dependence 2023*, United Nations, New York, https://unctad.org/system/files/official-document/ditccom2023d3_en.pdf. [73]

UN-HABITAT (2024), *Cities and Climate Action: World Cities Report 2024*, United Nations Human Settlements Programme, Nairobi, https://unhabitat.org/world-cities-report-2024-cities-and-climate-action. [94]

UN-HABITAT (2023), *Unlocking the Potential of Cities: Financing Sustainable Urban Development*, United Nations Human Settlements Programme, Nairobi, https://unhabitat.org/sites/default/files/2023/11/unlocking_the_potential_of_cities_-_financing_sustainable_urban_development_-_06-min.pdf. [90]

UNODC (2024), *Learn about UNCAC*, The United Nations Office on Drugs and Crime, https://www.unodc.org/corruption/en/uncac/learn-about-uncac.html. [68]

WHO (2023), *Climate change and noncommunicable diseases: connections*, World Health Organization, https://www.who.int/news/item/02-11-2023-climate-change-and-noncommunicable-diseases-connections. [84]

World Bank (2024), *Taxes & Government Revenue*, https://www.worldbank.org/en/topic/taxes-and-government-revenue. [59]

World Bank / UNODC (2024), *StAR Annual Report 2023*, https://star.worldbank.org/sites/default/files/2024-04/StAR-annual-2023-06%20%281%29.pdf. [69]

World Bank / UNODC (2023), *StAR Brochure: A brief introduction to StAR's mission, work and methodology*, https://star.worldbank.org/star-brochure-0. [70]

World Bank / UNODC (n.d.), *Stolen Asset Recovery Initiative: Asset Recovery Watch Database*, https://star.worldbank.org/asset-recovery-watch-database?cid=EFI_EM_AssetRecovery_EN_EXT (accessed on 16 November 2024). [71]

World Bank Group (2023), *State and Trends of Carbon Pricing (Executive Summary)*, https://openknowledge.worldbank.org/server/api/core/bitstreams/d14ff4b1-823f-4d70-927c-456449772089/content. [42]

World Bank Group (2017), *Tobacco Tax Reform: at the Crossroads of Health and Development*, https://documents1.worldbank.org/curated/fr/491661505803109617/pdf/119792-REVISED-v2-OctFINALWBGTobaccoTaxReformFullReportweb.pdf?utm_source=chatgpt.com. [83]

World Economic Forum (2023), *Global Gender Gap Report 2023: Insight Report*, World Economic Forum, https://www.weforum.org/publications/global-gender-gap-report-2023/digest/. [52]

World Health Organization (2021), *WHO Report on the Global Tobacco Epidemic 2021: Addressing New and Emerging Products*, https://www.who.int/publications/i/item/9789240032095. [47]

Notes

[1] Authors' calculation. The estimated mobilisation potential is derived from the increase in US dollars of tax-to-GDP using WB WDI GDP (USD current in 2020). The median tax-to-GDP ratio in LICs was 11.4% in 2020 compared with 15.7% on average in LMICs. In 2020, the total GDP of LICs stood at USD 646.8 billion.

[2] According to the Institute of New Structural Economics at Peking University database, 36% of the 127 new PDBs and DFIs established since 2006 are located LMICs; 33% in high-income countries, 19% in UMICs and 5% in LICs. See http://www.dfidatabase.pku.edu.cn/DataVisualization/index.htm.

[3] Improved inter-agency co-ordination and national strategies for a whole-of-government approach to combat IFFs can be achieved by leveraging the ten global principles for fighting tax crime developed by the OECD Task Force on Tax Crimes and other Crimes and by collaborating with the Global Forum on Transparency and Exchange of Information for Tax Purposes.

[4] Prioritising high-risk sectors such as commodity trading, guided for example by the OECD Guidance on Mitigating the Risks of Illicit Financial Flows in Oil Commodity Trading, can yield swift improvements in reducing IFF risks.

[5] A study published by the EU Tax Observatory found by billionaires in France, the Netherlands and the United States have effective tax rates of about 20%-30%, lower than for any lower-income groups. See https://doi.org/10.1787/8dbf9a62-en.

3 Domestic and International Private Business and Finance

This chapter reviews the Domestic and International Private Business and Finance action area of the Addis Ababa Action Agenda (AAAA) including progress, persistent challenges, and emerging areas as the international community prepares for the Fourth International Conference on Financing for Development (FfD4). It explores the progress and challenges in mobilising private sector support for sustainable development. Key advancements include increased adoption of policy instruments, expanded private sector engagement, and the growth of sustainable finance initiatives, such as ESG and impact investing. Despite this, challenges persist in areas like financing for Least Developed Countries (LDCs), high remittance costs, and insufficient private finance mobilisation for climate action. Emerging trends highlight the growing role of sustainable finance, the need for improved transparency and governance, and the importance of addressing de-risking to enhance cross-border financial access. Ensuring long-term investments aligned with sustainability goals is crucial for future success.

3.1. Data dashboard

Key Trends

Global financial assets increased by 47% between 2015 and 2023, with an increasing share held in developing countries.

In 2022, total global financial assets fell by 0.4%, the first decline in the non-banking financial institution sector since 2009 and driven by higher interest rates and lower asset valuations.

Most (79%) of the USD 461.2 trillion in global financial assets under management (stocks) in 2022 remain concentrated in developed countries (Figure 3.1). However, the share held in developing countries has increased over 2015-22 from 17% to 21%.

Figure 3.1. Global financial assets

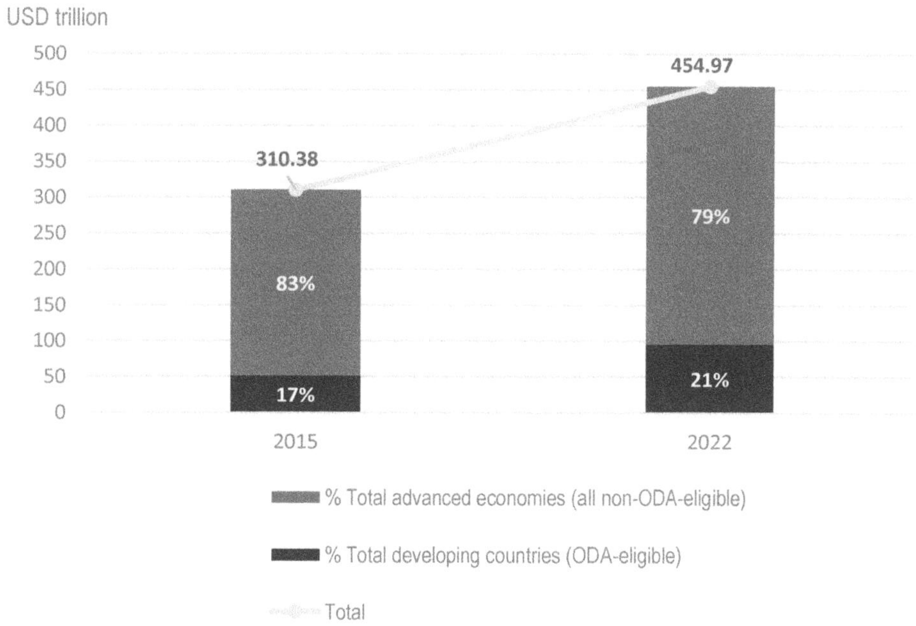

Note: The sum of jurisdictions is not equal to the total global financial assets reported to the Financial Stability Board. Global financial assets are those managed by entities including banks, central banks, insurance companies, pension funds, public financial institutions and other financial institutions. Non-bank financial intermediation includes investment funds, insurance companies, pension funds and other financial intermediaries.
Source: Authors based on Financial Stability Board (2023[1]), *Global Monitoring Report on Non-bank Financial Intermediation 2023*, https://www.fsb.org/2023/12/global-monitoring-report-on-non-bank-financial-intermediation-2023/.

Global foreign direct investment inflows have declined significantly from USD 2.4 trillion in 2015 to USD 1.3 trillion in 2023.

Global foreign direct investment (FDI) inflows dropped by 2% between 2022 and 2023 to USD 1.3 trillion, continuing a declining trend since 2015 (Figure 3.2). The latest available figures for global FDI flows indicate a further decline to USD 802 million in the first half of 2024 (OECD, 2024[2]).

Between 2015-22, FDI flows declined by 42% in least developed countries (LDCs) and 84% in other low-income countries (LICs) but decreased by only 2% in lower middle-income countries (LMICs) and increased by 8% in upper middle-income countries (UMICs). The LDC share of FDI going to developing countries decreased from 5.1% in 2015 to 3.6% in 2022 .

In addition to the volume of inflows, the quality of FDI and its impact on sustainable development matter to move from resource mobilisation to achieving Sustainable Development Goals (SDG). Importantly, Foreign investment is rapidly shifting to sectors that have lower job creation potential but are crucial for the green and digital transitions.

Figure 3.2. Foreign direct investments inflows

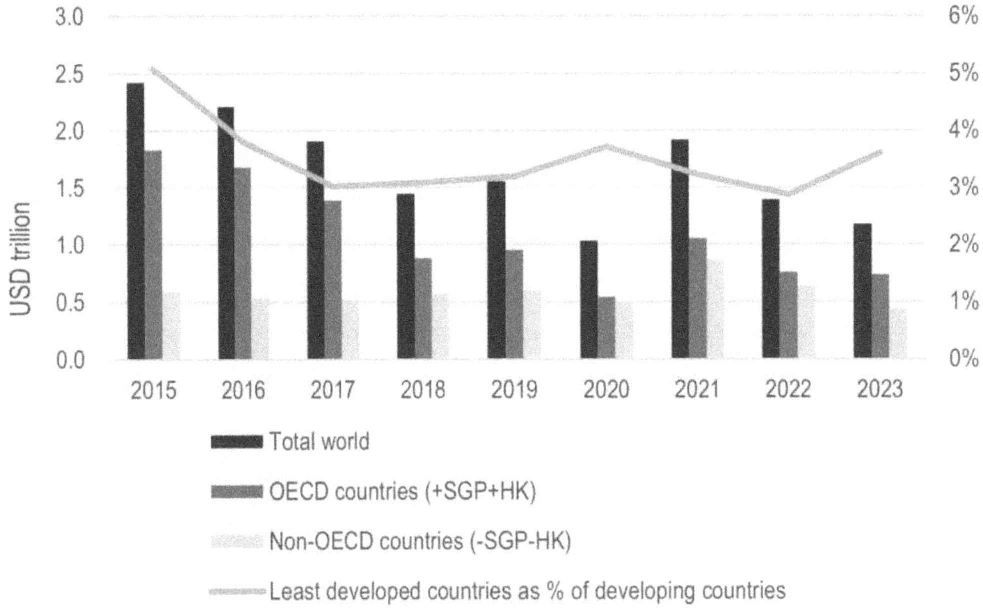

Notes: In the figure, HK = Hong Kong (China); SGP = Singapore. The calculation of FDI to LDCs as a percent of FDI to all developing countries is based on UN Trade and Development (UNCTAD) data. FDI inflows for OECD, non-OECD and World aggregates were compiled using directional figures when available, or asset/liability figures otherwise. Resident SPEs from Austria, Belgium, Hungary, Iceland, Latvia, Luxembourg, Mexico, the Netherlands, Portugal, and Switzerland are excluded.
Source: For total world, OECD and non-OECD countries: OECD (2024[3]) FDI statistics database available through the OECD Data Explorer (BMD4). For LDCs and the total for developing countries: UNCTAD (2024[4]), *World Investment Report 2024*, https://unctad.org/publication/world-investment-report-2024.

Remittance volumes are increasing though transfer costs remain high.

Total remittances to developing countries (excluding China) increased by 29% since 2015 to reach USD 476 billion in 2023. The volume of remittances has increased the most in UMICs (+49%) compared to LMICs (+20%) and LDCs (+27%). The transfer cost of sending USD 200 has declined from 7.7% to 6.4% but is still more than double the 3% SDG target (Figure 3.3).

Figure 3.3. Remittances in volume and transfer costs

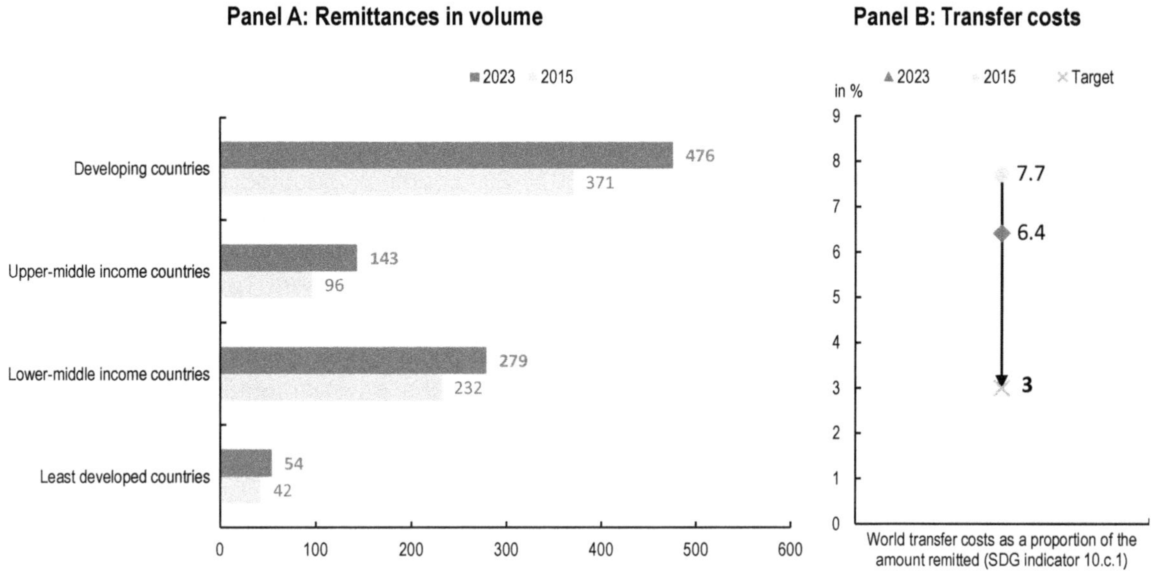

Note: Calculations are based on 2015 constant prices and deflated using the GDP deflator of the US Federal Reserve Bank of St. Louis. For transfer costs, the latest available data are from the first quarter of 2024. Developing countries are defined as ODA eligible countries, excluding China.
Source: World Bank (2024[5]), *World Development Indicators*, https://data.worldbank.org/topic/financial-sector?view=chart

Key performance indicators

↑	In 2021, 71% of adults in developing economies had a financial account, up from 63% in 2017.
↑	Greenfield FDI in renewable energies expanded sharply since 2019 in OECD countries and since 2022 in non-OECD countries, more than tripling overall.
↔	Energy intensity improvements have fallen short of the SDG 7.3 target of an average annual improvement of 2.6% between 2010-30, which is equivalent to doubling the average improvement rate observed over 1990-2010. To reach this target, annual progress of about 4% is needed between 2022 and 2030 (UN, 2024[6]).
↓	The global share of women holding management positions in 2022 declined to 27.5% from 28.5% in 2016 (UN, 2024[7]). Gender parity will take 176 years to be achieved at the current rate of change.

↓ Slight setback	↓ Setback	↔ No change, neutral	↔ Stagnant, possible issue	↑ Major progress	↑ Minimal progress
Minimal setback	↓ Major setback	Holding steady, slight concern	↔ Negative stagnation, concerning	Progress	↑ Negligible progress or progress contested

Note: Selected quantifiable commitments. Annex Table 3.A.1. contains the full list.

Resource mobilisation potential

- LDCs would have received USD 280 billion in FDI inflows since 2015, i.e. an additional USD 41 billion total since 2015, had their inflows increased at the same rate (17%) as in other developing countries over 2015-23 (UNCTAD, 2024[4]).
- An additional USD 16 billion could have been mobilised in support of developing country households by reducing remittance transfer prices to the 3 percentage point SDG target in 2023.[1]

3.2. Key areas of progress

The public sector has strengthened its approach to engaging the private sector as a key partner in support of sustainable development

Since 2015, governments have stepped up their adoption of policy instruments in support of sustainable consumption and production, including responsible business and investing, to help strengthen incentives for private sector alignment to the SDGs. From 2015-20, countries adopted 34 economic and fiscal instruments (up from 16 in 2015); 160 macro policy instruments (up from 51 in 2015); 81 regulatory and legal instruments (up from 37 in 2015); and 72 voluntary schemes (up from 30 in 2015) (UNEP, 2024[8]). In 46 of the 52 developing countries covered by the OECD 2022 Investment Tax Incentive database, at least one tax incentive supports an area related to the SDGs (Celani, Dressler and Wermelinger, 2022[9]). As of 2023, 75% of OECD countries have adopted a variety of due diligence-related regulations that require companies that require companies to manage and disclose the environmental and social impacts of activities within their global supply chains and investment portfolios.[2]

Several global initiatives also enhance private sector participation in sustainable development. Examples include the UN Global Compact, the world's largest corporate sustainability initiative that engages over 10 000 companies globally; the Global Investors for Sustainable Development Alliance, launched in 2019, that includes 30 corporate and financial leaders promoting sustainable investments; and the Principles for Responsible Investment network, comprised of more than 4 000 investors managing USD 121 trillion. Others are the Sustainable Stock Exchanges Initiative, which involves more than 100 stock exchanges and encourages investors to use responsible investment to enhance environmental, social and governance (ESG) transparency. In addition, the Business for 2030 initiative aligns corporate projects with the SDGs. Finally, the International Sustainability Standards Board (ISSB) builds on the Climate Disclosure Standards Board, the Task Force for Climate-related Financial Disclosures, the Value Reporting Foundation's Integrated Reporting Framework, and the industry-based Sustainability Accounting Standards Board Standards as well as the World Economic Forum's Stakeholder Capitalism Metrics and the International Platform on Sustainable Finance.

Development co-operation providers have also developed specific policies to more effectively engage the private sector including by supporting developing countries. official development assistance (ODA) eligibility rules ensure that donors' direct support to the private sector (i.e. private sector instruments) can be reported as ODA only if it ensures both financial or non-financial additionality (OECD, 2024[10]). By untying most of their ODA, donors also ensure that all companies can effectively compete and access donor funds and allow recipient countries more flexibility in procurement. For example, in 2015, approximately 80% of bilateral ODA was either untied or offered on the condition that it be used to procure goods or services from the provider of the aid. By 2022, the proportion had increased to over 85%, reflecting ongoing efforts to enhance the effectiveness of donors' private sector engagement3 (OECD DAC, 2022[11]). Another example is the Kampala Principles on effective private sector engagement in development co-operation, which promote partner country ownership of private sector engagement and ensure the alignment of projects and programmes with national sustainable development priorities (Global Partnership for Effective Development Co-operation, 2019[12]). The Kampala Principles Assessment is a novel component of the Global Partnership for Effective Development Co-operation (2023[13]) monitoring exercise that generates evidence to track and stimulate greater effectiveness on private sector engagement in development co-operation.

Finally, development co-operation providers have agreed several international standards to strengthen the commitment to effective private sector engagement. Among these are OECD DAC Blended Finance Principles and accompanying Guidance. While definitions of blended finance vary,[4] the principles and guidance provide development finance actors with tools to design and implement effective, efficient and transparent blended finance programmes and ultimately to mobilise more private finance for sustainable development. Progress is being made in disseminating and implementing responsible business conduct standards to enhance the environmental and social impact of businesses and generate positive spillover effects in developing countries through the due diligence process. Development co-operation plays an important role in this regard, helping to build capacities and ensure that all countries and entities can promote sustainable investment and improve opportunities to participate in global value chains.

Financial inclusion, including bank account ownership, has steadily advanced

More than half a billion people gained access to formal financial services between 2017-21 (UN, 2024[14]). Global bank account ownership rose from 51% in 2011 to 76% in 2021, notably increasing by 30 percentage points in developing countries to reach 71% in 2021 (UN, 2024[14]). However, progress varies by region, with only 15.7% of small-scale industries in sub-Saharan Africa having access to loans or lines of credit over 2006-23 compared with 44.2% in Latin America and the Caribbean (UN, 2024[14]).

Remittance volumes are increasing and transfer costs remain high

Remittance volumes grew to USD 838 billion in 2022, including USD 614 billion to all developing countries, and remain a crucial source of income for households and small and medium-sized enterprises (SMEs) (UN, 2024[14]). Remittances were expected to have reached USD 669 billion in 2023 (UN, 2024[14]). The highest remittances growth rate (21.6%) was in the Latin America and the Caribbean region, driven by economic recovery in the United States and migrants' responses to natural disasters in their home countries (UNCTAD, 2024[4]). In 2022, LDCs received USD 62 billion in remittances – twice the volume of FDI (USD 27 billion) received that year[5].

The global average cost to send USD 200 decreased from 7.7% in 2015 to 6.2% in 2023, largely due to migrants' greater access to digital instruments for transferring remittances. However, the global average cost of sending remittances is still more than double the SDG target of 3%. The World Bank's Smart Remitter Target (SmaRT), the simple average of the three cheapest qualifying services for sending remittances in each remittance corridor, stood at 3.5% in 2023 (World Bank, 2024[15]). However, transfer fees were higher than 5% in 20% of remittance corridors. Barriers to reducing the cost include lack of competition among money transfer operators, stiff regulatory requirements for even small transfers, and insufficient support to new digital players as well as de-risking, notably due to the absence of precise risk metrics for certain corridors.

Philanthropic financing for sustainable development in developing countries is on the rise

Philanthropic financing is growing, and domestic foundations in emerging countries are playing a growing role. Private philanthropy for development from 40 reporters grew from USD 4 billion in 2015 to 11 billion in 2022. Domestic foundations in emerging markets such as People's Republic of China, India and Mexico accounted for 19% of this financing over the period. Sub-Saharan Africa receives the largest share of total philanthropic funding, with significant contributions to support health and economic development. The Gates Foundation and other major foundations focus heavily on this region, particularly in the areas of disease eradication and healthcare improvement, and provided a total of USD 5 billion in 2022 (Ratha et al., 2019[16]).

3.3. Persistent challenging areas

FDI flows to developing countries overall are increasing but not to LDCs

Global FDI dropped by 2% between 2022 and 2023, to USD 1.3 trillion, continuing the declining trend since 2015 and lower than the pre-COVID-19 level for the second consecutive year (UNCTAD, 2024[4]). While FDI inflows to developing countries overall increased over the 2015-23 period, FDI to LDCs has declined in terms of both volume and share. FDI inflows to LDCs have not rebounded following COVID-19 to the same degree as they have to other developing countries due to the disproportionate impacts of food and energy and successive other global crises (UNCTAD, 2023[17]). LDCs received USD 31.3 billion in FDI in 2023, down from USD 37.6 billion in 2015, 3.6% of the total FDI inflows to developing countries and 2.4% of global FDI (a slight increase from the 1.8% share in 2015) (UNCTAD, 2024[4]). FDI often bypasses LDCs due to perceived risks in the form of political instability, weak infrastructure and limited market size. Additionally, Inadequate regulatory frameworks lack of skilled labour and other structural barriers deter investors. At the same time, globally, cross-border mergers and acquisitions activity continued a downward trend, hitting a record ten-year low in 2023. Greenfield investment activity stalled in 2023, yet trends in advanced economies and in emerging and developing economies diverged, with capital expenditures up by 21% in the latter group (OECD, 2024[18]).

Capital market development is needed in developing countries to allow firms and governments to finance their long-term investments

Capital markets support capital formation and investment diversification and help ensure long-term financing. However, capital markets remain small and underdeveloped in developing economies, hindering their growth opportunities. Capital markets consist of equity markets and bond markets, and both equity and bonds can be acquired through the primary market, where new securities are issued, or through the secondary market, which involves trading existing securities. By way of comparison, equity market capitalisation reached 131% of gross national product (GNP) in high-income countries in 2022 but just 34.4% of GNP in Latin America and the Caribbean, 16.2% of GNP in Central Europe and the Baltics, and 64.4% in non-high-income East Asia and Pacific countries. Equity markets in these regions lack liquidity, are concentrated in large companies and show a trend of negative net listings over the last two decades. On the other hand, bond markets in these regions tend to be concentrated in public sector issuances. (OECD, 2024[19]).

Private sector investment mobilised by official development finance intervention has increased though remains below expectations

Between 2012 and 2022, official development finance interventions mobilised over USD 416.4 billion from the private sector, mainly through direct investments, special purpose vehicles and guarantees (OECD, 2024[20]). Private finance mobilisation increased from USD 28 billion in 2015 to USD 62 billion in 2022, with multilateral development banks contributing 70% of the total funding during 2020-22. Most mobilised private finance targeted middle-income countries (87%); only 12% supported low-income countries (OECD, 2024[20]).

According to findings in a recent OECD (2023[21]) report on mobilisation, the primary mechanisms for mobilising private finance between 2018 and 2020 were direct investments in companies and project finance special purpose vehicles (38%) and guarantees (26%). The share of finance mobilised through direct investments increased over time. Guarantees, however, accounted for a declining share, dropping from 32% of finance mobilised in 2018 to 20% in 2020. Credit lines (12%), syndicated loans (10%), shares in collective investment vehicles (8%) and simple co-financing (5%) played smaller but contextually significant roles, especially in SME financing and small-scale projects (OECD, 2023[21]).

There are significant challenges to mobilising private finance for sustainable development, particularly in developing countries. High investment risk, low returns, lack of bankable projects and insufficient financial innovation are the key barriers. In LDCs, economic instability and lack of investment expertise further hinder private mobilisation. Additionally, private investors are less inclined to finance sectors such as health and education or policy objectives such as climate adaptation due to low returns and smaller project sizes. Increasing mobilisation will require innovative financial instruments, greater risk appetite from institutions, and improved data transparency to address misperceptions of investment risk. Survey respondents identified the availability of bankable investment opportunities, financial innovation and macroeconomic stability as among the main drivers of increased finance mobilisation. Other key drivers are improved investment returns as well as the Paris Agreement, and the SDGs. These latter frameworks incentivise the mobilisation of private finance by aligning financial opportunities with global climate and sustainability objectives, encouraging investments that yield both profit and societal impact.

Gender inequality in the labour market persists

The global labour force participation rate for women is 47% versus 73% for men. Women also earn significantly less, receiving 51 cents for every US dollar earned by men. Additionally, women spend 2.6 times more than men on unpaid care and domestic work, which further limits their economic opportunities. Regional disparities are pronounced: women in Northern Africa and Western Asia spend five times as many hours on unpaid care and domestic work than men while in Oceania, Europe and Northern America, women spend about twice as many hours as men on these (UN, 2024[14]).

3.4. New and emerging areas

Sustainable finance has gained prominence, driven by growing investor interest in non-financial or ESG factors

Global sustainable investing assets are investments that consider ESG factors to promote long-term sustainability across various sectors and aim for both financial returns and positive societal impact. The volume of these assets reached USD 30.3 trillion in 2022, a substantial increase over 2016 but slightly below the record highs of 2020 and 2021. Sustainable investment funds, mostly domiciled in developed countries and particularly Europe, captured 81% of the market and have received significant inflows, peaking at USD 558 billion in 2021 before declining to USD 72 billion in 2023. By the end of 2023, sustainable funds had accumulated USD 2.56 trillion in assets under management, accounting for about 10% of all sustainable assets. In absolute numbers, however, sustainable fund assets make up a small share of total fund assets under management, representing less than 5% of total global fund assets in 2023 (UN, 2024[22]). In impact investing – a more targeted form of investment that seeks to generate measurable, positive social or environmental impact alongside financial returns – assets under management exceeded USD 1.2 trillion in 2022, driven by the rise of green and sustainability-linked bonds. The cumulative issuance of green, social, sustainability and sustainability-linked (GSSS) bonds totalled USD 5.3 trillion in 2023 (World Bank, 2024[23]). The share of GSSS bonds that was issued by entities in developing countries dropped to 5% in 2023 from 13% in 2022. (OECD, 2024[24]).

Policies to enhance transparency, accountability and governance of sustainable financial and capital markets are having significant impact

Nearly half of global GDP is generated in countries that adopted climate-related disclosure legislation. The ISSB has made significant strides in consolidating major reporting standards to improve ESG data infrastructure.[6] As of July 2023, over 780 sustainable finance policy measures across 109 countries have been recorded, a 70% increase since 2015 (Green Finance Platform, 2019[25]). These measures include at least 30 taxonomies and 200 frameworks, standards and guidelines on sustainability and climate disclosures. However, in addition to the risk of market fragmentation which hampers access, many developing countries struggle with weak financial markets that further limit their ability to effectively attract sustainable finance. Though they contribute up to 40% of national income in emerging economies, for example, many SMEs face challenges to access finance and respond to emerging sustainability-related standards.

There has been progress in the information infrastructure. As of 2022, approximately 70% of monitored companies were publishing sustainability reports, a threefold increase since 2016 (United Nations Environment Programme, 2024[26]). However, data gaps and risks of greenwashing persist in developed and developing countries alike. In 2023, 30% of asset managers removed references to the abbreviation "ESG" and the phrase "net zero" from their marketing materials and websites in the United States (UN, 2024[22]). The banking and financial services sectors experienced a particularly sharp increase in greenwashing in 2023, with 148 cases reported compared with 86 in 2022. Over 50% of these cases involved misleading claims about fossil fuel involvement (RepRisk, 2023[27]).

Globally agreed sustainable finance taxonomies and legislation could help clarify rules for disclosure and minimise market distortions, risks of broader SDG washing and stalling on SDG targets – for example on SDG 8 on child labour, where no progress has been made since 2016 (United Nations, 2024[28]). Harmonisation efforts are ongoing. Further efforts to strengthen harmonisation include the collaboration between the Global Reporting Initiative and the ISSB and increasing adoption of the Taskforce on Nature-related Financial Disclosures However, disparities across jurisdictions highlight the need for global interoperability.

Private finance for climate action could be scaled up

Developed countries pledged to mobilise USD 100 billion annually in climate finance for developing nations by 2020 and extended the pledge through 2025 (AAAA § 49) (UN, 2015[29]). Climate finance surged by 30% after 2021 to reach USD 115.9 billion in 2022, surpassing the USD 100 billion target for the first time, with 60% of the financing allocated to mitigation efforts (UN, 2024[14]). Private finance mobilised by public climate finance, for which comparable data are only available from 2016, grew from USD 14.4 billion in 2021 to USD 21.9 billion in 2022 (a USD 7.5 billion or 52% increase) following several years of relative stagnation (OECD, 2024[30]). However, the UN Framework Convention on Climate Change estimates that nearly USD 6 trillion is needed for developing countries' climate action plans by 2030, which will require additional resource mobilisation and between USD 500 billion and USD 600 billion annually in private finance by 2030. Multilateral development banks and other financial institutions are expected to mobilise a large portion of these amounts (Bhattacharya et al., 2023[31]).

Several initiatives aim to inject and catalyse investment into quality, sustainable infrastructure and foster partnerships that facilitate lower-cost financing in developing countries. From 2013 to 2020, China invested more than USD 731 billion globally, launching the Belt and Road Initiative International Green Development Coalition in 2019 to align with the SDGs, for example, though carbon-intensive projects, including coal-fired power plants, continue to be financed (Nedopil, 2024[32]). The Blue Dot Network, announced at the 2021 Group of Seven summit, focuses on promoting high infrastructure standards, good governance and climate resilience through private investment in developing countries (OECD, 2024[33]).

Strengthening FDI qualities enhances sustainable development and supports the green and digital transitions

Foreign investment significantly contributes to sustainable development. But not all countries, population segments and territories benefit. Globally, over 10 million new jobs were created from greenfield FDI over 2019-23, 6.4 million of them in developing and emerging economies. Women are filling many of these jobs:

foreign firms have a bigger share of female workers than domestic companies. However, most of these new jobs are not senior management positions and are often in low-wage sectors (OECD, 2022[34]). Furthermore, the job creation intensity of FDI (i.e. the number of jobs created per million USD invested) is declining, including in developing and emerging economies, with adverse long-term impacts on the crucial role of FDI in providing much-needed jobs and incomes (OECD, forthcoming[35]).

It is important to ensure that FDI not only brings financial capital but also contributes to local economic development, environmental sustainability and social progress. By linking domestic firms to multinational enterprises, FDI can serve as a conduit for domestic firms to access international markets and integrate global value chains (OECD, 2022[36]).

Foreign investment also is rapidly shifting to sectors such as renewable energies, semi-conductors and ICT, activities that have lower job creation potential yet are crucial for the green and digital transitions. For instance, in developing and emerging economies, greenfield FDI in renewables has increased from USD 3.3 billion in 2003 (0.8% of total greenfield FDI) to USD 175.4 billion in 2023 (24.3% of total greenfield FDI). Nonetheless, FDI in fossil fuels still amounted to 12.7% of greenfield FDI in 2023 (OECD, forthcoming[35]). Swift policy intervention is required to reap the benefits of FDI for both sustainable and inclusive growth and the green and digital transitions. This includes orienting financial incentives to the right activities and population and rapidly adapting the workforce to emerging skills in demand by multinational enterprises, including through better reskilling and/or upskilling incentives to firms (OECD, 2022[36]).

De-risking hinders the development of safe, affordable cross-border payment systems and limits access to international financial markets

De-risking, the phenomenon of financial institutions terminating or restricting business relationships with clients or categories of clients to avoid rather than manage risk, can have severe consequences for developing countries. The total number of active correspondent banks fell by 29% during 2011-22 (Bank of International Settlements, 2023[37]). De-risking can raise the costs of remittance transfers, the largest source of external finance for many low- and middle-income countries. Addressing de-risking requires international co-operation to help countries meet global financial integrity standards, enhance their reputation in international markets, deter financial crime, increase capital inflows, and expand access to financial services for individuals and businesses, including trade finance. Such international co-operation needs to go hand in hand with safeguards to prevent sanctions evasion.

Extending the investment horizon can support long-term sustainable development goals

Commercial creditors usually provide loans with short-term maturities and high interest rates, inhibiting long-term investments and increasing liquidity risks in developing countries (Sachs et al., 2023[38]). Short-term profitability should not come at the expense of long-term productive and sustainable investment. Enhancing the availability and quality of ESG disclosures can encourage investors to make more long-term investment decisions. Moreover, there is room to better integrate sustainability into financial institutions' mandates and operations. A World Benchmarking Alliance (2023[39]) assessment of 400 financial institutions found that in 2022, only 37% had disclosed long-term net zero targets and that just 2% of commitments had been translated into interim targets for the institutions' financing activities, with only 1% of these backed by scientific evidence.

Annex 3.A. Domestic and International Private Business and Finance

Annex Table 3.A.1. Assessment of the action area: Domestic and international private business and finance

AAAA paragraph	Commitment	Specific target or objective	Matching Sustainable Development Goal (SDG) target (where available)	State of implementation or progress made since 2015, using selected SDG or other relevant indicators (proxies)
35	Calls on all business to engage as partners and invest in areas critical to sustainable development, including foreign direct investment (FDI) in countries most in need and long-term financing.	No	No SDG targets agreed by private sector actors. Target 12.1 Implement the ten-year Framework of Programmes on sustainable consumption and production patterns, all countries taking action, with developed countries taking the lead, taking into account the development and capabilities of developing countries.	Private sector actors have not formally agreed to the SDG targets and indicators framework. However, many networks and groups have helped strengthen partnerships with the private sector to align activities with the SDGs. These include the UN Global Compact, the UN Global Investors for Sustainable Development Alliance and the UN Principles for Responsible Investment (PRI), among others. (For a more comprehensive assessment of performance for SDG 12, see https://sdg12hub.org/ and Chapter 12 in https://unstats.un.org/sdgs/report/2024/extended-report/Extended-Report_Goal-12.pdf). SDG indicator 12.1.1 Number of countries developing, adopting or implementing policy instruments aimed at supporting the shift to sustainable consumption and production. As of 2023, 63 UN member states reported 516 policy instruments to accelerate the shift to sustainable consumption and production. Of these reported policies, 49% are national roadmaps or strategies (UN, 2024[40]). Between 2015-20, countries stepped up their adoption of policy instruments with 34 economic and fiscal instruments (up from 16 in 2015); 160 macro policy instruments (up from 51 in 2015); 81 regulatory and legal instruments (up from 37 in 2015); and 72 voluntary schemes (up from 30 in 2015) (UNEP, 2024[8]). FDI to developing countries, including countries most in need (UNCTAD) Over 2015-23, world FDI dropped from over USD 2.0 trillion to USD 802 billion. Inflows to ODA-eligible developing countries declined from USD 338 billion in 2015 to USD 286 billion in 2023. Over the same period, FDI inflows to least developed countries (LDCs) dropped from USD 37.6 billion to USD 31.3 billion, although LDCs' share of the total increased from 1.8% to 2.4%. Likewise, the volume of FDI to

AAAA paragraph	Commitment	Specific target or objective	Matching Sustainable Development Goal (SDG) target (where available)	State of implementation or progress made since 2015, using selected SDG or other relevant indicators (proxies)
				landlocked developing countries declined from USD 25.1 billion to USD 24.3 billion. However, FDI to small island developing states rose from USD 6.4 billion to USD 8.3 billion (UNCTAD, 2024[41]). FDI Qualities Indicators The FDI Qualities Indicators examine the contribution of foreign businesses to productivity and innovation, job quality and skills, gender equality, and green growth. Globally, over 10 million new jobs were created from greenfield FDI over the years 2019-23 – 6.4 million of them in developing and emerging economies (OECD, forthcoming[35]). Foreign investment is rapidly shifting to sectors such as renewable energies, semi-conductors, and information and communication technology, activities that have lower job creation potential yet are crucial for the green and digital transitions. For instance, in developing economies, greenfield FDI in renewables has increased from USD 3.3 billion in 2003 (0.8% of total greenfield FDI) to USD 175.4 billion in 2023 (24.3% of total greenfield FDI). Nonetheless, FDI in fossil fuels still amounted to 12.7% of greenfield FDI (OECD, forthcoming[35]). Investment gap and flows to sectors essential to the SDGs The SDG financing gap for infrastructure reached USD 2.2 trillion in 2022 (UNCTAD, 2023[42]). Between 2015-23, investment relevant to sustainable development in developing countries has varied by sector. The number of projects in infrastructure grew by 40%, in renewable energy by 76% and in health by 22%. However, the number of projects over the same period fell by 6% both in water, sanitation and hygiene and in agrifood (UNCTAD, 2024[43]).
36	Develop policies and/or regulatory frameworks for the quality of finance and alignment. Promote and create an enabling environment for inclusive and sustainable investment, including competition policies.	No	n.a.	Official development assistance (ODA) in support of private sector development Between 2015-22, ODA to economic infrastructure and services grew from USD 41.6 billion to USD 45.2 billion and ODA to production sectors increased from USD 15.8 billion to USD 20 billion, together accounting for 22% of total ODA The banking and financial services sector, for instance, received USD 5.8 billion and USD 6.4 billion of ODA support in 2015 and 2022, respectively (OECD, 2024[44]).

AAAA paragraph	Commitment	Specific target or objective	Matching Sustainable Development Goal (SDG) target (where available)	State of implementation or progress made since 2015, using selected SDG or other relevant indicators (proxies)
				Number of countries that are members of the International Competition Network The International Competition Network has grown from 15 founding institutions in 2001 to over 140 members from nearly 130 jurisdictions (Competition Policy International, 2020[45]) (ICN). The OECD Competition Trends database contains information about competition trends since 2018 for 77 jurisdictions along 34 variables (OECD, 2024[46]). OECD DAC Recommendation on Untying Official Development Assistance DAC members agreed to untie ODA to LDCs, Heavily Indebted Poor Countries, other low-income countries, and International Development Association (IDA)-only countries and territories in the DAC Recommendation on Untying ODA (last amended in 2018) and the 2022 OECD Untied Aid progress report. Effective private sector engagement in development co-operation: Kampala Principles Assessment part of the Global Partnership for Effective Development Co-operation monitoring exercise The Global Partnership for Effective Development Co-operation (2023[13]) covers four issue areas: the state of policies, inclusive dialogues, the quality of private sector engagement and the ease of partnering. The Kampala Principles Assessment (KPA) findings can be used to inform multi-stakeholder dialogues in participating countries with relevant evidence, identify and overcome bottlenecks for collaboration, and improve co-ordination among development actors, thereby building trust between public, private and civil society partners. By demonstrating the impact of public-private collaboration, the KPA can lead to greater investment, uptake and scaling up of such partnerships. OECD Recommendation and Policy toolkits on the Policy Framework for Investment and FDI Qualities See paras 35 and 37. Investment promotion: see para 46.
37	Promote business while protecting labour rights and health standards (ILO). Encourage sustainable and responsible business models and practices (Global Compact) and impact investment. Harmonise initiatives, identify gaps and	No	Many targets of SDG 8 are relevant, including the following: Target 8.8 Protect labour rights and promote safe and secure working environments for all	Many indicators associated with SDG targets are relevant, including the following: SDG indicator 8.8.2 Level of compliance with labour rights. The estimated number of children in child labour stood at 160 million worldwide at the beginning of 2020, that is almost one in ten of all children worldwide and one in four in sub-Saharan Africa (UN, 2024[47]). While the long-term global trend is decreasing,

AAAA paragraph	Commitment	Specific target or objective	Matching Sustainable Development Goal (SDG) target (where available)	State of implementation or progress made since 2015, using selected SDG or other relevant indicators (proxies)
	strengthen compliance including on gender.		workers. Target 12.6 Encourage companies, especially large and transnational companies, to adopt sustainable practices and to integrate sustainability information into their reporting cycle.	global progress against child labour has stalled since 2016. Global estimates indicate that 50 million people were living in modern slavery in 2021,10 million more than in 2016 (ILO / IOM, 2022[48]). Data on fatal and non-fatal occupational activities show significant progress over decades. The global average for SDG indicator 8.8.2 on national compliance with fundamental labour rights (freedom of association and collective bargaining) in 2022 stood at 4.81. For the period from 2015 to 2021, the situation in 43% of countries worsened by 0.55 points and in 35% it improved by 0.51 points. The number of international migrant workers has been growing continuously and reached 169 million in 2019 (UN, 2024[49]). SDG indicator 12.6.1 Number of companies publishing sustainability reports. In 2021-22, 73% of the companies included in the Refinitiv database, which covers data from over 10 000 mostly large public companies across the world, published sustainability reports and the number of companies doing so has tripled since 2016. This growth was observed in all regions in 2022. Latin America, Africa and Oceania demonstrated continuous progress while Europe, Asia and North America have the largest share of companies reporting on sustainability (UN, 2024[40]). Other forms of sustainability reporting by private sector actors The PRI network comprises over 4 000 investors managing USD 121 trillion. The Sustainable Stock Exchanges Initiative involves more than 100 stock exchanges to enhance environmental, social and governance transparency. The Global Compact includes more than 20 000 companies in over 160 countries (PRI, 2023[50]; SSE, 2024[51]; UN Global Compact, 2024[52]). OECD FDI Qualities indicators Job creation intensity of greenfield FDI (the number of jobs created per USD 1 million invested) is higher in non-OECD countries than in OECD countries. Between 2019 and 2023, 2.6 new jobs were created per USD 1 million invested in non-OECD countries compared with only 1.8 new jobs per USD 1 million in OECD countries. Job creation intensity declined over the past decade, including in developing economies, with important adverse impacts on job creation and incomes. This decline results from a shift in FDI to sectors with lower job creation potential such as renewable energies and semi-conductors (OECD, 2024[53]). *(For a more comprehensive assessment of performance on SDG 8 and other*

AAAA paragraph	Commitment	Specific target or objective	Matching Sustainable Development Goal (SDG) target (where available)	State of implementation or progress made since 2015, using selected SDG or other relevant indicators (proxies)
				relevant targets, see https://ilostat.ilo.org/data/ *and The UN SDGs 2024 Report,* https://unstats.un.org/sdgs/report/2024/ *, chapters 8,* https://unstats.un.org/sdgs/report/2024/extended-report/Extended-Report_Goal-8.pdf *and 12,* https://unstats.un.org/sdgs/report/2024/extended-report/Extended-Report_Goal-12.pdf *).*
38	Ensure that the policy and regulatory environment promotes financial market stability and financial inclusion (e.g. address risk mitigation side effects). Promote incentives for long-term performance and sustainability and reduce volatility.	No	n.a.	Global sustainable bonds issuance and inflows in sustainable investment funds Between 2018-23, global sustainable bonds issuance surged from USD 227 billion to USD 872 billion. While funds for SDG investment through sustainable finance products in global capital markets are still growing, the pace is slowing. Sustainable bonds showed marginal growth in 2023, while inflows in sustainable investment funds dropped by 60% (UNCTAD, 2024[4]).
39	Work towards full and equal access to formal financial services for all including through strategies, regulation, institutional support, innovative tools, peer learning and experience sharing (see Alliance for Financial Inclusion), capacity development, and mutual collaboration.	Yes Full and equal access to formal financial services for all.	Target 8.10 Strengthen the capacity of domestic financial institutions to encourage and expand access to banking, insurance and financial services for all.	SDG indicator 8.10.2 Proportion of adults (15 years and older) with an account at a bank or other financial institution or with a mobile-money-service provider. Financial inclusion has steadily advanced with more than half a billion people gaining access to formal financial services between 2017-21. Global bank account ownership rose from 51% in 2011 to 76% in 2021, notably increasing by 30 percentage points in developing countries to reach 71% in 2021 (Demirgüç-Kunt et al., 2022[54]). SDG indicator 8.10.1 (a) Number of commercial bank branches per 100 000 adults and (b) number of automated teller machines (ATMs) per 100 000 adults. While the number of commercial bank branches in the world declined between 2015-21 (from 15.0 to 13.7 per 100 000 inhabitants), it increased in LDCs (from 4.8 to 5.9 per 100 000 inhabitants). Regional disparities remain with a 4.1 ratio in sub-Saharan Africa. The number of ATMs per 100 000 inhabitants grew from 64.6 to 63.9 globally and from 12.4 to 10.8 in sub-Saharan Africa (UN, 2024[49]).
40	Ensure that adequate and affordable financial services are available to migrants and their families. Support national authorities to remove obstacles, increase co-ordination among regulatory authorities, and exploit new technologies for financial literacy and inclusion and data	Yes Reduce the average transaction cost of migrant remittances by 2030 to less than	Target 10.c By 2030, reduce to less than 3% the transaction costs of migrant remittances and eliminate remittance corridors with costs higher than 5%. Target 17.3	SDG indicator 10.c.1 Remittance costs as a proportion of the amount remitted. The cost of sending remittances from the Group of Twenty (G20) was 6.5% on average in 2023, higher than the global average (World Bank, 2023[55]). In 20% of remittance corridors, transfer fees remain above the 5% target (World Bank, 2023[55]). SDG indicator 17.3.2 Volume of remittances (in US dollars) as a proportion of total

AAAA paragraph	Commitment	Specific target or objective	Matching Sustainable Development Goal (SDG) target (where available)	State of implementation or progress made since 2015, using selected SDG or other relevant indicators (proxies)
	collection.	3% of the amount transferred. Ensure that no remittance corridor requires charges higher than 5% by 2030.	Mobilise additional financial resources for developing countries from multiple sources.	gross domestic product (GDP). Global remittance volumes have grown to an estimated USD 831 billion in 2022, including USD 647 billion to developing countries. The cost of sending remittances remains high. The global average cost of sending USD 200 decreased from 7.7% in 2015 to 6.2% in 2023 but is still more than double the SDG target of 3% (IOM, 2023[56]). Smart Remitter Target (SmaRT) indicator (WB) In 2023, the global SmaRT average cost – the cost that a savvy consumer with access to complete information could pay in each corridor – was 3.41% (World Bank, 2024[15]). Share of digital remittances In 2023, digital remittances accounted for 30% of total transactions. Mobile money was 35% less expensive than a bank transfer and the most cost-effective instrument to send remittances (World Bank, 2023[57]).
41	Commit to give women and girls equal rights and opportunities to those enjoyed by men, including through undertaking needed legislation and administrative reforms and encouraging the private sector to advance gender equality. (Reference to the UN Women Empowerment Principles and Global Compact.)	No	Many SDG 5 targets are relevant as are gender-specific targets in other SDGs.	Many indicators associated with SDG 5 targets are relevant as are other gender-specific indicators for other SDGs. As of 2022, 13% of the indicators used to assess progress are assessed as very far from the targets for 2030 set out under SDG 5, and 15% are far from target. Only 48% of the data needed to monitor progress on SDG 5 are available (UN Women, 2022[58]). Almost half of the 95 countries surveyed by UN Women and the UN Department of Economic and Social Affairs in 2020 continued to restrict women from working in certain jobs or industries, and women represented only 28% of managerial positions in the workplace (UN, 2024[7]). *(For a comprehensive assessment of performance for SDG 5 and other relevant SDGs, see https://data.unwomen.org/features/are-we-track-achieve-gender-equality-2030). See also reference in para 37 on SDG 8 tracking.*
42	Encourage philanthropic giving, co-operation with other actors, increased transparency and accountability, alignment with national priorities, and impact	No	n.a.	Private Philanthropy for Development (OECD) Between 2015 and 2022, private philanthropy for development grew from USD 3.5 billion to USD 9.9 billion, a 185% increase, and 48 philanthropic organisations now report their co-operation with developing countries. This increase was largely due to

AAAA paragraph	Commitment	Specific target or objective	Matching Sustainable Development Goal (SDG) target (where available)	State of implementation or progress made since 2015, using selected SDG or other relevant indicators (proxies)
	investment.			improved data coverage (OECD, 2024[59]).
43	Encourage lending to micro, small and medium-sized enterprises (MSMEs). (List of multiple measures and capacity building, ref. to IFC and new investment vehicles such as blended finance, new debt funding structure, risk mitigation instruments.)	No	Target 9.3 Increase the access of small-scale industrial and other enterprises, in particular in developing countries, to financial services and including to affordable credit, and their integration into value chains and markets.	SDG indicator 9.3.1 Proportion of small-scale industries in total industry value added. MSMEs make up over 90% of all firms, account on average for 70% of total employment and represent 50% of GDP worldwide. The small and medium-sized enterprise finance gap is estimated at USD 5.7 trillion or USD 8 trillion when informal enterprises are included (IFC, 2024[60]). SDG indicator 9.3.2 Proportion of small-scale industries with a loan or line of credit. Only 16.9% of small-scale industries in sub-Saharan Africa and 17.4% in LDCs have access to loans or lines of credit compared with 45.4% in Latin America and the Caribbean (UN, 2024[47]).
44	Develop domestic capital markets, including long-term bonds and insurance. Strengthen supervision, clearing, dispute settlement, risk management, regional markets and local currency lending. Enhance international support and capacity building.	No	n.a.	FSB NBFI Report Between 2015-22, the stock of global assets under management grew from USD 310 trillion to USD 455 trillion, with the share held in developing countries also growing from 17% to 21% (FSB, 2023[1]). ODA to financial sector ODA to banking and financial services remained stable over the 2015-22 period, growing from USD 5.8 billion to USD 6.4 billion. During the COVID-19 crisis, the ODA response triggered a spike in support to this sector, which peaked at USD 10.9 billion (OECD, 2024[44]). WBA Financial System Benchmark An assessment by the World Benchmarking Alliance of 400 of the world's largest financial institutions, including multilateral development banks, found that in 2022 only 37% disclose long-term net zero targets. Of these commitments, only 2% have been translated into interim targets applied across the institution's financing activities and only 1% are backed by scientific evidence (WBA, 2022[61]).
45	Encourage investment promotion and prioritise sustainable and transformational projects through financial and technical support and	No	Target 17.5 Adopt and implement investment promotion regimes for LDCs.	SDG indicator 17.5.1 Number of countries that adopt and implement investment promotion regimes for developing countries, including LDCs. Among the 50 countries with established outward foreign direct investment (OFDI) promotion mechanisms, only 18 developed economies (58%) and 5 developing

AAAA paragraph	Commitment	Specific target or objective	Matching Sustainable Development Goal (SDG) target (where available)	State of implementation or progress made since 2015, using selected SDG or other relevant indicators (proxies)
	capacity building. Use insurance, investment guarantees (ref. to MIGA) and other new instruments to incentivise FDI to countries most in need.			economies (26%) have put in place at least one instrument specifically designed to encourage OFDI in developing countries, including LDCs (UN, 2024[62]). OECD Investment Promotion Agency Network Created in 1995 by the UN Trade and Development and 50 investment promotion agencies (IPAs), the World Association of Investment Promotion Agencies (WAIPA) has 133 members in 2024. For their 2020 report on the state of IPAs in the world, the WAIPA and the World Bank surveyed 162 IPAs (WAIPA, 2023[63]). In 2016, the OECD created the Investment Promotion Agency Network, which includes 51 adherents to the 1976 OECD Declaration on International Investment and Multinational Enterprises; five of the adherents have become part of the IPA network since 2015 (OECD, 2024[64]). Multilateral Investment Guarantee Agency (MIGA) guarantees In FY2023, MIGA issued a record USD 6.4 billion in new guarantees across 40 projects to support USD 8.6 billion in total financing (from private and public sources): 27% of gross issuances went to IDA-eligible (lower-income) countries, 19% went to fragile and conflict-affected countries, and 28% of the total guaranteed investment of the projects contributed to climate finance (MIGA, 2023[65]). OECD Policy Framework for Investment and FDI Qualities Indicators, Recommendation and Policy Toolkit. The OECD FDI Qualities Recommendation calls on governments to facilitate and promote investment for sustainable development opportunities by addressing information failures and administrative barriers. Governments should: raise public and stakeholder awareness on impacts of investment on sustainable development. improve the link between investment promotion and sustainable development objectives, including in the areas of quality infrastructure, skills development and regional development improve the link between investment facilitation activities and sustainable development objectives, including by taking measures to make procedures for obtaining authorisations and permits transparent and ensure that they are efficiently managed and by enhancing business linkages between foreign investors and domestic firms.

AAAA paragraph	Commitment	Specific target or objective	Matching Sustainable Development Goal (SDG) target (where available)	State of implementation or progress made since 2015, using selected SDG or other relevant indicators (proxies)
46	Resolve to adopt and implement investment promotion regimes for LDCs. Offer financial and technical support (including for project and contract preparation, dispute resolution, risk insurance and guarantees). (Ref. to MIGA, enabling environment.) Reduce financing gaps in countries most in need. Encourage use of innovative mechanisms and partnerships.	No	Target 17.3 Mobilise additional financial resources for developing countries from multiple sources. Target 17.5 Adopt and implement investment promotion regimes for LDCs. Target 17.9 Enhance international support for implementing effective and targeted capacity building in developing countries to support national plans to implement all the SDGs including through North-South, South-South and triangular co-operation.	See paras 35 and 36. SDG indicator 17.3.1 Additional financial resources mobilised for developing countries from multiple sources. See para 54 in Annex 4.A. SDG Indicator 17.5.1 Number of countries that adopt and implement investment promotion regimes for developing countries, including LDCs. Building on the Addis Ababa Action Agenda, the 2022 Doha Programme of Action for LDCs aims to adopt and implement investment promotion regimes for LDCs. Capacity development programmes for IPAs and investment promotion in LDCs were subsequently created involving major related institutions. The UNCTAD annual World Investment Report contains analysis of investment policy trends, including on dispute resolution and international investment agreements, among other themes (UNCTAD, 2024[4]). SDG Indicator 17.9.1 Dollar value of financial and technical assistance (including through North-South, South-South and triangular co-operation) committed to developing countries. See paras 56 and 57 in Annex 4.A. Share of ODA in external financing flows LDCs remain largely dependent on ODA and remittances, which represent, respectively, 61% and 29% of their external financing flows compared with 12% and 12%, respectively, in other developing countries. Private financing flows (FDI and other private flows at market terms combined) represent only 1% of total external flows in LDCs compared with 22% in other developing countries (OECD, 2022[66]).
47	Imbed resilient and quality infrastructure investment plans in national strategies, strengthen the domestic enabling environment, and provide technical support for creating pipeline of projects (ref. to African Union Programme for Infrastructure Development in Africa AU-PIDA). Encourage long-term investment, including from institutional investors	No	Target 9.a Facilitate sustainable and resilient infrastructure development in developing countries through enhanced financial, technological and technical support to African countries, LDCs, landlocked developing countries and SIDS.	See paras 35 and 36. SDG Indicator 9.a.1 Total official international support (official development assistance plus other official flows) to infrastructure. Total official flows from all donors for infrastructure in developing countries reached USD 68.2 billion in 2022, an 11% increase since 2015 that is mainly due to greater flows for banking and financial services. However, as a percentage of total official flows, flows to this sector trended downward from 21% in 2015 to 17% in 2022 (UN, 2024[47]).

AAAA paragraph	Commitment	Specific target or objective	Matching Sustainable Development Goal (SDG) target (where available)	State of implementation or progress made since 2015, using selected SDG or other relevant indicators (proxies)
	and through adequate standard setting.			Total Official Support for Sustainable Development (TOSSD) (Pillar 1) amounted to USD 21.4 billion in 2022 for energy infrastructure, USD 23 billion for transport and storage, and USD 2.3 billion for communications. Mobilised private finance for these three sectors amounted to USD 8.4 billion, USD 8.1 billion and USD 3 billion, respectively (TOSSD, 2024[67]). A number of programmes and pledges for infrastructure development have been made. During its first Priority Action Plan (2012-20), the African Union Program Infrastructure Development for Africa (PIDA) developed 16 066 kilometres of roads and 4 077 kilometres of railway lines; established One-Stop Border Posts; and developed 7 gigawatts of hydroelectricity power production and 3 506 kilometres of transmission lines. An estimated USD 360 billion is required to implement all PIDA projects by 2040 (African Union Development Agency - NEPAD, 2023[68]). The quality of infrastructure standards has also progressed, for instance with the Blue Dot Network.
48	Build capacity to enter into public-private partnerships, including with regard to planning, contract negotiation, management, accounting and budgeting for contingent liabilities. Give careful consideration to the appropriate structure and use of blended finance instruments.	No	Target 17.17 Encourage and promote effective public, public-private and civil society partnerships, building on the experience and resourcing strategies of partnerships.	SDG Indicator 17.17.1 Amount in US dollars committed to public-private partnerships for infrastructure. No data submitted since 2016. Size of the blended finance market Between 2014-23, the blended finance market comprised 85 deals per year on average, with a median annual financing total of USD 15 billion. Climate blended finance transactions account for about half (49%) of the blended finance market in terms of deal count and 57% of aggregate financing, most of it in renewable energy (Convergence Blended Finance, 2024[69]). *See also data on private finance mobilised by official intervention included in Chapter 3 and in para 54 of Annex 4.A.*
49	Promote both public and private investment in energy infrastructure and clean energy technologies including carbon capture and storage technologies. Substantially increase the share of renewable energy. Enhance international co-operation	Yes Double the global rate of energy efficiency and conservation with the aim of	Beyond the three explicit targets (7.3, 7.1 and 13.a), many SDG 7 targets are relevant. Target 7.1 By 2030, ensure universal access to affordable, reliable and modern energy	Beyond the indicators associated with the three explicit targets, many indicators associated with other SDG 7 targets are relevant. *(For a comprehensive assessment of performance for SDG 7, see https://trackingsdg7.esmap.org/ by IEA, IRENA, UNSD, World Bank, WHO). See also https://unstats.un.org/sdgs/report/2024/extended-report/Extended-Report_Goal-7.pdf.*

AAAA paragraph	Commitment	Specific target or objective	Matching Sustainable Development Goal (SDG) target (where available)	State of implementation or progress made since 2015, using selected SDG or other relevant indicators (proxies)
	to provide adequate support and facilitate access to clean energy research and technology; expand infrastructure and upgrade technology for supplying modern and sustainable energy services to all developing countries, in particular LDCs and SIDS. (Ref. to UN Sustainable Energy for All, Power Africa, NEPAD Africa Power Vision, Global Renewable Energy Islands Network of IRENA.)	ensuring universal access to affordable, reliable, modern and sustainable energy services for all by 2030. A call for action on the recommendations of the UN Secretary-General's Sustainable Energy for All initiative, with a combined potential to raise over USD 100 billion in annual investments by 2020, through market-based initiatives, partnerships and leveraging development banks.	services. Target 7.3 By 2030, double the global rate of improvement in energy efficiency. Target 13.a Implement the commitment undertaken by developed country parties to the United Nations Framework Convention on Climate Change (UNFCCC) to a goal of mobilising jointly USD 100 billion annually by 2020 from all sources to address the needs of developing countries in the context of meaningful mitigation actions and transparency on implementation and fully operationalise the Green Climate Fund through its capitalisation as soon as possible. Target 12.a Support developing countries to strengthen their scientific and technological capacity to move towards more sustainable patterns of consumption and production.	SDG indicator 7.1.1 Proportion of population with access to electricity. In 2022, 91% of the world population had access to electricity compared with 84% in 2015, although there remained large disparities across regions: of the 685.2 million people in the world still lacking access to electricity in 2022, 569 million were living in sub-Saharan Africa (UN, 2024[6]). SDG indicator 7.1.2 Proportion of population with primary reliance on clean fuels and technology. In 2022, 74% of the global population had access to clean cooking fuels, but 2.1 billion people still relied on polluting sources such as charcoal and wood. While the access deficit has decreased from 36% to 26% since 2015, it is projected that 1.8 billion people will still lack access to clean cooking by 2030 if current trends continue (UN, 2024[6]). SDG indicator 7.3.1 Energy intensity measured in terms of primary energy and GDP. In 2021, primary energy intensity improved by 0.8%, below the 1.2% five-year average and far short of the 2.6% SDG 7.3 target. To meet the 2030 goal, annual progress of about 4% is needed between 2022 and 2030, a milestone aligned with the International Energy Agency's Net Zero Roadmap. The slow progress reflects the moderate pace of post-COVID recovery , with energy consumption rising by over 5%, the largest increase in 50 years (UN, 2024[6]). SDG indicator 13.a.1 Amounts provided and mobilised in US dollars per year in relation to the continued existing collective mobilisation goal of the USD 100 billion commitment through to 2025. In its seventh progress assessment towards the UNFCCC goal, the OECD found that in 2022, developed countries provided and mobilised USD 115.9 billion in climate finance for developing countries, surpassing the annual USD 100 billion target for the first time (OECD, 2024[30]). SDG indicator 12.a.1 Installed renewable energy-generating capacity in developing and developed countries (in watts per capita). The global installed renewable energy-generating capacity grew from 250 watts per capita in 2015 to 424 watts per capita in 2022. Capacity in sub-Saharan Africa remained well below this level at 39 watts per capita in 2022 compared with 28 watts per capita in 2015. To meet the target of doubling global progress on energy

AAAA paragraph	Commitment	Specific target or objective	Matching Sustainable Development Goal (SDG) target (where available)	State of implementation or progress made since 2015, using selected SDG or other relevant indicators (proxies)
				efficiency by 2030, global investment in energy efficiency would need to triple by 2030 (UN, 2024[40]). Global renewable energy share in total final energy consumption Between 2015-21, the global renewable energy share in total final energy consumption grew from 16.7% to 18.7%, with large disparities across regions. For instance, the share was just 32.3% in Latin America and the Caribbean but 69.9% in the sub-Saharan Africa region (IEA, IRENA, UNSD, World Bank, WHO, 2024[70]). FDI in renewables versus fossil fuel investments In non-OECD countries, greenfield FDI in renewables has increased from USD 3.3 billion in 2003 (0.8% of total greenfield FDI) to USD 175.4 billion in 2023 (24.3% of total greenfield FDI). In non-OECD countries, FDI in fossil fuels still amounted to USD 91.7 billion in 2023 (12.7% of greenfield FDI).

Note: The data points are mainly drawn from the UN's Sustainable Development Goals Extended Report 2024 and its statistical annexes. Trend data in are in constant USD 2015 prices unless otherwise indicated.

References

African Union Development Agency - NEPAD (2023), *Programme for Infrastructure Development in Africa (PIDA): First 10-Year Implementation Report*, AUDA-NEPAD, Midrand, South Africa, https://www.au-pida.org/wp-content/uploads/2023/09/PIDA-Progress-Report_WEB.pdf. [68]

Bank of International Settlements (2023), *CPMI Quantitative Review of Correspondent Banking Data (database)*, https://www.bis.org/cpmi/paysysinfo/corr_bank_data.htm (accessed on 13 July 2024). [37]

Bhattacharya, A. et al. (2023), *A Climate Finance Framework: Decisive Action to Deliver on the Paris Agreement – Summary*, Grantham Research Institute on Climate Change and the Environment and London School of Economics and Political Science, London, https://www.lse.ac.uk/granthaminstitute/wp-content/uploads/2023/11/A-Climate-Finance-Framework-IHLEG-Report-2-SUMMARY.pdf. [31]

Celani, A., L. Dressler and M. Wermelinger (2022), "Building an Investment Tax Incentives database: Methodology and initial findings for 36 developing countries", *OECD Working Papers on International Investment*, No. 2022/01, OECD Publishing, Paris, https://doi.org/10.1787/62e075a9-en. [9]

Competition Policy International (2020), *(Nearly) A Century with the ICN*, https://internationalcompetitionnetwork.org/wp-content/uploads/2021/10/ICN@20-Century-with-the-ICN.pdf. [45]

Convergence Blended Finance (2024), *The State of Blended Finance 2024*, Convergence Report, https://www.convergence.finance/resource/state-of-blended-finance-2024-climate-edition/view. [69]

Demirgüç-Kunt, A. et al. (2022), *The Global Findex Database 2021*, The World Bank, https://doi.org/10.1596/978-1-4648-1897-4. [54]

FSB (2023), *Global Monitoring Report on Non-bank Financial Intermediation 2023*, Financial Stability Board, https://www.fsb.org/2023/12/global-monitoring-report-on-non-bank-financial-intermediation-2023/. [1]

Global Partnership for Effective Development Co-operation (2023), *Annex 2: Guidance for the Kampala Principles Assessment*, https://www.effectivecooperation.org/system/files/2023-12/Annex%202_KPA%20Guidance%20%28ENG%29.pdf. [13]

Global Partnership for Effective Development Co-operation (2019), *Kamala Principles on Effective Private Sector Engagement in Development Co-operation*, https://www.effectivecooperation.org/system/files/2019-07/Kampala%20Principles%20-%20final.pdf. [12]

Green Finance Platform (2019), *Green Finance Measures Database*, https://www.greenfinanceplatform.org/financial-measures/browse (accessed on 10 July 2024). [25]

IEA, IRENA, UNSD, World Bank, WHO (2024), *Tracking SDG 7: The Energy Progress Report*, World Bank, Washington DC, https://www.iea.org/reports/tracking-sdg7-the-energy-progress-report-2024. [70]

IFC (2024), *MSME Finance*, International Finance Corporation, https://www.ifc.org/en/what-we-do/sector-expertise/financial-institutions/msme-finance. [60]

ILO / IOM (2022), *Global Estimates of Modern Slavery: Forced Labour and Forced Marriage*, International Labour Organization, International Organization for Migration, Geneva, https://www.ilo.org/publications/major-publications/global-estimates-modern-slavery-forced-labour-and-forced-marriage. [48]

IOM (2023), *Migration and Migrants: A Global Overview*, International Organization for Migration, https://worldmigrationreport.iom.int/what-we-do/world-migration-report-2024-chapter-2/international-remittances. [56]

MIGA (2023), *MIGA Annual Report 2023*, https://www.miga.org/sites/default/files/multilingual/2023-10/MIGA_AnnualReport2023_interior_toprint_R10.pdf. [65]

Nedopil, C. (2024), *China Belt and Road Initiative (BRI) Investment Report 2023*, Griffith University and FISF Fudan University, Brisbane and Shanghai, https://www.griffith.edu.au/__data/assets/pdf_file/0033/1910697/Nedopil-2024-China-Belt-Road-Initiative-Investment-report.pdf. [32]

OECD (2024), *Climate Finance Provided and Mobilised by Developed Countries in 2013-2022*, OECD Publishing, Paris, https://doi.org/10.1787/19150727-en. [30]

OECD (2024), *Data Explorer - DAC5: Aid (ODA) by sector and donor (database)*, http://data-explorer.oecd.org/s/xm (accessed on 3 July 2024). [44]

OECD (2024), *Data Explorer - Private Philanthropy for Development (database)*, http://data-explorer.oecd.org/s/xl (accessed on 20 July 2024). [59]

OECD (2024), *FDI in figures, October 2024*, https://www.oecd.org/en/publications/fdi-in-figures-october-2024_fcdc2fb2-en.html. [2]

OECD (2024), "FDI in Figures, October 2024", *FDI in Figures*, OECD Publishing, Paris, https://www.oecd.org/en/publications/fdi-in-figures-october-2024_fcdc2fb2-en.html. [18]

OECD (2024), *FDI main aggregates, BMD4 (database)*, http://data-explorer.oecd.org/s/111. [3]

OECD (2024), *Foreign Direct Investment Qualities and Impact (webpage)*, OECD Publishing, Paris, https://www.oecd.org/en/topics/sub-issues/foreign-direct-investment-qualities-and-impact.html (accessed on 15 November 2024). [53]

OECD (2024), *Investment Promotion Agency Network (webpage)*, OECD Publishing, Paris, https://www.oecd.org/en/networks/investment-promotion-agency-network.html (accessed on 5 November 2024). [64]

OECD (2024), *Latin American Economic Outlook: Financing Sustainable Development*, OECD Publishing, Paris, https://doi.org/10.1787/c437947f-en. [19]

OECD (2024), *Mobilised private finance for development (database)*, http://data-explorer.oecd.org/s/q (accessed on 1 July 2024). [20]

OECD (2024), *OECD Competition Trends 2024*, OECD Publishing, Paris, https://doi.org/10.1787/e69018f9-en. [46]

OECD (2024), "Private sector engagement", *Development Co-operation Fundamentals*, https://www.oecd.org/en/publications/development-co-operation-tips-tools-insights-practices_be69e0cf-en/private-sector-engagement_3153a116-en.html (accessed on 29 November 2024). [10]

OECD (2024), "Sustainability-linked bonds: How to make them work in developing countries, and how donors can help", *OECD Development Perspectives*, No. 44, OECD Publishing, Paris, https://doi.org/10.1787/7ca58c00-en. [24]

OECD (2024), "The Blue Dot Network begins global certification framework for quality infrastructure, hosted by the OECD", https://www.oecd.org/en/about/news/press-releases/2024/04/the-blue-dot-network-begins-global-certification-framework-for-quality-infrastructure-hosted-by-the-oecd.html. [33]

OECD (2023), *Private finance mobilised by official development finance interventions*, OECD Publishing, Paris, https://doi.org/10.1787/c5fb4a6c-en. [21]

OECD (2022), *External finance to least developed countries (LDCs): A snapshot*, https://one.oecd.org/document/DCD(2022)13/en/pdf. [66]

OECD (2022), *FDI Qualities Indicators 2022*, OECD Publishing, Paris, https://www.oecd.org/content/dam/oecd/en/topics/policy-sub-issues/fdi-qualities-and-impact/FDI-Qualities-Indicators-2022.pdf. [34]

OECD (2022), *FDI Qualities Policy Toolkit*, OECD Publishing, Paris, https://doi.org/10.1787/7ba74100-en. [36]

OECD (forthcoming), *FDI Qualities Indicators 2024*, OECD Publishing, Paris. [35]

OECD DAC (2022), *2022 Report on the Implementation of the DAC Recommendation on Untying*, ONE Members and Partners, https://one.oecd.org/document/DCD/DAC(2022)34/FINAL/en/pdf. [11]

PRI (2023), *About the PRI (webpage)*, Principles for Responsible Investment, https://www.unpri.org/about-us/about-the-pri. [50]

Ratha, D. et al. (2019), "Data release: Remittances to low- and middle-income countries on track to reach $551 billion in 2019 and $597 billion by 2021", *World Bank People Move blog*, https://blogs.worldbank.org/en/peoplemove/data-release-remittances-low-and-middle-income-countries-track-reach-551-billion-2019 (accessed on 29 November 2024). [16]

RepRisk (2023), *On the Rise: Navigating the Wave of Greenwashing and Social Washing*, https://www.reprisk.com/research-insights/reports/on-the-rise-navigating-the-wave-of-greenwashing-and-social-washing. [27]

Sachs, J. et al. (2023), "The case for long-term SDG financing", *SDSN Reflection Paper*, United Nations Sustainable Development Solutions Network, Paris, https://www.unsdsn.org/resources/the-case-for-long-term-sdg-financing/. [38]

SSE (2024), *Sustainable Stock Exchanges Initiative*, Sustainable Stock Exchanges Initiative, https://sseinitiative.org/. [51]

TOSSD (2024), *Total Official Support for Sustainable Development*, Total Official Support for Sustainable Development, https://www.tossd.org/. [67]

UN (2024), *Financing for Sustainable Development Report 2024*, United Nations Department of Economic and Social Affairs, New York, https://desapublications.un.org/publications/financing-sustainable-development-report-2024. [22]

UN (2024), *Progress Towards the Sustainable Development Goals - Report of the Secretary-General: Statistical Annex*, United Nations Economic and Social Council, New York, https://unstats.un.org/sdgs/files/report/2024/E_2024_54_Statistical_Annex_I_and_II.pdf. [47]

UN (2024), *The Sustainable Development Goals Extended Report 2024: Goal 12*, United Nations Statistics Division, New York, https://unstats.un.org/sdgs/report/2024/extended-report/Extended-Report_Goal-12.pdf. [40]

UN (2024), *The Sustainable Development Goals Extended Report 2024: Goal 17 Partnerships for the Goals*, United Nations Statistics Division, New York, https://unstats.un.org/sdgs/report/2024/extended-report/Extended-Report_Goal-17.pdf. [62]

UN (2024), *The Sustainable Development Goals Extended Report 2024: Goal 5*, United Nations Statistics Division, New York, https://unstats.un.org/sdgs/report/2024/extended-report/Extended-Report_Goal-5.pdf (accessed on 29 November 2024). [7]

UN (2024), *The Sustainable Development Goals Extended Report 2024: Goal 7*, United Nations Statistics Division, New York, https://unstats.un.org/sdgs/report/2024/extended-report/Extended-Report_Goal-7.pdf (accessed on 29 November 2024). [6]

UN (2024), *The Sustainable Development Goals Extended Report 2024: Goal 8*, United Nations Statistical Commission, New York, https://unstats.un.org/sdgs/report/2024/extended-report/Extended-Report_Goal-8.pdf. [49]

UN (2024), *The Sustainable Development Goals Report 2024*, United Nations Department of Economic and Social Affairs, New York, https://unstats.un.org/sdgs/report/2024/ (accessed on 29 November 2024). [14]

UN (2015), *Addis Ababa Action Agenda of the Third International Conference on Financing for Development*, https://sustainabledevelopment.un.org/content/documents/2051AAAA_Outcome.pdf. [29]

UN Global Compact (2024), *The world's largest corporate sustainability initiative*, United Nations Global Compact, https://unglobalcompact.org/what-is-gc. [52]

UN Women (2022), *Are we on track to achieve gender equality by 2030?*, United Nations Women, https://data.unwomen.org/features/are-we-track-achieve-gender-equality-2030. [58]

UNCTAD (2024), *FDI Data Explorer - World Investment Report 2024*, https://unctad.org/publication/world-investment-report-2024. [41]

UNCTAD (2024), "Global foreign investment weak in 2023, funding for sustainable development sectors drops over 10%", https://unctad.org/news/global-foreign-investment-weak-2023-funding-sustainable-development-sectors-drops-over-10. [43]

UNCTAD (2024), *World Investment Report 2024*, UN Trade and Development(UNCTAD), Geneva, https://unctad.org/publication/world-investment-report-2024. [4]

UNCTAD (2023), "Investment flows to least developed countries affected disproportionately by global crises", *Investment Trends Monitor*, No. 45, UN Trade and Development (UNCTAD), Geneva, https://unctad.org/publication/investment-flows-least-developed-countries-affected-disproportionally-global-crises. [17]

UNCTAD (2023), "Investment policies for the energy transition: Incentives and disincentives", *Investment Policy Monitor* 26, https://unctad.org/publication/investment-policies-energy-transition-incentives-and-disincentives (accessed on 29 November 2024). [42]

UNEP (2024), *SDG 12 Hub*, United Nations Environment Programme, https://sdg12hub.org/ (accessed on 29 November 2024). [8]

United Nations (2024), *Statistical Annex I and II: SDG Report 2024*, https://unstats.un.org/sdgs/files/report/2024/E_2024_54_Statistical_Annex_I_and_II.pdf. [28]

United Nations Environment Programme (2024), *Indicator 12.6.1*, https://www.unep.org/topics/sustainable-development-goals/why-do-sustainable-development-goals-matter/goal-12. [26]

WAIPA (2023), *About WAIPA*, World Association of Investment Promotion Agencies, https://waipa.org/about-waipa/. [63]

WBA (2022), *2022 Financial System Benchmark: assessing 400 global financial institutions on their progress to supporting a just and sustainable economy*, World Benchmarking Alliance, https://www.worldbenchmarkingalliance.org/publication/financial-system/. [61]

World Bank (2024), *Green, Social, Sustainability, and Sustainability-Linked (GSSS) Bonds Market Update, July 2024*, https://thedocs.worldbank.org/en/doc/dacb969cc71f53abde2d2758f1cc13ed-0340012024/original/GSSS-Quarterly-Newsletter-Issue-No-8.pdf. [23]

World Bank (2024), *Remittances Prices Worldwide Quarterly: An Analysis of Trends in Cost of Remittance Services*, https://remittanceprices.worldbank.org/sites/default/files/rpw_main_report_and_annex_q124_final.pdf (accessed on 29 November 2024). [15]

World Bank (2024), *World Development Indicators (database): Financial Sector*, https://data.worldbank.org/topic/financial-sector?view=chart (accessed on 10 December 2024). [5]

World Bank (2023), *An analysis of trends in cost of remittance services quarterly*, https://remittanceprices.worldbank.org/sites/default/files/rpw_main_report_and_annex_q423_final.pdf. [57]

World Bank (2023), *Remittance prices worldwide*, https://remittanceprices.worldbank.org/. [55]

World Benchmarking Alliance (2023), *2024 Annual Plan*, https://assets.worldbenchmarkingalliance.org/app/uploads/2024/03/2024-Annual-Plan-for-website.pdf. [39]

Notes

[1] The potential reduction is the authors' estimate based on the volume of remittances in developing countries (excluding China) in 2023 and the difference between the current world transfer cost (as a percentage of the amount transferred) and the UN SDG target.

[2]The OECD Guidelines for Multinational Enterprises on Responsible Business Conduct are recommendations addressed to multinational enterprises by governments for aligning their activities with sustainable development and conducting due diligence to avoid adverse impacts on people and the planet. Fifty-one countries have adhered to the Guidelines as of 2023.

[3] In the Recommendation, last amended in 2018, DAC members agreed to untie ODA to LDCs, Heavily Indebted Poor Countries, other low-income countries, and IDA-only countries and territories. See https://legalinstruments.oecd.org/en/instruments/OECD-LEGAL-5015.

[4] The OECD DAC defines blended finance as "the strategic use of development finance for the mobilisation of additional finance towards sustainable development in developing countries". See https://doi.org/10.1787/9789264288768-en.

[5]Authors based on World Bank, World Development Indicators, https://databank.worldbank.org/source/world-development-indicators/preview/on (accessed 25 July 2024).

[6] The major reporting standards consolidated by the ISSB are as follows: the Task Force on Climate-Related Financial Disclosures; the Climate Disclosure Standards Board, which included the Carbon Disclosure Project; the Value Reporting Foundation, which housed the Sustainability Accounting Standards Board; and the International Integrated Reporting Framework.

4 International Development Co-operation

This chapter reviews the International Development Co-operation action area of the Addis Ababa Action Agenda (AAAA) including progress, persistent challenges, and emerging areas as the international community prepares for the Fourth International Conference on Financing for Development (FfD4). It explores advancements in modernising official development assistance (ODA) and the recent creation of a more inclusive measurement framework with the introduction of the Total Official Support for Sustainable Development (TOSSD) framework. Persistent challenges such as unmet aid commitments, aid fragmentation, and insufficient gender equality funding are highlighted. Opportunities to strengthen development effectiveness, address multidimensional vulnerabilities, safeguard debt sustainability, and mobilise private sector resources for sustainable development, including through innovative finance and capacity building, are also presented.

4.1. Data dashboard

Key trends

Since 2015, total ODA provided by DAC member countries, including cross-border flows (CPA and humanitarian aid) and in-donor refugee costs, increased.

In 2023, total official development assistance (ODA) provided by DAC member countries rose to an all-time high of USD 223 billion in current prices or USD 194 billion in 2015 constant prices (OECD, 2024[1]).[1] This marks a 48% increase from 2015, rising from USD 131 billion (Figure 4.1). Between 2015 and 2022, disbursements from non-DAC providers to developing countries increased by 51% from USD 10.9 billion to USD 16.5 billion (OECD, 2024[1]).[2]

Both country programmable aid (CPA) and humanitarian assistance continued to rise over the period to a combined total of USD 90 billion in 2023. CPA alone, the subset of ODA flows to partner countries that is programmable, reached USD 67 billion in 2023, a 27% increase since 2015, though if support to Ukraine is excluded, CPA remained stable over the period (OECD, 2024[2]).

In-donor refugee costs rose to USD 28 billion in 2023 and humanitarian ODA amounted USD 23 billion, reflecting increases of 134% and 70%, respectively, since 2015.

Figure 4.1. ODA provided by DAC member countries, including cross-border flows (CPA and humanitarian aid) and in-donor refugee costs

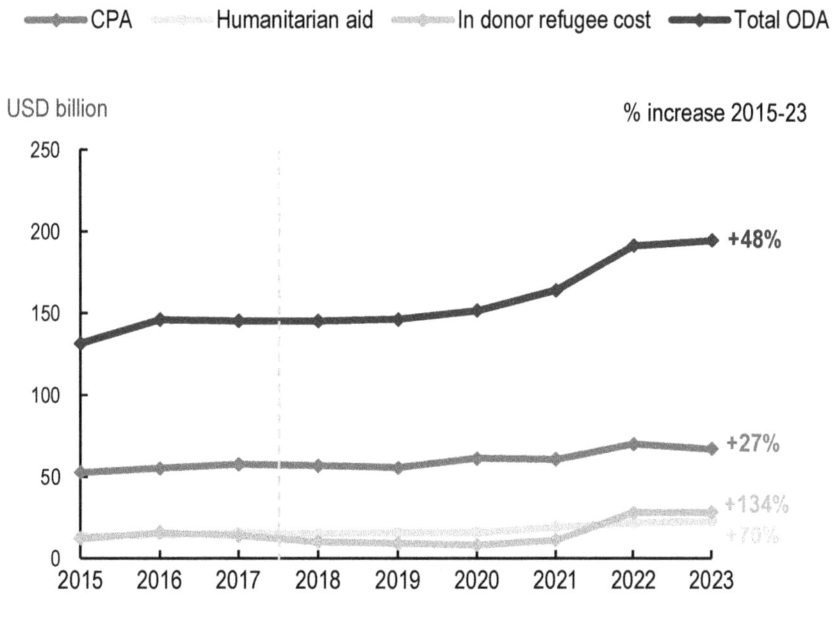

Note: Calculations based on disbursements, in 2015 constant prices. For total ODA, figures prior to 2018 are calculated using the cash flow method, while figures from 2018 onward are based on the grant equivalent method. Humanitarian and in-donor refugee costs are calculated based on net ODA. CPA calculations are derived from gross ODA.
Source: Authors' calculations based on OECD (2024[2]), OECD Data Explorer, Creditor Reporting System (database), http://data-explorer.oecd.org/s/c

Since Addis, ODA from DAC members to vulnerable countries has lagged behind total spending.

Though total ODA from DAC members increased over 2015-23 (+48%), ODA to several of the most vulnerable country groups did not keep pace with this growth (+28% on average) (Figure 4.2). ODA to small island developing states (SIDS) is the exception and has increased faster than total ODA volumes over the period.

ODA to countries most in need grew overall by 28% on average, it increased by 25% for least developed countries (LDCs), 17% for fragile states and conflict-affected countries (FS), 8% for landlocked developing countries (LLDCs) and 62%for small island developing states (SIDS).

Figure 4.2. Official development assistance (ODA) flows from DAC members to vulnerable countries

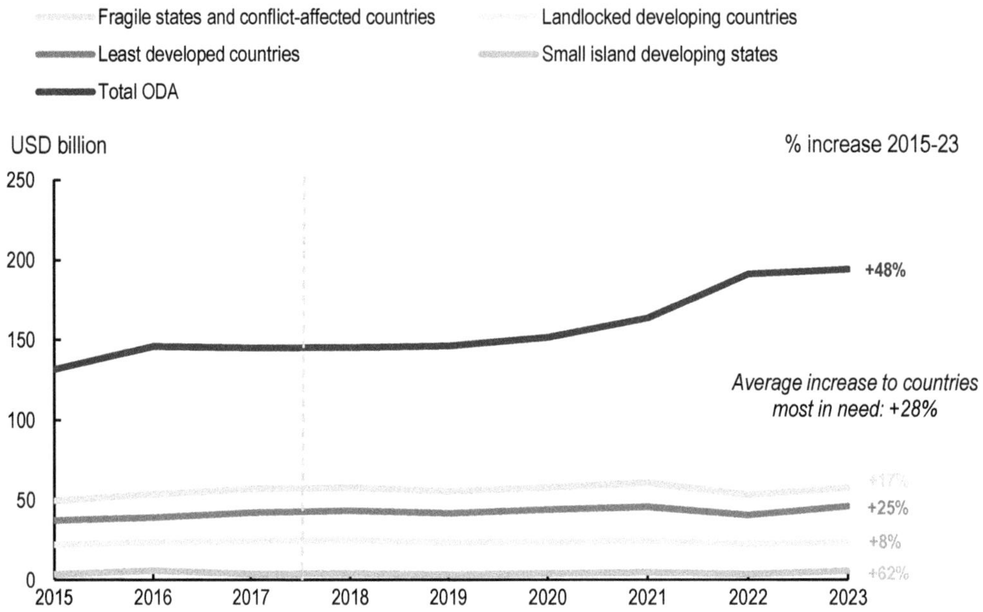

Note: Calculations based on disbursements, in 2015 constant prices. For total ODA, figures prior to 2018 are calculated using the cash flow method, while figures from 2018 onward are based on the grant equivalent method. Calculations for LDCs, LLDCs, SIDS and FS are based on net bilateral ODA and imputed multilateral ODA.
Source: Authors' calculations based on OECD (2024[3]), OECD Data Explorer, DAC 2a table, http://data-explorer.oecd.org/s/w.

Available data on the measure of cross-border total official support for sustainable development (TOSSD) have improved.

Cross-border TOSSD flows, or pillar 1, amounted to USD 315 billion in 2022. These flows included bilateral and multilateral grants, concessional loans, non-concessional loans, and in-kind support including South-South and triangular co-operation (Figure 4.3).

Multilateral TOSSD cross-border flows increased from 57% of the total in 2019 to 61% of the total in 2022. Pillar 2 of TOSSD, which tracks global and regional support to international public goods, totalled USD 126 billion in 2022.

Figure 4.3. Total official support for sustainable development (TOSSD) flows

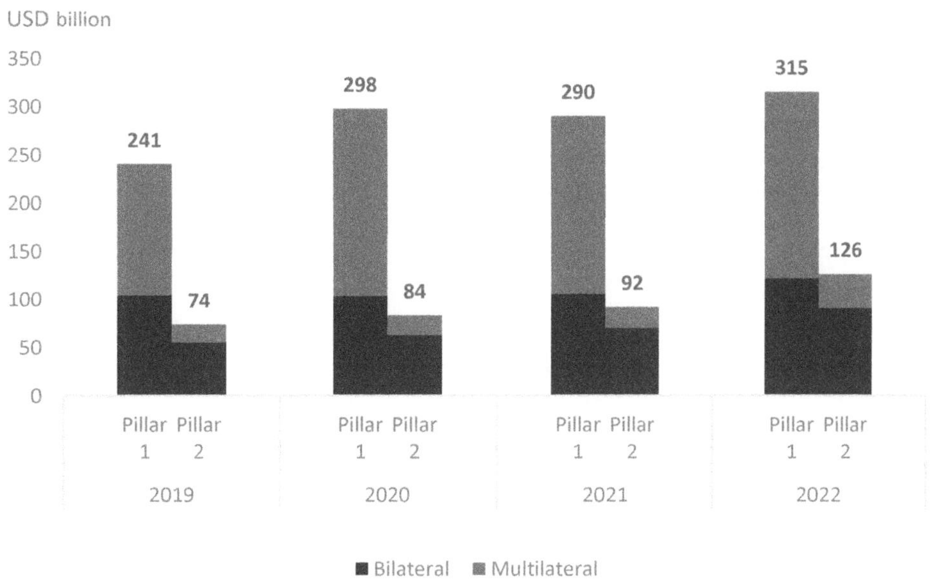

Note: Disbursements in 2022 constant prices. Country coverage varies by year (92 bilateral and multilateral reporters in 2019, 103 in 2020,112 in 2021 and 121 in 2022).
Source: International Forum on Total Official Support for Sustainable Development (2024[4]), TOSSD data visualisation tool (database) - Distribution of amounts by pillar, disbursements, 2022 constant prices. https://tossd.online/app.

Key performance indicators

↔	In 2022, the 16 DAC members that had committed to the target provided on average 0.54% of their total gross national income (GNI) in ODA to developing countries. Most (27 of 31) DAC members made progress towards the target since 2018, and 5 members reached the target in 2023.[1] In 2022, DAC members provided 0.08% on average, of their GNI to LDCs, below the target of 0.15% to 0.20% (OECD, 2024[5]).[2]
↔	In 2022, developing countries received a total of USD 276.6 billion in official resources including USD 55.3 billion from mobilised private finance and USD 10.2 billion in private grants, according to data reported by 101 bilateral and multilateral providers (UN, 2024[6]).
↔	Though most bilateral providers have enhanced their development planning since 2011, the use of country-owned results frameworks and planning tools by bilateral development co-operation providers decreased from 64% in 2011 to 57% in 2018 (UN, 2024[6]).

↓ Slight setback	↓ Setback	↔ No change, neutral	↔ Stagnant, possible issue	↑ Major progress	↑ Minimal progress
↓ Minimal setback	↓ Major setback	↔ Holding steady, slight concern	↔ Negative stagnation, concerning	↑ Progress	↑ Negligible progress or progress contested

1. The ODA grant equivalent methodology is used from 2018 whereby only the "grant portion" of the loan, i.e. the amount "given" by lending below market rates, counts as ODA. This indicator is measured as a percentage of GNI using million USD constant prices, using 2021 as the base year.
2. Calculations exclude the European Union.
Selected quantifiable commitments. Annex Table 4.A.1 contains the full list.

Resource mobilisation potential

- DAC members alone would have mobilised USD 200 billion in additional ODA in 2023 had they all committed to and met the 0.7% ODA/GNI target.[3] It should be noted that not all DAC members have committed to this target.
- Even under the optimistic scenario, additional multilateral development bank lending would amount to USD 40 billion per year – substantially less than the target set by the G20 Independent Expert Group (+USD 260 billion) (OECD, 2024[7]).

4.2. Key areas of progress

The modernisation of ODA has helped improve its integrity, transparency and accountability

The DAC's modernisation of the ODA measure has clarified eligibility rules for peace and security expenditures and for expenditures for hosting refugees. It also introduced new debt relief reporting and grant equivalent[4] accounting for financial instruments such as loans, guarantees and equities and adopted new reporting rules for private sector instruments, with data reported starting in 2023. These changes and accompanying safeguards that enhance the accuracy of the data as well as transparency and accountability reinforce the integrity of ODA and ensure that major changes in development co-operation, such as the diversification of financial instruments, are appropriately reflected in ODA reporting.

The creation of the TOSSD measurement framework and the International Forum on TOSSD has advanced transparency and comprehensive information on financial flows for sustainable development

Open, inclusive and transparent discussions led to the adoption of a new TOSSD measure that includes activity-level data on cross-border resource flows to developing countries (TOSSD Pillar 1), global and regional expenditures (TOSSD Pillar 2), and semi-aggregates on mobilised private finance. The UN Statistical Commission adopted TOSSD Pillar 1 as a data source for Sustainable Development Goal (SDG) indicator 17.3.1. Tracking of support for sustainable development in TOSSD has improved since 2019, with more data being captured and, in 2022, 121 reporters including 19 South-South providers (TOSSD, 2024[4]).

The independent International Forum on TOSSD was established in 2024. Its Steering Group is a balanced composition of traditional providers, dual providers and recipients, recipient countries, and multilateral organisations with strong involvement from the civil society and the UN.

The number of South-South co-operation activities reported to TOSSD increased by 64% between 2019-22 from 5 558 to 9 092. Triangular co-operation activities grew by 268%, from 382 to 1 404, over the same period (International Forum on Total Official Support for Sustainable Development, 2024[8]).

4.3. Persistent challenges

ODA/GNI commitments including to LDCs remain unmet

As of 2022, 16 DAC members had committed to achieving the 0.7% ODA/GNI target, and several of these commitments include a timeframe to achieve it by 2030 (OECD, 2023[9]). The weighted average of those members' ODA to GNI ratio in 2021 was 0.54%.[5] Several non-DAC countries have already achieved the 0.7% ODA/GNI target.[6]

While not all DAC members have committed to the target of 0.15% to 0.20% ODA/GNI for LDCs, the ratio on average among DAC members was stalled at about 0.09% ODA/GNI in 2022 (OECD, 2024[5]). In addition, LDCs received roughly the same volume of ODA, averaging USD 50 billion annually, over the period of 2015-22. Their 22% share of total ODA in 2022 was the smallest it had been since 1996, despite commitments to reverse the decline in ODA share (OECD, 2024[10]).

Development effectiveness, quality and impact accelerate delivery of the SDGs, but progress to improve these is mixed

A focus on quantitative targets alone does not suffice to achieve sustainable development. Proliferation and fragmentation of the aid system persists: more and more of recipient countries are dealing with 60 or more agencies; the number of ODA transactions rose sharply in 2019; and more than 200 international organisations and funds are channelling almost half of all ODA, leading to reduced project sizes and wider dispersion of resources (OECD, 2024[7]; OECD, 2023[9]). These and other challenges – in the use of country systems, trade-offs between country ownership and whole-of-society approaches, lack of donor co-ordination, and targeting the furthest behind – jeopardise the effectiveness, quality and impact of all types of development co-operation (OECD, 2023[9]). Strengthening the role of recipient countries in harmonising donor efforts, as emphasised in the principle of country ownership, is critical to ensuring alignment with national priorities and enhancing accountability. The development co-operation effectiveness principles provide guidance to address these challenges through evidence from the Global Partnership for Effective Development Co-operation (GPEDC) and its ongoing monitoring exercise, among others (OECD/UNDP, 2019[11]). Forthcoming guidance will also encourage more effective multilateral partnerships, greater coherence between bilateral and multilateral efforts, and support for the reform of the increasingly fragmented international development co-operation system. Sharing lessons on the effective use of all types of development co-operation, including South-South and triangular co-operation, is essential for mutual learning, identifying areas of common interest, and strengthening providers' systems.

To establish more equitable partnerships and greater agency of national and local actors, some providers are exploring new policy commitments and institutional reforms. For example, several DAC members are working to accelerate locally led development – development co-operation that gives affected people and local actors, from national governments to grassroot organisations, more agency in the design and implementation of development co-operation.

The mobilisation of private sector resources by official intervention has increased significantly but still falls short of needs

Since 2015, the volume of private sector resources mobilised[7] has more than doubled from USD 27.7 billion to USD 61.6 billion in 2022 (OECD, 2023[12]). Even this increase, however, falls far short of mobilising the trillions in financing needed in developing countries, and the amounts to date have largely bypassed countries most in need. Most of these resources (77%) are mobilised in middle-income countries (OECD, 2023[12]). The cumulative issuance of green, social, sustainability and sustainability-linked (GSSS) bonds totalled USD 5.3 trillion in 2023. (World Bank, 2024[13]). Yet, only 13% of all GSSS bonds were issued by entities in developing countries in 2022, and their share of the total market dropped to 5% in 2023 (OECD, 2024[14]). (More information on barriers and opportunities to mobilise the private sector is presented in Chapter 3 on domestic and international private business and finance.)

ODA in support of gender equality and the empowerment of all women and girls can be improved

The share of ODA with gender equality objectives has declined after nearly a decade of growth (OECD, 2024[15]). In 2021-22, gender equality was a policy objective in 42% of the programmes funded by DAC members' bilateral allocable ODA, amounting to USD 60.4 billion of the USD 143 billion in bilateral allocable ODA assessed against the OECD gender marker (OECD, 2024[15]). While in 2021-22 the total volume of such ODA was higher than the 2019-20 level of USD 57 billion, its share was down from 45% in 2019-20, the first relative drop after a period of growth from 2011 to 2020 (OECD, 2024[15]). The bulk of ODA with gender equality objectives was for programmes that integrate gender equality as one policy objective among others, and only 4% of aid was dedicated to programmes with gender equality as the principal objective (OECD, 2024[15]).

4.4. New and emerging areas

ODA increasingly responds to global crises including health, climate and conflict

Following successive global shocks, it remains unclear whether the increase in ODA is truly new and additional or reflects ODA redirected from existing commitments. The OECD estimates that DAC members' bilateral aid spending on what could be considered to be the provision of global public goods has grown from 30% of average bilateral ODA in 2006-10 to about 57% in 2016-20, due in large part to growing expenditures related to climate challenges, the costs for refugees in donor countries and infectious diseases (OECD, 2023[9]). ODA budgets are increasingly stretched as they respond to short-term demands while continuing to finance long-term development in developing countries and poverty reduction goals (OECD, 2022[16]).

Climate finance provided and mobilised by developed countries for climate action in developing countries, including and beyond ODA, nearly doubled from USD 59 billion in 2016 to USD 116 billion in 2022 in line with the UN Framework Convention on Climate Change target to mobilise USD 100 billion per year by 2020 in developing countries (OECD, 2024[17]). Climate finance provided and mobilised by developed countries just for SIDS tripled since 2016 to USD 3.2 billion in 2022 (OECD, 2024[17]). Developed countries also have made progress towards the goal of doubling the adaptation finance they provide and mobilise and are on track to achieve the target if current efforts are maintained (OECD, 2024[17]). Total bilateral climate-related development finance amounted to a two-year average of USD 50 billion in 2021-22 or 40% of total bilateral ODA (OECD, 2024[18]). In addition, bilateral providers increased their official development finance flows for biodiversity, which reached an all-time high of USD 15.4 billion in 2022 (OECD, 2024[19]).[8] Finally, ODA to protect oceans is on an upward trend (OECD, 2020[20]). (More information on climate finance, including private finance mobilisation for climate action, is presented in Chapter 3 on domestic and international private business and finance.)

At COP29, nations agreed on a New Collective Quantified Goal for climate finance, committing developed countries to mobilise at least USD 300 billion annually by 2035 to support developing nations in addressing climate change (COP29, 2024[21]). The conference also called for raising USD 1.3 trillion per year from all public and private sources in total by 2035 (UN, 2024[22]).

Debt sustainability safeguards for ODA have been strengthened

Since 2015, on average 85% of total ODA is in the form of grants (OECD, 2024[1]). ODA loans must comply with the World Bank and International Monetary Fund Debt Sustainability Analysis standards to ensure that they do not contribute to debt distress. In addition, they should remain highly concessional, particularly when extended to those most in need. However, the average grant element (measure of concessionality) of DAC members' ODA loans to LDCs declined from 78.4% in 2015 to 70.0% in 2022[9] due to higher interest rates, which doubled to 0.82%, and the shortened maturity of loans by 6 years (to 29.8 years in 2022) (OECD, 2024[2]).[10]

Multidimensional vulnerabilities, beyond GDP, are important to consider for countries approaching the graduation from development finance thresholds

It is important to develop other measures and indices of vulnerability as world poverty and inequalities shift and as climate change and debt increase risk levels. The use of GNI per capita, while imperfect, is grounded in robust evidence and is a good proxy for a country's welfare, vulnerabilities associated with lower levels of economic development, and resilience. While GNI per capita remains the key metric for determining the ODA eligibility of a country, including low- and middle-income countries as defined by the World Bank, GNI per capita is not the only measure of how development finance is allocated. SIDS, for example, are mainly MICs, yet face an anticipated annual adaptation gap of USD 7.3 billion on average per year until 2030, demonstrating continuing financing needs. The aim of the UN Multidimensional Vulnerability Index, initiated in 2020, is to help assess and raise awareness of vulnerabilities that are not captured by GNI per capita or by GDP (UN, 2024[23]). To further support countries as their GNI per capita reaches the threshold for ODA graduation, the DAC is exploring options for more open, inclusive and transparent partnerships in support of a smooth transition to broader sources of financing beyond ODA, particularly for those countries that are approaching the threshold for ODA eligibility and face specific vulnerabilities.

Total official development finance for capacity building and technical assistance is increasing and facilitates access to innovative finance

While innovative solutions for sustainable development finance have mushroomed in recent years, their impact and deployment has been limited in developing countries due to capacity constraints. Capacity building and technical assistance in vulnerable countries seeks to leverage innovations such as sustainable finance instruments and debt management tools. In 2022, total official development finance for capacity building and national planning amounted to USD 54.9 billion, a 50% increase over 2015 (OECD, 2024[2]). Policy reforms carried out through Integrated National Financing Frameworks (INFFs) in 17 countries have leveraged USD 16 billion for SDG investments and offer the potential to align an additional USD 32 billion (Integrated National Financing Frameworks, 2024[24]). The INFF Facility, launched in 2022, provides technical assistance to and supports capacity building in countries preparing or implementing INFFs to enable them to bring innovations to scale. It also is exploring the creation of new windows (including with South-South and DAC providers) to also help respond to growing demand.

Annex 4.A. International Development Co-operation

Annex Table 4.A.1. Assessment of the action area: International development co-operation

AAAA paragraph	Commitment	Specific target or objective	Matching Sustainable Development Goal (SDG) target (where available)	State of implementation or progress made since 2015, using selected SDG or other relevant indicator (proxy)
50	Increase all forms of international public finance support. Strengthen international development co-operation and maximise its effectiveness, transparency, impact and results (including principles and dialogue).	No	n.a.	Total official support for sustainable development (TOSSD) In 2022, cross-border (Pillar 1) TOSSD flows amounted to USD 315 billion, up from USD 290 billion in 2021. Global and regional expenditures and resources in support of international public goods (Pillar 2) totalled USD 126 billion in 2022, up from USD 92 billion in 2021 (TOSSD, 2024[4]).
51	Reaffirm the fulfilment of all official development assistance (ODA) commitments, including the pledge by many developed nations to reach the target of spending 0.7% of gross national income (GNI) on ODA and an ODA/GNI ratio of 0.15% to 0.20% for least developed countries (LDCs). Encourage ODA providers to consider establishing an ODA/GNI goal of at least 0.20% to LDCs.	Yes Target of 0.7% ODA/GNI to developing countries and 0.15% to 0.20% ODA/GNI to LDCs.	Target 17.2 Developed countries to implement fully their ODA commitments, including the commitment by many developed countries to achieve the target of 0.7% of GNI for ODA to developing countries and 0.15% to 0.20% of ODA/GNI to LDCs; ODA providers are encouraged to consider setting a target to provide at least 0.20% of ODA/GNI to LDCs.	SDG indicator 17.2.1 Net ODA, total and to LDCs, as a proportion of OECD DAC donors' GNI In 2023, ODA from DAC member countries amounted to USD 223.3 billion, accounting on average for 0.37% of their GNI. (UN, 2024[6]). In 2022, on average, DAC members allocated 0.09% of their total GNI to LDCs (OECD, 2024[5]). Between 2015 and 2023, ODA to countries most in need grew by 28% on average (i.e. up 25% for LDCs, 8% for LLDCs, 62% for SIDS, and 17% for fragile states and conflict-affected countries). In comparison, total ODA increased by 48% (OECD, 2024[5]).
52	Direct the most concessional resources to countries most in need. Pledge to reverse the decline in the proportion of ODA allocated to LDCs.	No	Target 17.2. See para 51.	SDG indicator 17.2.1. See para 51.

AAAA paragraph	Commitment	Specific target or objective	Matching Sustainable Development Goal (SDG) target (where available)	State of implementation or progress made since 2015, using selected SDG or other relevant indicator (proxy)
53	Ensure effective use of ODA to meet development goals. Encourage the publishing of clear, predictable and transparent plans for future development co-operation. Urge countries to track and report on resources allocated for gender equality and women's empowerment.	No	Target 1.a Ensure significant mobilisation of resources from a variety of sources, including through enhanced development co-operation, in order to provide adequate and predictable means for developing countries, in particular LDCs, to implement programmes and policies to end poverty in all its dimensions. Target 5.c Adopt and strengthen sound policies and enforceable legislation for the promotion of gender equality and the empowerment of all women and girls at all levels.	SDG indicator 1.a.1 Total ODA grants from all donors that focus on poverty reduction as a share of the recipient country's GNI In 2022, 9% of bilateral ODA grants (USD 27.2 billion) were allocated to basic social services and development food aid, focusing on poverty reduction (UN, 2024[25]). SDG indicator 5.c.1 Proportion of countries with systems to track and make public allocations for gender equality and women's empowerment Data from 105 countries and territories for the period 2018-21 show that 26% countries had comprehensive systems to track and make public budget allocations for gender equality and women's empowerment. In addition, 59% had some features of a system in place and 15% the minimum required elements of such systems (UN, 2024[25]).
54	Catalyse additional resource mobilisation from other sources, both public and private.	No	Target 17.3 Mobilise additional financial resources for developing countries from multiple sources.	SDG indicator 17.3.1 Additional financial resources mobilised for developing countries from multiple sources In 2022, financial resources for developing countries as reported by 101 bilateral and multilateral providers totalled USD 276.6 billion in official resources, USD 55.3 billion from private finance and USD 10.2 billion in private development grants. While the volume of sustainable development grants (both official and private) declined from 2021, sustainable concessional development loans rose by 6%, non-concessional loans fell by less than 1% and mobilised private finance increased by 21%, offsetting the decline in 2021 (UN, 2024[26]). *Data published under SDG 17.3.1 on private finance mobilised excludes OECD CRS survey on private finance mobilised in developing countries. Including amounts mobilised in developing countries, the amount reached USD 62 billion in 2022.*
55	Modernise the ODA measurement. Develop the proposed measure of total official support for sustainable development.	Yes Development of TOSSD measure.	n.a.	*The DAC's modernisation of ODA rules clarifies eligibility for peace and security spending and refugee hosting and introduces grant equivalent accounting for loans, guarantees and equities. These changes improve data accuracy, transparency and accountability, ensuring that the diversification of financial instruments is reflected in ODA reporting. Safeguards such as stricter concessionality measures, a ceiling on debt relief reporting and closer monitoring of refugee costs maintain ODA integrity.*

AAAA paragraph	Commitment	Specific target or objective	Matching Sustainable Development Goal (SDG) target (where available)	State of implementation or progress made since 2015, using selected SDG or other relevant indicator (proxy)
				The DAC is also exploring more open partnerships to support countries nearing ODA eligibility thresholds and facing vulnerabilities. (OECD, 2025[27]) *Open, inclusive and transparent discussions have been held on the TOSSD measure and an International Task Force (2017-23) was established to develop TOSSD. The methodology was reviewed in a UN Working Group (2020-21) of the Inter-Agency and Expert Group on SDGs. The UN Statistical Commission, in a March 2022 decision, adopted TOSSD Pillar 1 on cross-border resource flows to developing countries as a data source for SDG indicator 17.3.1 in the SDG indicator framework.* *The International Forum on TOSSD (established in 2024) and its predecessor task force have collected and published TOSSD data for four years (2019-22) of flows, with 2022 data covering resources provided by 121 reporters (countries and multilateral organisations) including 19 South-South co-operation providers. TOSSD data are available in a public online database and data visualisation tool that provide activity-level data on cross-border resource flows to developing countries (TOSSD Pillar 1), global and regional expenditures (TOSSD Pillar 2), and semi-aggregates on mobilised private finance* (TOSSD, 2024[4]).
56	Increase South-South co-operation.	No	Target 17.3 Mobilise additional financial resources for developing countries from multiple sources. Target 17.9 Enhance international support for implementing effective and targeted capacity building in developing countries to support national plans to implement all SDGs, including through North-South, South-South and triangular co-operation.	SDG indicator 17.3.1 *See para 54.* SDG indicator 17.9.1 Dollar value of financial and technical assistance (including through North-South, South-South and triangular co-operation) committed to developing countries Total official development finance for capacity building and national planning reached USD 54.9 billion in 2022, a 51.4% increase since 2015, with USD 27.2 billion directed to public administration, health and financial policy. Support for health policies grew by 26% in 2022 to USD 6.5 billion to address COVID-19 challenges. (UN, 2024[6]). Between 2019-22, while the number of South-South co-operation activities reported to TOSSD increased by 64%, from 5 558 to 9 092, the total volume declined from USD 12.8 billion in 2019 and USD 10.4 billion in 2022.[1] *In a global survey conducted by the UN Trade and Development (UNCTAD), 60 of 80 responding Southern countries requested immediate support to start collecting these data to fulfil their reporting obligations to the SDG indicator. UNCTAD with partners leads the work to strengthen the capacity of developing countries to accurately measure and report South-South co-operation, enabling them to effectively manage*

AAAA paragraph	Commitment	Specific target or objective	Matching Sustainable Development Goal (SDG) target (where available)	State of implementation or progress made since 2015, using selected SDG or other relevant indicator (proxy)
				and mobilise resources for achieving the goals set by the 2030 Agenda (UN, 2024[28])
57	Strengthen South-South and triangular co-operation and improve their development effectiveness.	No	Target 17.9 See para 56.	SDG indicator 17.9.1. See para 56 for South-South co-operation. Between 2019-22, triangular co-operation activities grew by 268% from 382 to 1 404, or the equivalent of USD 84.23 million in 2019 and USD 424.82 million in 2022.
58	Enhance the quality, impact and effectiveness of development co-operation by aligning with national priorities, reducing fragmentation and accelerating the untying of aid in line with agreed principles of development co-operation effectiveness. Promote country ownership, adopt programme-based approaches, strengthen partnerships, and increase transparency and predictability. Avoid requesting tax exemptions on goods and services provided as government-to-government aid, starting with the renunciation of value-added tax and import levy repayments.	No	Target 17.15 Respect each country's policy space and leadership to establish and implement policies for poverty eradication and sustainable development.	SDG indicator 17.15.1 Extent of use of country-owned results frameworks and planning tools by providers of development co-operation The use of country-owned results frameworks and planning tools by bilateral providers of development co-operation declined from 64% in 2016 to 57% in 2018 (Global Partnership for Effective Development Co-operation, n.d.[29]). Percentage of aid which is untied The proportion of untied ODA has risen from an average of 47% in 1999-2001 to 89% in 2022 (UN, 2024[30]) Percentage of country programmable aid (CPA) CPA alone, the subset of ODA flows to partner countries that is programmable, reached USD 67 billion in 2023, a 27% increase since 2015, though if support to Ukraine is excluded, CPA remained stable over the period (OECD, 2024[2]). *Launched in 2022, the OECD's Tax Treatment of Official Development Assistance (ODA) Hub is the first public resource to improve the transparency around the taxation of aid. The Hub includes country survey responses and links to additional resources. It presents approaches taken by 22 of the 30 DAC members that participated in the survey, representing over 80% of total bilateral ODA in 2020. Since 2015, 13 out of 22 donors on the Hub reported reviewing their policy since 2015. Of these, 4 never or rarely request exemptions, 3 sometimes request exemptions, 9 generally request exemptions and 6 have no general policy on the issue.* (OECD, n.d.[31]) *The UN through the subcommittee on the tax treatment of ODA projects produced guidelines on the tax treatment of government-to-government aid projects.* (United Nations Department of Economic and Social Affairs, 2023[32]) *The UN Tax Committee also adopted a recommendation on the Public Disclosure of Provisions*

AAAA paragraph	Commitment	Specific target or objective	Matching Sustainable Development Goal (SDG) target (where available)	State of implementation or progress made since 2015, using selected SDG or other relevant indicator (proxy)
				Concerning the Tax Treatment of Government-to-Government Aid Projects.
59	Acknowledge that the UN Framework Convention on Climate Change and its Conference of the Parties are the primary international and intergovernmental forums for negotiating the global response to climate change.	No	n.a.	n.a.
60	Deliver on the commitment made by developed countries to mobilise USD 100 billion annually by 2020 in climate finance for developing countries.	Yes Mobilise USD 100 billion in climate finance annually by 2020.	Target 13.a Implement the commitment undertaken by developed country parties to the UN Framework Convention on Climate Change (UNFCCC) to a goal of mobilising jointly USD 100 billion annually by 2020 from all sources to address the needs of developing countries in the context of meaningful mitigation actions and transparency on implementation and to fully operationalise the Green Climate Fund through its capitalisation as soon as possible.	SDG indicator 13.a.1 Amounts provided and mobilised in US dollars per year in relation to the continued, existing collective mobilisation goal of the USD 100 billion commitment through to 2025 According to the OECD's seventh progress assessment towards the UNFCCC goal, developed countries provided and mobilised USD 115.9 billion in climate finance in 2022 for developing countries, surpassing the annual USD 100 billion target for the first time, albeit with a two-year delay from the original target year (OECD, 2024[17]).
61	Welcome the initiation of the Green Climate Fund (GCF) and the Board's decision to aim for a 50:50 balance between mitigation and adaptation over time.	No	Target 13.a See para 60.	SDG indicator 13.a.1. *See para 60.* ODA allocated to mitigation and adaptation After a slight decrease in 2021, adaptation finance increased to USD 32.4 billion in 2022, a threefold increase from 2016. Mitigation continued to dominate, making up 60% of the total (OECD, 2024[17]). GCF disbursements and replenishments The GCF has increased disbursements from USD 10.3 billion at the time of initial resource mobilisation in 2014 by 24.3% to USD 12.8 billion in 2022 . As of December 2023, the GCF's second replenishment reached a record total of USD 12.8 billion

AAAA paragraph	Commitment	Specific target or objective	Matching Sustainable Development Goal (SDG) target (where available)	State of implementation or progress made since 2015, using selected SDG or other relevant indicator (proxy)
				over the next four years pledged by 31 countries (Green climate fund, 2024[33]).
62	Consider climate and disaster resilience in development financing to ensure the sustainability of development results. Strengthen the capacity of national and local actors to manage and finance disaster risk as part of national sustainable development strategies.	No	Target 11.b By 2020, substantially increase the number of cities and human settlements adopting and implementing integrated policies and plans towards inclusion, resource efficiency, mitigation and adaptation to climate change, and resilience to disasters and develop and implement holistic disaster risk management at all levels in line with the Sendai Framework for Disaster Risk Reduction 2015-30. Target 13.2 Integrate climate change measures into national policies, strategies and planning. Target 13.b Promote mechanisms for raising capacity for effective climate change-related planning and management in LDCs and SIDS, including focusing on women, youth, and local and marginalised communities.	SDG indicator 11.b.1 Number of countries that adopt and implement national disaster risk reduction (DRR) strategies in line with the Sendai Framework for Disaster Risk Reduction 2015-30 In 2023, a total of 129 countries reported having a national DRR strategy aligned with the Sendai Framework compared with 55 countries that did so in 2015. (UN, 2024[34]) SDG indicator 11.b.2 Proportion of local governments that adopt and implement local DRR strategies in line with national DRR reduction strategies. In 2023, 106 countries reported having local DRR strategies that align with national strategies. On average, 72% of local governments in these countries indicated they have such strategies in place (UN, 2024[35]). SDG indicator 13.2.1 Number of countries with nationally determined contributions, long-term strategies, national adaptation plans and adaptation communications, as reported to the secretariat of the UNFCCC. In 2023, 194 countries had nationally determined contributions, 154 had national communications (non-Annex I Parties) and 45 had national adaptation plans (UN, 2024[36]; UN, 2024[25]). SDG indicator 13.b.1 Number of LDCs and SIDS with nationally determined contributions, long-term strategies, national adaptation plans and adaptation communications, as reported to the secretariat of the UNFCCC. LDCs submitted 46 readiness proposals to the Green Climate Fund for National Adaptation Plans or other adaptation processes, with 31 approved and 26 already receiving disbursed funds (UNFCCC, 2024[37]). Additionally, 37 SIDS and 45 LDCs have submitted at least their first versions of nationally determined contributions and many countries have also begun submitting long-term strategies and adaptation communications to the UNFCCC (UNFCCC, 2024[37]).
63	Mobilise financial resources from all sources and at all levels to conserve and sustainably use biodiversity and ecosystems. Implement the global Strategic Plan for Biodiversity for	Yes Implement the global Strategic Plan for	Target 15.a Mobilise and significantly increase financial resources from all sources to conserve and sustainably use biodiversity	SDG indicators 15.a.1 and 15.b.1 (a) ODA on conservation and sustainable use of biodiversity; (b) revenue generated and finance mobilised from biodiversity-relevant economic instruments. In 2022, ODA on conservation and sustainable use of biodiversity amounted to USD

AAAA paragraph	Commitment	Specific target or objective	Matching Sustainable Development Goal (SDG) target (where available)	State of implementation or progress made since 2015, using selected SDG or other relevant indicator (proxy)
	2011-20 and its Aichi Biodiversity Targets. Commit to supporting the efforts of countries to advance conservation and restoration efforts. Provide support to countries that need to enhance the implementation of their national biodiversity strategies and action plans.	Biodiversity for 2011-20 and its Aichi Biodiversity Targets.	and ecosystems. Target 15.9 By 2020, integrate ecosystem and biodiversity values into national and local planning, development processes, poverty reduction strategies and accounts.	11 billion, up from USD 9.5 billion in 2015 (OECD, 2024[19]). SDG indicator 15.9.1 (a) Number of countries that have established national targets in accordance with or similar to Aichi Biodiversity Target 2 of the Strategic Plan for Biodiversity 2011–20 in their national biodiversity strategy and action plans and the progress reported towards these targets; (b) integration of biodiversity into national accounting and reporting systems, defined as implementation of the System of Environmental Economic Accounting. In 2022, 145 countries had established national targets in accordance with Aichi Biodiversity Target 2 of the Strategic Plan for Biodiversity 2011-20 in their national biodiversity strategy and action plans (UN, 2024[25]).
64	Ensure the conservation and sustainable use of the oceans and seas and of their resources for sustainable development.	No	Target 14.2 By 2020, sustainably manage and protect marine and coastal ecosystems to avoid significant adverse impacts, including by strengthening their resilience, and take action for their restoration in order to achieve healthy and productive oceans. Target 14.c Enhance the conservation and sustainable use of oceans and their resources by implementing international law as reflected in the UN Convention on the Law of the Sea, which provides the legal framework for the conservation and sustainable use of oceans and their resources	ODA allocated to the ocean economy In 2022, ODA for the ocean economy amounted to USD 3.5 billion, up from USD 2.1 billion in 2015, but this constituted only a small portion (1%) of total ODA. ODA for the sustainable ocean economy focused on enhancing the sustainability of ocean economy sectors and conserving the ocean rose to USD 2.4 billion, up from USD 1.1 billion in 2015, representing 69% of the total ODA allocated to the ocean economy (OECD, 2020[20]; OECD, 2024[7]).
65	Commit to enhancing support for coastal areas and low-lying coastal countries, including LDCs and SIDS, to address and adapt to rising global temperatures, sea level rise, ocean acidification and other climate change impacts.	No	Target 14.7 By 2030, increase the economic benefits to SIDS and LDCs from the sustainable use of marine resources, including through sustainable management of fisheries, aquaculture, and tourism	ODA allocated to the ocean economy See para 64. ODA allocated to LDCs and SIDS Between 2015 and 2023, ODA to LDCs and SIDS increased by 25% and 62%, respectively (OECD, 2024[5]).

AAAA paragraph	Commitment	Specific target or objective	Matching Sustainable Development Goal (SDG) target (where available)	State of implementation or progress made since 2015, using selected SDG or other relevant indicator (proxy)
66	Enable countries to prevent or combat situations of chronic crisis related to conflicts or natural disasters. Strengthen the capacity of national and local actors to both manage and finance disaster risk reduction and to enable countries to draw efficiently and effectively on international assistance when needed.	No	Target 11.b See para 62.	SDG indicator 11.b.1 *See para 62.* SDG indicator 11.b.2 *See para 62.*
67	Assist countries in accessing financing for peacebuilding and development in the post-conflict context.	No	n.a.	ODA to fragile contexts ODA to fragile contexts reached USD 89.1 billion in 2022, up from USD 75.5 billion in 2016 (OECD, 2024[5]). *Since 2016, the OECD has been evaluating fragility in numerous countries and contexts worldwide through a multidimensional framework that encompasses economic, environmental, human, political, security and societal dimensions. While conflict-affected areas are often fragile, most fragile contexts are not experiencing active war. Nevertheless, fragility heightens the risk of conflict or crisis* (OECD, n.d.[38]).
68	Support efforts by LDCs, LLDCs and SIDS to build their national capacity to respond to various kinds of shocks including financial crises, natural disasters and public health emergencies.	No	Target 10.b Encourage ODA and financial flows, including foreign direct investment, to states where the need is greatest, in particular LDCs, African countries, SIDS and LLDCs, in accordance with their national plans and programmes.	SDG indicator 10.b.1 Total resource flows for development by recipient and donor countries and type of flow (e.g. ODA, foreign direct investment and other flows) In 2022, developing countries received USD 499 billion in total resource flows, including USD 246 billion in ODA, of which 66% was from DAC countries, 7% from other bilateral donors and 27% from multilateral organisations. Asia received the largest share (38%), and lower middle-income countries were the main beneficiaries overall. Private flows rebounded post-COVID-19, contributing USD 200 billion, while the ODA share decreased from 54% in 2015 to 49% in 2022 (UN, 2024[39]).
69	Explore additional innovative mechanisms based on models combining public and private resources such as green bonds, vaccine bonds, triangular loans and pull mechanisms, and carbon pricing	No	Target 17.3 See para 54.	SDG indicator 17.3.1 See para 54. Annual global sustainable bond issuance

AAAA paragraph	Commitment	Specific target or objective	Matching Sustainable Development Goal (SDG) target (where available)	State of implementation or progress made since 2015, using selected SDG or other relevant indicator (proxy)
	mechanisms.			Annual global sustainable bond issuance – green, social, sustainability and sustainability-linked (GSSS) bonds – reached USD 946 billion in 2023, a 2.2% increase after a decline in 2022 (FSDR 2024). Sustainable bond issuance has grown fivefold since 2018, and the cumulative issuance of GSSS bonds totalled USD 5.3 trillion in 2023 (UN, 2024[30]; World Bank, 2024[40]). However, only 13% of the overall GSSS bond market was issued by entities in developing countries in 2022, and the share dropped to 5% in 2023 (OECD, 2023[41]). *Green, social and sustainability bonds finance specific sustainable activities. Sustainability-linked bonds are general purpose but tied to environmental or social performance targets. Green bonds remain the dominant instrument, making up 60% of total issuance, with a primary focus on climate mitigation* (UN, 2024[30]).
70	Acknowledge the crucial role of multilateral development banks and international financial institutions in financing sustainable development through both concessional and non-concessional lending.	No	n.a.	Development finance by multilateral providers In 2022, multilateral organisations committed a total of USD 213 billion from their core resources to support developing countries, up from USD 152 billion in 2015. Nearly half of these commitments, USD 92 billion in 2022 and USD 71 billion in 2015, were provided as concessional support (OECD, 2024[7]). DAC members' contribution to the multilateral development system In 2022, DAC members' total contribution to the multilateral system reached USD 98.5 billion, up from USD 60.7 billion in 2015 (OECD, 2024[7]).
71	Enhance support for middle-income countries (including concessional finance such as ODA).	No	n.a.	ODA to middle-income countries ODA disbursements (in constant prices) from DAC members to lower middle-income countries in 2022 amounted to USD 47.1 billion, an increase from USD 27.4 billion in 2015. For upper middle-income countries, disbursements totalled USD 13.1 billion in 2022, up from USD 10.2 billion in 2015 (OECD, 2024[3]).
72	Enhance support for middle-income countries, and address concerns about reduced access to concessional finance as incomes rise. Encourage multilateral development banks to adopt sequenced graduation policies while	No	n.a.	MIGA support to middle-income countries In FY2023, MIGA issued a record USD 6.4 billion in new guarantees across 40 projects, supporting USD 8.6 billion in total financing (from private and public sources). Almost all the MIGA projects supported at least one of its three priority areas: 27% of gross issuances went to International Development Association-eligible (lower-income) countries, 19% went to fragile states and conflict-affected

AAAA paragraph	Commitment	Specific target or objective	Matching Sustainable Development Goal (SDG) target (where available)	State of implementation or progress made since 2015, using selected SDG or other relevant indicator (proxy)
	exploring tailored assistance strategies and emphasising risk mitigation mechanisms such as those offered by the Multilateral Investment Guarantee Agency (MIGA).			countries, and 28% of the total guaranteed investment of the projects contributed to climate finance. As a result, FY2023 MIGA issuances are expected to help create 8 774 jobs and enable USD 2.6 billion in loans, including for small and medium enterprises and climate-related activities. MIGA projects also connected 55 million people to mobile telephone networks and 40 million to the internet (MIGA, 2023[42]).
73	Adjust the level of concessionality in international public finance based on recipient development indicators and project viability.	No	n.a.	See para 72.
74	Support the UN development system.	No	n.a.	All UN member states' support to the UN development system In 2022, contributions from all UN member states to the UN development system totalled USD 38.7 billion, an increase of roughly 100% from USD 19.3 billion in 2016 (OECD, 2024[7]). DAC members' support to the UN development system Of the total, DAC member countries contributed USD 36.8 billion in 2022, up from USD 17.9 billion in 2015 (OECD, 2024[7]).
75	Highlight development banks' role in financing infrastructure and development. Encourage effective safeguards and long-term investment in sustainability. Support new financing mechanisms for regional investments and organisations.	No	Target 9.a Facilitate sustainable and resilient infrastructure development in developing countries through enhanced financial, technological and technical support to African countries, LDCs, LLDCs and SIDS. Target 17.17 Encourage and promote effective public, public-private and civil society partnerships, building on the experience and resourcing strategies of partnerships.	SDG indicator 9.a.1 Total official international support (ODA plus other official flows) to infrastructure In 2022, the total official flows (gross disbursements) for infrastructure amounted to USD 68.2 billion, up from USD 61 billion in 2015 (+11%). However, as a share of total official flows, these dropped from 21% in 2015 to 17% in 2022. For LDCs, total official flows for infrastructure was USD 12.85 billion, up from USD 8.33 billion in 2015 (UN, 2024[25]). SDG indicator 17.17.1 Amount of US dollars committed to public-private partnerships for infrastructure. No data available since 2016. Development finance by public development banks *See Annex 2.A for more information on the role of public development banks in financing sustainability.*

AAAA paragraph	Commitment	Specific target or objective	Matching Sustainable Development Goal (SDG) target (where available)	State of implementation or progress made since 2015, using selected SDG or other relevant indicator (proxy)
76	Support multi-stakeholder partnerships.	No	Target 17.16 Enhance the Global Partnership for Sustainable Development, complemented by multi-stakeholder partnerships that mobilise and share knowledge, expertise, technology and financial resources to support the achievement of the SDGs in all countries, in particular developing countries.	SDG indicator 17.16.1 Number of countries reporting progress in multi-stakeholder development effectiveness monitoring frameworks that support the achievement of the SDGs. In 2018, 56 out of the 114 countries involved in consecutive assessments of effective development co-operation (36 of them recipients and 20 of them providers) had made overall progress in strengthening the effectiveness of multi-stakeholder partnerships for implementing the 2030 Agenda (UN, 2024[26]). In 2024, only one in five recipient countries with newly available assessments has shown overall progress in strengthening the effectiveness of these partnerships for development (UN, 2024[26]).
77	Support multi-stakeholder health partnerships such as Gavi and the Global Fund. Recognise the leadership of the World Health Organization (WHO) in international health co-ordination. Enhance global and national health systems, increase health financing, and strengthen the health workforce in developing countries. Support the implementation of the WHO Framework Convention on Tobacco Control and innovative funding for women and children's health, including the Global Financing Facility's contributions.	No	Target 3.8 Achieve universal health coverage, including financial risk protection, access to quality essential healthcare services, and access to safe, effective, quality and affordable essential medicines and vaccines for all. Target 3.a Strengthen the implementation of the WHO Framework Convention on Tobacco Control in all countries as appropriate. Target 3.b Support the research and development of vaccines and medicines for the communicable and non-communicable diseases that primarily affect developing countries and provide access to affordable essential medicines and vaccines in accordance with the Doha Declaration on the TRIPS Agreement and Public Health, which affirms the right of developing countries to use to the full the provisions in	SDG indicator 3.8.1 Coverage of essential health services. The universal health coverage service coverage reached 68% in 2021, up from 65% in 2015 (UN, 2024[25]). SDG indicator 3.8.2 Proportion of population with large household expenditures on health as a share of total household expenditure or income. In 2019, the proportion of population with large household expenditures on health (greater than 25%) as a share of total household expenditure or income was 3.8%, compared with 3.3% in 2015. The proportion of population with large household expenditures on health (greater than 10%) as a share of total household expenditure or income was 13.5%, compared with 12.7% in 2015 (UN, 2024[25]). SDG indicator 3.a.1 Age-standardised prevalence of current tobacco use among persons aged 15 years and older. The age-standardised prevalence of current tobacco use among persons aged 15 and older, both sexes, was 20.9% in 2022 versus 23.9% in 2015 (UN, 2024[25]). SDG indicator 3.b.2 Total net ODA to medical research and basic health sectors. The total net ODA disbursements to medical research and basic health sectors was USD 21.1 billion in 2022, compared with USD 10.5 billion in 2015. For LDCs, total net ODA for medical research and basic health sectors amounted to USD 6.4 billion in 2022, up from USD 4.9 billion in 2015 (UN, 2024[25]).

AAAA paragraph	Commitment	Specific target or objective	Matching Sustainable Development Goal (SDG) target (where available)	State of implementation or progress made since 2015, using selected SDG or other relevant indicator (proxy)
			the Agreement on Trade-Related Aspects of Intellectual Property Rights regarding flexibilities to protect public health and, in particular, provide access to medicines for all. Target 3.c Substantially increase health financing and the recruitment, development, training and retention of the health workforce in developing countries, especially in LDCs and SIDS.	SDG indicator 3.c.1 Health worker density and distribution. In 2021, health worker density in the world, by type of occupation, was 17.3 per 10 000 population for physicians but in LDCs was just 2.8 per 10 000 population. Though a recent study indicates that the projected global shortage of health workers by 2030 has decreased from 18 million to 10 million, the ageing world population is increasing health needs and further widening this gap. To maintain the current age-standardised density of health workers, an additional 1.8 million health workers are required across 54 countries, predominantly high-income countries. Data from 2014-22 show that Europe has the highest densities of medical doctors and dentists, with 40.4 and 6.9 per 10 000 population, respectively; North America leads in nursing and midwifery personnel and pharmacists, with 117.2 and 9.7 per 10 000 population, respectively. In contrast, sub-Saharan Africa has the lowest health worker densities, with just 2.3 medical doctors and11.6 nursing and midwifery personnel per 10 000 population, and fewer than 1 dentist and pharmacist per 10 000 population (UN, 2024[43]).
78	Provide quality education for all children. Ensure free, equitable and inclusive education from early childhood to secondary school. Strengthen initiatives such as the Global Partnership for Education. Increase the number of qualified teachers, particularly in developing countries and SIDS.	No	Target 4.1 By 2030, ensure that all girls and boys complete free, equitable and quality primary and secondary education leading to relevant and effective learning outcomes. Target 4.2 By 2030, ensure that all girls and boys have access to quality early childhood development, care and pre-primary education so that they are ready for primary education. Target 4.b By 2020, substantially expand globally the number of scholarships available to developing countries – in particular LDCs, SIDS and African countries – for enrolment in higher education, including vocational training, information and communications	SDG indicator 4.b.1 Volume of ODA flows for scholarships, by sector and type of study. The volume of ODA (gross disbursements) for scholarships amounted to USD 1.67 billion in 2022 compared with USD 1.39 billion in 2015 (UN, 2024[44]). SDG indicator 4.c.1 Proportion of teachers with the minimum required qualifications, by education level. In 2022, 15% of teachers were still not trained according to their country's national minimum standards, showing no progress since 2015. Significant disparities exist between regions: in sub-Saharan Africa, only 70% of teachers meet the national minimum qualification standards compared with 88% in Eastern and South-Eastern Asia (UN, 2024[44]). ODA in support of education Bilateral ODA commitments in support of education increased from USD 13.6 in 2015 to USD 14.4 in 2022 (OECD, 2024[45]).

AAAA paragraph	Commitment	Specific target or objective	Matching Sustainable Development Goal (SDG) target (where available)	State of implementation or progress made since 2015, using selected SDG or other relevant indicator (proxy)
			technology, and technical, engineering and scientific programmes in developed countries and other developing countries. Target 4.c By 2030, substantially increase the supply of qualified teachers, including through international co-operation, for teacher training in developing countries, especially LDCs and SIDS.	

Notes: The data points are mainly drawn from the UN's Sustainable Development Goals Extended Report 2024 and its statistical annexes. Trend data in are in constant USD 2015 prices unless otherwise indicated. 1. Based on data provided by International Forum on TOSSD.

References

COP29 (2024), *Breakthrough in Baku delivers $1.3 trillion 'Baku Finance Goal' with new core finance goal of $300 billion*, https://cop29.az/en/media-hub/news/breakthrough-in-baku-delivers-13tn-baku-finance-goal. [21]

Global Partnership for Effective Development Co-operation (n.d.), *The Global Partnership and SDG Target 17.15*, https://www.effectivecooperation.org/system/files/2023-06/SDG%2017.15.pdf. [29]

Green climate fund (2024), *Green climate fund*, https://www.greenclimate.fund/gcf-2. [33]

Integrated National Financing Frameworks (2024), *Making finance work for for people and planet: How countries are building their sustainable finance ecosystem through integrated national financing frameworks*, https://inff.org/resource/making-finance-work-for-people-and-planet-how-countries-are-building-their-sustainable-finance-ecosystem-through-integrated-national-financing-frameworks. [24]

International Forum on Total Official Support for Sustainable Development (2024), "About the data", *Total Official Support for Sustainable Development*, https://tossd.online/about (accessed on 30 November 2024). [8]

MIGA (2023), *Annual Report 2023*, Multilateral Investment Guarantee Agency, https://www.miga.org/sites/default/files/multilingual/2023-10/MIGA_AnnualReport2023_interior_toprint_R10.pdf. [42]

OECD (2025), *Modernising official development assistance (ODA)*, https://www.oecd.org/content/oecd/en/topics/sub-issues/oda-standards/modernising-official-development-assistance-oda.html (accessed on 25 January 2025). [27]

OECD (2024), *Biodiversity and Development Finance 2015-2022: Contributing to Target 19 of the Kunming-Montreal Global Biodiversity Framework*, OECD Publishing, Paris, https://doi.org/10.1787/d26526ad-en. [19]

OECD (2024), *Climate Finance Provided and Mobilised by Developed Countries in 2013-2022*, Climate Finance and the USD 100 Billion Goal, OECD Publishing, Paris, https://doi.org/10.1787/19150727-en. [17]

OECD (2024), *Development co-operation for a sustainable ocean economy in 2022: A snapshot*, https://one.oecd.org/document/DCD%282024%2921/en/pdf. [7]

OECD (2024), *Development Co-operation Report 2024: Tackling Poverty and Inequalities through the Green Transition*, OECD Publishing, Paris, https://doi.org/10.1787/357b63f7-en (accessed on 29 November 2024). [10]

OECD (2024), *Development Finance for Gender Equality 2024*, OECD Publishing, Paris, https://doi.org/10.1787/e340afbf-en. [15]

OECD (2024), *Multilateral Development Finance 2024*, OECD Publishing, Paris, https://doi.org/10.1787/8f1e2b9b-en. [47]

OECD (2024), *OECD Data Explorer, Aid activities targeting Global Environmental Objectives (dataset)*, http://data-explorer.oecd.org/s/m. [18]

OECD (2024), *OECD Data Explorer, Country programmable aid (CPA)*, http://data-explorer.oecd.org/s/1p. [46]

OECD (2024), *OECD Data Explorer, Creditor Reporting System (database)*, http://data-explorer.oecd.org/s/c. [2]

OECD (2024), *OECD Data Explorer, DAC 1 table (database)*, http://data-explorer.oecd.org/s/1c. [1]

OECD (2024), *OECD Data Explorer, DAC 2a table (database)*, http://data-explorer.oecd.org/s/w. [3]

OECD (2024), *OECD Data Explorer, DAC 3a table (database)*, http://data-explorer.oecd.org/s/y. [5]

OECD (2024), *OECD Data Explorer, DAC 5 table (database)*, http://data-explorer.oecd.org/s/u. [45]

OECD (2024), "Sustainability-linked bonds: How to make them work in developing countries, and how donors can help", *OECD Development Perspectives*, No. 44, OECD Publishing, Paris, https://doi.org/10.1787/7ca58c00-en. [14]

OECD (2023), *Development Co-operation Report 2023: Debating the Aid System*, OECD Publishing, Paris, https://doi.org/10.1787/f6edc3c2-en (accessed on 29 November 2024). [9]

OECD (2023), *Green, social and sustainability bonds in developing countries: the case for increased donor co-ordination*, OECD Publishing, Paris, https://www.oecd.org/content/dam/oecd/en/publications/reports/2023/06/green-social-and-sustainability-bonds-in-developing-countries_2c108396/1cce4551-en.pdf. [41]

OECD (2023), "Private finance mobilised by official development finance intervention", *OECD Development Perspectives*, No. 29, OECD Publishing, Paris, https://doi.org/10.1787/c5fb4a6c-en. [12]

OECD (2022), *Global Outlook on Financing for Sustainable Development 2023: No Sustainability Without Equity*, OECD Publishing, Paris, https://doi.org/10.1787/fcbe6ce9-en. [16]

OECD (2020), *Sustainable Ocean for All: Harnessing the Benefits of Sustainable Ocean Economies for Developing Countries*, The Development Dimension, OECD Publishing, Paris, https://doi.org/10.1787/bede6513-en. [20]

OECD (n.d.), *Conflict and fragility (webpage)*, https://www.oecd.org/en/topics/sub-issues/conflict-and-fragility.html. [38]

OECD (n.d.), *Tax treatment of official development assistance*, https://www.oecd.org/en/topics/policy-issues/tax-and-development/tax-treatment-of-official-development-assistance.html (accessed on 2024). [31]

OECD/UNDP (2019), *Making Development Co-operation More Effective: 2019 Progress Report*, OECD Publishing, Paris, https://doi.org/10.1787/26f2638f-en. [11]

TOSSD (2024), *TOSSD data visualisation tool*, International Forum on Total Official Support for Sustainable Development, https://tossd.online/ (accessed on 29 November 2024). [4]

UN (2024), *COP29 UN Climate Conference Agrees to Triple Finance to Developing Countries, Protecting Lives and Livelihoods*, https://unfccc.int/news/cop29-un-climate-conference-agrees-to-triple-finance-to-developing-countries-protecting-lives-and. [22]

UN (2024), *Financing for Sustainable Development Report 2024: Financing for Development at a Crossroads*, United Nations Department Social and Economic Affairs, Financing for Sustainable Development Office, New York, https://desapublications.un.org/publications/financing-sustainable-development-report-2024 (accessed on 20 November 2024). [30]

UN (2024), *History of the MVI*, United Nations Office of the High Representative for the Least Developed Countries, Landlocked Developing Countries and Small Island Developing States, https://www.un.org/ohrlls/mvi/history-of-mvi (accessed on 29 November 2024). [23]

UN (2024), *Progress Towards the Sustainable Development Goals - Report of the Secretary-General: Statistical Annex*, United Nations Economic and Social Council, New York, https://unstats.un.org/sdgs/files/report/2024/E_2024_54_Statistical_Annex_I_and_II.pdf. [25]

UN (2024), *SDGs - Extended Report*, United Nations Statistics Division, New York, https://unstats.un.org/sdgs/report/2024/extended-report/ (accessed on 29 November 2024). [28]

UN (2024), *The Sustainable Development Goals Extended Report 2024*, United Nations Statistical Commission, New York, https://unstats.un.org/sdgs/report/2024/extended-report/Extended-Report_Goal-17.pdf. [6]

UN (2024), *The Sustainable Development Goals Extended Report 2024*, United Nations Statistical Commission, New York, https://unstats.un.org/sdgs/report/2024/extended-report/Extended-Report_Goal-13.pdf. [34]

UN (2024), *The Sustainable Development Goals Extended Report 2024: Goal 10*, United Nations Statistical Commission, New York, https://unstats.un.org/sdgs/report/2024/extended-report/Extended-Report_Goal-10.pdf. [39]

UN (2024), *The Sustainable Development Goals Extended Report 2024: Goal 11*, United Nations Statistical Commission, New York, https://unstats.un.org/sdgs/report/2024/extended-report/Extended-Report_Goal-11.pdf. [35]

UN (2024), *The Sustainable Development Goals Extended Report 2024: Goal 11*, United Nations Statistical Commission, New York, https://unstats.un.org/sdgs/report/2024/extended-report/Extended-Report_Goal-11.pdf. [36]

UN (2024), *The Sustainable Development Goals Extended Report 2024: Goal 17*, United Nations Statistical Commission, New York, https://unstats.un.org/sdgs/report/2024/extended-report/Extended-Report_Goal-17.pdf. [26]

UN (2024), *The Sustainable Development Goals Extended Report 2024: Goal 3*, United Nations Statistical Commission, New York, https://unstats.un.org/sdgs/report/2024/extended-report/Extended-Report_Goal-3.pdf. [43]

UN (2024), *The Sustainable Development Goals Extended Report 2024: Goal 4*, United Nations Statistical Commission, New York, https://unstats.un.org/sdgs/report/2024/extended-report/Extended-Report_Goal-4.pdf. [44]

UNFCCC (2024), *Draft text on SBI 60 agenda item 11: Matters relating to the least developed countries*, https://unfccc.int/sites/default/files/resource/LDC_matters_SBI60.pdf. [37]

United Nations Department of Economic and Social Affairs (2023), *United Nations Guidelines on the Tax Treatment of Government-to-Government Aid Projects*, United Nations, https://doi.org/10.18356/9789210001083. [32]

World Bank (2024), *Green, Social, Sustainability, and Sustainability-Linked (GSSS) Bonds Market Update, July 2024*, https://thedocs.worldbank.org/en/doc/dacb969cc71f53abde2d2758f1cc13ed-0340012024/original/GSSS-Quarterly-Newsletter-Issue-No-8.pdf. [13]

World Bank (2024), *Green, Social, Sustainability, and Sustainability-Linked (GSSS) Bonds: Market Update – April 2024*, https://thedocs.worldbank.org/en/doc/2fa215f2779f95d970ef0601aa551cbc-0340012024/original/GSSS-Quarterly-Newsletter-Issue-No-7.pdf. [40]

Notes

[1] The headline total for ODA in 2023 is on a grant equivalent basis. The change in ODA volume since 2015 is based on net ODA figures.

[2] The amounts include ODA from non-DAC providers that report to the OECD Creditor Reporting System (CRS) and estimates of ODA from non-DAC providers that do not report to the CRS. (OECD, 2024[38]). Non-DAC providers that report to the CRS are Azerbaijan, Bulgaria, Croatia, Cyprus, Israel, Kazakhstan, Kuwait, Latvia, Liechtenstein, Malta, Monaco, Qatar, Romania, Saudi Arabia, Chinese Taipei, Thailand, Timor-Leste, Republic of Türkiye, and United Arab Emirates. Estimates were made for the following non-DAC providers: Argentina, People's Republic of China, India and South Africa.

[3] Estimate based on total ODA provided by DAC members and average DAC ODA/GNI in 2023 (0.37%).

[4] The grant equivalent accounting has made the measurement of ODA more objective and transparent and corrected previous flaws from use of the cash flow system. The new discount rates for official loans (between 6% and 9%) are also lower and more realistic than the discount rate (10%) applicable prior to the reform. All details of ODA data are available for public scrutiny. ODA data are still collected and published on a flow basis in addition to the grant equivalent system for the sake of transparency and comparability. See the https://web-archive.oecd.org/temp/2023-11-13/395130-modernisation-dac-statistical-system.htm.

[5] The countries that adopted a 0.7% or higher ODA to GNI target as of 2022 include: Austria, Belgium, Denmark, Finland, France, Germany, Iceland, Ireland, Italy, Luxembourg, Netherlands, New Zealand, Norway, Portugal, Spain, Sweden.

[6] The DAC and non-DAC countries that have achieved the 0.7% ODA/GNI target for one year or more since 2015 are Denmark, Kuwait, Germany, Luxembourg, Netherlands, Norway, Saudi Arabia, Sweden, Türkiye, United Arab Emirates and the United Kingdom.

[7] The term "mobilisation" describes the causal link between private finance made available for a specific project and an official intervention.

[8] The total is obtained by applying a 40% coefficient on a portion of data as having a significant objective (i.e. Biodiversity-specific ODF).

[9] The 1978 DAC Recommendation on the Terms and Conditions of Aid called on adherents to ensure an 86% grant element for all developing countries and 90% for LDCs. However, the Recommendation refers to the definition of ODA as it stood before 2014, including to a discount rate of 10% for calculating the grant element instead of discount rates differentiated by income group.

[10] See the 2024 DAC Working Party on Development Finance Statistics, https://one.oecd.org/document/DCD/DAC/STAT(2024)21/en/pdf.

5 International Trade as an Engine for Development

This chapter reviews the Trade as an Engine of Development action area of the Addis Ababa Action Agenda (AAAA) including progress, persistent challenges, and emerging areas as the international community prepares for the Fourth International Conference on Financing for Development (FfD4). It finds that South-South trade has surged, underpinned by digitalisation and regional integration, while trade facilitation measures have significantly reduced costs. However, the share of global trade in developing countries has stagnated since the 2010s, hindered by crises, decoupling, and technical barriers. LDCs face persistent challenges, including limited diversification, high tariffs, and the impacts of environmental norms. Emerging trends highlight trade's role in digital, environmental, and social transitions, with Aid for Trade increasingly aligned to Sustainable Development Goals.

5.1. Data dashboard

Key trends

The volume of global trade has grown, but the relative share of developing countries has remained stable.

Between 2015-23, total trade in goods and services increased by USD 10 trillion, or about 50%, up from USD 21 trillion in 2015 to USD 31 trillion in 2022 and down slightly to USD 30 trillion in 2023. At same time, the trade to gross domestic product ratio has remained stable at about 29.1% in 2023, comparable to the 2008 ratio of 29.6% (D'Andrea et al., 2024[1]). Least developed countries (LDCs) still represent only 1.0% of global trade and small island developing states (SIDS) just 3.2% (UNCTAD, 2024[2]).

Figure 5.1. Share of global exports

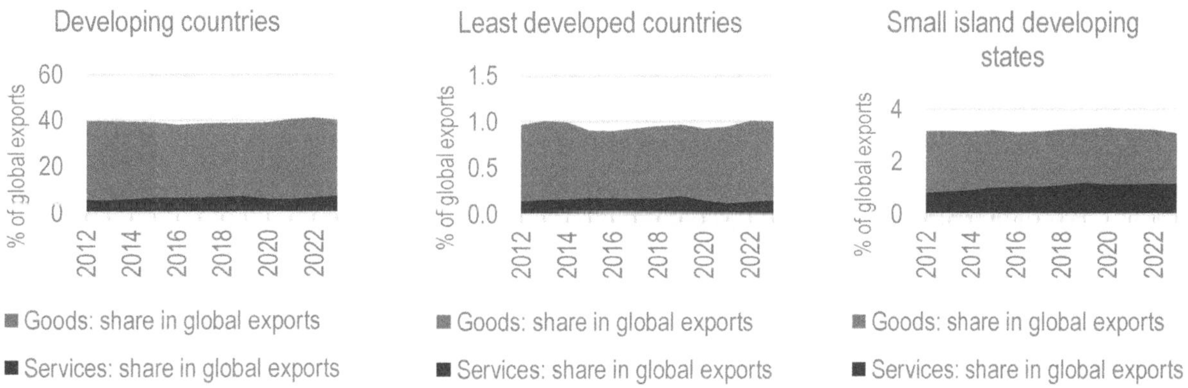

Source: UNCTAD (2024[2]), data available at: SDG Pulse, 2024, https://sdgpulse.unctad.org/trade-developing-economies/.

The global trade financing gap is widening.

The global trade finance gap, defined as the difference between requests and approvals for financing to support imports and exports, is now estimated to be USD 2.5 trillion annually, a substantial increase from 2016 and 2018 estimates of USD 1.5 trillion annually (ADB, 2023[3]).

Figure 5.2. Global trade finance gap

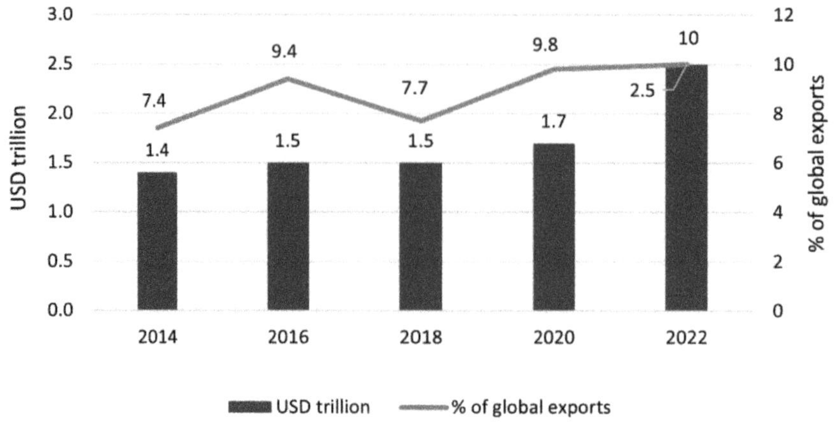

Source: ADB (2023[3]), "2023 Trade Finance Gaps, Growth and Jobs Survey", https://www.adb.org/publications/2023-trade-finance-gaps-growth-jobs-survey and WTO (2024[4]), Trade and tariff data, https://www.wto.org/english/res_e/statis_e/statis_e.htm.

Aid for Trade is growing but support to LDCs remains insufficient.

The total volume of Aid for Trade disbursements and the volume of support to LDCs reached a record of USD 51 billion and USD 14 billion (29% of the total) in 2022. Since the initiative was created in 2006, Aid for Trade disbursements have cumulated USD 689 billion, with 56% in economic infrastructure, 42% to build productive capacity, and 2% for trade policy and regulations. Of this total, USD 189 billion in disbursements went to LDCs and other low-income countries.

Figure 5.3. Aid for Trade disbursements and commitments, 2002-22

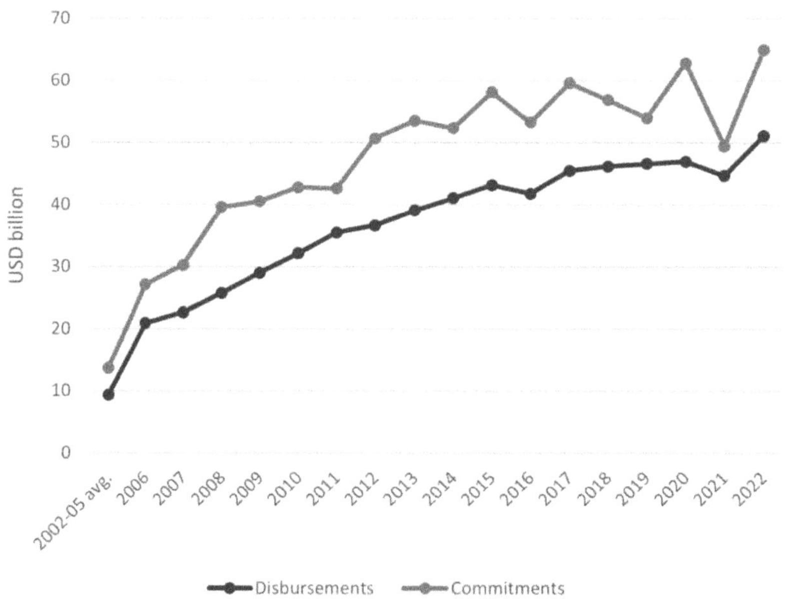

Source: Author's calculations based on OECD/WTO (2024[5]), Aid for Trade at a Glance 2024, https://doi.org/10.1787/7a4e356a-en.

Key performance indicators

↔	In 2022, Aid for Trade support to LDCs reached a record USD 14 billion in disbursements but represented a smaller share of total Aid for Trade than in 2021[1], which was at odds with the goal of doubling Aid for Trade disbursements to LDCs from 2018 levels by 2031.
↔	From 2012 to 2023, LDCs' share of global trade hovered at about 1% – far from the target of 2% (UNCTAD, 2024[2]).
↔	Digitally delivered services in LDCs have increased by 44% since 2015 though in the rest of the world, these services increased by 100% over the same period. As of 2024, the volume of digitally delivered services in LDCs is 73% smaller than the global average volume[2] (UNCTAD, 2024[2]).
↔	For 84 of 135 countries, the worldwide weighted average tariff under preferential status decreased over the period from 2015 to 2022.[3]

↓ Slight setback	↓ Setback	↔ No change, neutral	↔ Stagnant, possible issue	↑ Major progress	↑ Minimal progress
↓ Minimal setback	↓ Major setback	↔ Holding steady, slight concern	↔ Negative stagnation, concerning	↑ Progress	↑ Negligible progress or progress contested

Note: Selected quantifiable commitments. Annex Table 5.A.1 contains the full list.
1. Author's calculations based on OECD/WTO (2024[5]), Aid for Trade at a Glance 2024, https://doi.org/10.1787/7a4e356a-en.
2. Authors' calculations based on https://public.tableau.com/app/profile/tinotenda.mataire/viz/Digitallydeliveredservices/Dashboard2.
3. Authors calculations based on UN DESA (2024[6]) SDG Indicator database, https://unstats.un.org/sdgs/dataportal/database.

Resource mobilisation potential

- LDCs represent 1% of global trade, though they are home to 14% of the world's population. Doubling their share of trade to 2% could generate USD 230 billion per year.
- It is predicted that the African Continental Free Trade Area (AfCFTA) will increase African countries' trade income by USD 450 billion by 2035 and boost intra-African trade by more than 81% (Baker McKenzie, 2024[7]).
- The value of green exports from Africa such as green hydrogen, critical minerals and export credits could reach over USD 15 billion annually by 2050 (McKinsey & Company, 2024[8]).
- Trade increases women's wages and economic equality. Removing import tariffs would produce average real income gains for households headed by women that are 2.5% higher than for households headed by men. In Burkina Faso and Cameroon, for instance, such an increase for women-headed households would be equivalent to one year's spending on education or health (Rocha and Piermartini, 2023[9]). Reduction of gender-biased or so-called pink tariffs could reduce average tariffs by 6 percentage points in some countries (World Bank Group and World Trade Organisation, 2018[10]).

5.2. Key areas of progress

Developing countries have been the main driver of global trade growth.

Trade growth has been largely driven by trade between developing countries. Trade between developing countries as a share of global trade rose from 9.8% in 1995 to 24.6% in 2022. It represented 54% of all developing countries' exports. Developing countries also are increasingly integrated into the global economy, with backward and forward global value chain (GVC) participation rates increasing from 25.2% of total exports in 1995 to 44.6% in 2015 and 48.7% in 2022. These increases translated into a tripling of trade in intermediary goods since 2000 (UN, 2024[11]). Services trade has become a source of strong growth for developing countries in combination with digital trade opportunities. For instance, digitally delivered services exports doubled over 2005-15 and doubled again from 2015-23. After two decades of strong growth, however, the developing country share of world trade remained flat in the 2010s and early 2020s at about 40% and at 30% for services (UNCTAD, 2024[2]).

Regional trade integration between and with developing countries has progressed along with trade flows. South-South trade increased from USD 600 billion in 1995 to USD 5.3 trillion in 2021, and its volume now exceeds that of North-South trade and is growing faster than the world average (UNCTAD, 2023[12]). By eliminating barriers to trade in Africa, the AfCFTA could lift 30 million people out of extreme poverty and another 68 million people out of moderate poverty (African Union, 2024[13]).Interregional trade today, especially in developing countries, is often underestimated by official data sources. For example, the actual scale of interregional food trade in West Africa is much higher than reported in official statistics due to a substantial portion which occurs informally and goes unrecorded.

Helped by improved trade facilitation, tariffs and trade costs continue to decline.

It is estimated that full implementation of the World Trade Organization (WTO) Trade Facilitation Agreement (TFA), which entered into force in 2017, could reduce trade costs by an average of 14.3% and boost global trade by up to USD 1 trillion per year, with the biggest gains in the poorest countries (World Trade Organization, 2015[14]). As of 2024, implementation of TFA commitments is at 80.2% globally;74.1% for all developing countries; and 49% for LDCs alone (World Trade Organization, 2024[15]).

After two decades of decreases, when tariffs fell from 13.1% in 1996 to 9.1% in 2015, the simple average most-favoured nation tariff applied by WTO members stood at 8.8% in 2022. In 2022, LDCs had duty-free access on 62.9% of tariff lines, a level that has been stable since 2015. SIDS enjoyed duty-free access on 74.3% of product lines in 2022, a 12% increase from 2015 (UNCTAD, 2024[16]). However, tariffs applied in LDCs (including preferences) are seven times higher than those in developed regions (UNCTAD, 2024[16]).

Trade costs have been generally declining. For example, the tariff weighted average in LDCs has declined from 10.6% (most favoured nation) and 8.7% (including preferences), in 2015 to 9.2% and 7%, respectively, in 2022 (UN, 2024[17]).

The WTO's 2022 Agreement on Fisheries Subsidies aims to reduce the approximately USD 22 billion spent annually on harmful subsidies, thereby showcasing the potential of trade reform to redirect resources effectively (UN, 2024[11]). In 2023 and 2024, 52 WTO members ratified the agreement (World Trade Organization, 2024[18]).

Supporting developing countries' trade capacities through untying

One of the objectives of the DAC Recommendation on Untying Official Development Assistance (ODA) is to contribute to the integration of developing countries in GVCs by giving local companies access to ODA contracts and by promoting local procurement. In 2021-22, suppliers from developing countries were awarded 53% of the total number of untied contracts funded by DAC donors and 38% of the total in terms of value.

5.3. Persistent challenging areas

Developing countries have been increasingly marginalised in global trade amid the turmoil following the global financial crisis and the COVID-19 pandemic.

The 2008-09 global financial crisis and, more recently, COVID-19 pandemic-related trade tensions put an end to the rapid growth of the developing country share of global trade, which had been driven by the extension of GVCs and trade in intermediate goods in the early 2000s. Since the COVID-19 crisis, risks of decoupling have increased, with blocks experiencing 4%-6% lower growth in trade than internal trade within blocks (World Trade Organization, 2023[19]). Friend-shoring has risen by 6% since 2021. Near-shoring has shown stability with no clear trend observed, but trade concentration has increased by 5% over 2021 (UN, 2024[11]).

Technical barriers are increasing and affect 70% of all trade (UNCTAD, 2024[16]). Potentially trade-distortive state interventions surged after the pandemic and added to historical forms of subsidies. For example, agricultural support measures peaked at USD 851 billion in 2022 in high-income and emerging countries, hindering the competitiveness of LDCs and their global trade participation (OECD, 2023[20]). The growing use of government subsidies by large (OECD and non-OECD) economies to promote strategic industries also will likely undermine the trade competitiveness of most developing (and non-developing) countries that do not have the same fiscal space to compete subsidy with subsidy. It is for this reason that the International Monetary Fund, the OECD, the World Bank and the WTO have called for a co-ordinated approach towards subsidies (IMF; OECD; World Bank; World Trade Organization, 2022[21]).

The establishment of new environmental norms in advanced economies may also negatively impact developing countries' export capacities. For example, a study by the African Climate Foundation (2023[22]) of the impact of the European Union (EU) Carbon Border Adjustment Mechanism estimated it could result in a decrease in African exports to the EU of as much as 3.1% to 13.9% depending on the sector. Sectors in several countries, such as the cacao sector in Côte d'Ivoire and the coffee sector in Ethiopia are already impacted by the transition cost (Hochet-Bodin, 2024[23]). While such new norms in advanced countries aim to achieve legitimate environmental objectives, developing countries need additional support to cope with the adjustment cost (African Climate Foundation, 2023[22]).

Certain groups remain marginalised in international trade.

Fast-growing developing countries have driven the expansion of both trade and investment, but this growth has largely bypassed the poorest countries (OECD, 2023[20]). In 2021, the value of LDCs' services exports was 32% below pre-pandemic levels, reflecting the ongoing impacts of the crisis in these countries (UN, 2024[24]). Disparities in trade also persist. Male entrepreneurs are almost twice as likely as female entrepreneurs to internationalise (Korinek, Mourougane and Lieshout, 2023[25]), and tariffs continue to disproportionately affect sectors employing women and products consumed by women (World Bank Group and World Trade Organisation, 2018[10]).

Developing countries' exports remain poorly diversified and with low value-added.

In 2022, the exports concentration index of developing economies stood at 0.10 (and at 0.22 for LDCs and 0.26 for landlocked developing countries), which was notably higher than the 0.07 concentration index of developed economies. On average, about 65%% of the exports of LDCs and SIDS were directed to their top ten trading partners compared with 55% for developing countries as a group. In 2022, manufactured goods accounted for 66% of total merchandise exports from developing economies, up from 58% in 2012. Although the share of manufactured goods in total exports of LDCs increased from 22% in 2012 to 35% in 2022, LDCs' merchandise exports are largely focused on simple manufactured products such as textiles and clothing (UNCTAD, 2024[2]).

The reform of the multilateral trading system is still ongoing.

WTO members committed at the 2022 Ministerial Conference, and reaffirmed this commitment in the Abu Dhabi Ministerial Declaration in 2024, to work towards necessary reform of the WTO to improve all its functions and to acknowledge the progress made in this regard. The General Council will report progress at the 2025 Ministerial Conference on the work done to date to improve the daily functioning of WTO councils, committees and negotiating groups with a view to enhancing the WTO's efficiency and effectiveness and facilitate members' participation in WTO work. WTO members also are holding discussions aimed at having a fully and well-functioning dispute settlement system accessible to all members.

5.4. New and emerging areas

Trade is a driver of the triple transition (digital, environmental and social) and has an increasing role to play in sustainable development.

Trade and digital transformation

Digital connectivity has been crucial in cutting trade costs. A 1% increase in digital connectivity lowers domestic trade costs by 0.3% and international trade costs by 0.1%. Aid for Trade has significantly boosted information and communication technology support, with disbursements up 31% since 2020 and commitments having nearly doubled over five years (OECD/WTO, 2024[5]). Globally, exports of digitally delivered services nearly quadrupled since 2005, hitting USD 3.9 trillion in 2022 to represent 54% of total global services exports and surpassing growth in goods and other services exports (Botwright and Dabré, 2024[26]).

Trade and environmental transformation

In 2021-22, bilateral donors committed USD 20 billion to climate-related Aid for Trade, which accounted for 67% of total pledges. Pledges for mitigation projects increased by 18% but slightly declined for adaptation efforts. In 2021-22, 80% of Aid for Trade focused on mitigation, suggesting room for more adaptation funding (OECD/WTO, 2024[5]). Demand for critical minerals for clean energy is increasing and could potentially cause shortages. African countries, with 30% of global mineral reserves, aim to use the AfCFTA to build regional value chains and boost economic development (Botwright and Dabré, 2024[26]). Trade agreements increasingly include sustainability considerations – for instance the 2024 Agreement on Climate Change, Trade and Sustainability – although the harmonisation of standards and carbon border adjustment mechanisms remains a challenging issue.

Trade and social transformation

In the Abu Dhabi Ministerial Declaration, WTO members reiterated the centrality of the development dimension in the work of the WTO and the role that the multilateral trading system could play in contributing to achievement of the Sustainable Development Goals (SDGs). Aid for Trade projects target all SDGs: SDG 9 (industry, innovation and infrastructure) attracted the largest amount of Aid for Trade disbursements, followed by SDG 7 (affordable and clean energy), SDG 2 (zero hunger), SDG 11 (sustainable cities and communities), and SDG 8 (decent work and economic growth) (OECD/WTO, 2024[5]). A number of social and technological innovations can take place in GVCs, which could be made more resilient through adequate policies (Schwellnus, Haramboure and Samek, 2023[27]).

Annex 5.A. International Trade as an Engine for Development

Annex Table 5.A.1. Assessment of the action area: International trade as an engine for development

AAAA paragraph	Commitment	Specific target or objective	Matching Sustainable Development Goal (SDG) target (where available)	State of implementation or progress made since 2015, using SDG or other relevant indicator (proxy)
79	Promote a universal, rules-based, open, transparent, predictable, inclusive, non-discriminatory and equitable multilateral trading system under the World Trade Organization (WTO) as well as meaningful trade liberalisation.	No	Target 17.10 Promote a universal, rules-based, open, non-discriminatory and equitable multilateral trading system under the WTO, including through the conclusion of negotiations under its Doha Development Agenda (DDA).	SDG Indicator 17.10.1 Worldwide weighted tariff average In 2022, the global average tariff applied on all products was 3.1% (most-favoured nation) or 1.8% (including preferences) compared with.3.8% and 2.8%, respectively, in 2015. The average tariff was three times higher in least developed countries (LDCs) at 9.2% and 7%, respectively, in 2022 compared with 10.6% and 8.7%, respectively, in 2015 (UN, 2024[17]). Import and export restrictiveness and multilateral and preferential trade liberalisation International trade has been largely liberalised owing to both zero most-favoured nation (MFN) tariffs and preferential duty-free access. As of 2022, about two-thirds of international trade is free of tariffs, but tariffs applied to the remaining third are often very high. Agricultural trade is largely free from tariffs due to preferential access, but remaining tariffs are fairly high (averaging almost 20%). Preferential access is also important for manufacturing products, for which the simple average tariff is at almost 10%. Preferential access is of limited importance in the case of natural resources as trade in this category is largely tariff free under MFN rates and remaining tariffs are generally low (simple average about 6%) (UNCTAD, 2023[28]). Non-tariff measures frequency and coverage International trade is highly regulated through the imposition of technical barriers to trade, with more than 30% of product lines and almost 70% of world trade affected. Price control measures affect about 15% of world trade. Sanitary and phytosanitary measures affect almost 20% of world trade. Export measures are also frequently applied to international trade, though their use is largely related to agriculture (UNCTAD, 2023[28]). Services Trade Restrictiveness Index (STRI), Digital STRI and foreign direct

AAAA paragraph	Commitment	Specific target or objective	Matching Sustainable Development Goal (SDG) target (where available)	State of implementation or progress made since 2015, using SDG or other relevant indicator (proxy)
				investment regulatory restrictiveness Barriers to services trade continue to be high across countries and sectors as these are influenced by global economic and geopolitical challenges and the introduction in recent years of new policies, among them the 2023 policies affecting the supply of services through commercial presence and foreign investment. In 2023, the average STRI and Digital STRI for OECD countries were 0.19 and 0.14, respectively, in a maximum of 1 (e.g. most trade restricted) (OECD, 2024[29]).
80	Implement all the decisions of the Bali Package, including on LDCs, small economies and the Trade Facilitation Agreement (TFA).	Yes Ratify the TFA.	n.a.	TFA rate of implementation commitments The TFA entered into force on 22 February 2017 following its ratification by two-thirds of the WTO membership. The global rate of implementation commitments is at 80.2% in 2024 (WTO, 2024[30]).
81	Expand WTO-compatible trade finance (and call on development banks to provide solutions).	No	n.a.	Trade finance gap (estimates only, which vary significantly; see Asian Development Bank, based on survey) The trade finance gap increased over 2014-22 from USD 1.4 trillion (7.4% of global exports) to USD 2.5 trillion (10.0% of global exports) (Asian Development Bank et al., 2023[31]).
82	Increase world trade in a manner compatible with the SDGs and integrate sustainable development into trade policy. Support fuller integration of LDCs, landlocked developing countries (LLDCs), small island developing states (SIDS) and Africa into regional and world markets.	Yes Double the share of LDCs in global exports by 2020.	Target 8.2 Achieve higher levels of economic productivity through diversification, technological upgrading and innovation, including through a focus on high value added- and labour-intensive sectors. Target 17.11 Significantly increase the exports of developing countries, in particular with a view to doubling the LDCs' share of global exports by 2020.	SDG Indicator 17.11.1 Developing countries' and LDCs' share of global exports. (SDG trade monitor) The developing country share of global exports of merchandises reached 44.4% in 2021, up from 42.1% in 2015. LDCs' share stood at 1.1% in 2022 compared with 0.9% in 2015 (ITC; UNCTAD, 2024[32]). World trade as share of GDP World trade as a share of GDP was 56.5% in 2021 compared with 56.1% in 2015 (World Integrated Trade Solution, 2024[33]).
83	Conclude the negotiations on the DDA. Combat protectionism in all its	Yes Conclude the	Target 2.B Correct and prevent trade restrictions and	SDG Indicator 2.B.1 Agricultural export subsidies Export subsidy outlays notified to the WTO have decreased significantly from USD

AAAA paragraph	Commitment	Specific target or objective	Matching Sustainable Development Goal (SDG) target (where available)	State of implementation or progress made since 2015, using SDG or other relevant indicator (proxy)
	forms (including discipline on subsidies in agriculture and fisheries). Accelerate accession of all developing countries engaged in negotiations.	Doha Development Agenda; accession of all developing countries engaged in negotiations.	distortions in world agricultural markets, including through the parallel elimination of all forms of agricultural export subsidies and all export measures with equivalent effect in accordance with the mandate of the Doha Development Round.	6.7 billion in 1999 to USD 33 million in 2022. As of January 2024, only LDCs and net food-importing developing countries can use certain forms of export subsidies (ITC; UNCTAD, 2024[34]). Record of unilateral commercial policy interventions (GTA database) In 2015, the Global Trade Alert (GTA) database recorded 343 trade-discriminatory state interventions, down from 1 941 in 2023 (Global Trade Alert, 2024[35]). List of WTO members and accessions list Since 2015, four developing countries have completed their WTO accession process: Seychelles (2015), Kazakhstan (2015), Liberia (2016) and Afghanistan (2016). In 2024, Comoros and Timor-Leste handed over their acceptance of the Protocol of Accession, and another 22 countries are still engaged in negotiations (WTO, 2024[36]). Negotiations on the DDA have stalled. Nonetheless, multilateral negotiations delivered a number of advances such as the Nairobi Package, the revision of the TRIPS Agreement (access to medicine), the COVID-19 package and the Agreement on Fisheries Subsidies.
84	Implement and monitor special and differential treatment in accordance with WTO rules.	No	Target 10.A Implement the principle of special and differential treatment for developing countries, in particular LDCs, in accordance with WTO agreements.	SDG Indicator 10.A.1 Proportion of tariff lines applied to imports from LDCs and developing countries with zero tariff The proportion of tariff lines applied to imports from LDCs has increased from 48.1% in 2005 to 62.9% in 2022; for other developing countries with zero tariff it has increased from 40.7% to 55.2% over the same period (UN, 2024[17]). SDG Indicator 10.A.(i) Share of exports admitted duty free (SDG trade monitor) The share of exports admitted duty free to developed regions stood at 75.4% in 2022 for all developing countries compared with 71.4% in 2015 (+4 percentage points). For LDCs, the share declined from 85.4% to 85.0% over the same period but increased for both SIDS and LLDCs from 87.3% to 95.2% and from 94.4% to 95.9%, respectively (ITC; UNCTAD, 2024[37]). In 2022, the share of duty-free products was overall 34.7% (versus 32.3% in 2015) for all developing countries and 39.1% (versus 35.7% in 2015) for LDCs. The shares varied considerably across sectors in all developing countries versus in LDCs: 29.8% (26.9% in 2015) and 37.5% (33.2% in 2015), respectively, for agriculture; 37.5%

AAAA paragraph	Commitment	Specific target or objective	Matching Sustainable Development Goal (SDG) target (where available)	State of implementation or progress made since 2015, using SDG or other relevant indicator (proxy)
				(35.7% in 2015) and 41.1% (38.2% in 2015), respectively, for industry; 63.4% (61.7% in 2015) for oil; 26.2% (23% in 2015) and 31.7% (27.2% in 2015), respectively, for textile; and 20% (15.6% in 2015) and 25.4% (20.4% in 2015), respectively, for clothing (ITC; UNCTAD, 2024[37]).
85	Implement duty-free, quota-free for LDCs; facilitate market access for LDCs (including rules of origin).	No	Target 17.12 Realise timely implementation of duty-free and quota-free market access on a lasting basis for all LDCs consistent with WTO decisions, including by ensuring that preferential rules of origin applicable to imports from LDCs are transparent and simple and contribute to facilitating market access.	SDG Indicator 17.12.1 Average tariffs faced by developing countries, LDCs and SIDS (SDG trade monitor) Between 2015-22, the average tariff faced (including preferences) in developing countries on all products dropped from 1.7% to 1.3% (i.e. by 0.44 percentage points). The decrease was faster in LDCs (from 3.1% to 2.4%, or -0.7 percentage points) but slower in LLDCs (from 1.7% to 1.3%), -0.34 percentage points) and in SIDS (from 0.52% to 0.32%, -0.2 percentage points) (ITC; UNCTAD, 2024[38]).
86	Accept TRIPS amendment on access to medicines.	Yes Adoption of TRIPS amendment.	n.a.	Adoption of the TRIPS amendment The TRIPS amendment entered into force in January 2017. More than 50 WTO members have adopted the necessary legislation to use the system for export, and according to informal estimates, the system now covers about 80% of current global medicines export capacity (WTO, n.d.[39]).
87	Strengthen regional co-operation and regional trade agreements and coherence and compatibility with WTO rules. Increase support to regional trade integration and integration of small and medium-sized enterprises into global value chains. Address gaps in trade, transport and transit-related regional infrastructure (including for LLDCs, LDCs and SIDS).	No	n.a.	Number of trade agreements in force (WTO RTAIS and COMTRADE) The number of preferential trade agreements (PTAs) in force has approximately doubled from less than 150 in 2005 to more than 350 in 2022. More than half of all trade agreements in force go beyond tariff concessions to cover services and behind-the-border measures. After 2015, the upward trend has been largely driven by new trade agreements covering both goods and services (UNCTAD, 2024[40]). Share of trade between parties of PTAs (WTO RTAIS and COMTRADE) Although the number of PTAs has significantly increased, the percentage of trade between countries that are part of PTAs has not increased as much. Overall, and without considering trade within the European Union, about one-third of world trade took place between countries that share a deep trade agreement (UNCTAD, 2024[40]). Aid for Trade to all economic infrastructure subcategories

AAAA paragraph	Commitment	Specific target or objective	Matching Sustainable Development Goal (SDG) target (where available)	State of implementation or progress made since 2015, using SDG or other relevant indicator (proxy)
				Aid for Trade disbursements to all economic infrastructure subcategories experienced significant growth over the 2020-22 period, including an increase of 34% for transport and storage (to close to USD 14 billion); 23% for energy generation and supply; and 31% for communications (OECD/WTO, 2024[5]). Aid for Trade to regional integration, transport, transit-related infrastructure, etc. (OECD CRS) In 2022, 12% of Aid for Trade projects were not country specific; 87% of partner country respondents to the 2024 Aid for Trade Global Review survey said they see regional integration as a priority for Aid for Trade and 54% of respondents identified regional integration as an area where Aid for Trade has an impact (OECD/WTO, 2024[5]).
88	Strengthen domestic enabling environments and implement sound domestic policies and reforms conducive to realising the potential of trade (role of UNCTAD).	No	n.a.	Aid for Trade to trade policy and regulation (OECD CRS) A total of 72% of respondents to the 2024 Aid for Trade Global Review survey reported they are seeking support in the broader trade policy and regulations category. However, in 2022, total disbursements for trade policies and regulations reached USD 900 million, down from USD 1.4 billion in 2021 and USD 1.2 billion in 2020. Commitments have also slightly decreased between 2021 and 2022 (OECD/WTO, 2024[5]).
89	Endorse the United Nations Commission on International Trade Law.	No	n.a.	n.a.
90	Acknowledge role of Aid for Trade and increase the share for LDCs including to address specific challenges of women and trade- and transit-related logistics technical assistance for LLDCs. (ref. to Enhanced Integrated Framework)	Yes Increase the share of Aid for Trade to LDCs.	Target 8.A Increase Aid for Trade support for developing countries, in particular LDCs, including through the Enhanced Integrated Framework for Trade-related Technical Assistance to Least Developed Countries.	SDG Indicator 8.A.1 Aid for Trade commitments and disbursements (SDG trade monitor) A total of USD 648 billion has been disbursed for Aid for Trade programmes since 2006. After a drop in 2021, both disbursements and commitments soared in 2022, reaching USD 51.1 billion and USD 65 billion, respectively (OECD/WTO, 2024[5]). Aid for Trade disbursements to LDCs reached USD 14 billion in 2022. However, progress remains insufficient to meet the commitments made in 2018 to significantly increase Aid for Trade with the objective of doubling support by 2031 from 2018 levels (OECD/WTO, 2024[5]). Aid for Trade to transports and logistics; Aid for Trade with impact on gender (OECD

AAAA paragraph	Commitment	Specific target or objective	Matching Sustainable Development Goal (SDG) target (where available)	State of implementation or progress made since 2015, using SDG or other relevant indicator (proxy)
				CRS) Average Aid for Trade commitments from bilateral donors including an objective to promote gender equality grew by 6 percentage points between 2019-20 and 2021-22, reaching 46% of total Aid for Trade commitments compared with about 32% in 2015-16 (OECD/WTO, 2024[5]).
91	Craft trade and investment agreements with appropriate safeguards so as not to constrain domestic policies and regulation in the public interest. Implement in a transparent manner and provide capacity building (role of UNCTAD).	No	n.a.	Aid for Trade to trade policy and regulation (OECD CRS) See para. 88.
92	Combat poaching and trafficking of protected species, trafficking in hazardous waste, and trafficking in minerals (including through capacity building and international co-operation).	No	n.a.	n.a.

Note: The data points are mainly drawn from the UN's Sustainable Development Goals Extended Report 2024 and its statistical annexes. Trend data in are in constant USD 2015 prices unless otherwise indicated.

References

ADB (2023), *2023 Trade Finance Gaps, Growth, and Jobs Survey*, https://www.adb.org/publications/2023-trade-finance-gaps-growth-jobs-survey. [3]

African Climate Foundation (2023), *Implications for African Countries of a Carbon Border Adjustment Mechanism in the EU*, https://africanclimatefoundation.org/news_and_analysis/implications-for-african-countries-of-a-carbon-border-adjustment-mechanism-in-africa/. [22]

African Union (2024), *The African Continental Free Trade Area*, https://au.int/en/african-continental-free-trade-area. [13]

Asian Development Bank et al. (2023), *2023 Trade Finance Gaps, Growth, and Jobs Survey*, Asian Development Bank, https://doi.org/10.22617/brf230334-2. [31]

Baker McKenzie (2024), *Africa: The African Continental Free Trade Area Investment Protocol - The Start of a New Era in Sustainable Trade and Investment*, https://insightplus.bakermckenzie.com/bm/international-commercial-trade/africa-the-african-continental-free-trade-area-investment-protocol-the-start-of-a-new-era-in-sustainable-trade-and-investment. [7]

Botwright, K. and G. Dabré (2024), "Critical minerals are in demand. How do we make sure this trend drives development?", *World Economic Forum*, https://www.weforum.org/stories/2024/05/critical-minerals-are-in-demand-how-do-we-make-sure-this-trend-drives-development/ (accessed on 30 November 2024). [26]

D'Andrea, B. et al. (2024), "Thirty years of trade growth and poverty reduction", *WTO Data Blog*, https://www.wto.org/english/blogs_e/data_blog_e/blog_dta_24apr24_e.htm. [1]

Global Trade Alert (2024), *Independent Monitoring of Policies that Affect World Commerce*, https://www.globaltradealert.org/. [35]

Hochet-Bodin, N. (2024), *Ethiopian coffee is threatened by European deforestation regulations*, https://www.lemonde.fr/en/environment/article/2024/05/25/ethiopian-coffee-is-threatened-by-european-deforestation-regulations_6672600_114.html. [23]

IMF; OECD; World Bank; World Trade Organization (2022), *Subsidies, Trade, and International Cooperation*, OECD Publishing, Paris, https://doi.org/10.1787/a4f01ddb-en. [21]

ITC; UNCTAD (2024), "SDG indicator 10.A.(i): Share of exports admitted duty free", *SDG Trade Monitor*, https://sdgtrade.org/en/indicators/10-a-i/BC/3/. [37]

ITC; UNCTAD (2024), "SDG indicator 17.11.1: Developing countries' and least developed countries' share of global exports", *SDG Trade Monitor*, https://www.sdgtrade.org/en/indicators/17-11-1/BC/1/. [32]

ITC; UNCTAD (2024), "SDG indicator 17.12.1: Average tariffs faced by developing countries, LDCs and SIDS", *SDG Trade Monitor*, https://sdgtrade.org/en/indicators/17-12-1/BC/3/. [38]

ITC; UNCTAD (2024), "SDG indicator 2.B.1 Agricultural export subsidies", *SDG Trade Monitor*, https://sdgtrade.org/en/indicators/2-b-1/BC/1/. [34]

Korinek, J., A. Mourougane and E. Lieshout (2023), "Women are less engaged in trade: Why, and what to do about it", *Vox EU Column*, https://cepr.org/voxeu/columns/women-are-less-engaged-trade-why-and-what-do-about-it (accessed on 30 November 2024). [25]

McKinsey & Company (2024), *The Africa hydrogen opportunity*, https://hydrogencouncil.com/wp-content/uploads/2024/03/Hydrogen-Council-Africa-Hydrogen-Opportunity-.pdf (accessed on January 2025). [8]

OECD (2024), *OECD Services Trade Restrictiveness Index: Policy Trends up to 2024*, OECD Publishing, Paris, https://doi.org/10.1787/b9e5c870-en. [29]

OECD (2023), *Agricultural Policy Monitoring and Evaluation 2023: Adapting Agriculture to Climate Change*, OECD Publishing, Paris, https://doi.org/10.1787/b14de474-en. [20]

OECD/WTO (2024), *Aid for Trade at a Glance 2024*, OECD Publishing, Paris, https://doi.org/10.1787/7a4e356a-en. [5]

Rocha, N. and R. Piermartini (2023), *Trade Drives Gender Equality and Development*, International Monetary Fund, Washington, DC, https://www.imf.org/en/Publications/fandd/issues/2023/06/trade-drives-gender-equality-and-development-rocha-piermartini. [9]

Schwellnus, C., A. Haramboure and L. Samek (2023), "Policies to strengthen the resilience of global value chains: Empirical evidence from the COVID-19 shock", *OECD Science, Technology and Industry Policy Papers*, No. 141, OECD Publishing, Paris, https://doi.org/10.1787/fd82abd4-en (accessed on 30 November 2024). [27]

UN (2024), *Financing for Sustainable Development Report 2024: Financing for Development at a Crossroads*, United Nations Department of Economic and Social Affairs, New York, https://desapublications.un.org/publications/financing-sustainable-development-report-2024. [11]

UN (2024), *Progress towards the Sustainable Development Goals - Statistical Annex*, United Nations Statistical Commission, New York, https://unstats.un.org/sdgs/files/report/2024/E_2024_54_Statistical_Annex_I_and_II.pdf. [17]

UN (2024), *The Least Developed Countries in Facts & Figures*, https://www.un.org/ohrlls/sites/www.un.org.ohrlls/files/pamphlet.pdf. [24]

UN DESA (2024), *SDG Indicators Database*, https://unstats.un.org/sdgs/dataportal/database (accessed on November 2024). [6]

UNCTAD (2024), *Attaining the SDGs through trade – UNCTAD SDG Pulse 2024 (webpage)*, https://sdgpulse.unctad.org/trade-developing-economies/ (accessed on 27 January 2025). [2]

UNCTAD (2024), *Key Statistics and Trends in Trade Policy 2023*, UN Trade and Development, https://unctad.org/system/files/official-document/ditctab2024d2_en.pdf. [40]

UNCTAD (2024), "Tariff trends mostly downwards, but non-tariff measures increasingly used", *SDG Pulse*, https://sdgpulse.unctad.org/trade-barriers/ (accessed on 30 November 2024). [16]

UNCTAD (2023), *Key Statistics and Trends in Trade Policy 2022*, United Nations, Geneva, https://unctad.org/system/files/official-document/ditctab2023d2_en.pdf. [28]

UNCTAD (2023), *The South-South trade partnership for accelerating the SDGs achievement*, https://unctad.org/meeting/south-south-trade-partnership-accelerating-sdgs-achievement. [12]

World Bank Group and World Trade Organisation (2018), *Trade and Poverty Reduction: New Evidence of Impacts in Developing Countries*, World Trade Organization, Geneva, https://www.wto.org/english/res_e/booksp_e/wto_wbjointpublication_e.pdf. [10]

World Integrated Trade Solution (2024), *World Trade in % of GDP*, https://wits.worldbank.org/CountryProfile/en/Country/WLD/StartYear/2015/EndYear/2021/Indicator/NE-TRD-GNFS-ZS. [33]

World Trade Organization (2024), "Members submitting acceptance of Agreement on Fisheries Subsidies", https://www.wto.org/english/tratop_e/rulesneg_e/fish_e/fish_acceptances_e.htm (accessed on 30 November 2024). [18]

World Trade Organization (2024), *Trade faciliatation agreement database: Status of notification by measure (database)*, https://tfadatabase.org/en/notifications/categorization-by-measure (accessed on 30 November 2024). [15]

World Trade Organization (2023), *World Trade Report 2023: Re-globalisation for a Secure, Inclusive and Sustainable Future*, https://www.wto.org/english/res_e/booksp_e/wtr23_e/wtr23_e.pdf. [19]

World Trade Organization (2015), *World Trade Report 2015: Speeding Up Trade - Benefits and Challenges of Implementing the WTO Trade Facilitation Agreement*, https://www.wto.org/english/res_e/publications_e/wtr15_e.htm. [14]

WTO (2024), *Completed accessions*, World Trade Organization, https://www.wto.org/english/thewto_e/acc_e/completed_acc_e.htm. [36]

WTO (2024), *Implementation commitments dashboard*, World Trade Organization, https://www.tfadatabase.org/en/implementation. [30]

WTO (2024), *Trade and tariff data*, https://www.wto.org/english/res_e/statis_e/statis_e.htm. [4]

WTO (n.d.), *Amendment of the TRIPS Agreement*, World Trade Organization, https://www.wto.org/english/tratop_e/trips_e/tripsfacsheet_e.htm. [39]

6 Debt and Debt Sustainability

This chapter reviews the Debt and Debt Sustainability action area of the Addis Ababa Action Agenda (AAAA) including progress, persistent challenges, and emerging areas as the international community prepares for the Fourth International Conference on Financing for Development (FfD4). It explores advancements in debt relief and debt management support and capacity building which have expanded as well as trends in sovereign debt in developing countries. Persistent challenges such as rising interest rates, debt service levels, credit quality and transparency of debt are highlighted. Opportunities to strengthen the international debt architecture and innovative climate-related financial instruments to address debt challenges, are also presented.

6.1. Data dashboard

Key trends

The risk of external public debt distress has increased.

Deteriorating global financial conditions have significantly increased the risk of external public debt distress in developing countries. In 2022, the total amount of defaulted sovereign debt, including non-marketable debt, reached USD 470 billion, up from an average of about USD 200 billion in 2015.

In heavily indebted poor countries (HIPC), sovereign debt in default reached a record high of USD 127 billion in 2023 due in part to the slow pace at which some non-Paris Club official creditors are implementing debt relief (Beers, Ndukwe and Charron, 2024[1])..

Figure 6.1. Sovereign debt in default (2015-23)

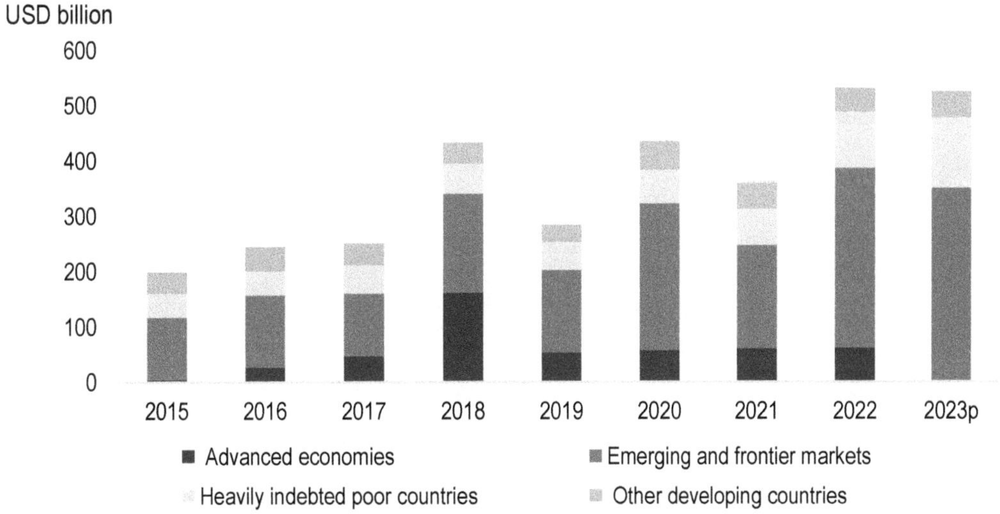

Note: A sovereign is in default or debt distress when it interrupts debt payments or seeks to renegotiate terms, including to reduce principal, lower interest rates or extend maturities. Once restructured, the debt is considered performing and not in default.
Source: Beers et al., (2024[1]), "BoC–BoE Sovereign Default Database: What's new in 2024?", https://www.bankofcanada.ca/wp-content/uploads/2024/07/SAN2024-19.pdf.

Sovereign restructuring has become more complex.

Sovereign debt restructuring has become more complex because of a rise in defaulted debt and a more diverse creditor base, with the private sector, China and Gulf states playing increasingly significant roles.

The composition of lenders to low-income countries (LICs) has changed significantly since 1996, when Paris Club creditors held 39% of their external debt and non-Paris Club and private creditors each held 8%. By the end of 2021, Paris Club creditors' share of the total external debt of LICs had dropped to 11% while the shares held by non-Paris Club creditors and private creditors more than doubled to 20% and 19%, respectively.

Figure 6.2. Creditor composition in LICs, % of public and publicly guaranteed external debt stock (1996-2021)

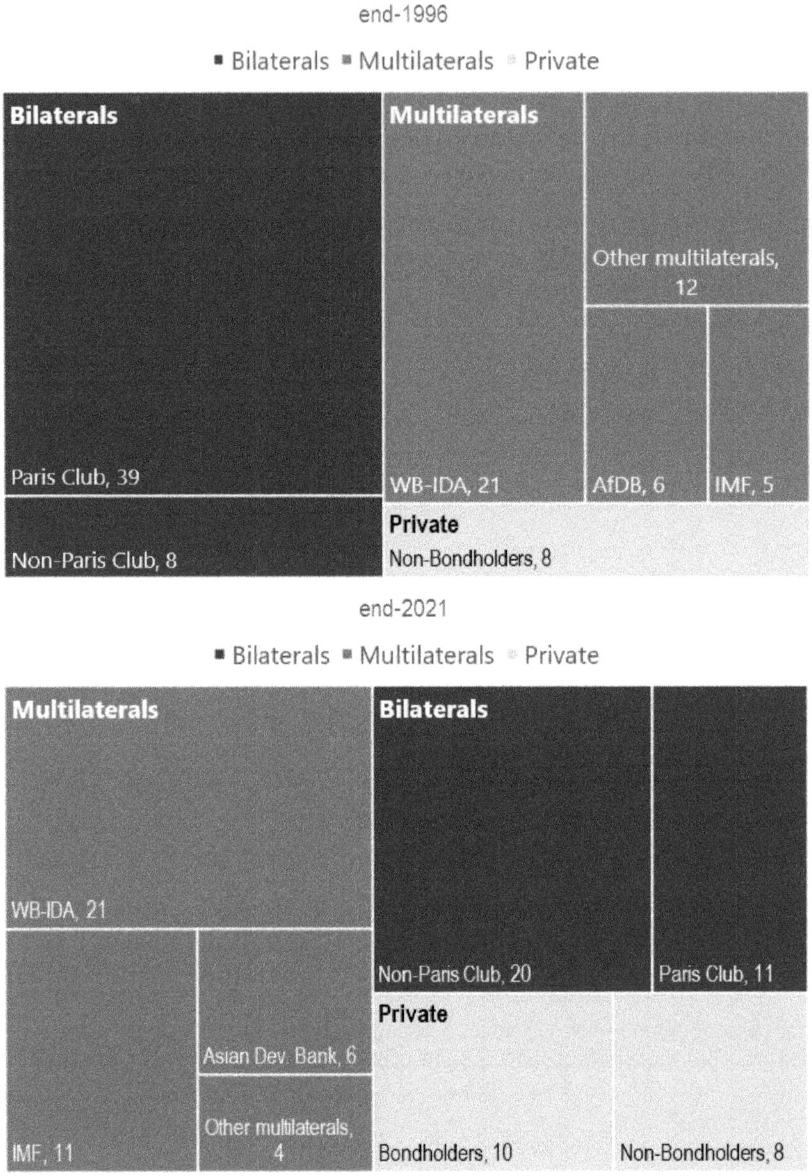

Note: The numbers indicate the share of total external debt the respective creditor holds in a given year, WB-IDA: World Bank International Development Association; IMF: International Monetary Fund; AfDB: African Development Bank.
Source: IMF 2023, https://www.elibrary.imf.org/view/journals/001/2023/079/article-A001-en.xml

Increasing debt service limits the fiscal space and borrowing capacity of developing countries

Debt service consumes over a fifth of tax revenue in 25 developing countries (Beers, Ndukwe and Charron, 2024[1]). Projections are that 92 countries will have spent more on external public debt service than on Sustainable Development Goal (SDG) investments in 2024 (Merling et al., 2024[2]).

In many sub-Saharan African countries, fiscal consolidation is necessary to achieve prudent debt targets, with adjustments of 2%-3% of gross domestic product (GDP) required over 2022-27 (Comelli et al., 2023[3]).

Approximately 20 LICs and lower middle-income countries (LMICs) are solvent but face illiquidity issues (i.e. a high debt service-to-revenue ratio) as creditors are reluctant to roll over loans out of concern that others will exit and leave them with riskier claims.[1]

Figure 6.3. Number of countries exceeding the IMF-World Bank debt service-to-revenue thresholds, by income group, 2015-25 (estimated)

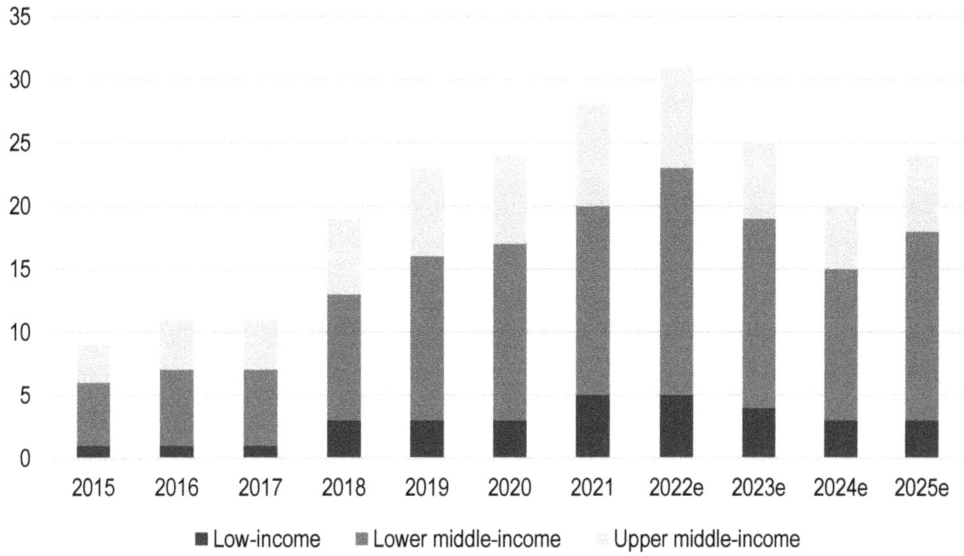

Note: e = estimated. The debt service-to-revenue threshold used in the International Monetary Fund (IMF)-World Bank debt sustainability analysis varies depending on a country's debt carrying capacity. The indicator is calculated as the ratio of a country's total debt service payments (interest and principal) to its government revenues. This metric provides insight into the fiscal burden imposed by debt service and the government's ability to generate sufficient revenue to cover these obligations without compromising other essential spending. After 2021, data are based on estimates.
Source: Adapted from Diwan, Songwe and Kessler (2024[4]), *A Bridge to Climate Action*, https://findevlab.org/a-bridge-to-climate-action/.

Key performance indicators

↓	Between 2015 and 2023, debt service on long-term external publicly guaranteed debt as a percentage of exports of goods and services in least developed countries (LDCs) nearly doubled from 7.6% to 13.2% while it remained stable in high-income developing countries at roughly 3.5% (UNCTAD, 2024[5]).
↓	The proportion of LICs in debt distress or at high risk of debt distress more than doubled, from 27% to 56% between 2015 and 2023 (World Bank, 2023[6]).
↓	In 2023, a record high of 54 developing countries, nearly half of them in Africa, had net interest payments exceeding 10% of their revenues (UNCTAD, 2024[7]).
↓	In 2020-22, a total 3.3 billion people resided in the 48 countries where interest payments exceed expenditures on either education or health (UNCTAD, 2024[7]).

↓ Slight setback	↓ Setback	↔ No change, neutral	↔ Stagnant, possible issue	↑ Major progress	↑ Minimal progress
Minimal setback	↓ Major setback	Holding steady, slight concern	↔ Negative stagnation, concerning	Progress	↑ Negligible progress or progress contested

Note: Selected quantifiable commitments. Annex Table 6.A.1 contains the full list. It should be noted that the chapter of the Addis Ababa Action Agenda on debt issues does not include quantifiable or timebound commitments.

Resource mobilisation potential

- Implementing an HIPC-like programme today would likely cost between USD 100 billion and USD 200 billion, considering inflation, current debt levels and the broader scope of economic challenges (Chuku et al., 2023[8]).
- Debt-for-nature swaps could help redirect USD 100 billion of debt in developing countries to nature restoration and climate adaptation.
- Up to USD 80 billion could be unlocked by rechanneling special drawing rights (SDRs) via multilateral development banks through the purchase of hybrid capital instruments.

6.2. Key areas of progress

Debt relief provided under the HIPC and Multilateral Debt Relief Initiative (MDRI) programmes provided crucial support.

By the end of 2020, the HIPC and related Multilateral Debt Relief Initiative (MDRI) programmes had relieved 37 participating countries, 31 of them in Africa, of more than USD 100 billion in debt. Implementing HIPC-like initiatives today would be more challenging due to hidden debt and a more diverse creditor landscape. Since the mid-1990s, private sector debt in LICs has more than doubled from 8% to 19%. Additionally, creditor co-ordination and geopolitical fragmentation might undermine the efficiency of these programmes (Chuku et al., 2023[8]).

The sovereign bond market in emerging markets and developing economies has grown significantly

The sovereign bond markets of emerging markets and developing economies (EMDEs) have expanded significantly since 2007, with particularly strong growth since the onset of the COVID-19 pandemic. The annual gross issuance of bonds by EMDEs has nearly quadrupled from approximately USD 1 trillion in 2007 to almost USD 4 trillion by 2023. China's share of this borrowing also rose significantly from 15% in 2021 to 37% in 2023 (OECD, 2024[9]). LICs experienced the most significant growth in sovereign bond issuances, with their markets expanding more than tenfold, followed by LMICs with a nearly ninefold increase.

The substantial growth in sovereign gross issuances for LICs and LMICs is primarily driven by efforts to finance net borrowing needs through marketable debt instruments rather than an increase in overall borrowing requirements. Between 2009 and 2019, net borrowing for LICs and LMICs remained between 4% and 6% of GDP, without a consistent upward trend. Thus, the rise in gross issuances reflects the growing reliance on bond issuances to meet borrowing needs, indicating the development of sovereign bond markets in LICs and LMICs (OECD, 2024[9]).

The proportion of EMDEs' local currency fixed rate sovereign bonds increased from 57% in 2000 to 66% in 2023, and the increase was accompanied by longer average maturities. However, both the volume and maturity period of this debt are still lower for EMDEs than for OECD countries, and the gap is particularly pronounced in smaller economies (OECD, 2024[9]).

By the end of 2023, the global outstanding value of official sector and corporate and sustainable bonds reached USD 4.3 trillion, a significant increase from USD 641 billion in 2018 (OECD, 2024[9]). Nonetheless and despite recent rapid growth, sovereign sustainable debt instruments still make up a small share of total sovereign bond issuances, averaging 2.2% for advanced economies and 8.1% for EMDEs in 2022. Green bonds dominate this market, representing over 75% of sovereign sustainable instruments, and are primarily issued by advanced economies (OECD, 2023[10]).

Debt management support and capacity building continue to expand

The IMF and World Bank, together with implementing partners, have been implementing a multi-pronged approach to address debt vulnerabilities including through the Debt Management Facility, which support more than 463 technical assistance initiatives across 78 countries and 20 subnational entities by December 2022 (World Bank, 2023[11]). The IMF spends about one-third of its resources on capacity-development activities, which include technical assistance and training programmes to strengthen debt management practices in developing countries (International Monetary Fund, 2024[12]). Regional multilateral development banks (MDBs) such as the African Development Bank are also actively engaged in capacity building for debt management, transparency and other activities.

Official development assistance rules have established new incentives to strengthen debt sustainability of concessional finance

The 2014 official development assistance (ODA) rules implemented a stricter measure of concessionality than previous guidelines, setting discount rates set at 9%, 7% and 6% and thresholds at 45%, 15% and 10% in contrast to the previous 10% discount rate and 25% threshold. Consequently, lenders are required to offer more concessional loans for these to qualify as ODA, which particularly affects LDCs. Additionally, the rules introduced new provisions in the ODA criteria concerning debt sustainability. Under these provisions, loans that do not adhere to the IMF Debt Limits Policy and/or the World Bank's Non-Concessional Borrowing Policy and Sustainable Development Finance Policy cannot be reported as ODA.

6.3. Persistent challenging areas

Rising interest rates and high refinancing needs threaten debt sustainability in developing countries

Developing countries' average interest cost on external borrowing is three times higher than that of developed countries (Spiegel and Schwank, 2022[13]). Every 1% increase in the interest rate represents an additional USD 35 billion in interest payments that LICs and middle-income countries must make to creditors (Walker et al., 2022[14]). LICs face significant debt repayments and need to refinance about USD 60 billion of external debt in 2024-26, which is triple the average over the ten-year period of 2010-20 (Holland and Pazarbasioglu, 2024[15]). Since 2016, Eurobonds and syndicated loans from private banks have surged while grace periods have become shorter and spreads have become more volatile (Chuku et al., 2023[8]).

High refinancing requirements in an environment of elevated interest rates could strain national budgets and jeopardise foreign market access for certain countries. Between 2024 and 2026, over USD 4.5 trillion in bond debt from EMDEs will mature The proportion of debt maturing in 2024 is particularly high, at approximately 20%, for LICs, and is nearly 25% for countries whose credit ratings indicate high credit risk or risk of default (i.e. a rating of single B or below) compared with an average of 15% in other income groups (OECD, 2024[9]).

Countries with low credit ratings are also more exposed to refinancing needs in foreign currency. For countries with credit ratings above single B, the average share of foreign currency debt maturing between 2024-26 is below 8%. In contrast, the average share exceeds 30% for countries with lower credit ratings. Among the 16 countries where more than 30% of foreign currency-denominated debt is due by end-2026, 10 have credit ratings of BB- (reflecting high risk) or lower. While defaults on local currency debt are rare, substantial refinancing needs in local currency during periods of high yields can significantly impact government budgets and reduce fiscal space for other priorities (OECD, 2024[9]).

Debt and debt service levels have risen, increasing the risk of debt default

Recent crises have increased risks of debt defaults as well as the cost of debt service. Currently, 13 countries – 7 of them LMICs or LICs – are in or nearly in default, according to credit rating agencies. This is the highest number in 24 years. As of 2023, these 13 countries collectively have about USD 1.4 trillion in GDP, or slightly over 1% of global GDP, and a combined population of nearly 400 million, or 5% of the world's population. Another 13 countries with total GDP of USD 1.7 trillion and a combined population of more than 700 million are at significant risk of default. Taken together, these two groups of countries at either substantial risk of default or in default account for about 3% of global GDP but 15% of the world's population (OECD, 2024[9]).

Countries eligible for the HIPC Initiative and the MDRI experienced the largest relative increases in sovereign debt default following the COVID-19 crisis of 62.70% and 52.56%, respectively.[2] In 2022, developing countries paid USD 49 billion more to their external creditors than they received in fresh disbursements, resulting in a negative net resource transfer. Developing countries also pay the highest price: Debt service on external public debt reached USD 365 billion in 2022, equivalent to 6.3% of export revenues. Over USD 4.4 trillion of EMDE bond debt matures between 2024 and 2026 (OECD, 2024[9]). The number of low-graded EMDEs accessing international markets fell from 20 on average in 2015-21 to approximately 10 in 2022-23.[3]

The Group of Twenty (G20) Debt Service Suspension Initiative (DSSI) provided temporary relief by pausing USD 12.9 billion in debt service payments for LICs from May 2020 to December 2021. In 2020, the G20 introduced the Common Framework for Debt Treatment, aimed at providing more structured debt relief for these countries. So far, only four countries – Chad, Ethiopia, Ghana and Zambia – have requested assistance under this framework. While Chad and Zambia have reached agreements with their creditors, the negotiations took well over a year to finalise (Alayza, Laxton and Neunuebel, 2023[16]). While public debt of developing countries in the Asia Pacific region increased sharply during the COVID-19 pandemic, opportunities for restructuring are often limited because a large portion of the debt is owed to MDBs that do not participate in the DSSI and the Common Framework in order to maintain their credit ratings and low funding costs. As a result, countries with significant MDB debt have fewer options to access relief.

While there is still room for improvement on the Common Framework progress, it remains an important innovation in the global financial infrastructure, and there has been considerable improvement in the process and timing for each subsequent restructuring. The Global Sovereign Debt Roundtable, established in 2023, aims to improve debt restructuring processes, but private creditor participation remains a challenge.

Credit quality in developing countries has deteriorated since the pandemic

From 2020 to the first quarter of 2024, there were 224 downgrades but only 105 upgrades for EMDEs. There were more upgrades than downgrades in high-income and upper middle-income countries in 2023 and the first quarter of 2024, while LICs and LMICs experienced more than twice as many downgrades as upgrades. By the first quarter of 2024, nearly 60% of the approximately 100 rated EMDEs were classified as low grade, and more than 10 countries were either near default or in default. The number of countries rated C or in default has reached a historic high, including the number of LICs and LMICs among this group, while the share of investment-grade countries globally fell to its lowest point in the first quarter of 2024 (OECD, 2024[9]). (Chapter 7 on addressing systemic issues presents additional information on credit rating agencies and the financial architecture.)

The transparency of sovereign debt remains low

Fiscal transparency is a critical element of effective public financial management as it can help build market confidence and reinforce economic sustainability. It also fosters greater government accountability and facilitates better-informed public debate regarding debt quality and sustainability. Opaque debt agreements, on the other hand, cause delays in debt restructurings. Hidden debt due to under-reporting accumulates during economic booms and tends to become evident in recessions and times of distress. In debt restructurings, higher hidden debt also is associated with larger credit losses (Horn et al., 2024[17]).

In 2020-21, 40% of low-income developing countries did not publish any sovereign debt data, and public debt data show discrepancies of up to 30% of GDP across different sources (Rivetti, 2021[18]). IMF analysis finds that of the 60 developing countries surveyed, just half have laws that require debt management and fiscal reports and fewer than a quarter require disclosure of loan-level information that is crucial for transparency (Ashcroft, Vasquez and Weeks-Brown, 2024[19]). Recent international efforts, including initiatives by the G20, IMF and Institute of International Finance (IIF), aim to enhance debt data reporting and disclosure practices. G20 countries endorsed principles of information sharing and transparency among creditors in their Operational Guidelines for Sustainable Financing agreed in 2017 (World Bank, 2023[20]). The World Bank's Debtor Reporting System and the IIF's voluntary principles for debt transparency are crucial for standardising and monitoring debt data, promoting accountability, and supporting sustainable economic development (World Bank, 2023[6]). Other initiatives such as the Joint Debt Hub (by the OECD, IMF, World Bank Group and Bank for International Settlements) also aim to improve statistics on the overall external debt of countries (World Bank, 2024[21]).

Domestic laws in creditor and debtor countries could strengthen the legal framework to prevent future debt burden

Several countries are working to strengthen the legal framework to support the litigation efforts of developing countries (UK Parliament, 2023[22]). Relatedly, there is an increased focus on regulating collateralised lending practices to ensure fairer terms and prevent excessive debt burdens on developing nations. However, a recent IMF study found that key vulnerabilities in domestic laws allow debt concealment, among them a limited definition of public debt, insufficient disclosure requirements, confidentiality clauses in public debt contracts and weak oversight (Ashcroft, Vasquez and Weeks-Brown, 2024[19]).

6.4. New and emerging areas

The international debt architecture can be strengthened to support sustainable development and climate goals and address financial inequalities

Governments, multilateral organisations and civil society have begun advocating for reform of the international debt architecture, with a focus on increasing low-cost public finance through reforms of MDBs and the IMF. Their focus is on improving governance and representation within these institutions, and enhancing the agility and flexibility of lending mechanisms, particularly for countries vulnerable to climate change. Proposals also emphasise improving risk assessments to attract investment, reforming debt governance to better manage crises, and fostering coalitions to drive advocacy and policy implementation. Key initiatives such as the Bridgetown Initiative; the United Nations SDG Stimulus; the High-level Working Group of African ministers of finance, planning and economic development: the Vulnerable Twenty Group (V20); and the Paris Pact for People and Planet, among others, collectively aim to address global financial inequalities and support sustainable development. (Chapter 7 on systemic issues provides more information on reform of the global financial architecture more broadly.)

Innovative climate-related financial instruments can help respond to finance needs and debt challenges

Climate change has increased the debt cost for the V20 countries by USD 62 billion over 2007-16, and the climate premium is expected to more than double from 2019-28 (Alayza, Laxton and Neunuebel, 2023[16]). Most of the public climate finance provided by developing countries – USD 63.6 billion or 69% – in the form of loans (OECD, 2024[23]).

While no single instrument can solve a country's debt situation, several climate-related financial instruments can help address both the climate finance needs and debt challenges of developing countries. These include debt-for-climate and debt-for-nature swaps, climate resilient debt clauses (CRDCs), and special drawing rights (SDRs). All of these have been used increasingly in recent years, though they come with trade-offs, and careful consideration is needed in applying these instruments. Another example is sustainability-linked bonds, forward-looking, performance-based debt instruments that can be linked to existing sustainability targets such as nationally determined contributions – and help incentivise action towards these.

In debt swaps for climate and nature, applicable to both sovereign and commercial debt, a portion of a country's debt is forgiven or restructured in exchange for the country's commitment to invest in climate-related projects, which ensures that the fiscal cost to the debtor does not exceed the value of the debt relief (Chamon et al., 2022[24]). Such agreements could help redirect USD 100 billion of debt in developing countries, including USD 33.7 billion for LDCs[4], to nature restoration and climate adaptation. Reducing transaction-related costs, which currently consume 40% or more of financial benefits, could make debt swaps a more viable opportunity for nearly 15% of developing countries. However, their relatively small scale compared to a country's debt burden, the conditionality of arrangements, and adequate governance and enforcement are among the matters that should be considered in contemplating such swaps.

CRDCs enable the temporary suspension, deferment or restructuring of debt payments when a country faces climate-related events such as a hurricane or flood. Several bilateral and multilateral lenders offer these clauses in contracts, and the International Capital Market Association has also announced that LICs would be able to include CRDCs in bonds. However, even with a CRDC, interest continues to accrue while debt is suspended, and a country must be able to fulfil repayment requirements. With these instruments, the parameters for trigger events and thresholds could be better harmonised.

SDR allocations have provided approximately USD 275 billion to developing countries, and 80 countries use them. By March 2024, the IMF gathered about USD 8.4 billion in commitments for its Resilience and Sustainability Trust to support climate activities in developing countries (International Monetary Fund, 2024[25]). By end-February 2024, commitments totalling USD 7.0 billion were approved, yet only USD 1.4 billion had been disbursed to 9 countries, with a further USD 3.4 billion scheduled for 2024 to be disbursed to another 17 countries scheduled (Hicklin, 2024[26]). SDR rechanneling through MDBs has been part of the MDB Capital Adequacy Framework agenda, and the G20 Independent Experts Group has called for MDBs to take steps to boost their lending capacity, including by exploring hybrid capital structures.

Annex 6.A. Debt and Debt Sustainability

Annex Table 6.A.1. Assessment of the action area: Debt and debt sustainability

AAAA paragraph	Commitment	Specific target or objective	Matching Sustainable Development Goal (SDG) target (where available)	State of implementation or progress made since 2015, using SDG or other relevant indicator (proxy)
93	Address debt sustainability challenges, especially for least developed countries and small island developing states, including through initiatives such as the Heavily Indebted Poor Countries (HIPC) initiative and Multilateral Debt Relief Initiative (MDRI). References smooth transition for graduated LDCs.	No	Target 17.4 Assist developing countries in attaining long-term debt sustainability through co-ordinated policies aimed at fostering debt financing, debt relief and debt restructuring, as appropriate, and address the external debt of HIPCs to reduce debt distress.	SDG indicator 17.4.1 Debt service as a proportion of exports of goods and services. In 2022, debt service in LDCs accounted for 8.4% of exports of goods, services, and primary income. This was an increase from 7.6% in 2015 (UN, 2024[27]). Debt service as percentage of government revenues. In 2023, developing countries' net interest payments on public debt amounted to USD 847 billion, a 26% increase over 2021. Also in 2023, a record 54 developing countries, 38% of the total, dedicated 10% or more of their government revenues to interest payments (UNCTAD, 2024[7]). Developing countries face significantly higher borrowing costs than do developed countries. Interest rates on sovereign debt in developing countries are 2 to 4 times higher than those in the United States and 6 to 12 times higher than those in Germany (UNCTAD, 2024[7]). Debt service as percentage of tax revenue. The fiscal positions of developing countries deteriorated more than those of developed countries due to the COVID-19 crisis. Debt service now accounts for more than 20% of tax revenue in 25 developing countries. (UN, 2023[28]). Debt relief provided by the HIPC and MDRI. The HIPC Initiative and the MDRI have relieved 37 participating countries of over USD 100 billion in debt since 1996 (World Bank, 2024[29]). Percentage of official development assistance (ODA) (grants and loans) provided as concessional loans

AAAA paragraph	Commitment	Specific target or objective	Matching Sustainable Development Goal (SDG) target (where available)	State of implementation or progress made since 2015, using SDG or other relevant indicator (proxy)
				An increasing portion of ODA is being delivered as concessional loans rather than grants. The proportion of loans in ODA to developing countries rose from 28% in 2012 to 34% in 2022 (UNCTAD, 2024[7]). The average grant element of ODA loans to LDCs decreased from 78% in 2015 to 70% in 2021 due to both higher interest rates (from 0.35% in 2015 to 0.63% in 2021) and shorter maturity periods (from 36 years in 2015 to 27 years in 2021) (OECD, 2023[30]). ODA allocated to debt-related actions. ODA resources dedicated to debt-related actions such as debt relief, swaps, and restructuring have reached a historic low, dropping from USD 4.1 billion in 2012 to only USD 300 million in 2022 (UNCTAD, 2024[7]). Smooth transition for least developed country (LDC) graduates. Since 2015, six countries have graduated from the LDC category and an additional five are recommended for future graduation (UN ECOSOC, 2024[31]). The United Nations (UN) Committee for Development Policy (CDP) contributed to the 2024 Economic and Social Council by conducting the triennial review and monitoring of LDCs and discussing graduation in a global context. The CDP monitored the development progress, including debt sustainability challenges, of nine countries that recently graduated or are graduating from the list of LDCs, finding that in several instances natural disasters and/or oil price fluctuations have negatively impacted the debt position of graduated LDCs (UN ECOSOC, 2024[32]). *(For more information see the UN Smooth Transition for LDCs website.)*
94	Assist developing countries in achieving long-term debt sustainability through co-ordinated policies on debt financing, relief, restructuring and management. Commit to supporting HIPC-eligible countries completing the process and consider initiatives for non-HIPC nations. Maintain support for countries that have already received relief and achieved sustainable debt	No	Target 17.4 See para. 93.	Number of countries eligible for the HIPC Initiative that have benefited from debt relief. Of the 39 countries eligible for the HIPC Initiative, all 36 countries that reached the decision point have now reached the completion point (IMF, 2023[33]). *Initiatives of the International Monetary Fund (IMF) and the World Bank, in collaboration with their partners, include the Debt Management Facility, which has supported over 463 technical assistance projects across 78 countries and 20 subnational entities as of December 2022* (World Bank Group, 2023[34]).

AAAA paragraph	Commitment	Specific target or objective	Matching Sustainable Development Goal (SDG) target (where available)	State of implementation or progress made since 2015, using SDG or other relevant indicator (proxy)
	levels.			Share of IMF resources allocated to capacity-development efforts. Approximately one-third of the IMF's resources are allocated to capacity-development efforts, which encompass technical assistance and training programmes aimed at reinforcing debt management practices in developing nations (IMF, 2022[35]).
95	Welcome IMF, World Bank and UN efforts to strengthen debt sustainability and management tools. Use IMF-World Bank debt sustainability analysis as a valuable tool to assess appropriate borrowing levels. Urge these institutions to continue improving their tools in an inclusive process in collaboration with the UN and stakeholders.	No	Target 17.4 See para. 93.	*The IMF has focused on several key areas to strengthen debt sustainability. In collaboration with the World Bank, for instance, it updated the Debt Sustainability Framework for Low-Income Countries in 2017. This framework helps assess the risks of debt distress in low-income countries (LICs) and guides them in managing their debt levels prudently. The updated framework incorporates more realistic stress-testing and broader macroeconomic factors.* *The IMF also revised its debt limits policy in 2020 to offer countries greater flexibility, allowing them to manage their debt according to their development needs while maintaining sustainability. This policy now includes tailored approaches based on country-specific circumstances and risk assessments.* *The World Bank has also undertaken several initiatives to improve debt management. For example, a cross-country comparison of Debt Management Performance Evaluations (DeMPA) shows that more than half of the assessed countries do not meet minimum standards for sound sovereign debt management practices. Key weaknesses include poor cash flow forecasting and coordination with debt management, leading to inefficient practices such as issuing new debt while holding surplus cash. Operational risk management is also a significant concern, exposing governments to potential data loss and process failures. However, improvements have been seen in aligning debt management with macroeconomic policies and enhancing legal frameworks* (World Bank, n.d.[36]). *Like the IMF, the World Bank also provides extensive technical assistance and training to strengthen countries' debt management capacities. It supports the development of medium-term debt management strategies and enhances countries' ability to manage public debt prudently.* *In addition, the UN plays a vital role in promoting debt sustainability through its various bodies and programmes. An example is the UN Trade and Development (UNCTAD) Debt Management and Financial Analysis System, which assists developing countries in managing their public debt effectively. The system further helps countries improve their capacity to record, monitor and analyse public debt*

AAAA paragraph	Commitment	Specific target or objective	Matching Sustainable Development Goal (SDG) target (where available)	State of implementation or progress made since 2015, using SDG or other relevant indicator (proxy)
				data, contributing to better debt sustainability.
96	Support ongoing efforts to establish standards and promote public access to data on sovereign and external debt and encourage comprehensive quarterly debt reporting. Advocate for the creation of a central data registry on debt restructurings and urge all governments to enhance transparency in debt management.	No	Target 17.4 See para. 93.	Number of International Development Association (IDA) countries with full debt data accessibility. The World Bank's Debt Reporting Heat Map provides an assessment of how various countries report their debt data, offering insights into debt transparency globally. In 2023, 74 IDA countries reported their data compared with 76 in 2020 (World Bank Group, 2023[37]). Percentage of low-income developing countries reporting sovereign debt data. About 40% of low-income developing countries did not disclose any sovereign debt data in 2020-21, and discrepancies of up to 30% of gross domestic product (GDP) were observed across various sources of public debt data (Rivetti, 2021[18]). *Recent international efforts, including initiatives by the Group of Twenty (G20), IMF and Institute of International Finance (IIF), are focused on improving debt data reporting and disclosure practices. The World Bank's Debtor Reporting System and the IIF's voluntary principles for debt transparency play a crucial role in standardising and monitoring debt data, fostering accountability, and supporting sustainable economic development. Additionally, initiatives such as the Joint Debt Hub (OECD, IMF, World Bank Group, Bank for International Settlements) aim to enhance overall statistics on countries' external debt.*
97	Enhance collaboration between debtors and creditors to prevent and resolve unsustainable debt situations. Establish global guidelines on debtor and creditor responsibilities in sovereign borrowing and lending, building on current initiatives (such as the UNCTAD principles on responsible sovereign lending and borrowing, the IMF and World Bank's debt limits policies, and the OECD Development Assistance Committee's new safeguards to enhance recipient countries' debt sustainability). Strengthen information	Yes Establish global guidelines on debtor and creditor responsibilities.	Target 17.4 See para 93.	*To date, there are no globally agreed guidelines on sovereign borrowing for debtors and creditors. However, many initiatives to design guidelines are in place. For instance, the G20 Common Framework, developed in response to the COVID-19 pandemic, builds on the G20's Debt Service Suspension Initiative (DSSI) to provide a structured approach to debt treatment involving both official and private creditors. The Paris Club of official creditors also has adopted principles and practices that serve as guidelines for restructuring bilateral debt. The IIF, which represents the global financial industry, has developed a set of voluntary principles – Principles for Stable Capital Flows and Fair Debt Restructuring – to guide private sector involvement in sovereign debt restructuring.* *Another example is the UN Basic Principles on Sovereign Debt Restructuring Processes, adopted by the UN General Assembly in September 2015 through Resolution A/RES/69/319. These principles aim to provide a framework for fair and orderly sovereign debt restructuring to ensure transparency, accountability and*

AAAA paragraph	Commitment	Specific target or objective	Matching Sustainable Development Goal (SDG) target (where available)	State of implementation or progress made since 2015, using SDG or other relevant indicator (proxy)
	sharing and transparency.			*equitable treatment of all creditors and debtors. To date, over 130 UN member states have expressed support for these principles. However, some major economies and financial centres have not fully endorsed them, citing concerns over how these principles would interact with existing legal frameworks and financial markets.* *In 2012, UNCTAD introduced the Principles on Responsible Sovereign Lending and Borrowing, which are voluntary and non-binding. No country has officially endorsed the principles.* *In 2020, the IMF revised its debt limits policy to provide greater flexibility for countries in managing their debt according to their development needs. The revised policy takes a tailored approach, considering each country's specific circumstances and risk profile.* *The IMF and the World Bank also updated the Debt Sustainability Framework for Low-Income Countries in 2017, incorporating more comprehensive stress-testing and broader macroeconomic factors. The updated framework provides a more nuanced assessment of debt risks and supports responsible borrowing.* ODA concessionality criteria (discount rates and thresholds). The 2014 ODA rules introduced stricter concessionality criteria than earlier guidelines, with discount rates of 9%, 7% and 6%, and thresholds of 45%, 15% and 10% that replaced the previous 10% discount rate and 25% threshold. As a result, lenders must provide more concessional loans in order for them to qualify as ODA, which particularly impacts LDCs. Additionally, these new rules included a new safeguard regarding debt sustainability in the ODA criteria. Under these provisions, loans that do not comply with the IMF debt limits policy and/or the World Bank's Non-Concessional Borrowing Policy and Sustainable Development Finance Policy cannot be reported as ODA (OECD, 2023[30]). The OECD Recommendation on Sustainable Lending Practices and Officially Supported Exports Credits was adopted by the OECD Council meeting (all OECD members adhere) at ministerial level in 2018. It was revised in 2024 to update the references to the World Bank's Sustainable Development Finance Policy. The purpose of the Recommendation is to ensure that officially supported export credits do not contribute to the build-up of unsustainable external debt in lower-income countries. To this end, the Recommendation presents practices that adherents should follow when they are considering the provision of official export credit support to public sector obligors or guarantors in such countries (OECD, 2024[38]).

AAAA paragraph	Commitment	Specific target or objective	Matching Sustainable Development Goal (SDG) target (where available)	State of implementation or progress made since 2015, using SDG or other relevant indicator (proxy)
98	Emphasises the importance of debt restructurings being timely, orderly, effective, fair and negotiated in good faith with the aim of restoring public debt sustainability and maintaining favourable access to financing.	No	Target 17.4 See para. 93.	Reducing the time from IMF staff level agreement to delivering financial assurance from creditors for program approval under the Common Framework. Restructurings under the Common Framework have demonstrated a reduction in the delay as stakeholders acquire greater familiarity with the process (IMF, 2024[39]).
99	Limit the presence of sovereign bonds lacking collective action clauses. Improve co-ordination between public and private sectors and debtors and creditors to reduce moral hazards and achieve fair burden sharing in orderly debt restructurings. Recognise ongoing efforts by the IMF and the UN in this area, including the Paris Club's Paris Forum initiative.	No	Target 17.4 See para. 93.	Share of Paris Club creditors to LICs. By the end of 2021, the composition of lenders to LICs had shifted significantly compared with the line-up in 1996. The share of Paris Club creditors dropped from 39% to 11%, the share of non-Paris Club creditors more than doubled to 20%, and private creditors' share also more than doubled to 19% (UN, 2024[40]). This shift indicates a rise in loans provided at market terms, complicating debt management for developing countries and restricting their access to affordable financing options. Share of developing countries' public debt out of the global public debt. Developing countries' public debt reached USD 29 trillion, representing 30% of the global public debt in 2023. This was a significant rise from 2010, when their share was only 16% share, highlighting the rapid expansion of public debt in developing countries. Public debt in developing countries is increasing twice as fast as in developed countries (UNCTAD, 2024[7]).
100	Urge global action against minority bondholders disrupting majority-supported debt restructurings. Support reforms (including pari passu and collective action clauses) to protect sovereigns from holdout creditors. Provide legal assistance to LDCs and enhance international support for advisory services, including monitoring post-restructuring creditor litigation. Encourage countries issuing bonds under foreign laws to introduce such clauses in all bond issuances. (ref to International Capital Market	No	Target 17.4 See para. 93.	n.a.

AAAA paragraph	Commitment	Specific target or objective	Matching Sustainable Development Goal (SDG) target (where available)	State of implementation or progress made since 2015, using SDG or other relevant indicator (proxy)
	Association and IMF)			
101	Acknowledge the rise in sovereign bonds issued in domestic currency under national laws. Voluntarily enhance domestic legislation to reflect guiding principles for effective, timely, orderly and fair resolution of sovereign debt crises.	No	Target 17.4 See para. 93.	EMDE sovereign bond debt. EMDE sovereign bond debt reached a record high of nearly USD 3.9 trillion in the 2023 (OECD, 2024[9]). EMDE borrowing costs. While EMDE borrowing costs in local currency have risen, most remain below early 2000s levels. Real yields at issuance in local currency rose from about zero to 3% between 2020-21 and the first quarter of 2024, to over 7% and 5%, respectively, for LICs and speculative-grade economies (OECD, 2024[9]). *Recent developments in creditor countries' domestic laws highlight an increasing commitment to safeguarding developing countries from unsustainable debt. For example, the United Kingdom government has proposed enhancements to the country's legal framework to bolster litigation support for developing countries and has begun efforts to improve the transparency of debt held by private creditors. Likewise, there is a growing emphasis on regulating collateralised lending practices to promote fairer terms and mitigate the risk of excessive debt burdens on developing countries.*
102	Natural disasters and other shocks can undermine sovereign debt sustainability. Notes importance that public creditors help to ease debt payments. Encourage debt rescheduling and cancellation following shocks as well as the use of new financial instruments where appropriate. References the potential of debt-to-health and debt-to-nature swaps.	No	n.a.	The volume of debt relief provided following environmental, global health and other shocks. The G20's DSSI offered temporary relief by deferring USD 12.9 billion in debt service payments for LICs from May 2020 to December 2021 due to the COVID-19 pandemic (World Bank Group, 2022[41]). Following the DSSI, the G20 introduced the Common Framework for Debt Treatment to provide more structured debt relief. In addition, the Global Sovereign Debt Roundtable in 2023 aimed to enhance debt restructuring processes (Cassimon, 2023[42]). In 2023, around 140 debt-for-nature swaps have been entered into. Using a methodology derived from previous international debt-reduction schemes, the International Institute for Environment and Development (IIED) estimates that debt swaps could free up to USD100 billion to restore nature and help climate change adaptation (Whiting, 2024[43]).

AAAA paragraph	Commitment	Specific target or objective	Matching Sustainable Development Goal (SDG) target (where available)	State of implementation or progress made since 2015, using SDG or other relevant indicator (proxy)
				The Global Fund has operated the Debt2Health programme since 2007. Under the programme, ten implementing countries have entered into debt swap agreements with creditor countries, and more than USD 226 million in cancelled debt repayments have been invested in domestic health programmes (The Global Fund, n.d.[44]).

Note: The data points are mainly drawn from the UN's Sustainable Development Goals Extended Report 2024 and its statistical annexes. Trend data in are in constant USD 2015 prices unless otherwise indicated.

References

Alayza, N., V. Laxton and C. Neunuebel (2023), “Commentary: Developing countries won’t beat the climate crisis without tackling rising debt”, *World Resources Institute*, https://www.wri.org/insights/debt-climate-action-developing-countries. [16]

Ashcroft, A., K. Vasquez and R. Weeks-Brown (2024), “Hidden debt hurts economies. better disclosure laws can help ease the pain”, *IMF blog*, https://www.imf.org/en/Blogs/Articles/2024/04/02/Hidden-Debt-Hurts-Economies-Better-Disclosure-Laws-Can-Help-Ease-the-Pain. [19]

Beers, D., O. Ndukwe and A. Charron (2024), “BoC–BoE Sovereign Default Database: What’s new in 2024?”, *Staff Analytical Note*, No. 2024-19, Bank of Canada, Ottawa, https://www.bankofcanada.ca/wp-content/uploads/2024/07/SAN2024-19.pdf. [1]

Cassimon, D. (2023), “Debtor (Non-)Participation in Sovereign Debt Relief: A Real Option Approach”, *IMF Working Papers*, Vol. 2023/187, p. 1, https://doi.org/10.5089/9798400248504.001. [42]

Chamon, M. et al. (2022), “Debt-for-climate swaps: Analysis, design, and implementation”, *Working Paper*, No. WP/22/162, International Monetary Fund, Washington, DC, https://www.imf.org/en/Publications/WP/Issues/2022/08/11/Debt-for-Climate-Swaps-Analysis-Design-and-Implementation-522184. [24]

Chuku, C. et al. (2023), “Are we heading for another debt crisis in low-income countries? Debt vulnerabilities: Today vs the pre-HIPC era”, *Working Paper*, No. WP/23/79, International Monetary Fund, Washington, DC, https://www.elibrary.imf.org/view/journals/001/2023/079/article-A001-en.xml. [8]

Comelli, F. et al. (2023), “Navigating fiscal challenges in Sub-Saharan Africa: Resilient strategies and credible anchors in turbulent waters”, *African Departmental Paper*, No. DP/2020/007, International Monetary Fund, Washington, DC, https://doi.org/10.5089/9798400230349.087. [3]

Diwan, I., V. Songwe and M. Kessler (2024), *A Bridge to Climate Action*, Finance for Development Lab (FDL), https://findevlab.org/a-bridge-to-climate-action/ (accessed on 28 January 2025). [4]

Hicklin, J. (2024), “The IMF’s resilience and sustainability trust: How conditionality can help countries build resilience”, *CGD blog*, https://www.cgdev.org/publication/imfs-rst-how-conditionality-can-help-countries-build-resilience. [26]

Holland, A. and C. Pazarbasioglu (2024), “How to ease rising external debt-service pressures in low-income countries”, *IMF Blog*, https://meetings.imf.org/en/IMF/Home/Blogs/Articles/2024/01/24/how-to-ease-rising-external-debt-service-pressures-in-low-income-countries. [15]

Horn, S. et al. (2024), “Hidden debt revelations”, *Policy Research Working Paper*, No. 10907, World Bank Group, Washington, DC, https://documents1.worldbank.org/curated/en/099436209162426807/pdf/IDU11e8447b910f541496b18a3018630cb1554dc.pdf?_gl=1*18q729i*_gcl_au*MTgxOTYzNDgwNS4xNzIyNTI2OTA5. [17]

IMF (2024), *Sovereign Debt Restructuring Process Is Improving Amid Cooperation and Reform*, International Monetary Fund, https://www.imf.org/en/Blogs/Articles/2024/06/26/sovereign-debt-restructuring-process-is-improving-amid-cooperation-and-reform. [39]

IMF (2023), *Debt Relief Under the Heavily Indebted Poor Countries (HIPC) Initiative*, International Monetary Fund, https://www.imf.org/en/About/Factsheets/Sheets/2023/Debt-relief-under-the-heavily-indebted-poor-countries-initiative-HIPC. [33]

IMF (2022), *Capacity Development*, International Monetary Fund, https://www.imf.org/en/About/Factsheets/imf-capacity-development. [35]

International Monetary Fund (2024), "IMF Executive Board concludes the review of the Fund's Capacity Development Strategy", https://www.imf.org/en/News/Articles/2024/04/09/pr24111-imf-executive-board-concludes-the-review-of-fund-capacity-development-strategy. [12]

International Monetary Fund (2024), "Interim review of the Resilience and Sustainability Trust and review of adequacy of resources", *Policy Paper*, No. 2024/031, https://www.imf.org/en/Publications/Policy-Papers/Issues/2024/06/24/Interim-Review-of-The-Resilience-and-Sustainability-Trust-and-Review-of-Adequacy-of-550939. [25]

Merling, L. et al. (2024), *The Rising Cost of Debt: An Obstacle to Achieving Climate and Development Goals*, Center for Economic and Policy Research, Washington, DC, https://www.cepr.net/report/the-rising-cost-of-debt-an-obstacle-to-achieving-climate-and-development-goals/. [2]

OECD (2024), *Climate Finance Provided and Mobilised by Developed Countries in 2013-2022*, Climate Finance and the USD 100 Billion Goal, OECD Publishing, Paris, https://doi.org/10.1787/19150727-en. [23]

OECD (2024), *Global Debt Report 2024: Bond Markets in a High-Debt Environment*, OECD Publishing, Paris, https://doi.org/10.1787/91844ea2-en. [9]

OECD (2024), *Recommendation of the Council on Sustainable Lending Practices and Officially Supported Export Credits*, https://legalinstruments.oecd.org/en/instruments/OECD-LEGAL-0442. [38]

OECD (2023), *DAC Working Party on Development Finance Statistics: monitoring ODA grant equivalents*, ONE Members and Partners, https://one.oecd.org/document/DCD/DAC/STAT(2023)25/FINAL/en/pdf. [30]

OECD (2023), *Sovereign Borrowing Outlook 2023*, OECD Publishing, Paris, https://doi.org/10.1787/09b4cfba-en. [10]

Rivetti, D. (2021), *Debt Transparency in Developing Economies (English)*, World Bank Group, Washington D.C., http://documents.worldbank.org/curated/en/743881635526394087/Debt-Transparency-in-Developing-Economies. [18]

Spiegel, S. and O. Schwank (2022), "Bridging the 'great finance divide' in developing countries", *Brookings Commentary*, https://www.brookings.edu/articles/bridging-the-great-finance-divide-in-developing-countries/. [13]

The Global Fund (n.d.), *Debt2Health: Collaboration Through Financial Innovation*, https://www.theglobalfund.org/media/12284/publication_debt2health_overview_en.pdf. [44]

UK Parliament (2023), *Debt Relief in Low-income Countries*, https://publications.parliament.uk/pa/cm5803/cmselect/cmintdev/146/report.html. [22]

UN (2024), *Financing for Sustainable Development Report 2024: Financing for Development at a Crossroads*, United Nations Department Social and Economic Affairs, Financing for Sustainable Development Office, New York, https://desapublications.un.org/publications/financing-sustainable-development-report-2024. [40]

UN (2024), *Progress Towards the Sustainable Development Goals - Report of the Secretary-General: Statistical Annex*, United Nations Economic and Social Council, New York, https://unstats.un.org/sdgs/files/report/2024/E_2024_54_Statistical_Annex_I_and_II.pdf. [27]

UN (2023), *United Nations Secretary-General's SDG Stimulus to Deliver Agenda 2030*, United Nations, https://www.un.org/sustainabledevelopment/wp-content/uploads/2023/02/SDG-Stimulus-to-Deliver-Agenda-2030.pdf?utm_source=chatgpt.com. [28]

UN ECOSOC (2024), *Enhanced monitoring of countries that are graduating or have graduated from the list of LDCs*, https://www.un.org/development/desa/dpad/wp-content/uploads/sites/45/CDP-excerpt-2024-3.pdf. [31]

UN ECOSOC (2024), *Report on the twenty-sixth session (4–8 March 2024)*, https://documents.un.org/doc/undoc/gen/n24/096/02/pdf/n2409602.pdf. [32]

UNCTAD (2024), *A World of Debt: A Growing Burden To Global Prosperity*, https://unctad.org/publication/world-of-debt. [7]

UNCTAD (2024), *Escalating debt challenges are inhibiting achievement of the SDGs (webpage)*, https://sdgpulse.unctad.org/debt-sustainability/ (accessed on 26 November 2024). [5]

Walker, J. et al. (2022), *Commitment to Reducing Inequality Index 2022*, Development Finance International Inc. and Oxfam, Washington, DC and Oxford, UK, https://oxfamilibrary.openrepository.com/bitstream/handle/10546/621419/rr-cri-2022-111022-en.pdf;jsessionid=83F5B359941D181B83223A7307738B55?sequence=33. [14]

Whiting, K. (2024), *Climate finance: What are debt-for-nature swaps and how can they help countries?*, World Economic Forum, https://www.weforum.org/stories/2024/04/climate-finance-debt-nature-swap/. [43]

World Bank (2024), *Heavily Indebted Poor Countries (HIPC) Initiative*, World Bank, https://www.worldbank.org/en/topic/debt/brief/hipc. [29]

World Bank (2024), *Joint External Debt Hub (database)*, https://databank.worldbank.org/source/joint-external-debt-hub (accessed on November 2024). [21]

World Bank (2023), *Brief - Debt Management Facility (DMF)*, https://www.worldbank.org/en/topic/debt/brief/debt-management-facility. [11]

World Bank (2023), *International Debt Report 2023*, https://www.worldbank.org/en/programs/debt-statistics/idr/products. [6]

World Bank (2023), *Preliminary Findings from the G-7 and Paris Club Countries Debt Data Sharing Exercise*, https://thedocs.worldbank.org/en/doc/6e72b0ded996306fa01f5db7a0c38b19-0050052021/related/G7-and-Paris-Club-Data-Reconciliation-Exercise-April-2023.pdf. [20]

World Bank (n.d.), *Debt Management Performance Assessment (DeMPA)*, https://www.worldbank.org/en/programs/debt-toolkit/dempa. [36]

World Bank Group (2023), *Debt Management Facility (DMF)*, https://www.worldbank.org/en/topic/debt/brief/debt-management-facility. [34]

World Bank Group (2023), *Debt Reporting Heat Map*, https://www.worldbank.org/en/topic/debt/brief/debt-transparency-report/2023. [37]

World Bank Group (2022), *Debt Service Suspension Initiative*, https://www.worldbank.org/en/topic/debt/brief/covid-19-debt-service-suspension-initiative. [41]

Notes

[1] Insolvent countries are those that cannot meet their debt obligations without either significant adjustments to their revenues and expenditures or external assistance. There is no definition of an insolvency threshold under the International Monetary Fund-World Bank debt sustainability analysis. Illiquid countries are identified as those that do not breach insolvency thresholds yet are exceeding or will exceed the debt service-to-revenue thresholds within the next five years. For more information, see https://findevlab.org/a-bridge-to-climate-action/.

[2] These estimates are calculated based on the Bank of Canada staff analytical note available at https://www.bankofcanada.ca/wp-content/uploads/2024/07/SAN2024-19.pdf.

[3] This decline is partly explained by high US dollar bond yields having exceeded the 10% mark in 15 countries in 2023, up from 2 countries in 2019.

[4] The value of debt-for-nature swaps has increased since 2020, particularly in countries Barbados, Belize, Ecuador, and Gabon, though the number of these swaps has not increased significantly. See https://www.iied.org/debt-swaps-could-release-100-billion-for-climate-action.

7 Addressing Systemic Issues

This chapter reviews the Systemic Issues action area of the Addis Ababa Action Agenda (AAAA) including progress, persistent challenges, and emerging areas as the international community prepares for the Fourth International Conference on Financing for Development (FfD4). Key trends highlight the declining capacity of global reserves and the growing impact of inflation on economic resilience, particularly in vulnerable and developing countries. Efforts to strengthen financial stability and crisis prevention have delivered improvements, though disparities in access to resources and representation persist. Persistent challenges include conflicts and forced migration, strained financing capacities, while emerging risks include climate change, pandemics, and geopolitical tensions. Progress in policy coherence, health systems, and multilateral development reforms points to potential solutions, but the need for enhanced global collaboration and governance remains central to achieving sustainable development goals. Addressing these issues requires aligning systemic reforms with long-term resilience and equity in the face of evolving global risks.

7.1. Data dashboard

Key trends

Global reserves (in months of imports ratio) decreased by a third between 2015 and 2022.

Total reserves worldwide went from 13 months of imports in 2015 to 8.9 months in 2022 (-32%). This trend is also visible in developing countries, where reserves have decreased by 21% for least developed countries (LDCs), 31% for landlocked developing countries (LLDCs) and 25% for small island developing states (SIDS) over the same period (UN, 2024[1]).[1]

Figure 7.1. Total reserves

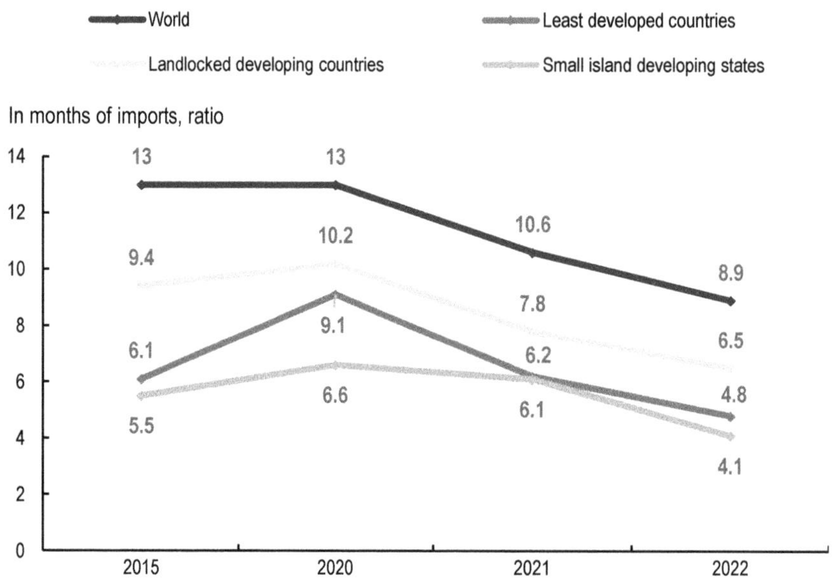

Note: Total reserves consist of monetary gold holdings, special drawing rights, International Monetary Fund (IMF) member reserves held by the IMF and foreign exchange assets managed by monetary authorities. This indicator represents reserves in terms of the number of months of imports of goods and services the reserves could cover, per the World Bank metadata glossary.
Source: Authors' calculations based on the United Nations (2024[2]), *Statistical Annex I and II: SDG Report 2024*, https://unstats.un.org/sdgs/files/report/2024/E_2024_54_Statistical_Annex_I_and_II.pdf.

Inflation has risen significantly globally and across all regions

Global inflation has surged from 1.4% in 2015 to 7.9% in 2022. This trend has been observed across all regions. Central and Southern Asia recorded the highest inflation rate, which reached 9.6% in 2022, up from 5.7% in 2015. Europe and Northern America experienced the largest increase, with inflation rising by 8.6 percentage points over the same period.

Figure 7.2. Annual inflation, consumer prices

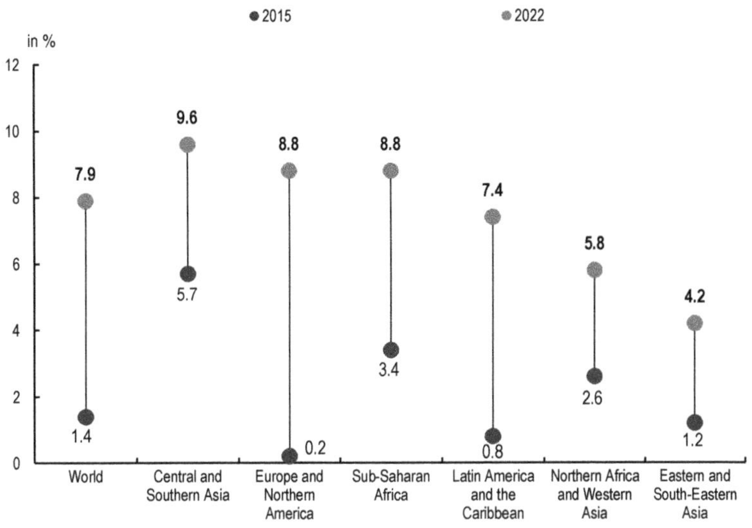

Source: Authors' calculations based on the United Nations (2024[2]), *Statistical Annex I and II: SDG Report 2024*, https://unstats.un.org/sdgs/files/report/2024/E_2024_54_Statistical_Annex_I_and_II.pdf.

Recorded food prices are high, particularly in developing countries.

High inflationary pressures in the global post-pandemic environment have taken a toll on all countries. In 2022, 58% of countries recorded abnormally high or moderately high food prices, up from 23% of countries in 2015.

The share of developing countries recording abnormally high or moderately high food prices has increased since 2015. In 2022, 45% of LDCs, 44% of SIDS and 50% of LLDCs recorded abnormally high or moderately high food prices compared with, respectively, 22%, 36% and 14% in 2015. The detrimental effect of high inflation on households has been higher for households in extreme poverty (OECD et al., 2023[3]).

Figure 7.3. Proportion of countries recording abnormally high or moderately high food prices

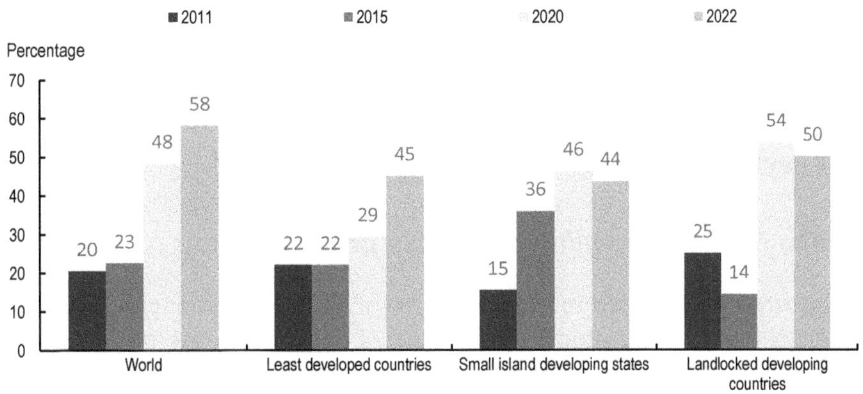

Note: Abnormally high values are defined as those for which the indicator of food price anomalies is equal to or exceeds 1. Moderately high values are defined as those for which the indicator is equal to or greater than 0.5 but strictly less than 1.

Source: Authors' calculations based on the United Nations (2024[2]), *Statistical Annex I and II: SDG Report 2024*, https://unstats.un.org/sdgs/files/report/2024/E_2024_54_Statistical_Annex_I_and_II.pdf.

Key performance indicators

↑	The global financial safety net was strengthened by the new 2021 allocation of USD 650 billion in special drawing rights. About one-third of this allocation went to developing countries, amounting to 0.42% of their gross domestic product (GDP) (United Nations, 2024[4]).
↔	Approximately half of the world's economies hold 97% of international reserves, with the remaining 3% held by a group of about 90 vulnerable emerging and low-income countries (UN, 2024[2]).
↔	Developing countries hold 37% of the voting rights at the IMF and 39% at the World Bank though they constitute 75% of the membership in these institutions (UN, 2024[2]).
↔	Non-bank financial intermediation represented 47.2% of total global financial assets in 2022 compared with 48.6% in 2015 (FSB, 2023[5]).
↔	In a 2023 survey by the OECD[1], 73% of responding countries identified lack of data and analysis on the transboundary impacts of policies as a key barrier to making progress on policy coherence for sustainable development.

↓ Slight setback	↓ Setback	↔ No change, neutral	↔ Stagnant, possible issue	↑ Major progress	↑ Minimal progress
Minimal setback	↓ Major setback	Holding steady, slight concern	↔ Negative stagnation, concerning	Progress	↑ Negligible progress or progress contested

Notes: 1. This refers to countries that have adhered to the OECD Council Recommendation on Policy Coherence for Sustainable Development, available at https://legalinstruments.oecd.org/en/instruments/OECD-LEGAL-0381.
Selected quantifiable commitments. Annex Table 7.A.1 contains the full list. It should be noted that the chapter of the Addis Ababa Action Agenda on systemic issues does not include quantifiable or timebound commitments.

Resource mobilisation potential

- Ongoing reforms of multilateral development banks aim to triple total lending volumes by 2030 to reach USD 400 billion per year.
- Climate change could cost the world economy an estimated USD 38 trillion per year by 2050, which would translate to a loss of 19% in income per capita around the world (Kotz, Levermann and Wenz, 2024[6]).
- The cumulative economic costs of the COVID-19 pandemic are estimated at about USD 13.8 trillion in global output loss through to 2024 (Sobrinho, Chun and Naidoo, 2022[7]; Imperial College London, 2023[8]).

7.2. Key areas of progress

Efforts to strengthen financial stability and crisis prevention are paying off

Financial stability measures accelerated in the aftermath of the global financial crisis in 2008-09. Thus, many of these measures were in place before the Addis Ababa Action Agenda (AAAA) was adopted in 2015, and they have since contributed to greater resilience in the international financial system. The Early Warning Exercise, a semi-annual assessment to identify and analyse potential risks to the global financial system that could lead to significant economic disruptions, was created in 2008. A year later, in 2009, the Financial Stability Board (FSB) was established to strengthen financial regulation and prevent future crises. In 2017, the IMF introduced a Macroprudential Policy Survey feeding the integrated Macroprudential Policy database, which facilitates quantitative analyses of macroprudential instruments. Basel III standards, a set of regulatory reform measures that cover banks' capital, leverage and liquidity, were finalised in 2018, with full implementation expected by end-2024. An evaluation of the impact and efficacy of these various reforms found that the overall resilience of the banking sector has increased without affecting the cost of capital of banks. In 2022, banks showed improved performance compared with 2015, a shift driven by ongoing recovery from the COVID-19 crisis. The share of countries reporting a return on assets (ROA) above 1% rose to 77.2%, up from 70.0% in 2021, and the median ROA increased to 1.56% from 1.34%.

However, there are concerns that tighter regulations have led to a reduction in cross-border lending by global banks to developing countries, including for financing infrastructure projects. Tightened bank regulations also gave rise to a greater role for non-bank financial intermediation (NBFI), which can exacerbate the volatility of international financial flows. NBFI grew by 31.7%, from USD 165.4 billion in 2015 to USD 217.9 billion in 2022. In relative terms, NGFI represented 47.0% of total global financial assets in 2022 compared with 48.6% in 2015, 42.0% in 2008 and a peak of 50.0% in 2019 (FSB, 2023[5]).

The global financial crisis also triggered a number of proposals and legislation aimed at strengthening the regulatory and supervisory framework for credit rating agencies (CRAs). In 2010, for instance, the FSB called for a reduction of reliance on CRA ratings, but little progress has been made since (see chapter 4). The big three CRAs (Moody's, S&P and Fitch Ratings) together hold 95% of the credit rating market and are frequently criticised for their perceived bias towards developing countries. The planned establishment of the pan-African CRA is expected to help make borrowing cheaper for African governments by providing more accurate assessments that take into account regional dynamics and geopolitical factors.

The global financial safety net is stronger but remains uneven

Countries' own reserves, the largest component of the global financial safety net, have increased in absolute terms but decreased in relative terms since 2015. Countries' reserves covered 8.9 months of imports in 2022, down from 13 months in 2015. The global network of bilateral swap lines provided prompt liquidity support during the pandemic, helping to stabilise the global financial markets and capital flows to emerging markets and developing economies. The network expanded substantially, from 6 swap lines in the early 2000s to 160 swap lines in 2024. However, very few developing countries have access to these facilities. According to the IMF, 97% of international reserves are held by approximately half of the world's economies, with a group of about 90 vulnerable EMDEs accounting for the remaining 3%.

The IMF has significantly expanded lending while adjusting its toolkit to address evolving needs, especially in developing and vulnerable countries. In FY2023, the IMF approved about USD 5.7 billion in new concessional lending commitments to low-income countries (LICs) – more than the three times the volumes in FY2015 (USD 1.8 billion). The Resilience and Sustainability Trust, created in 2022, helps countries build resilience to macroeconomic risks arising from longer-term structural challenges including climate change and pandemic preparedness. The allocation of an additional USD 650 billion in special drawing rights[2] (SDRs) helped countries address balance of payments needs and improve liquidity (see chapter 6). To date, a total of SDR 660.7 billion (equivalent to roughly USD 943 billion) have been allocated and constitute a significant portion of countries' international reserves. However, SDR distribution is based on IMF quotas, meaning that high-income countries receive the majority of the SDRs.

Calls to reform the international financial architecture abound

Bridgetown 3.0 (Global Policy Forum, 2024[9]), the United Nations Sustainable Development Goal (SDG) Stimulus (United Nations Secretary-General, 2024[10]), and the Paris Pact for People and the Planet (French Ministry for Europe and Foreign Affairs, 2023[11]) collectively call for a comprehensive reform of the international financial architecture to enhance support for climate action, sustainable development and economic resilience in vulnerable and developing countries. Reforms under way of multilateral development banks (MDBs) as part of these initiatives focus on increasing the scale and development impact of lending. The World Bank Group's evolution roadmap (World Bank, 2023[12]), updated in September 2023, suggests that it could boost its lending capacity by USD 50 billion, to USD 150 billion, over 2022-32 – an annual average increase of between USD 5 billion and USD 15 billion. In a joint Viewpoint Note (IDB, 2024[13]) released for the WBG and IMF Spring and Annual Meetings, ten MDBs estimated that they could collectively expand their lending headroom by an additional USD 300 billion to USD 400 billion over the coming ten years, equivalent to an annual average increase of USD 30 billion to USD 40 billion. The projected increases, however, would fall short of initial targets, such as the goal of an additional USD 260 billion per year set by the Group of Twenty (G20) Independent Expert Group (G20 Independent Experts Group, 2023[14]), in part because current reform initiatives are tilted towards increasing capital efficiency rather than increasing the general capital of MDBs.

Despite the repeated commitments to enhance the voice and participation of developing countries, their representation has not significantly changed in many international financial institutions and standard-setting bodies. Developing countries hold only 37% and 39%, respectively, of the voting rights in the IMF and World Bank but constitute 75% of the membership of these institutions. While there has been an increase in IMF quota allocations, the quota formula has not been updated to reflect the shifting economic weights of member countries in the world. The current IMF quota formula was agreed in 2008. The 14th General Review of Quotas entered into force in 2016 and the 15th review took place in 2020. The 16th review, which took place in 2023, approved a 50% increase in quota resources, with members' contributions to be in proportion to their current shareholdings – the equivalent of raising the IMF's permanent resources to USD 960 billion.[3]

7.3. Persistent challenges

The number of conflicts is growing, driving insecurity and placing additional burden on countries' financing capacities

The growing number of conflicts is taking a heavy toll on financing capacities. In 2023, there were 56 active conflicts, the highest number since the end of the Second World War (IEP, 2024[15]). The global economic cost of violence amounted to USD 19.1 trillion, or 13.5% of global GDP (IEP, 2024[15]). But spending on peacebuilding and peacekeeping amounted to USD 49.6 billion, accounting for less than 0.6% of total military expenditure in purchasing power parity terms (IEP, 2024[15]).

Migration is on the rise, bring with it opportunities and challenges for financing for sustainable development

An estimated 281 million people were living in a country other than their country of birth in 2020 – 32 million more than in 2015, 128 million more than in 1990 and more than triple the estimated number in 1970 (IOM, 2021[16]). As a consequence, the volume of remittances has also been increasing, representing a crucial source of income for households and small and medium-sized enterprises (see chapter 3).

At the same time, forced migration has increased steeply. At the end of 2022, the number of forcibly displaced people worldwide was estimated at 108.4 million, among them 62.5 million internally displaced persons, 35.3 million refugees and 5.4 million asylum seekers (UNHCR, 2022[17]). The majority (76%) of forcibly displaced people worldwide are hosted in low- and middle-income countries, straining the already stretched resources of these countries. (The cost of hosting refugees in donor countries is presented in chapter 4 on international development co-operation.)

Policy coherence for sustainable development demands greater political ambition to assess and address policy impacts

Achieving greater policy coherence for sustainable development (PCSD) remains a major challenge. The interconnected nature of the world economy and interconnectedness of economic, social and environmental challenges mean that individual countries' policies often have transboundary impacts[4] on other countries and the global commons. Despite commitments, governments have made limited progress to assess and address the impacts of their policies on global sustainable development (OECD, 2024[18]). This shortfall is mainly due to insufficient data, limited technical capacity, low political leadership and weak institutional mandates to implement measures. Lack of data and analysis on the potential transboundary impact of policies is a key obstacle. Governments must be better equipped to anticipate, address and adjust policies to systematically consider their impact on global sustainable development.

Failing to assess, monitor and address the interactions and impacts of different policies undermines key global objectives and negatively affects the sustainable development prospects of developing countries. For instance, the absence of global co-ordination and policy coherence hampers developing countries' access to climate finance and the equitable management of shared resources. Due to rising energy prices, direct fossil fuel subsidies rose to USD 1.53 trillion in 2022, a fivefold increase over 2020, that reversed progress towards the net zero transition (see chapter 2). Potentially trade-distortive state interventions surged after the COVID-19 pandemic, hindering the competitiveness and global trade participation of LDCs (see chapter 5).

7.4. New and emerging areas

A new context since the AAAA brings a shift in systemic issues beyond systemic financial risk

Since the AAAA was adopted in 2015, shifting global challenges have reshaped the nature of systemic risks, posing fresh threats to financing for development beyond those related to the global financial crisis of 2008-09. Emerging threats now include climate change, pandemics and limited fiscal space as well as risks posed by artificial intelligence and cybersecurity vulnerabilities. At the same time, geopolitical pressures, including war and violent conflict, have intensified, complicating collective decision making through international and intergovernmental bodies. There is a threat that the world will be divided into rival geopolitical blocs, which would reshape global trade and affect the cross-border allocation of capital. For example, a one standard deviation increase in geopolitical tensions between an investing country and a recipient country could reduce bilateral cross-border portfolio and bank allocation by about 15% (IMF, 2023[19]). The growing complexity and interconnected nature of these systemic risks make it all the more imperative for governments to strengthen their political commitment to PCSD and their tools to ensure this coherence and to ensure long-term policy making that takes into account the impact of policies now and into the future.

Climate change and biodiversity loss present a key systemic risk

Climate change presents a major systemic risk. If no additional measures are taken to address climate change, the negative impact on global annual GDP could range from 1.0% to 3.3% by 2060 (OECD, 2015[20]). In 2023, 129 countries reported having a national disaster risk reduction strategy that is aligned to the Sendai Framework. However, according to the United Nations Environment Programme, international adaptation finance flows to developing countries fall short of estimated needs (USD 300 billion annually by 2030) by a factor of five to ten (UNEP, 2022[21]). At COP27 in 2022, a Loss and Damage Fund was established with the aim of providing financial assistance to countries most vulnerable to and impacted by the effects of climate change. The Kunming-Montreal Global Biodiversity Framework, adopted in December 2022, aims to halt and reverse biodiversity loss that, unless addressed, could trigger a collapse in ecosystem services that would result in a USD 2.7 trillion annual decline in global GDP by 2030 (World Bank Group, 2021[22]). The Kunming-Montreal Global Biodiversity Framework includes targets to mobilise at least US*D 200 billion* per year in financial resources for biodiversity by 2030 from public and private sources.

There is widespread acknowledgement of the need to assess, manage and mitigate the financial vulnerabilities due to climate change, commonly referred to as climate-related financial risks. In 2021, the FSB published a comprehensive roadmap to address climate-related financial risks in four key policy areas: firm-level disclosures, data, vulnerabilities analysis, and regulatory and supervisory practices and tools. Starting in 2015, the now-disbanded Task Force on Climate-Related Financial Disclosures co-ordinated efforts to improve climate-related disclosures. The International Sustainability Standards Board currently is leading follow-up efforts.

The pandemic highlighted the systemic relevance of global health

The COVID-19 pandemic caused major disruptions to the global economy and heightened awareness of the critical relevance of global health for sustainable development (World Bank, 2022[23]). The G20 High Level Independent Panel estimates that a Global Health Threats Fund would require at least USD 10 billion in additional annual investment and that another USD 5 billion is needed to strengthen the World Health Organization (WHO) and other institutions.

Donor investments in global health have increased. The Pandemic Fund was established in 2022 to finance investments to strengthen pandemic prevention, preparedness and response capacities, with a focus on low- and middle-income countries. In 2023, WHO members agreed on a 20% increase in assessed contributions and the establishment of a replenishment mechanism to raise multi-year voluntary contributions. In 2022, 182 State Parties (representing 93% of anticipated submissions) reported on their implementation of the international health regulations (IHRs), which require countries to develop capacities to respond to public emergencies. Overall, according to the WHO, IHR capacities improved, albeit modestly, with the average global score rising from 64% in 2021 to 66% in 2022 (UN, 2024[2]). Total net ODA disbursements to medical research and basic health sectors totalled USD 21.1 billion in 2022, more than double the 2015 total of USD 10.5 billion (UN, 2024[2]).

Inflationary pressures cause cost-of-living spikes and diminish access to finance

High inflationary pressures in the global post-pandemic environment have taken a toll on developing countries. Annual inflation (consumer prices) rose to 7.9% in 2022, up from 1.4% in 2015. In LDCs, inflation reached 9.5% in 2022 compared with 4.0% in 2015. The share of countries experiencing moderately to abnormally high food prices hit a record high of 58.1% in 2022, a significant increase from 22.5% in 2015. Due to the spike in food prices, an estimated 29.6% of the global population – 2.4 billion people – did not have access to adequate food in 2022, 745 million more than in 2015.

Monetary tightening in response to inflation has exacerbated countries' struggle to secure stable and affordable long-term financing to support sustainable development. Developing countries' average interest cost on external borrowing is three times higher than that of developed countries (see chapter 6).

Cybersecurity risks could detract from available financing for sustainable development

See chapter 8 on science, technology, innovation and capacity building.

Annex 7.A. Addressing Systemic Issues

Annex Table 7.A.1. Assessment of the action area: Addressing systemic issues

AAAA paragraph	Commitment	Specific target or objective	Matching Sustainable Development Goal (SDG) target (where available)	State of implementation or progress made since 2015, using selected SDG or other relevant indicators (proxy)
103	Emphasise the importance of the coherence and consistency of the international financial and monetary and trading systems in support of development. Enhance global economic governance to develop a stronger, more coherent, inclusive and representative international framework for sustainable development while respecting the mandates of each organisation.	No	Target 17.13 Enhance global macroeconomic stability, including through policy co-ordination and policy coherence. Target 17.14 Enhance policy coherence for sustainable development. Target 17.15 Respect each country's policy space and leadership to establish and implement policies for poverty eradication and sustainable development.	SDG Indicator 17.13.1 Macroeconomic dashboard. • cash surplus and/or deficit as a proportion of gross domestic product (GDP) The global cash deficit was -8.0% of GDP in 2021, greater than the -3.7% of GDP in 2015. In least developed countries (LDCs), the deficit was -2.2% of GDP in 2018 versus -2.7% in 2015 (UN, 2024[1]). • annual inflation, consumer prices Global annual inflation (consumer prices) rose to 7.9% in 2022, up from 1.4% in 2015. In LDCs, inflation reached 9.5%, more than double the 4% in 2015 (UN, 2024[1]). • annual GDP growth Global GDP grew by 3.1% in 2022, marking a recovery from a decline of -3.1% in 2020 and matching the growth rate of 3.1% seen in 2015, but it was still lower than the 4.5% growth rate in 2000. For LDCs, GDP growth was 4.5% in 2022 following a contraction of -0.2% in 2020, a 2.7% growth rate in 2015 and a peak growth of 7.3% in 2005 (UN, 2024[1]). SDG indicator 17.14.1 Number of countries with mechanisms in place to enhance policy coherence of sustainable development. In most countries, governments lack dedicated resources, leadership and mechanisms to ensure policy coherence on sustainable development (PCSD), making it challenging to track progress on PCSD. In 2020, 27 countries reported their status by completing the relevant questionnaire, with scores ranging from 43% to 100% (UN, 2024[1]).

AAAA paragraph	Commitment	Specific target or objective	Matching Sustainable Development Goal (SDG) target (where available)	State of implementation or progress made since 2015, using selected SDG or other relevant indicators (proxy)
				In 2024, adherents to the OECD Council Recommendation on PCSD reported similar challenges including limited use of tools to assess the transboundary impacts of their policies. The share of adherents to the OECD Council Recommendation on PCSD that report using impact assessments to understand the transboundary impacts of their policies on developing countries was just 16%. (OECD, 2024[24]) SDG indicator 17.15.1 Extent of use of country-owned results frameworks and planning tools by providers of development co-operation. In 2018, it was estimated that 57% of bilateral providers used country-owned results frameworks and planning tools compared with 66% of multilateral providers (UN, 2024[1]).
104	Emphasise the need for robust financial market regulation and a global safety net since the 2008-09 financial crisis. Build on the progress made since Monterrey to build resilience, reduce vulnerability to international financial disruption and reduce spillover effects of global financial crises, including on developing countries. Strengthen International Monetary Fund lending capacity and leverage development banks' countercyclical roles during the crisis. Collaborate to reduce systemic risks. (ref. to Basel III).	No	Target 17.13 See para 103. Target 10.5 Improve the regulation and monitoring of global financial markets and institutions and strengthen the implementation of such regulations.	SDG Indicator 17.13.1 Macroeconomic dashboard • total reserves in months of imports Global total reserves, measured in months of imports, decreased to 8.9 in 2022, down from 13 in 2015. For LDCs, reserves dropped to 4.8 months in 2022, compared with 6.1 in 2015 (UN, 2024[1]). SDG indicator 10.5.1 Financial soundness indicator. In 2022, banks showed improved performance compared with 2015, a shift driven by ongoing recovery from the COVID-19 crisis. The share of countries reporting a return on assets (ROA) above 1% rose to 77.2%, up from 70.0% in 2021, and the median ROA increased from 1.34% to 1.56%. Asset quality also improved, with the median non-performing loans ratio falling from 4.07% in 2021 to 3.52% in 2022. At the same time, the capital buffer remained steady, with the median Tier 1 capital to risk-weighted assets at 16.8%, slightly down from 17% in 2021 (UN, 2024[1]). Allocations to the global financial safety net. Share of the allocation that goes to developing countries. Approximately half of the world's economies hold 97% of international reserves, with the remaining 3% held by a group of about 90 vulnerable EMDEs. Following the global financial crisis, the share of bilateral swap lines and regional financing arrangements has grown relative to that of the IMF, and IMF quota resources have decreased in relative terms compared to borrowed resources (IMF, 2023[25]). The global financial safety net was strengthened by the new 2021 allocation of USD

AAAA paragraph	Commitment	Specific target or objective	Matching Sustainable Development Goal (SDG) target (where available)	State of implementation or progress made since 2015, using selected SDG or other relevant indicators (proxy)
				650 billion in special drawing rights to help countries manage the economic impact of the COVID-19 pandemic. About one-third of this allocation went to developing countries, amounting to 0.42% of their GDP (UN, 2024[26]).
105	Pursue reforms of the international financial and monetary system to enhance global co-ordination and policy coherence for financial and macroeconomic stability. Mitigate the risk of financial crises, recognising the global impact of national policies. Address risks from volatile capital flows with macroprudential measures and, when necessary, capital flow management.	No	Target 17.14 See para. 103.	*See para. 103; see chapter 3 for more information on volatility of capital flows.* *In 2017, the IMF introduced a Macroprudential Policy Survey feeding the integrated Macroprudential Policy database, a comprehensive historical database that combines information on volatility from various sources and facilitates quantitative analyses. Participation in the annual survey has been increasing, and the database now covers 184 economies* (IMF, 2023[27]).
106	Increase the voice and participation of developing countries in international economic decision making and global economic governance (ref. to ratification and implementation of 2010 IMF reforms, governance reform of the IMF and World Bank) as well as the contribution of developing countries in norm-setting processes (ref. to Basel Committee on Banking Supervision and other standard-setting bodies). Support transparent, gender-balanced and merit-based leadership selections and the promotion of staff diversity in international financial institutions.	No	Target 10.6 Ensure enhanced representation and voice for developing countries in decision making in global international economic and financial institutions in order to deliver more effective, credible, accountable and legitimate institutions.	SDG indicator 10.6.1 Proportion of members and voting rights of developing countries in international organisations: (a) proportion of developing countries in the membership of international organisations (b) proportion of developing countries' voting rights at international organisations. EMDEs hold 40.9% of votes and 38.6% of quota shares at the IMF though they generate 58% of global GDP ((purchasing power parity (PPP)) and represent 86.4% of the global population. In contrast, advanced economies, with only 13.6% of the global population and 40.3% of GDP (PPP), hold 59.1% of votes and 61.4% of quotas at the IMF (Boston University Global Development Policy Center, 2025[28]). Developing countries hold 39% of the voting rights at the World Bank, despite constituting 75% of the membership (UN, 2024[1]). *The current IMF quota formula is a weighted average of GDP (weight of 50%), openness to the global economy (30%), economic variability (15%) and international reserves (5%). GDP is measured through a blend of GDP based on market exchange rates (weight of 60%) and on PPP exchange rates (40%). The current IMF quota formula was agreed in 2008. The 14th General Review of Quotas entered into force in 2016, and the 15th review took place in 2020.The 16th review, which took place in 2023, approved a 50% increase in quota resources, with members' contributions to*

AAAA paragraph	Commitment	Specific target or objective	Matching Sustainable Development Goal (SDG) target (where available)	State of implementation or progress made since 2015, using selected SDG or other relevant indicators (proxy)
				be in proportion to their current shareholdings – the equivalent of raising the IMF's permanent resources to USD 960 billion; the increase is to be effective in late 2024 when members with 85% of the votes will have ratified changes in their quota contributions (IMF, 2023[29]). *A new process for World Bank reform has been underway since 2021. The Intergovernmental Group of Twenty-Four proposed new targets for the IMF and World Bank Group (WBG) reforms. At the WBG and IMF Spring and Annual Meetings, the WBG announced that member states committed a total of USD 11 billion for three new financial instruments: the Portfolio Guarantee Platform, the Hybrid Capital Mechanism and the Livable Planet Fund. These resources should enable the WBG to leverage additional lending worth more than USD 63 billion* (Global Policy Forum, 2024[30]). *A joint MDB Viewpoint Note estimates that the ten main multilateral development banks could collectively expand their lending headroom by an additional USD 300 billion to USD 400 billion over the coming ten years, equating to an annual average increase of USD 30 billion to USD 40 billion. These gains fall short of the G20 Independent Expert Group target of raising an additional USD 260 billion per year* (G20 Independent Experts Group, 2023[14]).
107	Strengthen the international financial safety net and maintain a robust, quota-based IMF with adequate resources. Support collaboration between the IMF and regional financial arrangements, improve early warning systems for financial risks, and advocate for more flexible IMF support for developing countries. Promote financial risk management and capacity building in developing countries, ensuring that international standards align with the SDGs and the post-2015 agenda.	No	n.a.	Allocations to the global financial safety net. Share of the allocation that went to developing countries. See paras. 104 and 106 (on IMF quotas, global safety net). Development and efficiency of early warning systems. Created in 2008 at the request of the G20, the Early Warning Exercise (EWE) is a semi-annual assessment conducted jointly by the IMF and the Financial Stability Board (FSB). Its primary purpose is to identify and analyse potential risks to the global financial system that could lead to significant economic disruptions. The results of the EWE are presented to senior officials at the WBG and IMF Spring and Annual Meetings (IMF, 2023[31]).
108	Implement measures to avoid excessive volatility of commodity prices, including for food and	No	Target 2.c Adopt measures to ensure the proper	SDG indicator 2.c.1 Indicator of food price anomalies The share of countries experiencing moderately to abnormally high food prices hit a

AAAA paragraph	Commitment	Specific target or objective	Matching Sustainable Development Goal (SDG) target (where available)	State of implementation or progress made since 2015, using selected SDG or other relevant indicators (proxy)
	agriculture, and mitigate impact on global food security and nutrition. Urge regulatory bodies to facilitate timely, accurate and transparent market information (acknowledging the Agricultural Market Information System managed by the Food and Agriculture Organization). Support small-scale artisanal fishers by providing access to marine resources and markets while adhering to sustainable management practices and enhancing the value of their products.		functioning of food commodity markets and their derivatives and facilitate timely access to market information, including on food reserves, in order to help limit extreme food price volatility. Target 14.7 By 2030, increase the economic benefits to small island developing states (SIDS) and LDCs from the sustainable use of marine resources, including through sustainable management of fisheries, aquaculture and tourism. Target 14.b Provide access for small-scale artisanal fishers to marine resources and markets.	record high of 58.1% in 2022, a significant increase from 22.5% in 2015. For LDCs, this share was 45% in 2022 compared with 22% in 2015. The surge was largely due to major disruptions in logistics and food supply chains following Russia's full-scale invasion of Ukraine, which led to higher food and energy prices, especially in the first half of 2022 (UN, 2024[1]). SDG indicator 14.7.1 Sustainable fisheries as a proportion of GDP in SIDS, LDCs and all countries. The contribution of sustainable fisheries to global GDP fell below 0.10% in 2019. The most significant decline occurred in LDCs, where it dropped from 1.20% of GDP in 2017 to 0.88% in 2019. With nearly 200 million people employed directly or indirectly in fisheries and aquaculture, the sustainable development of this sector is crucial for supporting the livelihoods and food security of many of the world's poorest communities (UN, 2024[1]). SDG indicator 14.b.1 Degree of application of a legal, regulatory, policy and institutional framework which recognises and protects access rights for small-scale fisheries. The global application of legal, regulatory, policy and institutional frameworks recognising and protecting access rights for small-scale fisheries was highest in 2022, with a score of 5 out of 5 based on available data. However, this score reflects input from a reduced number of reporting countries. The International Year of Artisanal Fisheries and Aquaculture 2022 was a pivotal event to promote these frameworks, and the upcoming 2024 reporting period is expected to include results from a larger number of countries than in 2022 (UN, 2024[1]).
109	Acknowledge the FSB's efforts on financial market reform and commit to strengthening macroprudential regulation and countercyclical buffers. Support reforms in financial market regulation, focusing on reducing systemic risks in shadow banking, derivatives, securities lending and repurchase agreements. Address too-big-to-fail risks and improve cross-border resolution of systemically important financial	No	n.a.	Non-bank financial intermediation (NBFI) volumes as a share of total. (FSB) NBFI represented 47.2% of total global financial assets in 2022 compared with 48.6% in 2015 and a peak of 50.4% in 2019. In volumes, NBFI grew from USD 165.4 billion in 2015 to USD 217.9 billion in 2022 (FSB, 2023[5]). *The FSB was established in 2009 in response to the global financial crisis to strengthen financial regulation, improve the resilience of financial institutions and prevent future crises. It monitors and makes recommendations about the global financial system to promote stability. The FSB regularly reports to the G20, but has a broader membership and since 2011, has established six regional consultative groups that enable it to reach out to 70 non-G20 member countries and*

AAAA paragraph	Commitment	Specific target or objective	Matching Sustainable Development Goal (SDG) target (where available)	State of implementation or progress made since 2015, using selected SDG or other relevant indicators (proxy)
	entities.			*jurisdictions* (FSB, 2023[5]).
110	Reduce reliance on credit rating agency assessments, including in regulations. Improve the quality of rating, promote competition, address conflicts of interest and support greater transparency in credit rating agencies' evaluation standards (ref. FSB). Continue to address these issues, including within the United Nations.	No	n.a.	*The 2008-09 global financial crisis triggered a number of proposals and legislation aimed at strengthening the regulatory and supervisory framework for credit rating agencies (CRAs). Among these were the European Union rules adopted in 2009 and 2013 and the creation in 2011 of the European Securities and Market Authority. In 2010, the FSB called for a reduction of reliance on CRA ratings, but little progress has been made since* (European Commission, n.d.[32]; FSB, 2023[5]). *The big three CRAs (Moody's, S&P and Fitch Ratings) together hold 95% of the credit rating market.*
111	Engage globally to ensure safe, orderly migration while respecting human rights. Enhance co-operation on benefit portability, recognition of foreign qualifications and lower recruitment costs. Combat unethical recruiters, promote positive narratives about migrants and fight xenophobia. Support social integration, protect migrants' rights and uphold the human rights of all migrants, especially women and children, regardless of their status.	No	Target 10.7 Facilitate orderly, safe, regular and responsible migration and mobility of people, including through the implementation of planned and well-managed migration policies.	SDG indicator 10.7.2 Proportion of countries with migration policies that facilitate orderly, safe, regular and responsible migration and mobility of people. In 2021, 62.3% of countries worldwide had migration policies designed to facilitate orderly, safe, regular and responsible migration and mobility, and 58.1% of LDCs had such policies (UN, 2024[1]). Estimated number of international migrants and forcibly displaced people worldwide. The estimated number of international migrants has increased to reach 3.6% of the global population in 2020. An estimated 281 million people were living in a country other than their country of birth in 2020 – 32 million more than in 2015, 128 million more than in 1990 and more than triple the estimated number in 1970. Europe and Asia hosted, respectively, about 87 million and 86 million international migrants, or 61% of the global international migrant stock (IOM, 2024[33]). Remittances are increasing as a result (see chapter 3). At the end of 2022, the number of forcibly displaced people worldwide was estimated at 108.4 million, among them 35.3 million refugees and 5.4 million asylum seekers (UNHCR, 2022[17]). Proportion of refugees hosted by country groups. Low- and middle-income countries hosted 76% of the world's refugees and other people in need of international protection. LDCs provided asylum to 20% of the total. (UNHCR). In 2021, the estimated average annual cost of providing education to refugee students in low-, lower middle- and upper middle-income host countries was USD 4.85 billion (World Bank and UNHCR, 2021[34]).

AAAA paragraph	Commitment	Specific target or objective	Matching Sustainable Development Goal (SDG) target (where available)	State of implementation or progress made since 2015, using selected SDG or other relevant indicators (proxy)
112	Enhance regional, national and local institutions to prevent violence, combat terrorism and crime, and eliminate human trafficking and exploitation, especially of women and children. Strengthen national efforts to fight money laundering, corruption and terrorism financing. Improve global co-operation to build capacity, particularly in developing countries. Ensure the effective implementation of the United Nations Convention against Transnational Organized Crime (UNTOC).	No	Target 16.4 By 2030, significantly reduce illicit financial and arms flows, strengthen the recovery and return of stolen assets, and combat all forms of organised crime.	SDG Indicator 16.4.1 Total value of inward and outward illicit financial flows (in current US dollars). *(See chapter 2 for information on illicit financial flows.)* *The UNTOC Review Mechanism was established October 2018. As of August 2024, 80 reviews account for 42.4% of UNTOC parties* (UNODC, 2024[35]). *Transnational organised crime is estimated to generate USD 870 billion a year* (UNODC, n.d.[36]).
113	Enhance the coherence and alignment of multilateral financial, investment, trade, development and environmental institutions and platforms. Increase co-operation among major international institutions while respecting their mandates and governance structures. Improve the use of relevant United Nations forums to promote universal coherence and reinforce global commitments to sustainable development.	No	Target 17.14 See para. 103. Target 17.16 Enhance the Global Partnership for Sustainable Development, complemented by multi-stakeholder partnerships that mobilise and share knowledge, expertise, technology and financial resources to support the achievement of the SDGs in all countries, in particular developing countries.	SDG indicator 17.14.1 See para. 103. SDG indicator 17.16.1 Number of countries reporting progress in multi-stakeholder development effectiveness monitoring frameworks that support the achievement of the SDGs. *(For information on multi-stakeholder development effectiveness, see chapter 4.)*

Note: The data points are mainly drawn from the UN's Sustainable Development Goals Extended Report 2024 and its statistical annexes. Trend data in are in constant USD 2015 prices unless otherwise indicated.

References

Boston University Global Development Policy Center (2025), *Counting on the International Monetary Fund: aligning the IMF quota system with global need*, Boston University Global Development Policy Center, https://www.bu.edu/gdp/files/2023/10/GEGI-Report-Quotas-FIN.pdf. [28]

European Commission (n.d.), *Regulating credit rating agencies*, European Commission, https://finance.ec.europa.eu/capital-markets-union-and-financial-markets/financial-markets/regulating-credit-rating-agencies_en. [32]

French Ministry for Europe and Foreign Affairs (2023), *The Paris Pact for People and the Planet (4P)*, https://www.diplomatie.gouv.fr/en/french-foreign-policy/summits-and-global-affairs/the-paris-pact-for-people-and-the-planet-4p/ (accessed on 13 December 2024). [11]

FSB (2023), *Global Monitoring Report on Non-Bank Financial Intermediation*, Financial Stability Board, https://www.fsb.org/2023/12/global-monitoring-report-on-non-bank-financial-intermediation-2023/. [5]

G20 Independent Experts Group (2023), *Strengthening Multilateral Development Banks: The Triple Agenda*, Center For Global Development, https://www.cgdev.org/publication/strengthening-multilateral-development-banks-triple-agenda (accessed on 13 December 2024). [14]

Global Policy Forum (2024), *Bridgetown Initiative 3.0 released: What´s the news?*, https://www.globalpolicy.org/en/news/2024-06-05/bridgetown-initiative-30-released-whats-news (accessed on 13 December 2024). [9]

Global Policy Forum (2024), *International financial architecture reform at the 2024 Spring Meetings of IMF and World Bank: High ambitions meet piecemeal results*, Global Policy Forum, https://www.globalpolicy.org/en/news/2024-04-30/international-financial-architecture-reform-2024-spring-meetings-imf-and-world-bank. [30]

IDB (2024), *Multilateral Development Banks: Working as a System for Greater Impact and Scale*, Inter-American Development Bank, https://www.iadb.org/en/home/idbimpact/mdbs-working-system-impact-and-scale (accessed on 13 December 2024). [13]

IEP (2024), *Global Peace Index 2024: Measuring Peace in a Complex World*, Institute for Economics & Peace, https://www.economicsandpeace.org/wp-content/uploads/2024/06/GPI-2024-web.pdf. [15]

IMF (2023), *Global Financial Safety Net*, International Monetary Fund, https://www.imf.org/en/Publications/fandd/issues/2023/12/PT-global-financial-safety-net. [25]

IMF (2023), *Global Financial Stability Report: Safeguarding Financial Stability amid High Inflation and Geopolitical Risks*, International Monetary Fund, https://www.imf.org/en/Publications/GFSR/Issues/2023/04/11/global-financial-stability-report-april-2023?cid=bl-com-spring2023flagships-GFSREA2023001. [19]

IMF (2023), *The IMF-FSB Early Warning Exercise*, International Monetary Fund, https://www.imf.org/en/About/Factsheets/Sheets/2023/Early-Warning-Exercise. [31]

IMF (2023), *The Macroprudential Policy Survey*, International Monetary Fund, https://www.elibrary-areaer.imf.org/Macroprudential/Pages/Home.aspx. [27]

IMF (2023), *What are IMF quotas?*, International Monetary Fund, https://www.imf.org/en/About/Factsheets/Sheets/2022/IMF-Quotas. [29]

Imperial College London (2023), *Jameel Institute Annual Report*, Imperial College London, https://www.imperial.ac.uk/media/imperial-college/research-centres-and-groups/jameel-institute/public/Jameel-Institute---General---Dec-23-report.pdf. [8]

IOM (2024), *World Migration Report 2024*, International Organization for Migration, Geneva, https://worldmigrationreport.iom.int/msite/wmr-2024-interactive/. [33]

IOM (2021), *World Migration Report 2022*, International Organization for Migration, https://publications.iom.int/books/world-migration-report-2022. [16]

Kotz, M., A. Levermann and L. Wenz (2024), "The economic commitment of climate change", *Nature*, Vol. 628/8008, pp. 551-557, https://doi.org/10.1038/s41586-024-07219-0. [6]

OECD (2024), *Report on the Implementation of the OECD Recommendation on Policy Coherence for Sustainable Development*, https://one.oecd.org/document/C(2024)92/en/pdf. [24]

OECD (2024), *Unleashing Policy Coherence to Achieve the SDGs: An Assessment of Governance Mechanisms*, OECD Publishing, Paris, https://doi.org/10.1787/a1c8dbf8-en. [18]

OECD (2015), *The Economic Consequences of Climate Change*, OECD Publishing, Paris, https://doi.org/10.1787/9789264235410-en. [20]

OECD et al. (2023), *Latin American Economic Outlook 2023: Investing in Sustainable Development*, OECD Publishing, Paris, https://doi.org/10.1787/8c93ff6e-en. [3]

Sobrinho, N., S. Chun and K. Naidoo (2022), "The Impact of the IMF's COVID-19 Support to Developing and Emerging Economies", *IMF Working Papers*, Vol. 2022/261, p. 1, https://doi.org/10.5089/9798400229114.001. [7]

UN (2024), *Financing for Sustainable Development Report 2024: Financing for Development at a Crossroads*, United Nations Department Social and Economic Affairs, Financing for Sustainable Development Office, New York, https://desapublications.un.org/publications/financing-sustainable-development-report-2024 (accessed on 20 November 2024). [26]

UN (2024), *Progress Towards the Sustainable Development Goals - Report of the Secretary-General: Statistical Annex*, United Nations Economic and Social Council, New York, https://unstats.un.org/sdgs/files/report/2024/E_2024_54_Statistical_Annex_I_and_II.pdf. [1]

UN (2024), *UN ECOSOC (2024), Progress towards the Sustainable Development Goals - Statistical Annex.*, United Nations, https://unstats.un.org/sdgs/files/report/2024/E_2024_54_Statistical_Annex_I_and_II.pdf. [2]

UNEP (2022), *What you need to know about the COP27 Loss and Damage Fund*, United Nations Environment Programme, https://www.unep.org/news-and-stories/story/what-you-need-know-about-cop27-loss-and-damage-fund (accessed on 13 December 2024). [21]

UNHCR (2022), *Global trends: forced displacement in 2022*, United Nations High Commissioner for Refugees, https://www.unhcr.org/sites/default/files/2023-06/global-trends-report-2022.pdf. [17]

United Nations (2024), *First session of the Preparatory Commi2ee for the fourth Interna5onal Conference on Financing for Development: Mul5-Stakeholder Round Table Discussion on "Addressing systemic issues" (concept note)*, United Nations, https://www.uneca.org/eca-events/first-session-of-preparatory-committee-for-ffd4. [4]

United Nations Secretary-General (2024), *SDG Stimulus Leaders' Group*, https://www.un.org/sg/en/content/sg/personnel-appointments/2024-06-05/sdg-stimulus-leaders-group (accessed on 13 December 2024). [10]

UNODC (2024), *UNTOC Review Mechanism Statistics*, United Nations Office on Drugs and Crime, https://www.unodc.org/unodc/en/organized-crime/intro/review-mechanism-untoc/review_process.html. [35]

UNODC (n.d.), *Transnational organized crime: the globalized illegal economy*, United Nations Office on Drugs and Crime, https://www.unodc.org/toc/en/crimes/organized-crime.html. [36]

World Bank (2023), *Ending Poverty on a Livable Planet: Report to Governors on World Bank Evolution*, World Bank, Development Committee Meeting, https://www.devcommittee.org/content/dam/sites/devcommittee/doc/documents/2023/Final%20Updated%20Evolution%20Paper%20DC2023-0003.pdf. [12]

World Bank (2022), *World Development Report 2022: Finance for an Equitable Recovery*, The World Bank, https://doi.org/10.1596/978-1-4648-1730-4. [23]

World Bank and UNHCR (2021), *The Global Cost of Inclusive Refugee Education*, World Bank, https://documents1.worldbank.org/curated/en/159281614191477048/pdf/The-Global-Cost-of-Inclusive-Refugee-Education.pdf. [34]

World Bank Group (2021), *Protecting Nature Could Avert Global Economy Losses of $2.7 Trillion Per Year*, World Bank Group, https://www.worldbank.org/en/news/press-release/2021/07/01/protecting-nature-could-avert-global-economic-losses-of-usd2-7-trillion-per-year (accessed on 13 December 2024). [22]

Notes

[1] Authors' calculations based on the United Nations (2024), Statistical Annex I and II: SDG Report 2024, https://unstats.un.org/sdgs/files/report/2024/E_2024_54_Statistical_Annex_I_and_II.pdf.

[2] International reserve assets created by the IMF to supplement member countries' official reserves.

[3] Note that while the 16th General Review of Quotas was approved, member countries are still seeking approvals at the domestic level to make the 50% increase in quota effective.

[4] Transboundary impacts are defined by the OECD as any effect – intended or not – originated in one country that crosses national borders through flows of capital, goods, human and natural resources and that is able to affect positively or negatively the sustainable development prospects of another country. See https://legalinstruments.oecd.org/en/instruments/OECD-LEGAL-0381.

8 Science, Technology, Innovation and Capacity-building

This chapter reviews Science, Technology, Innovation and Capacity-Building efforts under the Addis Ababa Action Agenda with a focus on trends in research and development (R&D), environmentally sound technologies (ESTs), Internet access, and official development assistance. It highlights the impact of rising R&D spending and global EST trade on technological progress, noting persistent income disparities, as well as the rapid expansion of Internet access alongside significant connectivity gaps, particularly in least developed countries. The chapter underscores the importance of international support for digital infrastructure and capacity building for sustainable development, highlighting the transformative potential of renewable energy, artificial intelligence, climate technology and other emerging areas that could reduce costs of a sustainable transition. Finally, it reviews the importance of data privacy, cybersecurity and equitable digital access for building resilient systems globally.

8.1. Data dashboard

Key trends

Research and development (R&D) expenditure as a proportion of gross domestic product (GDP) has risen globally since 2015 but has flatlined in developing countries.

Global R&D expenditure as a proportion of GDP rose by 12% since 2015 and 25% since 2000, reaching 1.93% in 2021. However, in countries most in need, the R&D share has remained flat since 2000, and in many, it declined in 2021 since GDP grew faster than R&D spending, particularly in the recovery period after the COVID-19 crisis (Figure 8.1).

Figure 8.1. Research and development expenditure as a proportion of GDP

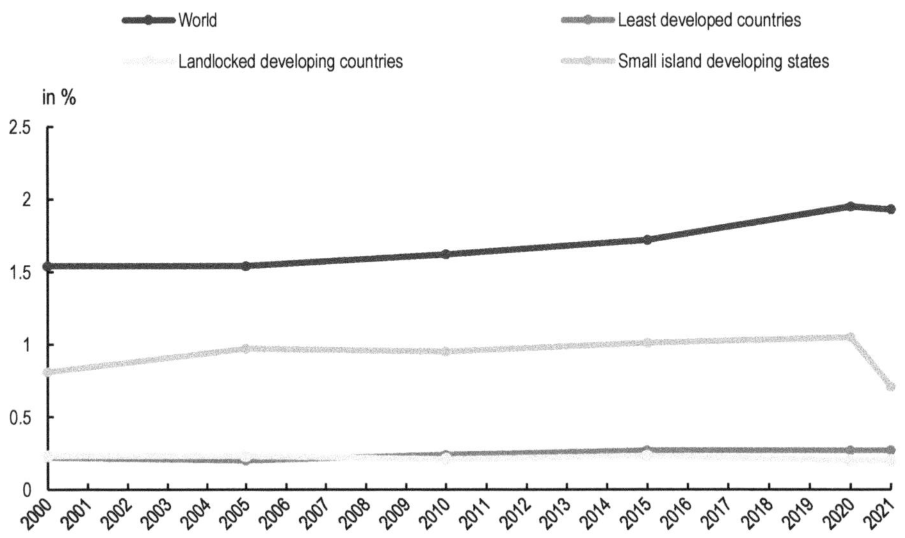

Source: Authors' calculations based on UN (2024[1]), *Progress Towards the Sustainable Development Goals - Report of the Secretary-General: Statistical Annex I and II*, https://unstats.un.org/sdgs/files/report/2024/E_2024_54_Statistical_Annex_I_and_II.pdf.

Trade in tracked environmentally sound technologies (ESTs) has increased globally but decreased in least developed countries (LDCs).

Global trade in ESTs, which are technologies traded that are deemed environmentally sound according to specific sectors,[1] totalled USD 2.36 trillion in 2020, an increase of 5% from USD 2.25 trillion in 2015. However, for LDCs, trade in ESTs declined by 43% from USD 15.28 billion in 2015 to USD 8.78 billion in 2020 (Figure 8.2).

Figure 8.2. Global trade in tracked environmentally sound technologies (ESTs)

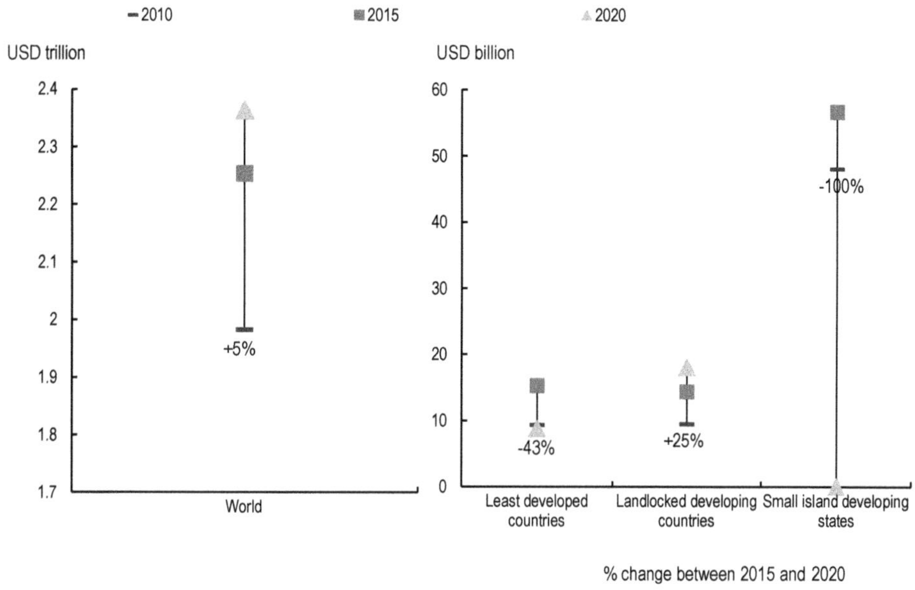

Source: Authors' calculations based on UN (2024[1]), *Progress Towards the Sustainable Development Goals - Report of the Secretary-General: Statistical Annex I and II*, https://unstats.un.org/sdgs/files/report/2024/E_2024_54_Statistical_Annex_I_and_II.pdf.

The share of the world population using the Internet significantly increased since 2015.

Globally, the proportion of people using the Internet increased from 40% to 67% between 2015 and 2023, or by nearly 70% (Figure 8.3). In LDCs, the growth rate was significantly higher, with a threefold increase, from 11% to 35%, in the share of individuals using the Internet increasing[2] (UN, 2024[1]).

Despite the rapid increase in the share of the population using the Internet in countries most in need, universal connectivity remains a distant goal in both LDCs and landlocked developing countries, where only 35% and 39% of the population, respectively, were online in 2023. In small island developing states, two-thirds of the population were online, in line with the global average.

Figure 8.3. Share of world population using the internet

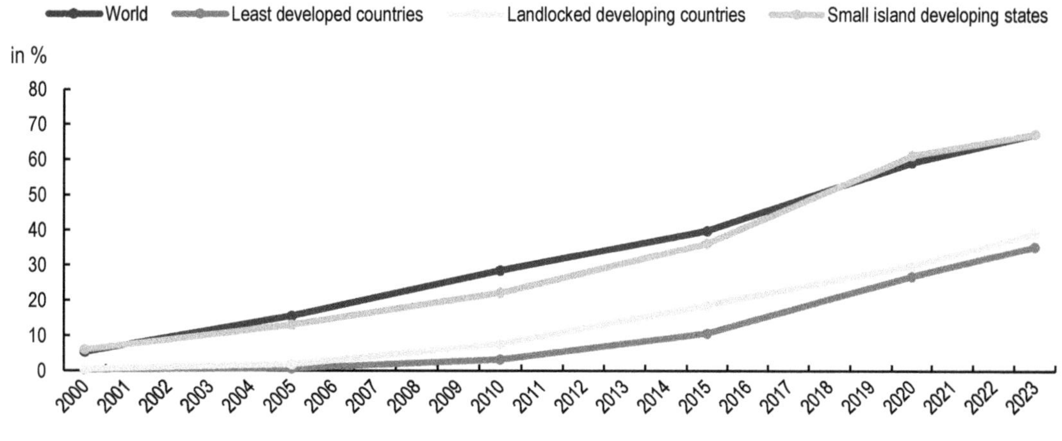

Source: Authors based on UN (2024[1]), *Progress Towards the Sustainable Development Goals - Report of the Secretary-General: Statistical Annex I and II*, https://unstats.un.org/sdgs/files/report/2024/E_2024_54_Statistical_Annex_I_and_II.pdf.

Key performance indicators

↑	Total official development assistance (ODA) disbursements to science, technology and innovation (STI) increased from USD 7.69 billion in 2015 to USD 9.33 billion in 2022, reflecting 21.33% growth over this period (OECD, 2024[2])..
↑	The global coverage of at least a 3G mobile network for the population notably rose from 78% to 95% between 2015 and 2023, approaching universal access. Coverage in LDCs also grew significantly from 53.2% to 82.0% over the same period.
↑	Fixed broadband subscriptions steadily increased at an average annual growth rate of 6.4% between 2015 and 2023, reaching a global proportion of 19 subscriptions per 100 inhabitants in 2023 from 11 per 100 inhabitants in 2015. Progress has been faster in LDCs, with 1.8 subscriptions per 100 inhabitants in 2023, more than doubling from 0.8 in 2015.
↓	The contribution of medium- and high-tech manufacturing value added to total value added has remained stable globally, accounting for 46.2% in 2021, 46.3% in 2015 and 45.8% in 2000. In LDCs, however, the contribution to total value added decreased to 8.4% in 2021 from 9.1% in 2015 and 14.5% in 2000 (UN, 2024[3]).

↓ Slight setback	↓ Setback	↔ No change, neutral	↔ Stagnant, possible issue	↑ Major progress	↑ Minimal progress
Minimal setback	↓ Major setback	Holding steady, slight concern	↔ Negative stagnation, concerning	Progress	↑ Negligible progress or progress contested

Note: Selected quantifiable commitments. Annex Table 8.A.1 contains the full list.

Resource mobilisation potential

Increasing Internet access to 75% of the population in developing countries would increase these countries' GDP by USD 2 trillion and create 140 million new jobs (Broom, 2023[4]).

Boosting women's participation in the science, technology, engineering and mathematics, or STEM, field could increase women's cumulative earnings by USD 299 billion over the next ten years (Tilghman, 2017[5]; Sayed, 2023[6]).

8.2. Key areas of progress

Progress is being made towards universal and affordable access to the Internet by 2030

To bridge the digital divide, digital connectivity must be enhanced globally.[3] Approximately 67% of the world's population, or 5.4 billion people, were online in 2023, a nearly 50% increase since 2015 that was accelerated by the COVID-19 pandemic. Significant progress has also been made in expanding mobile network coverage. The global population coverage of at least a 3G mobile network increased from 78% in 2015 to 95% in 2023, nearing universal access. Coverage also grew substantially, from 53.2% to 82.0%, in LDCs over the same period. However, there is a significant digital infrastructure investment gap, with approximately USD 428 billion per year required to connect the remaining 3 billion people aged ten and older who are not online to broadband Internet by 2030 (International Telecommunication Union, 2020[7]).

Support to strengthen country-driven capacity building has increased

In 2022, development finance for capacity building and national planning reached USD 54.9 billion, a 50% increase over 2015, with significant support directed towards the public administration, health and financial policy sectors. Support to health policies and administration in developing countries increased by 26% to USD 6.5 billion, primarily in response to the COVID-19 pandemic. Knowledge sharing is central to South-South and triangular co-operation modalities. From 2019 to 2022, South-South co-operation activities grew by 64%, though the total volume decreased from USD 12.8 billion to USD 10.4 billion. Triangular co-operation activities also rose substantially from USD 84.23 million in 2019 to USD 424.82 million in 2022, a 268% increase.

International flows in support of STI have increased, due in part to increased funding of medical research and COVID-19 control

Total ODA disbursements to STI increased from USD 7.69 billion in 2015 to USD 9.33 billion in 2022, representing growth of 21.33% over this period (OECD, 2024[2]). Since 2015, ODA to STI as a proportion of total ODA has generally increased, ranging from a share of about 0.9% in 2015 to a peak of roughly 1.6% in 2018, then stabilising at 1.2% to 1.4% from 2019 to 2021. However, estimates of ODA in support of STI vary as there is no internationally agreed methodology. For example, another OECD study found that total development finance supporting STI, including concessional and non-concessional financing from official providers and private philanthropy, averaged USD 14 billion annually between 2010 and 2016.

Among STI-related sectors, substantial portions of ODA consistently supported research and/or scientific institutions and medical research, with each accounting for approximately 0.2% to 0.5% over 2015-22. In 2022, total net ODA for basic health and medical research reached USD 21.1 billion, more than double the USD 10.5 billion in ODA allocated in 2015. COVID-19 response accounted for a significant share, or 42%, ODA for basic health care, with USD 8.8 billion dedicated to control and USD 1.6 billion specifically as COVID-19 vaccines donated by ODA providers. The Access to COVID-19 Tools Accelerator (ACT-A) and its COVID-19 Vaccines Global Access, or COVAX, facility played crucial roles in distributing vaccines to low- and middle-income countries, although vaccine nationalism and delayed agreements limited the timely delivery of doses. By October 2022, only 25% of the population in low-income countries had received at least one vaccine dose in stark contrast to 72% in high-income countries. ODA disbursements from OECD DAC countries to developing countries in the information and communications technology sector more than tripled, from USD 68.9 million in 2015 to USD 246.0 million in 2022. Among other research categories, fishery research and educational research consistently received smaller ODA shares to the sector of less than 0.1% each from 2015 to 2021 (OECD, 2024[2]).

8.3. Persistent challenging areas

The concentration of innovation and investment stifles technological progress in developing countries

Innovation activity has been highly concentrated in a few countries, with the top ten countries accounting for at least 87% of global patent applications. This concentration is even more pronounced in specific sectors: 90% of patenting activity in smart manufacturing occurs in just ten countries, and industrial firms from just seven countries represent 90% of all patenting activity in green technology (UN, 2024[8]). Additionally, there is a significant imbalance in health research funding, with developing countries bearing 90% of the world's disease burden but receiving only 10% of such related research funding (Sarewitz and Pielke, 2007[9]).

Global innovation trends tracked by the World Intellectual Property Organization in its 2023 Global Innovation Index suggest that investment in innovation produced mixed results in 2022. The number of scientific publications, R&D, venture capital deals and patents continued to grow, for instance, but at a slower pace than the exceptional increases observed in 2021. The contribution of medium- and high-tech manufacturing value added to total value added has remained stable globally, accounting for 46.2% in 2021, 46.3% in 2015 and 45.8% in 2000. In LDCs, however, the contribution to total value added decreased to 8.4% in 2021 from 9.1% in 2015 and 14.5% in 2000 (UN, 2024[1]).

An enhanced enabling environment and more strategic use of intellectual property rights could further unlock innovation, boost trade, attract investment and promote technological upgrading

Intellectual property rights have the potential to be a game changer for developing countries, including LDCs. In Cambodia, for example, the registration of premium pepper originating from the city of Kampot as a geographic indication helped farmers more than triple their incomes since 2010. Likewise, in Ethiopia, trademarking has contributed to a 275% increase in coffee exports since the early 2000s. However, an innovation gap persists: In LDCs, the average annual number of applications for trademarks was 2 197 between 2017 and 2021, far below the global average of 26 034 and the average of 24 789 in other developing countries. Annual applications in LDCs for patents and utility models, both of which protect inventors' rights, totalled just 55 and 24, respectively, over the same period. LDCs, which often rank at the bottom of the Global Innovation Index, also have the lowest level of productive capacities and readiness to harness frontier technology (UNCTAD, 2024[10]).

The gender gap in global Internet usage persists despite progress towards parity

In 2022, 63% of women globally used the Internet compared with 69% of men. The gap was even wider in lower-income countries, where only 21% of women were online compared with 32% of men. In 2023, 65% of women and 70% of men worldwide used the Internet. The gender parity score worldwide, which indicates parity at between 0.98 and 1.02, has improved from 0.90 in 2019 to 0.92 in 2023. This score does not fully capture the extent of the divide since women, who make up about half of the global population, make up an increasing percentage of people who are offline; the gap between women and men not using the Internet stood at 17% in 2023, up from 11% in 2019 (International Telecommunication Union, 2023[11]).

Countries most in need, particularly LDCs, still struggle to narrow the costly digital divide

The Doha Programme of Action for the Least Developed Countries for the Decade 2022-31 highlights STI alongside structural transformation as crucial for overcoming economic, social and environmental challenges facing LDCs. In LDCs, 18% of the population still lack access to 3G mobile broadband, and fixed broadband penetration remains low at just 1.8 subscriptions per 100 inhabitants in 2023 (UN, 2024[1]). The cost of broadband access in LDCs exceeds the affordability target set by the Broadband Commission for Sustainable Development (International Telecommunication Union, 2023[12]). Despite a more than threefold increase in digital connectivity from 11% to 35% between 2015 and 2023, universal access remains a distant goal in LDCs.

Efforts to improve digital infrastructure face numerous challenges including frequent Internet shutdowns due to political and security issues as well as unreliable power systems and other infrastructure shortcomings. There also are significant barriers related to usability, cost-effective technology and financial constraints (Walko, 2022[13]). Of the 32 LDCs assessed on the Global Innovation Index, 21 are in the bottom quartile, evidence of a persistent lag in innovation and adoption of new technologies. Limited infrastructure, insufficient financial and technical resources, and inadequate investment in education, skills development and STI R&D further contribute to the gap.

International mechanisms established to facilitate technology transfer to countries most in need struggle to secure funding

The United Nations (UN) technology facilitation mechanism (TFM) was established by the Addis Ababa Action Agenda in 2015. The TFM consists of four key elements: the UN Interagency Task Team on STI for the SDGs; the 10-Member Group of High-level Representatives; the annual Multi-stakeholder Forum on

STI for the SDGs; and the TFM 2030 Connect online platform, which serves as a central hub for accessing information on existing STI initiatives, mechanisms and programmes (UN, 2022[14]). The TFM also supports the development of STI roadmaps. Six pilot countries (Ethiopia, Ghana, India, Kenya, Serbia and Ukraine) and two international partners (the European Union and Japan) have participated in the first phase of the programme since 2019.

The UN General Assembly agreed to establish the Technology Bank for LDCs on 23 December 2016 (UN, 2017[15]). To date, the government of Türkiye is the sole volunteer donor of the Technology Bank and provides USD 1.7 million annually, an amount that covered only 60% of staff costs in 2023 (UN, 2022[16]).

Notable efforts have been invested in technology transfer for climate. Technology-related climate development finance grew substantially from USD 13.3 billion in 2015 to USD 28.6 billion in 2019. During this period, the proportion of climate-related activities with a technology transfer component increased from 27% to 36% and mitigation-related technology transfer comprised 69% of the total technology-related climate development finance. The primary sectors targeted were energy, transport and storage, and agriculture. Debt instruments were the most frequently used financial tools for climate technology transfer projects, accounting for 68% of total development finance resources, while grants represented 30% and equity investments 2% of such tools (UNEP; OECD, 2022[17]).

8.4. New and emerging areas

Renewable energy and climate technologies can help developing countries transition towards more circular and greener economies

Technological advances have significantly reduced the costs of some renewable energies, making them competitive with fossil fuels. For example, the cost of solar photovoltaic technology, which was 710% higher than that of fossil fuels in 2010, became 29% cheaper than the least expensive fossil fuel option by 2022 (UN, 2024[8]). Global trade in ESTs, which have the potential to significantly improve environmental performance relative to other technologies, increased but total trade of ESTs in LDCs dropped over the same period. The Global Environment Facility (GEF) remains the largest public sector funding source for transferring ESTs, with a record USD 5.33 billion pledged by 29 donor governments for its eighth replenishment cycle (2022-26) – a 30% increase over the previous cycle (Global Environment Facility, 2022[18]). Technology transfer has been a major component in most adaptation projects the GEF has carried out in LDCs, addressing climate resilience in diverse fields such as water management, disaster risk management, food security and agriculture, coastal management, and infrastructure development.

A shared digital future: generative artificial intelligence, data privacy and safety

The artificial intelligence (AI) market could add USD 15.7 trillion to the world economy by 2030, with the greatest economic gains of 27% in China (PwC, 2017[19]). For developing countries, the AI market presents opportunities in precision agriculture, medical diagnostics, teacher support and virtual tutoring, and efficient use of water and energy (Thapa, 2024[20]).

An analysis of 14 OECD countries indicates that the share of online vacancies requiring AI skills increased by 33% between 2019 and 2022 (Borgonovi et al., 2023[21]). Over 2000-21, nearly half of the 438 619 AI-related publications issued were published in just three countries: China, the United Kingdom and the United States (UNCTAD, 2023[22]). Many countries, especially the least developed ones, have been left behind, often confined to the role of being data providers (UNCTAD, 2023[23]). AI technology, however, present high-level risks, including the amplification of misinformation, increased harmful bias and discrimination, privacy breaches, and data governance risks at various levels (OECD, 2024[24]). The Global Digital Compact, adopted at the Summit of the Future with the aim of addressing such risks, is an initiative to establish common principles for a secure, open and inclusive digital future (UN, 2024[25]). It is expected to tackle issues such as digital connectivity, Internet fragmentation, data protection and the application of human rights in the online sphere.

Cybersecurity risks could cause disruption to financing for sustainable development

Cyberattacks are almost twice as frequent as they were before the COVID-19 pandemic. While most reported losses from these attacks are relatively minor, averaging about USD 500 000, the potential for severe losses (of up to USD 2.5 billion) and systemic disruption has grown significantly (IMF, 2024[26]). Cyberattacks against the financial sector in particular could threaten economic stability by eroding confidence in the financial system, disrupting critical services or causing spillovers to other institutions. However, cybersecurity policy frameworks, especially in developing countries, are often insufficient. For example, only about half of the countries surveyed recently by the International Monetary Fund reported having a national financial sector-focused cybersecurity strategy or dedicated cybersecurity regulations (IMF, 2024[27]).

Annex 8.A. Science, Technology, Innovation and Capacity-building statistical annex

Annex Table 8.A.1. Assessment of the action area: Science, technology, innovation and capacity-building

AAAA paragraph	Commitment	Specific target or objective	Matching Sustainable Development Goal (SDG) target (where available)	State of implementation or progress made since 2015, using selected SDG or other relevant indicators (proxy)
114	Promote information and communications technology infrastructure and rapid, universal and affordable access to the Internet in least developed countries (LDCs), small island developing states (SIDS) and land-locked developing countries (LLDCs). Advance access to technology and science for women, youth and children while enhancing the availability of accessible technology for persons with disabilities.	Yes Universal and affordable access to the Internet	Target 9.c Significantly increase access to information and communications technology and strive to provide universal and affordable access to the Internet in LDCs by 2020 Target 17.6 Enhance North-South, South-South, and triangular regional and international co-operation on and access to STI; enhance knowledge sharing on mutually agreed terms, including through improved co-ordination among existing mechanisms, in particular at the United Nations level, and through a global technology facilitation mechanism	SDG indicator 9.c.1 Proportion of population covered by a mobile network, by technology. In most developing countries, mobile broadband (3G or above) is the primary means of Internet access, available to 95% of the global population. However, the remaining 5% – especially in Oceania, sub-Saharan Africa and LDCs – still lack coverage, with gaps as high as 31% in Oceania and 17% in sub-Saharan Africa. In LDCs and LLDCs, 18% of the population does not have access to mobile broadband. These regions continue to fall short of SDG target 9.c, which aims for universal and affordable Internet access in LDCs by 2020 (ITU, 2023[28]). Since 5G deployment began in 2019, coverage has expanded to reach 40% of the global population in 2023. 4G serves as a strong alternative where 5G is unavailable, and 90% of the world's population is now covered by 4G. Of those without access, 55% live in low-income countries (LICs); in these countries, only 39% of the population is covered by 4G or above, with 3G being the dominant and often sole technology for Internet access (ITU, 2023[28]). SDG indicator 17.6.1 Fixed broadband subscriptions per 100 inhabitants, by speed. Fixed broadband subscriptions globally continued to grow steadily at an average annual growth rate of 6.4% between 2015 and 2023. In contrast the growth rate of subscriptions in LDCs was at 10.7% over the same period, from 0.8 in 2015 to 1.8 subscriptions per 100 inhabitants in 2023 (ITU, 2023[28]).

AAAA paragraph	Commitment	Specific target or objective	Matching Sustainable Development Goal (SDG) target (where available)	State of implementation or progress made since 2015, using selected SDG or other relevant indicators (proxy)
				SDG indicator 17.8.1 Proportion of individuals using the Internet. In 2023, 67% of the global population, or 5.4 billion people, were online, up 4.7% from 2022 and up 3.5% from 2021. While Internet use surged during the COVID-19 pandemic, growth rates have returned to pre-pandemic levels over the past three years. Universal connectivity also remains a distant prospect in LDCs and LLDCs, where only 35% and 39% of the population, respectively, are online (ITU, 2023[28]). *For more information, see SDG extended Report Goal 9 and 17.*
115	Calls for the creation of multi-stakeholder partnerships to strengthen country-driven capacity building and human resource development (including for public finance, debt management, gender-responsive budgeting, financial regulation, climate services, etc.) in developing countries, including LDCs, LLDCs, SIDS, African nations, and countries in conflict or post-conflict situations. Strengthening institutional capacity and human resource development, emphasising the importance of national capacity-building efforts in developing countries across areas such as public finance, social and gender-responsive budgeting, agriculture, debt management, climate services, and water and sanitation.	No	Target 17.9 Enhance international support for implementing effective and targeted capacity building in developing countries to support national plans to implement all the SDGs, including through North-South, South-South and triangular co-operation Target 17.19 By 2030, build on existing initiatives to develop measurements of progress on sustainable development that complement gross domestic product (GDP) and support statistical capacity building in developing countries.	SDG indicator 17.9.1 Dollar value of financial and technical assistance (including through North-South, South-South and triangular co-operation) committed to developing countries. Between 2019-22, the number of South-South co-operation activities reported under total official support for sustainable development, or TOSSD, increased by 64% from 5 558 to 9 092 while the total volume declined from USD 12.8 billion in 2019 to USD 10.4 billion in 2022. Triangular co-operation activities grew by 268% from 382 to 1 404. This was equivalent to USD 84.23 million in 2019 and USD 424.82 million in 2022 (OECD, 2024[29]). SDG indicator 17.19.1 Dollar value of all resources made available to strengthen statistical capacity in developing countries. The Partner Report on Support to Statistics by PARIS21 showed a resurgence in international support for data and statistics development, which amounted to USD 799 million in 2021, a 14% increase from 2020 and a 44% increase from 2015. Sub-Saharan Africa and LDCs received an increasing share of this funding. This renewed support helped mitigate pandemic-induced impacts on national statistical systems. For the first time, multilateral aid providers became the primary source of statistics funding in 2021. (PARIS21, 2023[30]). However, one donor drove most of the increase, with contributions from other donors decreasing, while funding for gender data remained low at USD 65 million. Funding is projected to increase by less than 5% for 2022. (PARIS21, 2023[30]) *The INFF Facility, launched in 2022, provides technical assistance to and supports capacity building to countries preparing or implementing INFFs to enable them to bring innovations to scale in line with growing demand.* (INFF Facility, 2024[31]).

AAAA paragraph	Commitment	Specific target or objective	Matching Sustainable Development Goal (SDG) target (where available)	State of implementation or progress made since 2015, using selected SDG or other relevant indicators (proxy)
				(See para 9 of the Addis Ababa Action Agenda and chapter 4 for more on INFFs.)
116	Incentivise research and innovation, recognise the importance of an enabling environment, including regulatory and governance frameworks, nurturing science and innovation (including social), the dissemination of technologies and industrial diversification, and the protection of intellectual property (including patent pooling).	No	Target 9.b Support domestic technology development, research and innovation in developing countries, including by ensuring a conducive policy environment for industrial diversification and value addition to commodities, among other things.	SDG indicator 9.b.1 Proportion of medium- and high-tech industry value added in total value added. The contribution of medium- and high-tech manufacturing value added to the total value added has remained stable globally, accounting for 46.2% of the total value added in 2021, 46.3% in 2015 and 45.8% in 2000. In LDCs, however, the contribution to total value added decreased sharply to 8.4% in 2021 from 14.5% in 2000 and 9.1% in 2015. (UNIDO, 2024[32]). Patent and utility model applications by LDCs. While international patent filings in LDCs are increasing, these still represent a small portion of the global total. Between 2017 and 2021, LDCs averaged 2 197 trademark applications annually, far below the global average of 26 034. Annual applications in LDCs for patents and utility models, both of which protect inventors' rights, totalled just 55 and 24, respectively, over the same period (UNCTAD, 2024[33]). World Intellectual Property Organization (WIPO) Global Innovation Index and Tracker. The World Intellectual Property Organization's 2023 Global Innovation Index, which uses 80 indicators to track global innovation trends in over 130 economies, found that results of investments in innovation were mixed in 2022. Scientific publications, research and development (R&D), venture capital deals, and patents continued to increase. However, growth rates were lower than the exceptional increases seen in 2021. In addition, the value of venture capital investment declined, and international patent filings stagnated in 2022. (WIPO, 2023[34]).
117	Foster knowledge sharing and promote co-operation and partnerships among stakeholders – including governments, businesses, academia and civil society – in sectors that contribute to achieving sustainable development goals. Promote entrepreneurship (ref. to business incubators); facilitate	No	n.a.	Official development assistance (ODA) to science, technology and innovation (STI) Total ODA disbursements to STI increased from USD 7.69 billion in 2015 to USD 9.33 billion in 2022, reflecting 21.33% growth over this period (OECD, 2024[2]). Since 2015, ODA to STI as a percentage of total ODA has generally increased, ranging from about 0.9% in 2015 to a peak of roughly 1.6% in 2018 and stabilising at about 1.2% to 1.4% from 2019 to 2021 (OECD, 2024[35]).

AAAA paragraph	Commitment	Specific target or objective	Matching Sustainable Development Goal (SDG) target (where available)	State of implementation or progress made since 2015, using selected SDG or other relevant indicators (proxy)
	technology, knowledge and skills transfers; and protect traditional knowledge.			ODA to ICT sector Disbursements from Development Assistance Committee (DAC) countries to developing countries in the ICT sector more than tripled from USD 68.9 million in 2015 to USD 246.0 million in 2022 (OECD, 2024[35]).
118	Consider using public funding to keep critical projects in the public domain and strive for open access to research from publicly funded projects where appropriate. Explore establishing innovation funds, on an open and competitive basis, to support innovative enterprises, particularly during the research, development and demonstration phases.	No	n.a.	n.a.
119	Increase investment in science, technology, engineering and mathematics, or STEM, education, and enhance technical, vocational and tertiary training, ensuring equal access for women and girls. Increase number of scholarships for students from developing countries to pursue higher education. Strengthen co-operation to bolster tertiary education systems and increase access to online education focused on sustainable development.	No	Target 4.5 By 2030, eliminate gender disparities in education and ensure equal access to all levels of education and vocational training for the vulnerable, including persons with disabilities, Indigenous peoples and children in vulnerable situations Target 4.b By 2020, substantially expand globally the number of scholarships available to developing countries, in particular LDCs, SIDS and African countries, for enrolment in higher education, including vocational training and information and communications technology, technical, engineering and scientific programmes, in developed countries and other developing countries	SDG indicator 4.5.1 Parity indices (female/male, rural/urban, bottom/top wealth quintile and others such as disability status, Indigenous peoples and conflict-affected as data become available) for all education indicators on this list that can be disaggregated SDG indicator 4.b.1 Volume of ODA flows for scholarships by sector and type of study The volume of ODA (gross disbursements) for scholarships amounted to USD 1.67 billion in 2022 compared with USD 1.39 billion in 2015. The volume in 2022 was 1.8% lower than the level in 2019, which was a peak year (UN, 2024[36]). SDG indicator 17.9.1 See para 115.

AAAA paragraph	Commitment	Specific target or objective	Matching Sustainable Development Goal (SDG) target (where available)	State of implementation or progress made since 2015, using selected SDG or other relevant indicators (proxy)
			Target 17.9 See para 115.	
120	Encourage environmentally sound technologies to developing countries on favourable terms, including concessional and preferential terms (refer to environmentally sound technologies) Enhance international co-operation, including ODA, in support of more sustainable patterns of consumption and production, including through implementation of the ten-year framework of programmes on sustainable consumption and production patterns and particularly for LDCs, LLDCs, SIDS and African nations. References sustainable consumption and production, ten-year framework programmes.	Yes Implementation of ten-year framework programmes on sustainable consumption and production	Target 12.a Support developing countries to strengthen their scientific and technological capacity to move towards more sustainable patterns of consumption and production Target 17.7 Promote the development, transfer, dissemination and diffusion of environmentally sound technologies to developing countries on favourable terms, including on concessional and preferential terms, as mutually agreed.	SDG indicator 17.7.1 Total amount of funding for developing countries to promote the development, transfer, dissemination and diffusion of ESTs. The global trade in tracked ESTs totalled USD 2.36 trillion in 2020, up from USD 2.25 trillion in 2015. However, for LDCs, ESTs trade declined from USD 15.28 billion in 2015 to USD 8.78 billion in 2020. (UN, 2024[36]). *See para. 35 in the chapter 3 on international and domestic private business and finance for the latest progress report on the ten-year framework of programmes on sustainable consumption and production patterns* (ECOSOC, May 2024) and the OECD report on climate finance provided and mobilised by developed countries in 2013-21 (OECD, 2023[37]).
121	Support the R&D of vaccines, medicines and preventive measures for both communicable and noncommunicable diseases, with a focus on those that disproportionately affect developing countries. (ref. Gavi, the Vaccine Alliance) Increase investment and international co-operation in agriculture and technology to boost food security and productive capacity	No	Target 2.a Increase investment, including through enhanced international cooperation, in rural infrastructure, agricultural research and extension services, technology development and plant and livestock gene banks in order to enhance agricultural productive capacity in developing countries, in particular least developed countries.	SDG indicator 2.a.2 Total official flows (official development assistance plus other official flows) to the agriculture sector. From 2015 to 2021, total official flows to the agriculture sector increased initially, peaking at USD 16.6 billion in 2020, before declining to USD 14.2 billion in 2021. For LDCs, flows rose consistently, reaching USD 4.0 billion in 2021. Landlocked Developing Countries (LLDCs) peaked at USD 3.5 billion in 2020, declining to USD 2.9 billion in 2021. Small Island Developing States (SIDS) showed fluctuating trends, peaking at USD 0.6 billion in 2020, then declining to USD 0.4 billion in 2021 (UN, 2024[36]).

AAAA paragraph	Commitment	Specific target or objective	Matching Sustainable Development Goal (SDG) target (where available)	State of implementation or progress made since 2015, using selected SDG or other relevant indicators (proxy)
	in developing countries, especially LDCs. (ref to plan and livestock gene banks) Increase scientific knowledge in marine technology for ocean health and marine biodiversity, particularly in SIDS and LDCs. (ref to Criteria and Guidelines on the Transfer of Marine Technology by Intergovernmental Oceanographic Commission)		Target 3.8 Achieve universal health coverage, including financial risk protection, access to quality essential healthcare services, and access to safe, effective, quality and affordable essential medicines and vaccines for all Target 3.b Support the R&D of vaccines and medicines for the communicable and noncommunicable diseases that primarily affect developing countries; provide access to affordable essential medicines and vaccines in accordance with the Doha Declaration on the TRIPS Agreement and Public Health, which affirms the right of developing countries to use to the full the provisions in the Agreement on Trade-Related Aspects of Intellectual Property Rights regarding flexibilities to protect public health; and, in particular, provide access to medicines for all	SDG indicator 3.b.1 Proportion of the target population covered by all vaccines included in the national programme. In 2022, coverage for the third dose of the diphtheria, tetanus, and pertussis vaccine increased to 84%, up from 81% in 2021 but still below the 86% level achieved in 2019. (UN, 2024[36]). *Global immunisation efforts have saved at least 154 million lives over the past 50 years. For each life saved through immunisation, an average of 66 years of full health were gained, with a total of 10.2 billion full health years gained over the five decades* (WHO, 2024[38]). *At the start of the COVID-19 pandemic, the international community launched the Access to COVID-19 Tools Accelerator (ACT-A) to provide vaccines, tests, treatments and personal protective equipment to low- and middle-income countries, with the COVID-19 Vaccines Global Access, or COVAX, Facility receiving the most funding (USD 16 billion in commitments) to purchase vaccines for LICs and LMICs through its Advance Market Commitment using donor-raised funds. Largely due to the vaccine nationalism of HICs, by the first quarter of 2022, COVAX had delivered just 1.4 billion of the 2.3 billion doses it aimed to distribute* (Pushkaran, Chattu and Narayanan, 2023[39]). *Most (60%-75%) of the delay in COVID-19 vaccine deliveries to LMICs was attributable to their having signed purchase agreements later than HICs did, which highlights the need for preparation and preparedness support. There were 92 LICs eligible to receive free doses and support thanks to more than USD 12 billion in donor funding for Gavi, the Vaccine Alliance COVAX Advance Market Commitment. Nearly 90% of the nearly 2 billion doses provided through the Facility went to lower-income economies* (GAVI, n.d.[40]). *As of October 2022, only 25% of the population living in LICs, versus 72% of the population in HICs, had received at least one dose of a vaccine in contrast to 72% of the population in HICs* (Duroseau, Kipshidze and Limaye, 2023[41]). SDG indicator 3.b.2 Total net ODA to medical research and basic health sectors. Total net ODA disbursements to medical research and basic health sectors was amounted to USD 21.1 billion in 2022 compared with USD 10.5 billion in 2015. For LDCs, total net ODA to these two sectors amounted to USD 6.4 billion in 2022, up from USD 4.9 billion in 2015 (UN, 2024[36]). ODA in support of COVID-19 pandemic activities. DAC donors spent 10.5% of their combined net ODA, or a total of USD 18.7 billion, on COVID-19-related activities in 2021, up from USD 16.6 billion or 10.2% of total

AAAA paragraph	Commitment	Specific target or objective	Matching Sustainable Development Goal (SDG) target (where available)	State of implementation or progress made since 2015, using selected SDG or other relevant indicators (proxy)
				DAC ODA in 2020 (OECD, 2022[42]). International finance in support of agriculture and technology in developing countries. From 2017 to 2021, food security and nutrition received less than a quarter of total ODA and other official flows, or an average of USD 76 billion annually, and only 34% of these flows targeted the primary causes of food insecurity and malnutrition (FAO; IFAD; UNICEF; WFP; WHO, 2024[43]). ODA alone in support of food security increased from USD 10.243 billion in 2018 to USD 11.650 billion in 2022 (OECD, 2024[44]). ODA in support of marine technology in developing countries. ODA in support of the ocean economy remained flat at roughly USD 2.6 billion in both 2015 and in 2021, though it spiked in 2017 to USD 5.6 billion (OECD, 2024[45]).
122	Strengthen coherence and synergies among UN initiatives such as the Commission on Science and Technology for Development, the UN Framework Convention on Climate Change Technology Mechanism, the Climate Technology Centre and Network, the WIPO's capacity building, and the UN Industrial Development Organization's National Cleaner Production Centres.	No	n.a.	n.a.
123	Establish a technology facilitation mechanism (TFM), now set to be launched at the UN summit for adopting the post-2015 development agenda, that aims to support the SDGs (ref. to TFM).	Yes Establish a Technology Facilitation Mechanism (TFM)	Target 9.5 Enhance scientific research; upgrade the technological capabilities of industrial sectors in all countries, in particular developing countries, including, by 2030, encouraging innovation and substantially increasing both the number of R&D workers per 1 million people and public and private R&D spending	SDG indicator 9.5.1 R&D expenditure as a proportion of GDP. From 2015 to 2021, global R&D expenditure as a proportion of global GDP increased from 1.72% to 1.93%, in line with a consistent upward trend apart from a slight decline in 2021. R&D expenditure in LDCs remained very low at 0.27% from 2015 to 2021 (UN, 2024[36]). Enhance international co-operation and co-ordination through a global TFM. The UN TFM was established by the AAAA in 2015 and reaffirmed in paragraph

AAAA paragraph	Commitment	Specific target or objective	Matching Sustainable Development Goal (SDG) target (where available)	State of implementation or progress made since 2015, using selected SDG or other relevant indicators (proxy)
			Target 17.6 Enhance North-South, South-South, and triangular regional and international co-operation on and access to STI; enhance knowledge sharing on mutually agreed terms, including through improved co-ordination among existing mechanisms, in particular at the UN level, and through a global TFM.	70 of the 2030 Agenda. The TFM consists of four key elements: the UN Interagency Task Team on STI for the SDGs, the 10-Member Group of High-level Representatives, the annual Multi-stakeholder Forum on STI for the SDGs and the TFM 2030 Connect online platform. The TFM also supports the development of STI roadmaps. Six pilot countries (Ethiopia, Ghana, India, Kenya, Serbia and Ukraine) and two international partners (the European Union and Japan) have participated in the first phase of the programme since 2019. For more information, see the UN TFM platform.
124	Await the recommendations of the UN Secretary-General's High-level Panel on the feasibility and operations of a proposed technology bank and innovation capacity-building mechanism for LDCs. Consider its advice on the bank's scope, functions, and organisation, aiming to make it operational by 2017, while fostering synergies with the TFM. (ref to the Technology Bank for LDCs).	Yes Operationalise the Technology Bank and STI capacity-building mechanism for LDCs by 2017.	Target 17.8 Fully operationalise the Technology Bank and STI capacity-building mechanism for LDCs by 2017 and enhance the use of enabling technology, in particular ICT	*The UN General Assembly approved the establishment of the Technology Bank for LDCs on 23 December 2016* (UN, 2017[46]). *To date, the government of Türkiye is the sole volunteer donor of the Bank, providing USD 1.7 million annually, an amount that covered only 60% of staff costs in 2023* (UN, n.d.[47]). *The Doha Programme of Action for the Least Developed Countries for the Decade 2021-2030, endorsed by the UN General Assembly in March 2022, calls for the Technology Bank to serve as "a focal point" for LDCs "to strengthen their science, technology and innovation capacity towards building sustainable productive capacities and promoting structural economic transformation".* *The support that the Technology Bank provides to LDCs is currently focused in four thematic areas – agriculture, environment, health and education – that are derived from the 14 technology needs assessments that the Bank has completed to date.* *For more information, see the Technology Bank for LDCs platform.*

Note: The data points are mainly drawn from the UN's Sustainable Development Goals Extended Report 2024 and its statistical annexes. Trend data in are in constant USD 2015 prices unless otherwise indicated.

References

Borgonovi, F. et al. (2023), "Emerging trends in AI skill demand across 14 OECD countries", *OECD Artificial Intelligence Papers*, No. 2, OECD Publishing, Paris, https://doi.org/10.1787/7c691b9a-en. [21]

Broom, D. (2023), "These are the places in the world where internet access is still an issue – and why", *World Economic Forum Stories*, https://www.weforum.org/stories/2023/09/broadband-no-luxury-basic-necessity/. [4]

Duroseau, B., N. Kipshidze and R. Limaye (2023), "The impact of delayed access to COVID-19 vaccines in low- and lower-middle-income countries", *Frontiers in Public Health*, Vol. 10, https://doi.org/10.3389/fpubh.2022.1087138. [41]

FAO; IFAD; UNICEF; WFP; WHO (2024), *The State of Food Security and Nutrition in the World 2024*, https://doi.org/10.4060/cd1254en. [43]

GAVI (n.d.), *The global pooled procurement and distribution mechanism at the heart of COVAX.*, https://www.gavi.org/covax-facility. [40]

Global Environment Facility (2022), *Funding - GEF-8 Replenishment (webpage)*, https://www.thegef.org/who-we-are/funding/gef-8-replenishment (accessed on 11 December 2024). [18]

IMF (2024), *Global Financial Stability Report: The Last Mile: Financial Vulnerabilities and Risks*, International Monetary Fund, https://www.imf.org/en/Publications/GFSR/Issues/2024/04/16/global-financial-stability-report-april-2024. [27]

IMF (2024), *Global Financial Stability Report: The Last Mile: Financial Vulnerabilities and Risks*, International Monetary Fund (IMF), Washington, DC, https://www.imf.org/en/Publications/GFSR/Issues/2024/04/16/global-financial-stability-report-april-2024. [26]

INFF Facility (2024), *Making finance work for people and planet: how countries are building their sustainable finance ecosystem through integrated national financing frameworks*, https://inff.org/resource/making-finance-work-for-people-and-planet-how-countries-are-building-their-sustainable-finance-ecosystem-through-integrated-national-financing-frameworks. [31]

International Telecommunication Union (2023), *Digital Inclusion of All*, https://www.itu.int/en/mediacentre/backgrounders/Pages/digital-inclusion-of-all.aspx/. [12]

International Telecommunication Union (2023), *The gender digital divide*, https://www.itu.int/itu-d/reports/statistics/2023/10/10/ff23-the-gender-digital-divide/. [11]

International Telecommunication Union (2020), *Connecting Humanity: Assessing Investment Needs of Connecting Humanity to the Internet by 2030*, https://www.itu.int/hub/publication/d-gen-invest-con-2020/. [7]

ITU (2023), *Facts and Figures 2023*, International Telecommunication Union, https://www.itu.int/itu-d/reports/statistics/facts-figures-2023/. [28]

OECD (2024), "AI, data governance and privacy: Synergies and areas of international co-operation", *OECD Artificial Intelligence Papers*, No. 22, OECD Publishing, Paris, https://doi.org/10.1787/2476b1a4-en. [24]

OECD (2024), *Data Explorer (database)*, https://data-explorer.oecd.org/?lc=en&tm=oda&pg=0&snb=42. [35]

OECD (2024), *Development co-operation for a sustainable ocean economy in 2022: A snapshot*, https://one.oecd.org/document/DCD%282024%2921/en/pdf. [45]

OECD (2024), *OECD Data Explorer, Creditor Reporting System: DAC5: Aid (ODA) by sector and provider (database)*, http://data-explorer.oecd.org/s/122 (accessed on 10 November 2024). [2]

OECD (2024), *OECD Data Explorer, DAC 5 table (database)*, http://data-explorer.oecd.org/s/u. [44]

OECD (2024), *TOSSD Data Visualisation Tool*, https://tossd.online/. [29]

OECD (2023), *Climate Finance Provided and Mobilised by Developed Countries in 2013-2021: Aggregate Trends and Opportunities for Scaling Up Adaptation and Mobilised Private Finance*, Climate Finance and the USD 100 Billion Goal, OECD Publishing, Paris, https://doi.org/10.1787/e20d2bc7-en. [37]

OECD (2022), *COVID-19 assistance to developing countries lifts foreign aid in 2021 - OECD*, https://www.oecd.org/en/about/news/press-releases/2022/04/covid-19-assistance-to-developing-countries-lifts-foreign-aid-in-2021-oecd-.html. [42]

PARIS21 (2023), *The PARIS21 Partner Report on Support to Statistics*, https://www.paris21.org/sites/default/files/media/document/2023-11/press-2023_0.pdf. [30]

Pushkaran, A., V. Chattu and P. Narayanan (2023), "A critical analysis of COVAX alliance and corresponding global health governance and policy issues: a scoping review", *BMJ Global Health*, Vol. 8/10, p. e012168, https://doi.org/10.1136/bmjgh-2023-012168. [39]

PwC (2017), *Sizing the Prize: What's the Real Value of AI for Your Business and How Can You Capitalise?*, https://www.pwc.com/gx/en/issues/artificial-intelligence/publications/artificial-intelligence-study.html. [19]

Sarewitz, D. and R. Pielke (2007), "The neglected heart of science policy: Reconciling supply of and demand for science", *Environmental Science & Policy*, Vol. 10/1, pp. 5-16, https://doi.org/10.1016/j.envsci.2006.10.001. [9]

Sayed, Z. (2023), *The STEM Skills Gap: A Growing Challenge for Countries to Overcome*, HRForcast, Munich, https://hrforecast.com/the-stem-skills-gap-a-growing-challenge-for-countries-to-overcome/. [6]

Thapa, R. (2024), *Developing AI for development*, World Bank, Washington, DC, https://accountability.worldbank.org/en/news/2024/Developing-AI-for-development (accessed on 11 December 2024). [20]

Tilghman, G. (2017), "Girls' STEM education can drive economic growth", *CFR Voices from the Field blog*, https://www.cfr.org/blog/girls-stem-education-can-drive-economic-growth. [5]

UN (2024), *Financing for Sustainable Development Report 2024: Financing for Development at a Crossroads*, United Nations Inter-agency Task Force on Financing for Development, New York, https://desapublications.un.org/publications/financing-sustainable-development-report-2024. [8]

UN (2024), *Global Digital Compact*, United Nations General Assembly, New York, https://www.un.org/global-digital-compact/sites/default/files/2024-09/Global%20Digital%20Compact%20-%20English_0.pdf. [25]

UN (2024), *Progress Towards the Sustainable Development Goals - Report of the Secretary-General: Statistical Annex*, United Nations Economic and Social Council, New York, https://unstats.un.org/sdgs/files/report/2024/E_2024_54_Statistical_Annex_I_and_II.pdf. [36]

UN (2024), *Progress Towards the Sustainable Development Goals - Report of the Secretary-General: Statistical Annex I and II*, United Nations Economic and Social Council, New York, https://unstats.un.org/sdgs/files/report/2024/E_2024_54_Statistical_Annex_I_and_II.pdf. [1]

UN (2024), *Statistical Annex I and II: SDG Report 2024*, United Nations, https://unstats.un.org/sdgs/files/report/2024/E_2024_54_Statistical_Annex_I_and_II.pdf. [3]

UN (2022), *The UN Technology Facilitation Mechanism - Informal note by the Secretariat on the first phase (2015-2022) and food for thought on the way forward*, United Nations Department of Economic and Social Affairs, New York, https://sdgs.un.org/sites/default/files/2023-01/TFM%20informal%20note%20by%20the%20Secretariat%20-17Oct2022%20rev.pdf. [14]

UN (2022), *United Nations Technology Bank for Least Developed Countries: Strategic Plan 2022-2024*, https://www.un.org/technologybank/sites/www.un.org.technologybank/files/strategic_plan_-_2022-2024_final_tt_p1.pdf. [16]

UN (2017), *Resolution 71/251 - Establishment of the Technology Bank for the Least Developed Countries*, United Nations General Assembly, New York, https://documents.un.org/doc/undoc/gen/n16/466/20/pdf/n1646620.pdf. [15]

UN (2017), *Resolution adopted by the General Assembly on 23 December 2016*, United Nations, https://documents.un.org/doc/undoc/gen/n16/466/20/pdf/n1646620.pdf. [46]

UN (n.d.), *United Nations Technology Bank for Least Developed Countries: Strategic Plan, 2022-2024*, United Nations, https://www.un.org/technologybank/sites/www.un.org.technologybank/files/strategic_plan_-_2022-2024_final_tt_p1.pdf. [47]

UNCTAD (2024), *Harnessing intellectual property rights for innovation, development and economic transformation in Least Developed Countries*, UN Trade and Development, https://unctad.org/publication/harnessing-intellectual-property-rights-innovation-development-and-economic. [33]

UNCTAD (2024), "Intellectual property: A potential game-changer for least developed countries", https://unctad.org/news/intellectual-property-potential-game-changer-least-developed-countries. [10]

UNCTAD (2023), "In an AI-driven digital economy, how can developing countries keep up?", https://unctad.org/news/ai-driven-digital-economy-how-can-developing-countries-keep. [23]

UNCTAD (2023), *Technology and Innovation Report 2023*, UN Trade and Development, New York, https://unctad.org/system/files/official-document/tir2023_en.pdf. [22]

UNEP; OECD (2022), *Technology Transfer for Climate Mitigation and Adaptation: Analysing Needs and Development Assistance Support in Technology Transfer Processes*, https://unepccc.org/wp-content/uploads/2023/06/tech-transfer-policy-brief-oecd.pdf. [17]

UNIDO (2024), *SDG 9 indicators (database)*, https://stat.unido.org/data/table?dataset=sdg. [32]

Walko, P. (2022), "Internet access as a tool for boosting economic and social equality", *LSE Digitalisation and ICT blog*, https://blogs.lse.ac.uk/internationaldevelopment/2022/11/29/internet-access-as-a-tool-for-boosting-economic-and-social-equality/. [13]

WHO (2024), *Global immunization efforts have saved at least 154 million lives over the past 50 years*, World Health Organization, https://www.who.int/news/item/24-04-2024-global-immunization-efforts-have-saved-at-least-154-million-lives-over-the-past-50-years. [38]

WIPO (2023), *Global Innovation Index 2023*, https://www.wipo.int/en/web/global-innovation-index/2023/index. [34]

Notes

[1] EST sectors include air pollution control, wastewater management, solid and hazardous waste management, renewable energy, environmentally preferable products, water supply and sanitation, energy storage and distribution, and land and water protection and remediation. For more information, see https://unstats.un.org/sdgs/metadata/files/Metadata-17-07-01.pdf.

[2]The source for these figures is the authors based on https://unstats.un.org/sdgs/files/report/2024/E_2024_54_Statistical_Annex_I_and_II.pdf.

[3] SDG target 9.c is to "significantly increase access to information and communications technology and strive to provide universal and affordable access to the Internet in least developed countries by 2020".

www.ingramcontent.com/pod-product-compliance
Ingram Content Group UK Ltd.
Pitfield, Milton Keynes, MK11 3LW, UK
UKHW051500290926
15471UKWH00008B/1327

9 789264 549067